DAVID McCUMBER

THE MITCHELL BROTHERS

A True Story

of Sex, Money,

and Death

SIMON & SCHUSTER

NEW YORK LONDON TORONTO SYDNEY TOKYO SINGAPORE

SIMON & SCHUSTER
SIMON & SCHUSTER BUILDING
1230 AVENUE OF THE AMERICAS
NEW YORK, NEW YORK 10020

SIMON & SCHUSTER AND COLOPHON ARE REGISTERED TRADEMARKS
OF SIMON & SCHUSTER INC.
DESIGNED BY PEI LOI KOAY
MANUFACTURED IN THE UNITED STATES OF AMERICA

1   3   5   7   9   10   8   6   4   2

LIBRARY OF CONGRESS CATALOGING IN PUBLICATION DATA
McCumber, David.
X-rated : the Mitchell brothers : a true story of sex, money, and
death / David McCumber.
p.   cm.
Includes index.
1. Mitchell, Jim.   2. Criminals—California—San Francisco—
Biography.   3. Murderers—California—San Francisco—Biography
4. Murder—California—San Francisco—Case studies.   5. Pornography—
California—San Francisco—Case studies.   6. Mitchell, Artie.
7. Murder victims—California—San Francisco—Biography.   I. Title.
HV6248.M62M33   1992
364.1'74'0979461—dc20   92-30316
CIP
ISBN: 0-671-75156-5

PHOTO CREDITS
Georgia Mae Mitchell: 1, 2, 3, 4, 6, 8
Georgia Mae Mitchell/ Rita Benton: 5
VCA Studios: 7
Missy Manners: 9
Joanne Scott: 10, 11, 14
Kristal Rose: 12
Bana Witt: 13
Marin Independent Journal/Robert Tong: 15
Marin Independent Journal/Martin E. Klimek: 16, 17
Richard Johnson Photo/Graphics: 18, 19, 20, 21, 22, 23

For Annette, and Max, and Andy,

the family I always wanted.

CONTENTS

Prologue 9

Part 1
THE BOYS FROM ANTIOCH 11

Part 2
THE FANTASY FACTORY 29

Part 3
"WOULD YOU LIKE SOME COMPANY?" 95

Part 4
"I'M A HELL OF A FUN GUY" 143

Part 5
MITCHELL BROTHER, SINGULAR 285

Part 6
"THERE ARE ONLY VICTIMS HERE" 339

Epilogue 457

Acknowledgments 460

Index 461

PROLOGUE

It was early in September 1951, and Jenny Downing's brand-new first-grade class was about to let out for recess.

There were twenty or so of the rambunctious little newcomers to Adelia Kimball Elementary School, and they were ready for a break from this strange new prison of desks and chalk dust and Mrs. Downing's hushes and admonitions and demands for their attention. They squirmed in their seats, looking out their windows at the brilliance of a fall day in the Sacramento River Delta, a fall that still seemed like summer. The sun was high and hot in the clear electric-blue sky, and for months now the grass on the knobby little hills that ringed the town of Antioch had been baked to a caramel brown.

The kids didn't know they were part of the country's biggest-ever bumper crop of babies. They could not know of the amazing years that were ahead of them, the agonies that bumper crop would suffer and the power it would wield, the forces that would reach down into this poor little mill town forty miles from San Francisco and change it forever: JFK and civil rights and freedom of speech and LSD and Vietnam and the sexual revolution and all the rest.

They didn't know any of this, of course. They just knew they wanted to get the heck out of that classroom for a while, run around, maybe play some kickball or hopscotch. Thank goodness, Mrs. Downing was finally opening the door.

When she did, she found another little boy waiting outside. He was a couple of years older than the kids in her class, and he looked quite solemn and grown-up as he stood there.

Jim Mitchell was in the third grade, and he had come to take care of his little brother, Artie, during recess.

It is February 27, 1991, forty years less six months later. San Francisco is cold and wet on this night, and the hookers in the Tenderloin district look a little bedraggled as they peer into passing cars, seeking eye contact with the cruising johns. There's a recession going on; business is tough and there's plenty of competition.

Some of the women look enviously through the drizzle at the liquid swirls of neon on the corner of Polk and O'Farrell streets. The big brick building there, lit up like the midway at a county fair, is just a little way off the "stroll," where the street hookers set up shop, and for many in the sex business here in sexy San Francisco, it is the ultimate place to work: the Mitchell Brothers O'Farrell Theatre.

Tonight, the marquee blazes: "The Place to Go in SF—Playboy" and "Carnegie Hall of Sex—HST." That somewhat cryptic reference is to gonzo journalist Hunter S. Thompson, who once labeled the theater "The Carnegie Hall of Public Sex in America."

Like Thompson, Jim and Artie Mitchell had become icons of the baby boom generation. The brothers from Antioch had come into San Francisco when the 1960s were in full flower and claimed the city for their own, in the name of the sexual revolution.

Time after time, they had fought in court to protect their constitutional rights to be purveyors of erotic movies and live sex shows, and time after time, they had won. They had become millionaires in their twenties. Now, in their forties, they are world-famous.

But on this night, James Lloyd Mitchell is grim-faced.

He goes into his garage and unlocks the cabinet where he keeps his guns.

He straps on a shoulder holster and slips a loaded Smith and Wesson .38 Special into it, then puts on a dark leather jacket. He picks up a .22 rifle, loads it, and puts it in the backseat of his maroon and silver Ford Explorer, so new it does not yet have license plates. He drives northward, through the rain, through the unearthly fog-shrouded yellow light on the deck of the Golden Gate Bridge.

Jim Mitchell is on his way to take care of Artie, one more time.

PART

THE BOYS FROM ANTIOCH

James Robert and Georgia Mae Mitchell raised their two little boys in a little brown wood-frame house at 405 Grangnelli Avenue in Antioch. They sure weren't rich but they weren't poor either, not by Antioch standards and not by the standards of their own childhood.

Both of Jim and Artie's parents were raised in grinding rural poverty, she in Arkansas, he in Oklahoma. To this day, Georgia Mae is justifiably proud of her family. She has traced her father's lineage back to royalty in the person of a seventh-century Welsh baronet. A thousand years later, the Guyn family emigrated to Virginia, where one of them was killed by the redcoats in the Revolutionary War. Later, the family moved west, first to Tennessee, then to Arkansas, where her grandfather was a prominent preacher—until, as a fifty-nine-year-old widower, he had the temerity to marry a nineteen-year-old Indian woman and start a brand-new family. It was not until she began doing her genealogical research in later life that Georgia Mae Mitchell discovered she was one-quarter Cherokee.

Georgia Mae came to California in the early 1940s, when she was still a schoolgirl. A few members of her family moved west, looking for a way to live a little better than they could in the woods around Hazen, Arkansas. Some of her brothers and sisters didn't want to leave the only life they knew, but nothing was going to keep Georgia Mae from this adventure and the dreams of a shining new life that went with it.

Before long one of those schoolgirl dreams came to life in the form of a tall, dashing Oklahoman. He was considerably older than she was, and he had some hard miles on him. He had even done a little stretch in the Texas prison system in the 1930s, although no record of exactly what his crime was remains.

His record notwithstanding, J.R. Mitchell had come a long way from the privations of his youth and of his pioneer family. His father, James Samuel Mitchell, grew up on a farm in Mississippi, near the Tennessee border. The family also operated a livery across the state line, in Memphis.

James Samuel thought he could do better elsewhere, and he emigrated to the Indian territory of Oklahoma. In 1893 he married Minnie Lee Corbett, who was fourteen at the time. They would have eleven children.

James Robert Mitchell was born to them on June 8, 1907, in a cabin near Mannsville, Oklahoma, down by the Texas border. He and his ten siblings were raised in labor camps scattered across the river-bottom land of southeastern Oklahoma, often camping in tents and eating whatever they could hunt or catch. One night when he was ten, Robert and his father and brothers treed seven raccoons in one tree. His father went up and scared them down, and Robert and his brothers and the dogs all were wrestling raccoons until his father could get back down.

Occasionally, Robert's father would just disappear. He would be gone for months at a time, leaving Minnie to raise the eleven children by herself. Then he would come back and pick up his life again as though he had been gone for an hour, not half a year.

Not much was said about it; the family just kept on about the all-consuming task of subsistence.

One day, when the Mitchells were living in a tent on the banks of the Clear Boggy River, Robert and his enterprising siblings decided to toss some dynamite in the river. Sure enough, the fish came up, stunned, to the surface, and the boys shucked their clothes and leaped into the river to get as many of them as they could.

The Mitchell youngsters were forever getting bruises and broken bones. Robert's older brother Charlie was bitten twice by rattlers, but each time their long-suffering mother, Minnie, prepared a poultice of soda and kerosene, and drew out the poison.

Then there was a mishap no poultice could cure. James Samuel Mitchell's life ended on one of his hunting trips when a shotgun propped against a fence discharged. Minnie and the rest of the family struggled on.

In 1923, a few years before drought and wind took all the topsoil in

Oklahoma and sent it somewhere else, the Mitchell boys had a great year farming corn and cotton. Robert, who was sixteen, and his brother Charlie, eighteen, cleared $600 when the crops were sold, and right away they took a train to Oklahoma City to buy their first car.

It was a Model T Ford, and they bought it on the condition that the salesman teach them how to drive. So he drove them to the edge of town, gave them a few rudimentary lessons, then caught a streetcar back and left them to figure out the rest.

The boys headed back toward home, but decided to pull over for the night because they didn't know how to operate the headlights. Then a squall came up, and Robert tried to turn the car around to shelter them from the rain and drove into a ditch. That stranded them until the next morning, when they found someone to pull them out, and on home they went. The Mitchell boys and their new Ford were the toast of Wapanucka.

After his Texas troubles, Robert Mitchell headed west like the thousands of other "Okies" fleeing their ruined land for the golden dream of California. Unlike many, he found the life he was looking for. He found Georgia Mae Guyn, and although he worked occasionally at factory jobs, Rob Mitchell quickly found his real career—gambling.

When he met the pretty dark-haired girl he was to marry, he was working at the Lathrop plant in Stockton, a defense-industry factory on the grounds of an army depot. It was good, steady work, but James Robert Mitchell soon would discover he could make more sitting at a card table. He played poker in card rooms all over Northern California, and occasionally he would go on the road to play elsewhere—Nevada, Southern California, anywhere there was a game.

He and Georgia Mae lived in the Delta town of Manteca for a while, and for the rest of his gambling life he would be known in the card rooms of California as Manteca.

His game of choice was California lowball, a draw poker game in which the object is to make the lowest possible hand without a pair. (A-2-3-4-5 is the perfect hand, "the wheel" in lowball parlance. Next best is A-2-3-4-6, the next A-2-3-5-6, and so on.)

The players and dealers who remember him are old men now, but they all agree on one thing: Manteca Mitchell was the best lowball player they ever saw.

"He was a jam-up player. He wouldn't just play sure hands. He'd gamble with you, raise the pot up, and he'd win," recalls J.D. Sipes, one of Mitchell's closest friends. "He could have won all the time if he wanted, but every once in a while he'd lose a little, just because it was good advertisement.

"He was so good he didn't have to cheat," says Sipes. "But if somebody tried to cheat him, he would turn it back on them and destroy them."

Manteca had a great trick. On the draw, if he drew one card to his opponent's two, he would say as his card came in, "I'll just bet you in the dark," indicating he hadn't yet looked at the draw, and was counting on the fact that his opponent had to draw two cards. But he had the ability to get his pinky just barely under the card as it arrived so he could get a glimpse of what it was as it landed on the felt tabletop. Calling Manteca's "bet in the dark" was a good way to lose money.

The card rooms of California were a wide-open proposition. There was a whole culture surrounding the games, lowball and draw poker and stud and Texas hold 'em. It was a milieu familiar to a lot of Okies like Mitchell and Sipes, who had survived many gambles in daily life, coming from boom-and-bust Oklahoma. A good player could make a lot of money, and a bad player—even a decent but unlucky player— could lose whatever he had.

The Mitchell family moved around a fair bit at first. Jim was born November 30, 1943, in Stockton. Artie arrived December 17, 1945, in Lodi. A third Mitchell boy, Robert Lewis Mitchell, was born on his daddy's fortieth birthday, June 8, 1947, in Stockton.

About the time the third Mitchell brother was born, the oldest brother was learning a few of life's lessons, courtesy of J.R. Jim was four, and not very big for his age. And every time he would go outside into the front yard to play, there was another little boy, a head taller, who would make his life miserable. He'd push Jim down in the dirt. It got so that Jim dreaded going outside, and his dad figured he better do something.

He bought boxing gloves and a heavy bag. For his four-year-old. Every day, he worked with little Jimmy, showing him how to protect himself, and how to punch. Then one day J.R. invited the other boy to put on the gloves too, and he watched as the preschoolers went at it. Jim took the older kid apart, just as J.R. knew he would, and from that day on Jim Mitchell played outside without a problem. Nobody would ever intimidate him again.

Nobody.

Jim's brand-new brother never got a chance to win a fight. Bobby's time would be shockingly short.

When he was just shy of four months old, he got an intestinal bug that was going around, and he developed severe diarrhea. His worried parents put their youngest boy in the hospital. Right away, he got better. After four days, the doctors told Georgia Mae she could come get him the next day, and she went out and bought him an outfit to wear home. But suddenly, late that evening, he developed lobar pneumonia, and on the following afternoon, October 2, 1947, he died.

It was a hard lesson about the fragility of life for the two little surviving brothers, but they bounced back quickly, as little boys do, and the family stayed strong.

J.R. had pretty much taken to gambling full-time, and they looked around for a good place to live, somewhere that would be good for gambling and good to raise kids too.

They chose Antioch. Rob's sister lived there, and in visiting her, he had discovered two bars, Jack's and Blu's, that had promising card rooms. There were lots of soldiers stationed at Camp Stoneman, just outside Antioch, and lots of mill workers too, and the bars roared with activity.

Most days in Antioch, Manteca played in Blu's Club, a bar on Second Street. "He was one of my best customers," recalls George Cito, who ran Blu's for more than forty years. "But he almost never drank, and he never got out of line."

Unlike almost every other chronic gambler, what J.R. Mitchell did was win. He took a steady income out of Blu's, regularly trimming the soldiers, factory workers, traveling salesmen, local merchants, and whoever else wandered into the smoky club and made that fateful left turn into the card room. "There weren't many who beat the game, but he did, and he beat it more than anyone," recalls Sipes.

Rob Mitchell has been dead twenty years, and the red-velvet surface on the lowball table at Blu's is faded and scarred with cigarette burns. But the players who sit there, even the youngsters, invoke his name with near reverence. "Manteca was the best card player ever in this place," a twenty-two-year-old bartender says solemnly. After a pause, he adds, "Hearing the stories about him in this place, it's kind of like Wyatt Earp, and Tombstone, and the O.K. Corral."

Back in those days, Antioch was indeed a good gambling town, but it was also a pleasant, livable town, a good place to raise kids. Jim and Art thrived, and people were kind to the young family.

Frank Grangnelli, who owned the entire hill where the Mitchells lived, was one of the richest men in town, but he still ran a fruit stand and drove a watermelon truck. He would make deliveries up and down the street, never failing to stop and buy some Kool-Aid from an entrepreneurial set of brothers who set up shop out in front of Number 405.

He'd leave his watermelon truck parked on the street at night, and often in the summer the Mitchell boys would ask to camp out in the backyard. Their ulterior motive, of course, was to wait until everything was quiet in the neighborhood and swipe a watermelon off the back of the truck. They didn't know that Frank Grangnelli was well aware of their nighttime raids, and always set a melon or two out near the back of the truck so they wouldn't go rooting through his entire stock.

J.R.'s gambling prowess may have become the stuff of legend, but at the time it wasn't security enough for Georgia Mae. When the kids got into school, she went back to school herself, getting her GED, then taking classes at Diablo Valley Junior College.

She had another motive, beyond the financial. "Life was passing me by," she says. "I was just doing everything for Rob and the kids, and not doing anything for me, and I was losing my sense of purpose. School offered a whole new perspective."

This woman who left school in the eighth grade and got married when she was sixteen sensed there was more to life than diapers and dinner, and she was right. Her husband may have been a good-old-boy gambler, but he was completely supportive of her quest for knowledge. She worked her schedule around so that she could take her classes while the kids were at school, but when she had to be away Rob was there for the boys.

She went to the junior college for a year and a half, plus two summers, staying up half the night to do her term papers after cooking supper and tending to her family. Then she started substitute teaching while she worked toward her bachelor's degree at San Francisco State. Her long, successful struggle for education was a manifestation of the strength of character that would serve her and her family so well in later life.

Georgia Mae got a full-time teaching job in the Oakley School District, outside Antioch, on a provisional certificate while she completed her education. Her first teaching contract called for an annual salary of $4,000. Nothing fancy, but it certainly made life a little easier.

The Mitchell boys were well groomed, well dressed, and always had a little spending money in their pockets. Any social discomfort created by the fact that daddy was a professional gambler was more than compensated for by the fact that mom was a schoolteacher. The family was liked and respected.

Georgia remembers substitute teaching at Adelia Kimball Elementary, where her boys were going. Jim's homeroom teacher came to her and said, "I just don't know what to do with Jim. I can't seem to control him at all. Last week he got every word right on the spelling test, and this week he missed every one of them on purpose."

Georgia Mae sympathized. She knew Jim could be ornery. But she also knew what to do about it. "Involve him in a project," she told the teacher. "But don't put him on somebody else's committee. Put him in charge and let him choose who he wants to help him. He'll get so involved in doing the job that he'll forget all about acting up."

The teacher took her advice, and it worked to perfection. "You should see what they've done," the teacher marveled. "There's just no end to it." Jim was put in charge of a class building project, making models of early California history figures, and pretty soon the display went all the way around the room.

Problem solving was to be Jim's strong suit throughout his life. He was never so effective as when he had a specific problem to work on— as long as he was the one making the decisions, devising the solutions.

Compared to his mischievous, full-of-the-devil little brother, Jimmy quickly became a model student. One fourth-grade teacher who had first Jim, then Artie, was totally unprepared for the younger model. "Oh, why can't you be good like Jim!" she scolded him in frustration one day.

That sentiment would be voiced often in Artie's life, and it would mark him indelibly. He always had a lot of living up to do—living up to his big brother, and, of course, to his father.

The two boys could not have been closer to their father. There was nothing in the world that would ever matter more to J.R. than Jim and Art, and all during their growing up they felt the same way about him. He was more than a role model. He was an object of worship, and he was also their best friend.

If his boys were still awake when he got home from the card room, J.R. would greet them with a ritual they loved. He would take the night's profits and toss them into the air, the hard-won bills fluttering to the floor all over the living room of the little wood-frame house. Laughing and scrambling, the little boys would pick it all up and count it. That's how they learned to count money, and it was a lesson they learned very well.

Of a Saturday morning, he would take them down to Second Street to get their hair cut, and then the Mitchell menfolk would stop in Blu's. He would lift the little boys up, sit them on the bar, and buy them Cokes. He'd take them fishing in the big muddy Sacramento for stripers and catfish. There was a great spot for bank fishing down where Wilbur

Avenue ran into the river, and the three of them would head there often. It was there that J.R. taught them the difference between "river talk" and polite conversation.

He told them the handful of swear words they would be hearing anyway as they grew. "You can use 'em down here on the river," he said, "but not at home. The women don't like them, and it's not polite. And don't use them at school. The teachers will get after you."

But down at the river, it was deliciously naughty and fun to try these forbidden words out. The boys would call the undersized fish they caught "fart knockers" and throw them back, waiting for Mr. Big to come along and bite. What a great private man-joke! That man's world was one they would inhabit all their lives—and eventually dominate.

Although they would grow up hippies, believing in free love, civil rights, the Great Society, and an end to war, their attitudes regarding gender were considerably less modern, and may be traced in part right back to those afternoons on the banks of the Sacramento, where they learned that women were to be catered to, loved, appreciated, taken care of, even indulged, but not necessarily treated as equals.

J.R. also took them hunting for small game, squirrel and rabbit and pheasant and duck. He could never forget the hunting tragedy that took his father, and he always taught his boys to be extra careful with guns.

When it came to raising their boys, Rob and Georgia Mae saw pretty much eye to eye. But not completely. Georgia still remembers the time she decided her husband was being a little too hard on Artie.

The younger Mitchell was all set to play baseball for the Kay Contractors team in the Babe Ruth League—which, in the summer of 1961, was about as important as anything could be for a fifteen-year-old in Antioch. Artie was small and slender, as he would be all his life, but he was quick and well coordinated, he had a great arm, and he was a tough competitor. Some of his best friends were on the team, too— J.D. Fluty, Bill Boyer, Billy Del Colletti.

But Artie insisted he could not play with his beat-up old glove. He had to have a new glove, and not just any glove. He wanted the best. The glove that caught his eye cost $30, an astounding sum of money at that time. His father, perhaps remembering his growing-up days camping on the Clear Boggy, demurred. It was just too much money. The Mitchell family was not about to spend $30 for a baseball glove, and that was final.

Artie, heartbroken, told his parents that he couldn't possibly play without it, and said he would have to quit the Babe Ruth team.

J.R. was obdurate, but Georgia Mae could tell how much the glove meant to Art. She took him aside, quietly, and told him that she had managed to put back $20 or so, and she could get the rest, but not to tell his father.

And so the glove was purchased surreptitiously, and Artie played Babe Ruth baseball. The *Antioch Ledger* sports page told the town on May 8 that the Kay Contractors had whipped the Stars 16–6: "The Stars took an initial lead but a bases-clearing triple by Artie Mitchell put the victors ahead for good in the second inning." Artie ended up leading the league that year with a .634 batting average.

The glove stayed tucked away in the back of Artie's closet between games. He let his friend J.D. Fluty use it too, and one day the next-door neighbor noticed J.D. crawling in a window of the Mitchell house when no one was at home. She confronted him on his way out, and he told her he was just borrowing Artie's glove, narrowly avoiding a trip to the police station.

Narrowly avoiding scrapes was a big part of being a teenager in Antioch, and Artie had an incredible success rate. Jim, not as good.

It was a rough place to grow up. The high school boys were always at risk from older toughs who worked at the Fibreboard factory or the steel mill, and cruised the high school parking lot looking for the young girls the high school guys figured were rightfully theirs. But their older rivals had cars, money, jobs, and what seemed to be amazing sophistication, and most of the time it was no contest.

That's not to say that the brothers didn't have girlfriends. They did. From the first, they both were immensely popular. Both of them were small in size, but that just led the girls to think of them as cute and harmless. Friends remember both of them profiting handsomely from this during high school, particularly Artie, who combined "cute" with a studied hard-to-get act that kept the girls anxious to please.

His best girl during high school was Catherine Page, daughter of a prominent Antioch doctor, cute as only a sixteen-year-old girl with a pug nose and devilish eyes can be. "She was the love of his life," Georgia Mae remembers. "She just came along too early."

She had a lasting influence on him, though, and may have been responsible for sparking his lifelong interest in politics. Her parents were active in the local Democratic Party, and in the year immediately following Art's graduation, when Lyndon Johnson and Barry Goldwater offered the country two radically different paths, a group called the Contra Costa Young Democrats sprang up in Antioch.

The group's first president was Artie Mitchell, vice president was Jeff Armstrong, and Catherine Page was secretary. The prez was quoted in the *Antioch Ledger* as saying, "We intend to interest young people in behind-the-scenes politics and government." Speaker at the group's first meeting was Alan Cranston, then California's controller and starting his first race for the U.S. Senate.

Girlfriends were great, but the Mitchell boys had the most fun when they were out with the guys.

They had to be inventive. That older crowd was always around, at the touch football game in the park, at the Panther drive-in, everywhere. "In Antioch, you couldn't have a party, invite some friends, because if you did, the older guys would always crash it, trash the place, beat somebody up, steal something, break everything in sight," remembers a classmate of Artie's. "So we outsmarted them."

It is Friday night. Artie gets himself slicked up, looking good, every brush-cut hair Brylcreemed into place, and makes his escape from the house: going to the movies, see you later.

Freedom, ah, freedom. Meet the guys at the pool hall. Play a game of snooker, then pool your resources, see what's in the kitty. Artie has a little money. Bill Boyer's mom is really poor, but he works at the pool hall five nights a week, so he's flush too. Jeff Armstrong kicks in a buck or two. As usual, J.D. is a hair short, but nobody cares. He is the muscle—a big, hulking kid whose physical stature and fearlessness long ago made him a leader. They buy gas. On this night, the only one with a car is Boyer, whose industriousness has netted him a '53 Pontiac sedan, four-door, with a straight 8 and a very useful back seat. Now they are out in earnest, on a mission they quaintly refer to as "cunt hunting."

What it really amounts to is: find an old rummy who—for the price of a few cans for himself—will buy them some beer. A quick run out to the sand dunes east of town, and the guzzling is rapidly accomplished. Then back into town, full of all the crazy high horny hell that a case of beer will invariably bring out in four seventeen-year-old males, oh yes, cruising on the prescribed route: starting at the Panther drive-in on tenth, down G Street, past the Stamm Theater, to Second Street, hang a left, by the pool hall (and, unavoidably, the police station), flip a U, back down Second Street, right on G, all the way out to Somersville Road, about two miles, right turn out to Hazel's. The cars are stacked up six deep, carhops delivering vertical Hazel burgers, stacked high with lettuce, tomato, and onion, and the *au courant* soft drink—vanilla Coke with coffee cream. Then back on the street, stacking laps around the track, hooting and hollering at the girls who are doing the same, probably without benefit of the case of Busch Bavarian.

As usual, this expedition is not successful in its stated purpose. (J.D. got a lot of blame for this pattern of failure. "Hell, as soon as we had some girls kind of interested, talking to them nice at Hazel's or out on the drag, he'd belch or fart or say something gross. Every damn time," one participant would recall.) But so what? They are out on the street on a Friday night with a beer buzz and gas in the tank.

After that last part inevitably changes—Boyer's Pontiac gets about 10 to the gallon—they end the night where they started, at the pool hall. Open a bag of Planter's peanuts, the old, greasy kind that predated dry roasting and cholesterol paranoia, dump them in the top of a bottle of Double Cola. Sit back, watch guys from the mill in 9-ball duels for five dollars a rack until closing time. Then Artie makes it home and stumbles into bed, luckily avoiding J.R.'s attention.

Another narrow escape. It happened all the time. The summer of '62: Boyer and Artie and a younger boy named Ron Pritchard, who would later play football in the NFL, want to play basketball, but it is 100 degrees on the Delta, and the heat shimmers in waves off the blacktop on the outdoor courts. So they decide to break into the high school via a skylight and drop down into the gym. Immediately, Boyer (who happens to be student body president at the time) and Pritchard are caught, kicked out and reported to the police. But Artie, who is still on the roof at the time of the bust, gets away clean.

A few months later. It is Christmas vacation, and Boyer and Artie and J.D. and Mike Pirazoli make the run to Tijuana, driving J.D.'s brother's car 100 mph through the ground fog of the Central Valley, then through L.A., San Diego, finally across the border. They hit one bar after another, and pretty quickly after they arrive Artie meets a girl—"a nice girl, not a stripper or anything," Boyer remembers. "She could have been the mayor's daughter"—and despite the language barrier, the new couple make plans to go to the dog races. Meanwhile, the other three keep bar hopping, end up in a whorehouse, where J.D. doesn't like something that happens and starts some trouble and suddenly there are what seems like fifty hostile Mexicans and they try to fight their way out and Pirazoli catches a board or a pipe or something in the back of the head. So the luckless drunken trio, laid low by horrible tequila nausea, manage to crawl to the U.S. consulate, where Pirazoli's head gets stitched up. Then they meet Artie at the agreed-upon rendezvous point, battered and bloody and sick, and Artie is happy as can be. He and his newest sweetie won at the races.

Jim isn't so lucky. He doesn't always get away clean.

While he is in high school, one of the boys' older cousins leaves a car in their garage for a few months. Jim and friend Charles Creecy can't resist, and they keep taking the car out for little joyrides, nothing big, just around the block and back, maybe a cruising lap, before his parents get home. Their next-door neighbor—the same one that apprehended J.D. when he sneaked in the window—would see them leave, but refused to tell on them. "They were always so careful!" she would tell Georgia Mae later.

But eventually, Jim's luck runs out. He and Creecy are out for a ride, and he sees his parents coming down the street, returning home quicker than he expected. Rather than face the music, the two boys take off. They are gone for three days, but finally J.R. goes out and finds them and brings Jim home in disgrace. Again, Artie escapes. He had ridden with them before, but this time he is home, like an angel, when the crisis strikes.

The brothers had grown up close, but when Jim was a junior and Artie was a freshman, Georgia Mae despaired of them ever growing up to be friends. They argued constantly that year. One of the sorest points was clothing. They were the same size, and invariably one brother would be wearing the shirt the other wanted.

One night, Artie was getting ready to go out to a dance, and he let out an agonized howl. "My shoes!" he cried. "My best shoes! Jim's got them on and he left!" The ever-patient J.R. knew there was only one way out of this. "Come on, Artie," he said. "Let's go for a ride and get another pair."

By the following year, when Jim was a senior, the brothers were buddies again.

Both brothers were average students, not exceptional. Test results indicated above-average intelligence, but do not reflect the abundance of creativity and innovation they would both display later in life. Overall, their school achievements gave little hint of the success that was to come.

Their transcripts show that the worst subject for both of them in high school was drama. They got Ds. But how many of the other Antioch High drama students would become millionaires producing movies?

Neither brother was an athletic star at the high school level, although both were quick, well coordinated, and exuded the requisite toughness that growing up male in a mill town demanded.

Indeed, Artie made up for his lack of size by having the biggest mouth in town. "He was scrawny. When everybody else was bulking up for football, here was this little runty guy with a cocky grin and a smartass remark," recalls one classmate.

But he always had someone around to protect him, get him out of trouble. Often, of course, it was Jim. Sometimes, it was the intimidating J.D. Fluty. This happy circumstance earned Artie the high school nickname Johnny Concho, after the Frank Sinatra character in the movie of the same name.

In the movie, Frank Sinatra is a little guy who terrorizes an entire town because of the reputation of his brother, Red Concho, the most famous gunfighter in the West. He wins poker hands because nobody dares call him; he drinks for free; and he talks rough to everybody in town and gets away with it.

Of course, in the movie, the inevitable happens: word reaches the town that Red Concho has been killed, and Johnny finds himself in a lot of trouble.

An editorial in the June 16, 1961, *Antioch Ledger* exhorted Jim and his 269 fellow graduates to go out and help America grow even greater. "Maybe there's a future diplomat in the crowd, or an inventor, or a state senator," the editorial rhapsodized. "Maybe a couple of the lads will kick up some of that dust on the moon."

Kick up some dust, yes. Moon, well, sort of. The writer didn't foresee that the one member of the class to become world-famous would do so by making dirty movies.

Of course, Jim had no idea either. He just knew he wanted to get out of town and have some fun.

The change that was dawning across the country in the early 1960s deeply affected Jim and Artie and their friends. Both sets of friends had the overwhelming conviction that they wanted to break the pattern, do something different. They thought: don't get stuck in a job in the mill right out of school, buy a car, cruise the high school, get married, stay in Antioch.

Jim and most of his friends started the breaking-away process by going into the service. It was an option that looked good to his classmates: of the 130-plus boys in the Class of '61, more than ninety enlisted.

Jim's decision to do so may well have been hastened by yet another narrow escape that he didn't quite make. Jim and the boys he ran around with—Richard Lackey, Fred Aquaviva, Richard Ceccini, and a few others— modestly christened themselves the Studs. One night a bunch of them went around spray-painting things like "Studs '61" on railroad trestles, public buildings, and such.

It wasn't too difficult to track down the culprits, and soon they were before a judge who gave them a choice: pay a fat fine or enlist. Jim went to Fort Ord for training, where he earned honors as a crack marksman, and then went on to Okinawa.

Jim came back to Antioch on leave after his overseas duty, and he and some friends headed for a bar, naturally, to tell stories and catch up on each other's lives. Artie went too.

The next day, a police officer knocked on the door of 405 Grangnelli, and Georgia Mae answered the door. "Ma'am, I'd like to talk to you about Artie," the cop said. It turns out that somebody in the bar had a grudge against young Johnny Concho, and had called the police to let them know that Artie Mitchell was drinking in a bar underage.

Artie had managed to do this by showing the skeptical bartender an expertly forged driver's license, showing him to be three years older than he actually was.

Just then, J.R. got home and took over the palaver with the police. Of course, Artie was providentially not at home when the heat arrived. The officer found J.R. a little tough to deal with. Playing his cards close to the vest, J.R. adamantly refused to do what the officer wanted, which was to bring Artie down to the station for booking when he came home.

What good would it do for the boy to get in trouble, J.R. said, eyes narrow and hooded as he sized up the cop. No, he wouldn't do that. But here's what he would do. He would personally guarantee to the officer that as soon as the young man came home, J.R. would confiscate the bogus license, and that would be the end of it. No more problem for anybody.

Sure, the officer said, folding his hand. Sure, Mr. Mitchell. That would be fine.

When Artie did get caught, it was because he wanted to, and he wasn't alone.

In May 1963, a couple of weeks before Artie was to graduate, the Class of '63 had itself a memorable party. It was a school-sponsored function, the annual "Ditch Day" senior class picnic. But what went on was definitely not authorized by school authorities. Despite the presence of six woefully outmanned chaperons, a goodly portion of the class proceeded to get smashed.

This was made possible by superior planning. Some students managed to go to the picnic site the day before and stash some booze. Others smuggled in bottles and cans in hollowed-out loaves of bread. Still others took the way of brute force and simply broke into a nearby archery clubhouse and stole, according to the sheriff's report, "$107.50 worth of beer, candy, cigarettes and potato chips, including 23 six-packs of beer."

Three students brazenly signed the club's guest register. Artie was too smart for that.

Two days later Principal Otis Mercer and school district Superintendent James Reusswig, full of outrage and disgust with what they presumed were a few bad apples in the otherwise illustrious class, called a class assembly.

This insult to their authority had already become a political problem of some magnitude. Mercer had announced the day before that the senior class ball would be canceled, and then was inundated by angry parents at a school board meeting that evening. The parents said it wasn't fair to penalize the whole class for the actions of a few, and anyway, the Ditch Day event had not been adequately chaperoned. Which seemed to be an understatement.

So at the assembly, the two men told the class, "This is your last chance to come forward and admit your involvement." They expected maybe fifty to confess.

Instead, they got 120—nearly half of the class.

At that point, the principal reinstated the senior ball.

After high school, Artie too enlisted in the army, and he faced a new danger: Vietnam. Artie visited the chaplain in his unit at boot camp, telling him he didn't want to go kill people and just didn't know if he could.

He called home, and told J.R. and Georgia Mae the same thing. J.R. didn't want his son to run away by himself, and he didn't blame him for the way he felt. "Come on home, Art, and we'll go over the hill together," he told his son.

But Art and his daddy didn't have to go to Canada. Everybody else in Artie's unit went to 'Nam. Somehow—perhaps with a little help from the chaplain—he got orders to Germany. Another narrow escape.

When Jim returned to Antioch after his military service, he found himself right where he didn't much want to be—in his hometown, and unemployed.

But his travels in the military had broadened him, and redoubled his desire to get out, do something in life besides get a factory job and a factory house and a factory wife. At Jim's insistence, a few of his classmates actually got together and tried to come up with some venture they could all work in to escape Antioch.

It didn't come to much, and Jim decided his best move was to use his brand-new VA entitlement to get himself an education.

He started at Diablo Valley College, majoring in English, doing well, and transferring from the two-year-school to San Francisco State, where he began taking film and photography classes. Jim had to make a film for an end-of-term assignment, and he headed for the beach, where he managed to talk a girl into removing her top. The class dozed as most of the films were shown, but Jim's certainly got attention—and applause.

PART 2

THE FANTASY FACTORY

San Francisco has always been a center of sexual commerce. From the gold rush days of the '49ers, through the heyday of sailing ships, when the bawdy port was known as the Barbary Coast, there were always men with hard-earned cash and a hankering for company to be taken care of.

This was not Boston with its pursed lips and Puritan morals, or Chicago with its Midwestern uptightness. This center of hedonism was more like New Orleans, or Rio de Janeiro. People came to San Francisco to have fun, and the City by the Bay was more than happy to oblige.

Certainly, in the 1960s, that was never more true. What a convergence of time and place! The Free Speech movement, the Summer of Love, acid-zonked hippies humping like rabbits in Golden Gate Park, in the Haight, everywhere. The Grateful Dead and the Airplane and Janis and all the rest!

Still, all that free love didn't mean there wasn't a market for dirty movies. Far from it: people were beginning to be a lot less hung up about wanting to see them. And there was a ready source of acting talent out there, perfectly willing to do what came naturally for the price of a few lids of pot or a few meals. It was a perfect milieu for a couple of randy Delta boys out to revolutionize the celluloid version of the world's oldest profession.

· · ·

Artie got back from Germany just in time for the fun. While Jim was going to school at San Francisco State, he had worked part-time at a burlesque house, the Follies, as a doorman for $1.25 an hour. He would take the bank bag down and make the deposit every night, and the bulge in the bag was not lost on him. By the time Artie showed up Jim had already started a modest little pornie business, taking seminude pictures and selling them to the newsstands and stores along Market Street.

At the time, high school pal Bill Boyer was at the *Antioch Ledger*, having failed to get out of his hometown but having succeeded in getting a good job in his career of choice, journalism. Artie and Jim found out that the *Ledger* had recently purchased a drum print dryer, a vast improvement over the old-fashioned dryer they were using, and so before long, after Boyer processed his sports pictures and made the final deadline, nude photos were rolling off the *Ledger*'s brand-new dryer in the middle of the night. Dean Lesher, crusty, conservative owner of the *Ledger* and a dozen other East Bay newspapers, would have been scandalized, of course, but no one was the wiser.

It was not long before the brothers were making loops, the pneumatic little ten- to twenty-minute smut films that viewers watched for twenty-five cents a minute. The market for them was brisk, and it became evident that this was a paying proposition. The brothers were on to something. They began to put together a team to expand.

Quite naturally, they looked to the people they grew up with, the people they could trust. They surrounded themselves with boys from Antioch—" 'tiochers," in the Delta vernacular—people like Jon Fontana, who graduated with Jim and becomes the outfit's top cameraman; Jeff Armstrong, who graduated with Artie, then went on to get his business degree from Cal; and Richard Mezzavilla, who was in the class between the two Mitchell boys and was destined to become the company's controller. Richard Ceccini, who graduated with Jim, was an all-around assistant, and became a wizard at locating props, costumes, locations. He took care of a thousand details on each shoot, making sure things went smoothly. Russ Mitchell, no relation but another Antioch friend, also did many different tasks, some lighting, backup on the camera, props, production assistance. Before long, Art and Jim's first cousin, Curtis "Rocky" Davidson, joined the inner circle, doing carpentry and maintenance chores as well as some production work.

They needed a scriptwriter, or at least they thought they did. And they wanted Boyer, because they knew him and trusted him. He had gone from the *Ledger* to a PR job at Harrah's Casino at Tahoe, for

$900 a month, half again the salary Lesher had paid him. For a guy in his early twenties who came from nothing he was making damn good money, so the first time crazy Johnny Concho and his big brother knocked on his door, he laughed at them. You want me to come write dirty movies? I'm rubbing shoulders with the governor of Nevada here, doing a flashy job in a flashy town for seriously good money.

He quit laughing when two things happened: one, they offered him even more than he was making at Harrah's, $1,200 a month or so, and two, he became infected with their excitement. Even then, the brothers had a way of getting you into their camp. They were both charismatic, and they had a great shared vision. All these boys were going to get rich making dirty movies, he could see that, and they were going to have a hell of a good time doing it. Before long, Boyer was on the team.

The Mitchells leased a cavernous old warehouse at 20th and Tennessee on San Francisco's Potrero Hill, and the team, doing the labor themselves, turned it into the city's largest soundstage.

After work, it is an Antioch flashback: they would choose up sides and play Shirts and Skins basketball out in front of the lot, then head down the hill to drink some beer and look for women.

Their success rate, of course, had improved dramatically since Antioch. Everybody was making love in San Francisco in those days, and the brothers and their friends were certainly no exception.

Shoot, they were *hiring* people to make love. On camera. And for their efforts they were making a hell of a lot more money than the boys back at the Fibreboard plant.

From the first, J.R. and Georgia Mae were comfortable with their boys' new enterprise.

"We knew before they knew we knew," their mother remembers. "They had a tiny little projector that they'd borrowed from someone. They left it with one of the films at the house one day, and Rob and I were curious as all get-out, so we got in there and turned it on right away, to see what the boys were into."

They found out.

Many mothers would have agonized. But not Georgia Mae. She had learned long ago to be open-minded about choices of profession. After all, her husband had become a professional gambler.

"I had learned not to pass judgment on people. Of course, you hope they don't pass judgment on you, but it doesn't work that way," she says.

J.R. thought it was just fine too. This was the daddy who had offered to go over the hill with Artie. And when Jim had grown his hair long after the service, he had firmly shushed any criticism. "It's his hair, and if he wants to wear it long it's his business. It doesn't affect what's underneath it," he said.

Married twenty-five years now, they were happy to have reared such strong, handsome boys. Georgia Mae was secretly thankful that she and J.R. had moved from Antioch to Sacramento. The little town where the boys had grown up was buzzing with talk, she was sure.

But it wouldn't have mattered so much. They were proud of those boys, at first for striking out on such a bold venture, then, as time passed, proud of them for succeeding.

And fighting to keep what was theirs.

Jim and Artie weren't always Jim and Artie around the studio. They went by Big Bob and Little Bob—another gesture of respect to their daddy. They'd be forever joking around with each other, Hey, Bob? Yeah, Bob? Hey, Bob, what are you doing, Bob? Nothing much, Bob, just editing this little fuck movie here, Bob, what are you doing, Bobby? Nothing, Little Bobby, nothing, how about going out for a beer, Bob? Sure, Bob, sure. Take your car, Bob?

Jim, of course, was Big Bob.

Soon, Big Bob and Little Bob set about the work of simultaneously revolutionizing a back-alley industry and fighting a war with the San Francisco District Attorney's office.

But first, they had some more plain old-fashioned carpentry to do. They had to fix up another ancient building—a big brick pile at the corner of Polk and O'Farrell in downtown San Francisco. The location was seedy enough to be cheap and close enough to the Civic Center and busy Van Ness Avenue to ensure lots of traffic.

After months of work, putting in seats, carpeting, projection equipment, the works, the brothers opened the O'Farrell Theatre on July 4, 1969, jumping into the lust-house scene with both feet. It was their mother, Georgia Mae's, forty-fourth birthday.

The movie house was the linchpin of the brothers' astonishing plan to redefine the skinflick business. They weren't going to be satisfied with making loops and selling them wholesale forever. They wanted control. All the way along the line.

"Jim always said the sex movie business should be run along the lines of the traditional movie studios, like MGM and Paramount," one early friend remembers. "He wanted to make the films, own the films, market the films, show the films, all within the same company. He wanted to make money on both ends of the business and everywhere in between."

Suddenly, the brothers were poised to do just that. They had a production crew. They had a soundstage. They could cast and produce and edit and package themselves. And they had a theater to show the films. From the moment the star got naked on the set to the time the credits rolled in front of the viewers' glazed eyes, they had control.

Now they got busy making movies. They graduated from loops to "featurettes"—thirty- to sixty-minute films that could be advertised and shown at the O'Farrell. They aimed for one a month, and came pretty close to that pace for about a year.

These little films were not high art, and they were not different in any major way from what was already on the market, although from the first the Mitchells aimed for higher production values than most of their competitors.

The brothers also became well known in the trade for the fresh young faces and bodies they featured. They would put casting calls in the newspapers, and in those post–Summer of Love days they would get an unbelievable number of applicants. They would spot the hookers and professionals right off and weed them out, opting instead for the enthusiastic young hippies that proliferated in the sexiest city in America.

They would shoot on location and at the studio, depending on what the wafer-thin plot line was. Often, an available location was the determining factor in the plot. For instance, they had a Delta friend with a paper bag factory, so they made a movie there.

They learned quickly too that in marketing these little films the title was everything. The paper bag flick was originally titled, with a wink in the direction of Erle Stanley Gardner, *The Case of the Badgered Bag-Makers*.

Cute, but about as sexy as yesterday's pot roast. It died. So in a while they re-released it under the name *Flesh Factory* and it packed 'em in.

Artie was responsible for a lot of the catchy titles. One super-low-budget production that absolutely roared at the box office was a little featurette titled by Artie *Rampaging Nurses*. It was easy to make: Just put the women into and out of white uniforms, and stand back.

The newspaper ads for these titles were masterpieces of the cheap double entendre ("She Was No Farmer's Daughter, but She Could Make Things Grow") and featured breathless "warnings" to anyone who might be offended by "every conceivable variation of the act of love" to stay away. They also featured manufactured review snippets by a movie critic with a catchy name. The June 1970 ad for a featurette

called *Thin Silva Saga* carried this tagline from the eminent critic:
" 'This time they may have gone too far—even for me'—B. Wakefield
Boyer."

The ads would exhort: "Bring a date—Chicks love it!" Soon, they
were advertising: "New projection equipment—100% brighter picture."

The brothers were really getting into the art of porn. "I'm a voyeur,"
Artie told the *San Francisco Chronicle*'s Maitland Zane in an early
interview. "I make movies for voyeurs. To make a good erotic movie
what you need is, like, real energy coming from the people who are
making love. What the best films offer is heavy doses of heavy energy,
pure emotion."

Jim would define it more simply: "It's good if it gives you an erection."

Zane went down one day to watch a film being made. Jim, bending
low as he directed the action, reminded Zane of an umpire poised to
make the call on a close play at the plate, with Artie exhorting from
the sideline: "Just get it on, forget the camera's there!"

What a new, strange thing this was! These two young bucks, so
recently cruising by the Stamm Theater in their innocence, looking for
girls to flirt with, now crouching over copulating couples, still strangely
innocent for all their audacity and bravado, still filled with curiosity
and wonder at this incredible force that would keep them, keep so many
people stacking those laps around the circuit forever, searching for that
perfect experience.

They were changing, though: around the time Neil Armstrong made
his Giant Leap for Mankind, the brothers made their leap, hippies to
businessmen, pranksters to hard-nosed fighters, boys to men, men in
a very tough racket.

Their movie mill kept rolling. They would take a week to write a
script, find the locations and the props, hire the talent, do all the
preproduction stuff. Then they'd take another week to shoot. Another
week getting prints and editing, then a week to schedule, advertise,
and voila! About a month after the initial concept, the movie opened
at the O'Farrell. Some of the early efforts included *Choi Oi,* a film
about a VC massage parlor in Saigon, *Soft, Ruby Lafayette, Riverboat,
Isabelle,* and *It Happened in Muskogee.*

Artie and Boyer would knock out the scripts and Jim and Jon Fontana
would turn them into reality on the technical end.

Fontana was a workhorse. He was instrumental in keeping the place
going in the early years. Regardless of what crazy ideas were dreamed

up in a cloud of smoke in the brothers' office, the success or failure of the movies came down to the ability of the guy with the camera to get it onto film. If Jim and Art weren't around for some reason—or if they had a fight and left the set and the shooting had to be finished—Fontana was the guy who could take charge, know what to do, motivate people, finish the job.

The brothers did have creative disagreements on the set, and sometimes they would be bitter and scary, particularly to the people who were depending on the brothers for their livelihood.

The first time it happened after Boyer came down from Tahoe, he thought, what is this? The company's dead, right here and now. But invariably, the day after an argument, the two would be tighter than ever. They could be screaming obscenities into each other's faces from six inches away. It didn't matter. One of them would call the other one that evening, they would sort it out, and the next day on the set they would be like nothing had ever happened.

Boyer made the mistake a couple of times, when there was a disagreement between the two brothers, of offering an opinion. "Suddenly, instead of witnessing a fight between two people, you'd have a pair of wolverines at your throat," he said.

Fontana told him, man, don't do that, sit back, they'll work it out, if you take one side or the other, they'll turn on you every time. Whoever you disagree with, the other one will immediately defend him, even though you're on his side. They're brothers, and that's the way they operate. One brother is threatened from the outside, the other one is there in a heartbeat. But they fight like wild dogs between themselves.

"When they get like that," he was told, "stay the fuck out of their way."

Later in 1969, Artie met a smart, pretty young hippie that had a lot more to offer than the women he was seeing at the theater.

Meredith Bradford was no ordinary working-class waif. She was an aristocratic Bostonian. The Bradfords were a Mayflower family; William Bradford, first governor of Massachusetts, was a direct ancestor, and her father was a prominent surgeon. But in 1969, Meredith cared nothing for all that. The place to be was California; there was a whole new revolution going on out there, and she wanted to be part of it. So when she graduated from Cornell she went to Los Angeles for the summer with some friends to see what it was all about.

She met Artie through friends, and decided to move to San Francisco to be with him. Besides, San Francisco was where it was *really* happening, and this impish, handsome, quick-witted boy was right in the middle of it.

Before long, blue-blooded Bostonian Meredith Bradford was carrying Cherokee-blooded Okie Artie Mitchell's baby.

They got married in a San Francisco tavern. Meredith's sister Jennifer came to town for the event, which must have seemed bizarre in the extreme to the Brahmin Bradfords. Artie had no money and no ring, so Jim gave him one to use. It was a fancy tooled-gold ring he had bought with his army mustering-out money.

On July 29, 1970, Artie became a daddy. He chose his little girl's name, and it was a dandy. It was hip, it was appropriate to both halves of her heritage, and it had a lot to do with what her daddy believed in.

He called her Liberty.

To the District Attorney's office, San Francisco's sex-soaked history was just that—history. And while the City may have been the capital of Free Love, the D.A. sure didn't care for flicks that showed folks just how it was done.

It didn't take long for the law to discover this band of renegade Delta boys and their home-grown, home-shown dirty movies. The authorities were feeling besieged enough at the events of the past few years in the Haight and Golden Gate Park. They sure didn't welcome a new outpost of salaciousness a couple of blocks from City Hall.

On July 25, 1969, just three weeks after it opened, plainclothes cops walked in on a showing of the Mitchells' featurette *Lessons in Love,* scaring the hell out of scores of patrons who had paid four dollars to see the show, and arrested one James Lloyd Mitchell, twenty-five, who posted $500 bail and vowed to fight the charge.

In August, the police took the fight a step further, raiding several theaters and arresting patrons. They didn't actually arrest O'Farrell patrons, targeting Alex De Renzy's Screening Room Theater instead, but they might as well have. The crackdown kept most of the customers away. Anyway, the cops got around to the O'Farrell soon enough.

"I remember Art calling us, really discouraged," Georgia Mae said. "It was like he was ready to give up. I told him, 'Art, fight with everything you've got. They do not have the right to come in there and say those films are illegal. It hasn't been proved in court.' They would have kept up the fight anyway, I know, but I think it did Art good to hear that we were behind him all the way."

On August 14, showing the political savvy and skill with the media that was to become their trademark, the Mitchells struck back. They held a press conference at the theater at which they vowed to file a suit in federal court to get the police off their back—and just to prove their movies had artistic merit, they showed one to the (male) reporters sent to cover the story.

The film would now be a collector's item, and it has a ghoulish resonance today. Titled *Requiem,* it opens in a graveyard, with a woman in black beside her husband's headstone.

Reporter Charles Howe, who attended the "press screening," told the next morning's *San Francisco Chronicle* readers that in the movie "the young woman performed an act moralists a few generations ago denounced as 'self abuse.' "

The media play worked, of course. Howe's story was spread over three columns, headed, "Erotic Movie Displayer Intends to Strike Back" and carried a one-column photo of an already balding, mustachioed young entrepreneur with the caption: James Mitchell/"Honest eroticism."

The brothers vowed to name Mayor Joseph Alioto specifically in their suit against the city, charging that he was conspiring against them because he had a financial interest in several competing theaters. (Alioto later admitted that he had had an interest along with his brother Frank in the company Syufy Enterprises, but claimed that he had divested himself of that interest before he became mayor.)

No stroke of good fortune would ever mean more to either of the brothers than the one that led them to hire attorney Michael John Kennedy.

The alliance was one more benefit the Mitchells derived from their network of close friends. Jim had served on Okinawa with Kennedy's brother, and they had kept in touch. When the brothers found themselves in urgent need of counsel, Jim's service buddy recommended his brother, who had just set up shop in San Francisco.

The fiery young defense attorney had already begun to build a national reputation with his potent mix of skilled advocacy and political activism. Displaying long hair, Sergeant Pepper's clothing, and wonderful, calculated bombast, Michael Kennedy was the quintessential radical-chic lawyer. When he and partner Joe Rhine decided to open a practice in San Francisco in 1969, their timing was as impeccable as the Mitchell Brothers'. Hippies, lefties, people of color were being harassed and arrested all over the Bay Area, and there was quite a market for a true believer who was also a hell of a good lawyer.

Kennedy's client list was studded with 1960s heavies: Tim Leary, Bernardine Dohrn, Huey Newton.

The Kennedy legend got its start in the famed Chicago Eight trial, where he was cited for contempt, but it was not his first or his last brush with the legal establishment.

He was hated by San Francisco police and prosecutors alike after his successful defense of Los Siete de la Raza, seven Latino men charged with killing a cop in a street brawl in San Francisco's Mission District. After he had won the case, an angry judge cited him with nearly 100 acts of contempt of court. A bar investigation later exonerated him.

"The Mission was an armed camp at that time," Kennedy remembers. "It was being run like a police state, every bit as much as the dictatorships of Somoza and Batista. Any Latino on the street was subject to police pressure and harassment."

The Los Siete acquittals had a huge impact, and Kennedy remains very proud of that. "After we won that case, the police in the Mission were never quite as free to abuse their power," he says.

Not surprisingly, with Kennedy—and, not incidentally, the First Amendment—in their corner from the start, the brash young brothers instantly became a potent legal force.

The three men got along wonderfully. Kennedy easily fitted into the brothers' tight circle. He thought like they did. He *got the joke*. Perhaps most importantly, he understood their dynamic, the way they worked together: Jim would say, "We've got to do this," and Art, with his soaring, free-ranging, devilish imagination, would suggest fifteen ways they could do whatever it was—from tormenting the mayor to making the next movie. Then the brothers would sit down and work out the details.

Quite simply, Kennedy's job was to preserve their right to keep on doing it, and he wasted no time. He won a federal court order banning further arrests of movie house patrons, which ensured the customers would keep coming through the door, but that was merely the first shot on Fort Sumter in this rebel uprising. San Francisco's acting police chief, Al Nelder, warned, "We will continue to arrest operators."

And arrest they did. Both Jim and Artie, who was then president of the Mitchells' corporation, were arrested dozens of times over the next year. As soon as the feature at the theater changed, they would be arrested and charged all over again.

In those early days, the policemen responsible for putting together the cases against the Mitchells were two porn detail partners, Sergeant Sol Weiner and Officer Pete Maloney. It got so that Maloney would call Artie or Jim and say, "You're about to be arrested. You want to come on down to the station?" and they'd say, "Sure, Pete. Be right down."

Of course, they continued to defy the cops and kept making and showing movies, completely defying convention. Most porntrepreneurs quietly paid their fines and eventually, if the heat persisted, folded up and went elsewhere.

The D.A. couldn't believe it. The hubris of these punk kids from Antioch! Here they are, nothing but a couple of goddamn hippie college kids with a camera, the company has a twenty-three-year-old *president*, for God's sake, and his twenty-five-year-old brother was still a student at San Francisco State! They should have wilted faster than one of their stars after the show. And here they are hiring hot-shit lawyers and embarrassing the mayor!

He quickly found out that Jim and Artie Mitchell weren't raised quitters. And they sure didn't like anybody pushing them around. The Antioch in them, the Okie in them, meant they were going to fight if somebody got in their way. Fight savagely. Just like J.R. had taught Jim to do, with the little boxing gloves he still kept as a reminder. There was never a question of doing anything else.

"Here's where the Mitchell Brothers really began to show how special they were," remembers one O'Farrell insider. "The police raid you and raid you. Now, if you have a soft spot in the middle, as most of us do, you might back off. If, like they were at that time, you were just getting the business going, you might reconsider, think about cutting your losses and running.

"But Jim and Art were solid to the core. No soft spots. Jim's thinking was, look, if the police are going to storm in here for us showing soft-core porn, we might as well show it all.

"In those days the key word wasn't hard-core, it was penetration. In other words, nobody was actually showing the penetration. So I think what Jim did was basically say, 'Fuck it, it's either free speech or it isn't, I'm either going to win or lose, and the police are coming through the door anyway so let's go all the way.' That defiance of the police, believing in their right of free speech, basically saved the porn industry in the city."

Another key person from those days says, "You know, the cops may have done exactly what they didn't want to do. I don't know if the Mitchell Brothers would necessarily have stayed with pornography. A lot of us figured it would be just a temporary thing, a kick. But after the first few raids by police, you get mad and you dig in, and also you have to start hiring attorneys, and you have to have big cash flow to pay them. They were really swept away by events.

"And, of course, because of who they were, when somebody pushed, they pushed back."

Dennis Roberts, who was a partner with Kennedy and Rhine and would play a significant role in the brothers' legal fights for the next twenty-plus years, remembers walking over to the Hall of Justice and looking at the Municipal Court docket and seeing every line on the docket be a Mitchell Brothers prosecution. Every one of them California Penal Code 311.2. Production, distribution or exhibition of obscene matter. Dirty movie prosecutions.

It was a year and a half before the first case finally made it into court. The stage was set for one of the longest-running, most entertaining courtroom circuses in the Bay Area.

The prosecutor: Deputy District Attorney Jerome Benson, upright, uptight, clean-cut, morally outraged. For the defense: the flamboyant, needling, wisecracking Kennedy, resplendent in wild suits and pageboy hairdo, cleverly deflecting attention from his two dapper little clients.

That first trial was an indication of the way things would go almost every time a jury considered whether the films the brothers were showing met the statutory definition of obscenity.

Benson put a psychiatrist named Louis Noltimier on the stand to testify that the movies were "unhealthy." The defense retaliated with John Wasserman, enormously popular *Chronicle* film and theater critic, who testified that the films "tended to broaden one's horizons," and that many Hollywood movies were merely "gussied-up" versions of what the Mitchells were showing.

Kennedy spent a day banging away at the unfortunate Sergeant Weiner, declaring that the cop's opinions on pornography reflected those of "old women and religious groups." He told Weiner scornfully, "Save your speeches for the PTA."

In a ripping two-hour final argument, Kennedy suggested that police would better spend their time arresting muggers and burglars. This was to become a keystone of final arguments in these cases: "If you're robbed or mugged and you need help," Kennedy would boom, "try to get to the nearest dirty movie house. There will be at least two cops inside."

Kennedy hammered home the point that there was no evidence to indicate watching pornography created harmful effects, and said that taxpayers' money was being wasted trying to tell people what they could and couldn't see.

Benson responded that the police were required to enforce all the laws on the books, and that community standards, not potential harmful effects, were the issue.

The jury deliberated for ten hours before announcing it was hopelessly deadlocked, voting 11–1 for acquittal on one film and 7–5 for conviction on two others.

Benson vowed to keep up the fight. Jim, ebullient in victory, promised to keep showing films despite the continuing police pressure. "Our position is that people want to see these movies," he said. He did deny a newspaper report that the Mitchells made films showing sex with animals, and said he and Art had decided not to make films showing torture or violence of any kind.

"We're clean-cut, All-American boys," he said. "We're going to stick with clean-cut little fuck movies."

The obscenity trials provided Kennedy and Rhine with their first real income, and allowed them to take on many of the glamorous pro bono clients that added to their legend. They also provided Kennedy with a wonderful showcase for his talent.

He really liked these brothers. They were smart and funny, and there was not an ounce of quit in them. And as he won victory after victory, Kennedy delighted in baiting the increasingly frustrated Benson.

Roberts, who describes his former partner as "an intuitive genius in court," says that one of Kennedy's great strengths was pushing Benson's button, teasing him in court until he was literally quaking with rage.

"One of the funniest things I ever saw was Mickey Kennedy, trying a case against Benson. He had a long fingernail on his pinky and as he walked past Jerome as he's sitting there at the D.A.'s table he runs that fingernail lightly across the nape of Benson's neck. Benson came absolutely unglued, just went nuts."

D.A. baiting was great sport. They were such sincere, straight-up, Boy Scout types, such easy targets for the raffish, wily, quick-witted defense attorneys. Roberts handled a Mitchells case in which another young D.A. had worked himself into an evangelical fury in his closing argument, and in the process of making one of his high moral pronouncements turned toward Roberts and roared, "Why, even Mr. . . . Mr. . . ." and in his feverish zeal totally blanked on Roberts's name.

"He looked at me with these appealing eyes as he sputtered, like 'For God's sake, help me,' " Roberts remembers. Instead, Roberts silently but clearly mouthed the words 'Fuck you,' sending the guy into new paroxysms of stuttering. Finally he flashed on "Dennis," and said, "Even Mr. Dennis—"

"Objection!" Roberts yelled, getting to his feet in mock fury. "I resent this attorney's attempt to imply he is on a first-name basis with me. I abhor everything he stands for." The jury laughed and the guy just shuffled through his notes and crumpled back into his seat, and another case was in the bag.

The cops' presentation was unintentionally humorous too. Weiner and Maloney. They became famous in the legal community for their terse, matter-of-fact reports about what was going on in the movies they watched: *WFA [white female American] orally copulates WMA. Two minutes. WFA leaves room. BFA enters room. Copulates with bedpost. Three minutes.*

"I used to want to publish them. They would be like the world's dumbest dirty books. They would go on and on. They were pathetic," Roberts said.

"I actually liked those two. They were wonderful guys," he added. "Maloney was just a typical blustery Irish cop, but Weiner I would torture. Solly Weiner was so Yiddish you couldn't believe it, but he went to San Francisco State and somehow or other became an Irish Catholic.

"I would see him in the Hall of Justice and I would yell down the hall to him, I'd wait until he was as far away as possible but still in earshot, 'Solly!' I'd bellow. 'Solly, does your mother know you sit in dirty movies all day long? That's what she raised you for, Solly?' His ears would turn red.

"The poor guys, they eventually got transferred to the pawnshop detail, like it was their fault they couldn't get a conviction, which of course it wasn't."

The whole show had a freakish aspect to it, the Merry Pranksters vs. the Keystone Kops. It was, in fact, two cultures in collision: the 1950s vs. the 1960s, Law and Order and God and Church and Family and America vs. Hippies, Free Love, LSD, Sex for Fun, If It Feels Good Do It, Make Love Not War, Question Authority. On top of that you had the old-time San Franciscans mad as hell anyway about what was happening to their city, being overrun by flower children and topless dancers and now porno palaces, being forced to see, as Kennedy kept reminding Benson, that times had changed, most people just didn't care about that stuff anymore, San Francisco *was* liberal now, everybody else was out of step. And the results of the trials confirmed it. Community standards were that issue, and the fact was that most of the community just didn't mind folks going to see dirty movies if that was what they wanted to do.

The brothers weren't the only porn merchants being hauled into court. There was Gino Del Prete, owner of the Expo 69 Theater on Kearny Street. There was Les Natali, who managed six theaters, including De Renzy's Screening Room; and, of course, De Renzy himself, who was probably San Francisco's first porn millionaire and would become one of the giants of the sex movie business.

But the brothers were the lightning rods. When others in the business preferred to tiptoe around the legal jungle, the Mitchells hacked their way through with machetes and dared prosecutors to bust them if they could. They became resigned early on to allocating a big chunk of the cash flow to legal fees. They paid their bills and they never backed away from a fight, even when that meant going against their lawyers' advice.

As the obscenity trials continued, Kennedy and Rhine and Roberts refined their act, putting together an impressive stable of defense witnesses. Hooker celebre Margo St. James, founder of the prostitutes' rights organization COYOTE (Call Off Your Old Tired Ethics). The *Chronicle*'s Wasserman. Ted McIlvenna, president of the Institute for Advanced Study of Human Sexuality—a sexologist—who would tell juries that the films were of value as "remedial sex education for the general public." A grandfatherly psychiatrist, Dr. Spotswood, who would say in his kindly way, "There is nothing wrong with sex." Who could argue? Another psychiatrist, Martin Blinder, who would become famous later for proffering Dan White's famed "Twinkie Defense" which claimed in essence that White's predeliction for junk food was a contributing factor in his killing of Mayor George Moscone and gay Supervisor Harvey Milk, the City Hall double slaying that electrified San Francisco in 1979.

The lawyers weren't above cheap theatrics. Occasionally, they'd get the boys' dignified parents to come and sit in the front row. And after Artie's daughter, Liberty, was born, they would make sure she came down the aisle to see Daddy. "When she was a toddler, she'd have her little sand pail and shovel, and she'd be dressed so cute, and she'd go right down to the front to see him."

And, of course, the brothers themselves played well before the jury.

Kennedy believed that the social value of pornography was to serve as a shield for the rest of art and literature, and he was arguing not just to protect the brothers, but to preserve that shield.

In the 1990s, the resonance of those pioneer obscenity cases with the fight over the NEA and the works of artists like Robert Mapplethorpe is obvious. "Our juries were telling us the same thing that the Cincinnati jury said in the Mapplethorpe trial," Kennedy remembers. "They said, 'We don't like this stuff, it's not our cup of tea, but they've got a right to do it.' "

Trial after trial, Kennedy and the brothers got hung juries and outright acquittals. Only once were they convicted on a 311.2, and that result was overturned on appeal. Kennedy remembers, though, that the conviction significantly raised the stakes. A second conviction could bring five-year jail terms for the brothers. But that never happened. They just kept on winning.

At the same time, they were helping to finance some of Kennedy's most memorable pro bono work: political defenses of Huey Newton, Angela Davis, and others. When Richard Mezzavilla needed an attorney to fight for his status as a conscientious objector, the brothers paid and Kennedy won the case.

Back on the porn front, the enemy was weakening.

Some of the D.A.'s and politicians came to Kennedy and said, look, we don't want to keep fighting. Just get them to tone it down a little bit. Their idea of "toning down" was no nipples, pubic hair, or penetration, and Kennedy's response was, "You're hypocrites and my clients aren't and you can go to hell."

In 1971, Mayor Alioto's own Crime Commission recommended easing enforcement pressure on "victimless crimes," including homosexuality, gambling, prostitution, and pornography. This enraged Chief Nelder and Benson, and they responded with a new wave of porno busts, all of which would prove to be fruitless.

Kennedy was forever coming up with new gambits. In a 1972 obscenity case involving the Mitchells' movie *Reckless Claudia,* he contracted with Field Research Corpation, the respected California polling firm, to survey attitudes about pornography. In trial, the pollster testified that only one in four adult Californians thought pornography should be banned. Kennedy won an acquittal, and afterward jurors expressed the opinion that the case should never have been brought.

Finally, after dozens of reversals, Benson grudgingly gave up. Like a cavalry officer with his horse shot out from under him, he was fighting to protect a community standard that, according to jury after jury, just did not exist.

Years later, they would face a whole new round of prosecutions in connection with their live entertainment. But for the time being, after paying some hefty legal fees to Kennedy and Rhine, the Mitchell Brothers' right to give San Francisco an erection was intact.

The brothers were doing more than making dirty movies and getting busted. First and last, they would always value having fun.

In that spirit, the O'Farrell hosted "The People's Nickelodeon," a freaky-deaky montage of old movies and live vaudeville-style entertainment, a couple of nights a week in the early 1970s.

The Nickelodeon would follow the porn flicks at midnight. Tickets were a sternly enforced five cents apiece, and usually somewhere around a couple hundred of the city's fun-loving hippie types and a few oldsters with a sense of humor would come to guffaw at a chorus line of demurely clad, outrageously funny young women called the Nickelettes, who would do spunky song-and-dance routines with much more enthusiasm than finesse, which was just great with the cannablissed audience.

It was a goof, a way for the brothers to say to the city, hey, we don't take this seriously, why should you? And it went a long way toward establishing the brothers' enduring image as fun-loving, mischievous boys who just happened to be porno producers as well.

Nevertheless, winning legal battles and polishing their image didn't solve all of the brothers' problems. They were doing okay, but not great. The movies they were making wouldn't run for the month it took to make the next one. They would open and almost always have a great first week. If they were really hot they'd do well for a second week. But sometimes they'd die the second week and be gone by the third. So they were having a tough time keeping the theater filled.

Also, the movies had almost no distribution potential beyond the O'Farrell. They had a few other small-time outlets, but in order to make big money, they had to make something that would sell in New York, something with a hook, something particularly marketable. That meant a feature-length, higher-budget movie, something with some legs, with some staying power.

That meant some wrenching changes in the organization. If they were going to go out of production with the shorter features, they not only didn't need some of their key people, they also wouldn't be maintaining the same cash flow.

It was typical of the "sabbaticals" that Mitchell insiders had to endure in the early years. Boyer recalls his shock and dismay the first time it happened. Hey, I thought we were friends here, close friends, and we were going to get rich together. What do you mean, you're laying me off for a while? I left a hell of a good steady job to take this.

The veterans who had preceded him in the group—Fontana, Mezzavilla—were prepared, because it had happened to them before. They had known to stash some cash when things were fat, to take them through the times that weren't. But Boyer wasn't. He was feeling a little weird anyway, having left a promising journalism/PR career to go to work for these crazies. Much of what he had wanted to do in scriptwriting was useless in these little plotless pornies. And the dialogue he wrote often sounded ridiculous when it came from the mouths of the amateurish players they used. So when another sportswriting job came up, he grabbed it.

"B. Wakefield Boyer" would eventually return to the fold, but by then the Mitchell Brothers would be world-famous. They accomplished that with creativity, hard work, great instincts, and a tremendous dose of gambler's luck.

Artie had brought back a crazy story idea from the service, in which a young woman's sexual fantasies became real, and a wild mythological epic that he'd heard in a mess hall in Germany, which he and Boyer turned into the rough script for a film called *Behind the Green Door*.

When they ran an ad in the San Francisco newspapers that said, "Now Casting for a Major Motion Picture," one of the hundreds who showed up at the big warehouse on Tennessee Street was a nineteen-year-old hippie girl named Marilyn Chambers who had done quite a bit of modeling and had worked as a topless dancer.

She had called to make an appointment, then called back when she realized she would be late, and the person who answered the phone at the big soundstage on Tennessee Street told her, don't bother, we've already cast the film.

But she went anyway, and she was handed a form to fill out. One of the first questions was, "Do you want a balling or nonballing role?"

"I thought, Oh, God, I'm in the wrong place," she remembers. She had never done a porn film. It just wasn't a hip thing to do. There was no such thing as a "major" porn film then. All she knew about were the stag films that she thought were more funny than sexy.

She was about to turn around and leave, but Jim and Art, ever sharp-eyed, had seen her from the top of the stairs that led to their office. One of them shouted, "Wait! We want to talk to you!"

So she went upstairs and into their office, taking the measure of these two guys barely older than she was, discovering that they seemed like really nice guys, not at all what she would expect porno movie producers to be like.

"Art had on this sweater vest and a button-down shirt, really preppie. I'm from the East Coast and I was so used to that preppie shit. I felt comfortable with them somehow. But nobody in California wore those clothes! It was totally Antioch!"

They began to tell her about themselves, what they wanted to do with the movie, and her disbelief grew. They were just regular guys, almost square. Artie told her about his baby girl. They were totally family-oriented, down to earth, and seemed absolutely honest. She related to them strongly right away.

"We clicked. I showed them my modeling portfolio and they said, 'You're just what we're looking for. We're looking for the girl next door.'" This was, after all, the sexy Sixties, and the girl next door didn't have to *be* a virgin, she just had to look like one. In fact, it was okay if she *loved* sex. And that was what they were after.

Marilyn thought the idea for the movie was fantastic. She was confident that she could act well enough to pull it off. Maybe it was something she could be proud of despite the sex part, she thought. The nudity didn't bother her at all. She had done some topless modeling, and some topless dancing. And this was, after all, in the time of the flower children. "Everyone walked around naked if they could," she said, displaying a firmer understanding of the popular culture than Jerome Benson had at the time.

The brothers had really put her at ease, and she wasn't at all inhibited when they asked her to pose for a topless Polaroid. They didn't leer at her at all. They were completely professional and matter-of-fact about it.

But this little hippie chick with the gorgeous bone structure had some business savvy. When they asked her, then and there, if she wanted the part, she set the hook.

"I told them what I wanted—a bunch of money and a piece of the film, a percentage of the revenue. They looked at me and said, 'No way.' So I left."

She remembers that in about an hour they called her and agreed to her terms, and so she became a porno star.

The Mitchells knew they had a great story, the right star, and a good chance to make a better porno movie than they or anyone else had made before. They even had a little gimmick.

A friend had introduced them to big, bad Ben Davidson, a defensive end with the Oakland Raiders. Davidson was a local celebrity. He had a restaurant, Big Ben's, out in the East Bay, and tremendous name ID, particularly in the Bay Area.

So the Mitchells offered him $500 for a cameo role in *Behind the*

Green Door. They put him in a tuxedo and made him the doorman, the keeper of the Green Door. It was pretty hokey—he took a football, squeezed it, and it exploded—but it was a publicity hook and it gave them a name to advertise, a way to make the film more distributable.

So Art fashioned this barracks legend into a rough script, and they started shooting. The Mitchells did something unprecedented: they did not lowball costs at the expense of quality, as was de rigueur in the porn biz. They filmed in high-quality, expensive 35mm. All in all, they would spend $60,000 to make the movie—an absolutely unheard of amount in those days.

On the set, no one would guess that they were risking everything they had for this movie. "They were so laid back," Chambers recalls.

George McDonald, one of the movie's male stars, said, "I could never have done porno acting were it not for Jim and Artie. They made you feel relaxed, as though you were with friends. They always provided catered meals." Of course there was always plenty of pot and beer around too.

As she began work, Marilyn had another surprise in store. She met one of her co-stars—Johnny Keyes—and discovered that he was black. She loved it. "It was a tremendous taboo, which is ridiculous, but it really turned me on," she told interviewer Lisa Palac years later.

She remembers her first porno movie as a pleasurable experience, thanks in great measure to the way the brothers treated her. "They always made me feel like I was the best. They gave me a lot of confidence and took as much time with me as they possibly could. They never rushed me, they were never mean to me, they never yelled at me. They always treated me like a little sister.

"I'm sure there was some of the 'producer falls in love with the star' thing, but I never looked at them like that. I liked them, but I was never in love with them. I always thought of them as my older brothers. They always protected me from everything."

She had a surprise for them, too. Boy, did she.

Finally, the film was finished and they were planning for its nationwide release, which meant New York, and their first shot at the big time.

Just then, Marilyn told them about an old modeling job she'd done that was about to become quite public. She'd done some work for Procter & Gamble. They were looking for a new face to put on their boxes of Ivory Snow. Well, they must have liked her girl-next-door looks too. Because they had decided to put her on the box, and it was about to come out.

The brothers were stunned.

They couldn't have asked for anything better. What a monster hook. This made Ben Davidson insignificant. Here they were with a beautiful, hot new porno star who was on the Ivory Snow box, nuzzling a baby, looking ninety-nine and forty-four one-hundredths percent pure herself. What a wonderful prank to pull on the Establishment, what a fantastic publicity coup.

It was like winning the lottery, striking gold, finding the Hope Diamond. They could not have asked for anything better. It was like getting dealt the wheel in the highest-stake lowball game of their lives. They played those cards to perfection, calling AP and UPI just as they left for the movie's world premiere in New York.

"They flipped their lid," Marilyn recalls. "It became international news, of course. The controversy of good girl/bad girl shot us all to fame."

And, of course, completely embarrassed Procter & Gamble, which finally managed to change faces on their box, but of course the damage was done.

Not only was the movie a hit, it changed the public perception about pornography. This was a movie that a normal couple could go to together, in a decent theater, and enjoy. Suddenly, it was okay, even hip, to go to a porn film. You didn't have to skulk around in grimy old sleaze palaces anymore. In a single stroke, they took porn from the raincoat crowd and gave it to the entire adult population.

The movie that people would call the *Gone with the Wind* of pornography would firmly establish the Mitchell Brothers as giants in the industry. And not incidentally, it would let the brothers rake in one of the biggest pots of their career. It would eventually gross more than $35 million.

Not bad for a couple of Okie lads from Antioch, barely out of their teens.

During that time of whirlwind action and excitement, the brothers lost their mentor, the lodestone of their personality and strength.

On September 6, 1972, J.R. and Georgia Mae decided to go to Nevada City to visit his sister Bessie and her husband, Pete Davidson. The four liked to get together and play dominoes and talk. Bessie and Pete's boy, Curtis "Rocky" Davidson, was one of the brothers' key employees, and the boys' exploits were always great fodder for conversation.

But the weekend of chitchat about Jim and Artie and Rocky over dominoes would not happen. As he drove into Nevada County, J.R. suffered a heart attack and died there by the side of the road as Georgia frantically sought help.

J.R. had been inordinately proud of his two boys. He could see that they were going to be successful beyond his dreams. They had inherited his toughness, his cunning, and his ability to exploit the weaknesses of lesser men. He had carefully clipped every story about the boys, every advertisement for their films, out of the papers and put them into a scrapbook.

In just the same way, Jim and Art revered their father. His mix of cold-eyed toughness and open-minded tolerance set the stage for what they were to become, and they knew it. Both of them felt his loss profoundly. They were glad that J.R. had lived to see the beginnings of their success; very often, over the next two decades, they would dedicate their further efforts to his spirit. And each year, they would host a lowball tournament at the theater in his memory.

Artie won it more often than anyone.

Having a nationally distributed hit movie was nice, but the brothers would discover, as many had before, that success breeds its own set of problems. And legal fees.

As they later told the FBI, New York mob figure Robert DeSalvo tried to persuade them to sign over half their profits in what he characterized as a deal for distribution rights and they saw clearly as a shakedown. He told them that if they refused, pirated versions of the film would play in several cities within a week. They refused him, and bootleg versions opened in Miami, Dallas, and Las Vegas, cutting into their take in those cities. "Before we could stop them, they hurt us badly," the Mitchells later reported.

It wasn't just the mob. They found that almost nobody respected copyrights in the porn business. Bootleg copies of *Green Door* proliferated, and the brothers realized that if they ever wanted to be able to distribute their own films effectively, they had to fight right away.

Again, this was a departure from the norm. Copyright battles were expensive and time-consuming, and most porno producers didn't bother. But the Mitchells did, pursuing every bootlegger ruthlessly until they made it clear that it just didn't pay to rip them off. Along the way, they are credited with strengthening copyright law with their court battles. Despite their antipathy toward the police, the brothers had no compunction enlisting the FBI, with its interest in the mob, on their side in the copyright battle. The big red-and-white FBI warning you see now at the beginning of videotapes is brought to you in part by the Mitchell Brothers—which amused the brothers endlessly.

One of the cases, *Mitchell Brothers Film Group* v. *Cinema Adult Theater,* made it to the Fifth Circuit of the U.S. Court of Appeals before the brothers won, but win they did.

It was a fascinating case, and it proved to be of vital importance to the industry, and significant to copyright law as a whole.

A couple of Dallas theater companies had obtained bootleg copies and showed them. The Mitchells sued. One company failed to appear, and the the Mitchells won a default judgment. But the other used an interesting defense, one that threatened the very core of the Mitchells' business. The defense claim was that because the film was obscene, the copyright was invalid and the Mitchells were not entitled to any relief under the law. U.S. District Court Judge Robert M. Hill thought that sounded just fine, and found in favor of the defendants.

In a starkly worded opinion dated October 16, 1979, the Fifth Circuit dismantled that argument and preserved the entire concept of copyright law, regardless of the content of the material copyrighted.

It was one more example of the Mitchells applying innovative thought and following it with squint-eyed, mule-headed, make-my-day toughness to produce new results in the business. To the police, to the mob, to the garden variety ripoff artist, to the competition, the message was plain: Don't fuck with the Mitchell Brothers. All it will bring you is pain, and it just isn't worth it. Let them be.

Meanwhile, the brothers in question were having a rather nice time. And why not? Before either of their thirtieth birthdays, they were unquestionably millionaires. Bootleggers or no, *Green Door* was bringing in spectacular profits. The Mitchells and their lascivious girl-next-door star were Big Names now. And they had vanquished the puritanical police putsch that threatened to put them out of business before they hit their stride.

The brothers thought, what now? Their instinct told them to ride the tiger, play the rush while the cards were hot. They had created a market that needed to be tended to. They wanted to push the porn market closer and closer to the mainstream, to keep improving plots, production values, acting, everything. And they wanted to take advantage of what they had learned on the distribution side as well. So they began tooling up to make more porn blockbusters.

Come on back, they told a skeptical Boyer. We want to make better and better movies. Your scripts are just what we need now. Boyer was unconvinced. He remembered the lean times, the layoffs, the fights between Jim and Artie, the frustrations and uncertainties.

But he couldn't argue with success. Look at what they had done with *Green Door* while he was gone. Plus, even though Dean Lesher was offering him a promotion, he knew that despite his column-writing talent his chances of breaking into the big-time sports market of the Bay Area with any of the metro papers was really slim. The jock columnists around the Bay were firmly entrenched, making good money, protected by the Newspaper Guild. He wasn't going to get one of those jobs anytime soon.

And, of course, the Mitchells were offering big money again, once more almost doubling what Lesher could offer him. So reluctantly, with reservations intact but with no option more attractive, Boyer returned to the fold.

The next major film the team produced was another vehicle for Chambers, *The Resurrection of Eve,* and it also sold extremely well.

Becoming millionaires changed the brothers far less than might be expected. Yes, it was important; yes, it was the signal that they were succeeding beyond their dreams. But it was not important *in itself.*

They had learned many lessons about money from their father, who was so world-wise, so aware of what could be done with steel nerve and an intimate knowledge of the weaknesses in the human psyche. They had learned not just how to win money, how to count the winnings after they fluttered to the floor. They had learned what it was. It wasn't the answer, the ultimate. It wasn't a thing to be worshiped above all else. It was merely the vehicle to a better life, to enjoyment, the way to go from camping on the Clear Boggy with nothing in your pocket but red dust to driving down the main street of Wapanucka in a shiny new Model T.

There is nothing like the great swell of hubris that comes with making your first million before you're thirty. The Mitchells knew that they would always be able to make money, so why worship money? Why hoard it? Why do anything with it but have fun?

They bought toys, they bought fun, but they didn't try to buy status or pretension. When Artie bought a Porsche and drove it around for a while, he got sick of fellow Porsche owners flicking their lights at him as they passed. What was this? Some sort of stupid status thing, some inside joke, some club he never applied to? So he took his Porsche home and put it in the driveway and got a gallon of cheap gray paint and took a brush and covered every inch of the car with it, slathered it over fenders, tires, bumpers, everything. *Then* he went out with his mischievous puckish humor and flicked his lights at the other Porsches as if to say, here you go, sport, want to be in the club? I just changed the rules.

They bought an eighty-foot fishing boat, the *Graciosa,* and they took it out for the first pull, the huge net as big as the boat, and you've got to be careful out there because a boat that big just doesn't automatically do what you want it to, you've got current and wind and whatnot, and they did what you can't do, hooked the net up somehow on the bottom and pulled the mast right off the boat and almost killed themselves. And they sneaked back into port sheepishly with their brand-new boat dismasted. So what? Get it fixed.

How Jim could spend money! Art used to give him endless grief about it, as if he really cared, but it was something to chivy his big brother about, and that was the real fun. Jim bought a huge, tricked-out equipment van, room for a whole workshop in it. Never carried more than a pair of pliers in it. Bought a Great Dane that ate the upholstery. Later, he would buy an old '40 Ford Coupé, tear it apart, and restore it to perfection, piece by piece. By the time he had finished, he had the most beautiful Ford in California, after spending twice what it would cost to buy one cherried out. So what? Only money, let's have some fun.

Artie went down Van Ness Avenue one day, past the Chevy dealership around the corner from the theater, and they had a bright orange Corvette in there. He walked in, a bottle of beer in his hand, and said, I want that. Just like his dad and the Model T. But this time, the salesman thought he was a flake, and blew him off. Artie was mad as hell, and went back to the theater and told Jim, hey, bro, they won't lease me this Corvette, and I want it. Jim, in the practical, cut-to-the-chase way he had, Jim the problem-solver, said bullshit, any company can rent anything from anybody if they've got the money, and had the accountant call, and Art had the car that day. And hated it. Gave it to Boyer to drive for a while. No big deal.

At the same time, they kept right on being hard-nosed about *making* the money. Now that they had the means, the brothers moved to make the vertical diversification they had dreamed of a reality. They began to expand their theater horizons. By the mid-1970s, they had eleven lust houses across the state, including one in Los Angeles and one in Santa Ana, the heart of reactionary Orange County. In years to come, that theater would become one of the nation's highest-grossing porn houses as well as the focus of a legal battle royal.

Of course, their immediate legal situation became more complicated as various authorities elsewhere tried the same tactics that the San Francisco police had. Los Angeles Police Chief Ed Davis, who would later become an ultraconservative state senator, went after the brothers with a vengeance, arresting patrons and managers alike.

Georgia Mae flew to Los Angeles once for an obscenity trial, expecting to witness another victory. The boys had her met at the airport with a limousine; it was all quite exciting. She got to court in time to see what she least expected: Artie being hustled off to jail.

The brothers were in the habit of having one represent both at trials, so they weren't both tied up in court. That had always worked in San Francisco, but this Los Angeles judge wasn't having any of it. He wasn't satisfied when Jim showed up alone. "Where's Art Mitchell?" he demanded. "Get him here." Court recessed, and Artie flew down; but when he arrived the judge found him in contempt and sentenced him to three days in jail.

As they led him away, Georgia Mae called out to him, "Hi, Artie! A mother hasn't lived until she's seen her son taken away to jail!" Knowing he would get a chuckle out of it.

Jim was furious. "Get my brother out of jail!" he thundered at the lawyers. Finally, they did, after Artie spent one night in the can. But one was better than three.

In one of the brothers' most memorable trials, *Behind the Green Door* was found by a Los Angeles jury not to be obscene. Because of all the furor surrounding the film, and because it was Los Angeles, the trial got huge publicity, and it was one of Kennedy's most satisfying victories.

The judge was enraged by the result. After the jurors had reached their verdict, he lectured them angrily: "This movie would violate the community standards of Sodom and Gomorrah!"

That bellow of frustration would have a huge impact on the brothers' lives.

If ever a gauntlet thrown down was picked up before it hit the floor, that judge's scolding was it. The fiendish fraternal brain-in-two-heads went wild with the potential. Sodom and Gomorrah was the Biblical embodiment of lust and evil, and the brothers immediately saw it as fertile ground for sacrilegious humor. It was an opportunity to take a shot at everything they thought silly and stodgy about Hollywood. The Cecil B. DeMille epic was a perfect template for their satire.

This pissant judge had pitched them a beautiful batting-practice fastball, grapefruit-fat and just as juicy, and they *would* take a rip at it. They missed, but what a swing they took.

This was to be the porn epic of epics. It would make *Green Door* look like a loop. It was going to blister their fascist critics and enemies, amuse, satirize, *and* titillate.

In the summer of '74, they leased a ranch out in the scorching-hot hills of Livermore where the East Bay meets California's Central Valley. The landscape was intended to duplicate the arid hills of Palestine, and it sure did.

But the Mitchells' creative landscape was just as dry. They had hit a barrier constructed of their own ambitions for the film, coupled with their excesses and conflicting visions.

Soon the location shooting in Livermore turned into a nightmare. It was broiling hot, and nothing worked. The logistics of transporting a "cast of thousands" into the country every day were horrifyingly complicated. Casting itself was difficult. The hippie days had come and gone, and there weren't as many good-looking women willing to make porno anymore.

"The movie was so huge in scope that everything was magnified, including the problems," Boyer said. "If just Jim were involved, it would have gotten done just fine. Or if just Art were involved, it would have been fine. But they couldn't agree on anything. It was just this weird, two-headed monster, and everybody got really discouraged."

The brothers' creative differences, usually resolvable, turned ugly. An elaborate set piece would be built according to Artie's specifications, and Jim would order it torn down and done again. The bills soared with the temperature and the tension.

But the booze and drugs flowed by the truckload.

Boyer remembers, "It was a bummer of a production process but it was a hell of a party."

The usual catered food was scaled back considerably because of the location. The cast and crew had to content themselves with cold lunch trucked in from the city. Mezzavilla would recall, "I was living on Coca-Cola and Southern Comfort and in a few weeks I was lean and tan. And going nuts. We shot 27,000 feet of film and spent $700,000."

The problems weren't all on the set. Jim's wife, Adrienne, shocked everybody by running off with one of the male stars. Artie's marriage was also being strained by the work pressure.

Boyer, nominally the screenwriter, got a bagful of headaches from the brothers' stress-induced erratic behavior. "They would change the story every day. I would go, 'Wait a minute, there's no continuity, this doesn't work, it doesn't make sense.'

"Then the female lead took off to Mexico or someplace in the middle of shooting and we had to replace her. Things were getting so bizarre that Jim just shut down shooting altogether for a month. Which caused another incredible set of problems. These people are transient anyway. You just can't do that and expect to get them back.''

With each new setback, the conflict between the brothers intensified. "The higher the artistic stakes, the more creativity that was involved, the higher the tension level got between them," Boyer recalled.

For a couple of lucky boys with the Midas touch, things sure were going south in a hurry.

When it was finally done, the film performed about like Lot's wife in the theaters. Reviewer Stanley Eichelbaum wrote in the *Chronicle,* "It's not a breakthrough or a milestone, but an abysmally shoddy spectacle of sex and violence that purports to kid the pants off the old Cecil B. DeMille extravaganza, but does it without humor, imagination, or production values."

Even Jim was to admit later, "We were on a crusade. We were determined to make a political statement, to overthrow the government, to be satirical. Only it didn't work."

Only some masterful distribution successes, the lessons learned since *Green Door,* saved the brothers from an even greater disaster.

Jeff Armstrong was proving to be a tower of strength in the brothers' Antioch management roster. He was beginning to handle the tough stuff for the brothers, distribution, a lot of the business relationships with others in the industry. And he did it with consummate style. His reputation nicely complemented Jim and Artie's: straight shooter, tough, honest, quick brain, sense of humor, tough, articulate, diplomatic, resourceful, tough. Tough tough tough. Not somebody you want to jack around.

"There's nobody better on the telephone than Jeff, and there's nobody more equipped to out-argue some shyster in Detroit, to represent the logic in a way that the schmuck would get it," a Mitchell insider says.

Jeff grew up middle-class by Antioch standards, the son of Red Armstrong, a tremendously well-liked and respected foreman at the Fibreboard plant. Jeff survived some wild times with J.D. Fluty and Artie and the rest of the '63 crowd, played football, learned to hustle a little 9-ball, more than held his own when fists and feet started flying, but kept it together in school. He did well enough, in fact, to get into the University of California, and when he graduated with a degree in business, he was both the pride of his family (the first to get a college degree) and a real jewel for the Mitchells to snag.

Jim, Artie, and Jeff planned the assault on New York for the opening of *Sodom*. It was New Year's week, and although it was important, work-wise, it was also a chance to kick loose. After the marathon trauma of this movie, everybody needed it.

The brothers assembled a huge troupe of Antioch boys—maybe fifteen or sixteen of them, all the key people, Fontana, Jeff, Mezz, Boyer, Rocky, Russ Mitchell, and a bunch more. They got them all on a plane, which was quite a feat. Some of them had never flown before, never been out of the Bay Area, for God's sake, and here they were in their fisherman's watch caps and blue jeans and work boots, freezing their butts off in New York City!

They wanted to headquarter near Times Square, naturally, so they took over a floor of the Edison Hotel on 47th Street and had a good old-fashioned Antioch beer bust, all-night hoohah, enough pot to stone the entire hotel, poker game running all the time. At noon every day they would all fan out across the city, into the Bronx, Harlem, everywhere the movie was playing, which was a lot of pretty gritty neighborhoods, because, after all, it wasn't exactly *National Velvet*.

One guy would go to each theater and *stand* there, in the box office, and count the take. None of the locals could believe it: *Here's this weird-looking honky guy, funny clothes, funny accent, but don't really look like somebody to mess with, you know, hanging out all day in the box office, say he's supposed to be there, well, shit, I guess it's his funeral.*

Then it was back onto the subway and back to the Edison, where the party would be in progress.

That was pretty much a sure thing because Jim and Artie, the bastards, reserved the theaters in Times Square, like two blocks away, for themselves. Everybody else had to go out in the boroughs. So they would roll out last, come back first, that's what they get for owning the joint.

The strategy paid off. Sure enough, the distributors, knowing they were dealing with out-of-town producers, tried to lowball them on the gate. The Mitchells were able to fire right back, here's the box office, every day, every joint, pay up, motherfuckers. "I'll pay you all of it, no problem, I just want to know how you got that," one flummoxed distributor told them.

In the 1970s, dealing porn in New York, there were a few people you had to have, and the Mitchells went out and got them. They dealt straight and they were refreshing. They were so obviously the real thing, strong enough to be taken seriously, yet they were charming, funny, totally different from anyone in the New York culture, curiosities, really.

A little hard to deal with because they were always smoking pot, being crazy.

"I had a tough time with the drug thing," says one former distributor. "Maybe because they were from San Francisco, you know, but a lot of people in porn in New York got out of that scene quick because they didn't want any excuse to get popped when they knew the cops were looking for one. It was part of the Mitchells' persona, part of their defiance of authority, but it got in the way of business a lot. Armstrong, though, was good as gold. You could trust what he said and you knew you couldn't run anything on him."

One of the people they dealt with was Mickey Zaffarano, the late theater owner–mob figure, who had the same reputation they did: honest, honorable within his circle, tough. He treated the Mitchells much differently than DeSalvo had.

Zaffarano, who produced the porn classic *Debbie Does Dallas,* bought advance distribution rights to the Mitchells' *Autobiography of a Flea,* and dealt with them on several other projects. They once had him met at the San Francisco airport with a limousine and a stripper, whom he eschewed, but he was reportedly touched by the gesture. When he died of a heart attack, the Mitchells attended his funeral.

"Hey, he was an all-right guy," Artie said later. "He never tried to twist our arms or act like a mobster."

The key to Times Square was a hard-bitten old man named Maurer, a little guy with a big cigar. Everybody called him the Jockey because he loved the nags and he was maybe five feet tall. He did his business out of a Mercedes he always had parked around Times Square, and he owned a lot of theaters, including the old Latin Quarter on 47th. He got into the porn biz by default when he had a bunch of empty theaters and had to show something in them and did not give a damn about the inevitable grief he would take over showing the stuff.

Jim Buckley, who co-founded *Screw* magazine with Al Goldstein and would produce a few movies himself, remembers the Jockey's wonderful instinct for the business.

"Within an hour of a film opening he could tell you how much it would do in his theater, how long it would run and what it would eventually make across the country. We opened a film with him, he told us, meet me at my office, that Mercedes of his, always had a driver sitting there with him. He tells us, $452 in an hour, you've got a hit, you'll make a lot of money, it'll run three months.

"We had a hit. It ran thirteen weeks, and it made a lot of money."

Maurer liked the brothers. He would do a lot of business with them, with Armstrong, and he would become a real ally. Once, meeting in his "office" with a guy who was threatening to bootleg a Mitchell movie, the old man got some local muscle to appear magically on the surrounding street corners. "Get the fuck out of here," said the ninety-pound septuagenarian, "before we kick your ass all over Times Square." Exit thug, sniveling.

Buckley had a fair amount in common with the Mitchells. Almost by accident, he was an early porno player, caught some breaks, made some more of his own, and made a lot of money. Unlike the Mitchells, he got out.

Buckley got a job out of the service as a typesetter at a rag called the *New York Free Press*. In those days, with a publication like that, it wasn't all that unusual for someone to go from typesetter to managing editor, and that's just what Buckley did.

He met Al Goldstein when Al submitted a first-person piece to the *Free Press* about being an industrial spy for the Bendix Corporation. Although Al didn't always trade in the truth as an editor of a publication called *Hush Hush Confidential,* this episode in his career was indeed true.

The piece was all about Goldstein going up to Utica to photograph some Bendix competitor's equipment. Getting into the New Journalism mode here, injecting a lot of himself into this story, Goldstein wrote about how he thought the possibilities for getting laid in Utica were probably minuscule, so for company, as it were, he took a rubber item billed as an "artificial vagina" with him, and further wrote, as sort of a consumerist sidelight, about how disappointed he was with its performance.

Buckley, editing the piece, thought the riff was good detail—ah, the travails of the traveling industrial spy—and left it in. The *Free Press* publisher, as publishers will eternally do, disagreed with his managing editor on this fine journalistic point.

"Are you nuts?" he asked rhetorically, and took it out.

Buckley considered this. He considered that in Goldstein's editorial capacity at *Hush Hush Confidential* he was given photos of scantily clad dead people, usually women, often decapitated, and told to write a story to go with the photos. And he considered how Goldstein was always told, heavy on the gore, but don't get into the sex part.

He thought, why is this? Why can't people deal honestly with sex? He knew whenever the *Free Press* ran a seminude woman on the cover, sales tripled. And he knew that a competing publication, the *East Village Other,* was practically unreadable but sold anyway because it had sexy classifieds.

So why not do a sex magazine that talks frankly about sex, deals with sexual politics, censorship, all the issues, fights for the freedom to talk about sex, show sex, etc.? Nobody's really doing it, there's got to be a market, he thought.

So he got Goldstein to go along, and each one of them put up $150, then grudgingly another $15 apiece, and they did the first issue. Which the distributor left in his office for three weeks, then dumped back in their hands, saying, my wife won't let me touch this, it's smut.

But Goldstein had been smart enough to put a November date on the thing, even though this was August. So Buckley and Goldstein, who before being the James Bond of Bendix had been an insurance salesman, went out and sold the magazine to newsstand operators. Sell it for a quarter, they said, we'll give you fifteen cents of it and take just a dime. This was about three times what newsies were being paid by other publications, so suddenly *Screw* got great newsstand position and started selling. They never had to put up another nickel.

Both Goldstein and Buckley would become good friends of the Mitchells, allies in the censorship battles.

At the same time the Mitchells were shooting *Behind the Green Door* on Potrero Hill, Buckley was making a movie called *It Happened in Hollywood,* which it didn't. It happened in an old vaudeville theater, the Anderson, at Second Avenue and East Fourth Street. As the Mitchells were doing, Buckley had huge sets painted, and shot the whole thing inside the theater, which he leased for a thousand bucks.

His movie did well, but although his star had the bankable stage name Felicity Split, she had not modeled for the Ivory Snow box, and his film didn't become a monster like *Green Door.*

He soon tired of the game.

"I think I ran into the same thing the Mitchells did," Buckley says now. "You start out with the ideals, wanting to defend the right to do sex shows, and the bucks start coming in a flood, and you get lost in it, suddenly you get mired in it. I wasn't writing about the business, I was *in* the business. I was a pornographer. And I didn't want to spend my life that way so I sold out, got out.

"I don't think Jim really wanted to spend his life that way either. But it was his identity, and it was easier for me to get out. I wasn't in it with my brother."

That awful summer of *Sodom*, the summer of treachery and tantrums and paranoia in the desert, had been the nadir, the deepest dip yet in the brothers' roller-coaster lives. It was almost as if the God they were making fun of had visited some sort of terrible Old Testament retribution upon their blasphemous balding heads.

Broke, in debt for the first time after an apparent embezzlement, marriages in ruins, sleeping in the loft at the O'Farrell, the law still nipping at their heels, drinking and drugging at a legendary pace, the boys from Antioch were in trouble.

Cash flow was seriously curtailed. They continued to make movies, but for the core group the sabbaticals started again.

This time Boyer knew what to expect. He understood the business a little better, and knew that when they were in production, all the jobs were needed, and when they were shut down for whatever reason, they weren't.

The layoffs affected almost everybody: Boyer, Ceccini, even Armstrong a few times. Ceccini already had a photography business on the side, so it worked fine for him. The others mostly used the time to kick back, get out of the pressure cooker, have some fun.

Usually, the brothers would ask, do you want to do something else for some bucks in the meantime until we get going again? Be a theater manager somewhere, or the night man, or something? But Boyer didn't. He really didn't have any interest in that side of the business, so he spent his time on the golf course, the tennis court, traveling, skiing, whatever.

Despite the layoffs, the entire crew remained intensely loyal. And for good reason. The Mitchells continued to treat them like family.

"Art would come by, have lunch, say, 'Are you okay, do you need some money?' " Boyer remembers. "They were good at building allegiances, at drawing people close."

Boyer would usually just rent an apartment in one of the huge complexes out on the Emeryville mud flats, near the Bay Bridge, where there were tennis courts and loads of single women, sit back, collect unemployment, do a few freelance PR and writing jobs, and wait it out.

He and Armstrong had a standing joke: "You know what? They're actually going to hire us back any minute, pull us back because they can't stand seeing us have this much fun. We're enjoying ourselves too much. They're going to say, get back on the set, back to the insanity."

When they were working, they would kid Jim and Art: "When's the next layoff? We need to do some vacation planning," and the brothers would glare at them in mock anger.

The feature-length movies kept rolling: *Inside Marilyn Chambers.* A craze-exploiter called *CB Mamas,* directed solo by Artie, to favorable reviews. A well-regarded period porn effort, *Autobiography of a Flea*. To keep the crews busy and keep the cash rolling in, they also went back to doing loops, introducing a super-slick, high-quality, but super-raunchy line of shorts called "Ultra-Core."

But the rest of the industry was eclipsing the Mitchells in volume. Porn was proliferating like never before.

Then the Mitchells got the second huge break of their career: video happened.

There was never a more perfect meeting of medium and message. Porn and video went together like Marilyn Chambers and John Holmes. Now people could get their sexy movies and watch them at home. No stigma. No risk of being seen ducking into the O'Farrell. And, of course, whatever activities might eventuate from watching the movie could be done at home too.

This was the sort of thing the Mitchells were great at. It was a nimble business move that did not require a huge creative debate between the brothers and a cast of thousands. Video became Jeff Armstrong's baby, and the company's response was nothing short of brilliant.

Porn was way out in front of the rest of the movie business in exploiting the video market, and the Mitchells were at the vanguard of the industry. They took an old friend, Ben Saia, and set him up in the video manufacturing business, and cut their costs to the bone in the process. They were making videos for fifty cents a copy that were selling for $100 and more. Suddenly, the brothers were riding another hot streak. The boys from Antioch were awash in dollars again.

Artie's marriage was breaking up, and he just couldn't believe it.

There were three children now; Liberty had been followed by a boy named Storm Sundown. (Artie had wanted to name him Sundown so he could say "Put my son Sundown down." But cute as that may have seemed to a dope-smoking porn prince, Meredith knew it wouldn't play well back east, where anything more unconventional than John or William was likely to raise eyebrows. So they had settled for the comparatively conservative first name of Storm. Still not exactly Mayflowerish, but it would do.) Then, in 1973, their youngest girl, Mariah, was born.

Sure, he stayed away from home late almost every night, out with the boys or in with the girls, but when he *was* home they all had a great time, didn't they? And he always provided money, didn't he? Just what did Meredith expect, for God's sake? He was still a kid, not yet thirty, with a lot more hell to raise. She knew she married a pornographer, and his work was important to him. What the hell did she want from him, anyway?

She wanted a family life, some semblance of normalcy. She wanted to eat dinner at six. Okay, seven. But not ten or eleven, after Artie had been out doing God knows what. She wanted him home at night.

She was tired of making soufflés that rose and fell long before he arrived, tired of overdone roasts and congealed sauces and cold potatoes. So she quit cooking for him altogether, and that really upset him, because Artie did like his homecooked meals. But it didn't bring him home.

Finally, Meredith did something few of Artie's women ever did: she left him.

Liberty was six at the time. She remembers it with acute pain. She had been a carefree little girl who worshiped her dad and wished she could see him more. Suddenly, she became mom's helper raising the two littler kids, confused because of her mother's bitterness and anger, feeling guilty because she didn't feel it too, missing her daddy more than ever.

Artie, for his part, was shocked and wounded that someone would actually leave him. He saw the betrayal all on Meredith's side. He just assumed that the family would stay together no matter what he did. For all his enlightened hippie attitudes, he expected old-fashioned Okie subservience at home. Also, he would tell friends later, he really loved Meredith, and his father's death was the only thing in his first thirty years that hurt him more than losing her.

Georgia Mae too was shocked. She had stood by J.R. through thick and thin, and of course, her love for Artie was unreserved. How could Meredith even think of leaving him? And those three little grandchildren! What would become of them? She grieved for them, and for Artie too, because she knew that the family structure was good for him, and without it, goodness knows what he would do.

The mother who was totally accepting about her sons making pornography had a lot harder time understanding divorce.

At the theater, things were getting better in a hurry. Harvard MBA students could use the Mitchells' response to video as a phenomenal example of how to adapt to changing market conditions. Not only did the Mitchells make a fortune on the front end of the market, selling videos retail, but they also turned a potential problem on the back end into another bonanza.

When video rental happened, everything changed again. Video sales prices dropped, and the profit margin on sales dropped too, from astronomical to merely opulent. And as people took videos home from the store for a buck a night, demand for public theater porn screenings dropped like a rock. The business solution the brothers adopted would propel them to even greater notoriety, provoke a new rash of legal battles, and make them a ton more money.

They cut the number of theaters down from eleven to four, made the movie screenings a sidelight, and actually found a new wrinkle in the world's oldest profession. In fact, they pioneered a whole new sex industry: customer-contact live shows.

The brothers had seen a few primitive customer-contact shows in bars and strip joints around the country, and they sent manager Vince Stanich around to see a few others. After seeing what there was out there, they did something completely new and different.

They opened three live shows in the O'Farrell in quick succession: the Ultra Room. Then the Kopenhagen. Followed shortly thereafter by the New York Live.

All three made sex-show history. All three aroused audiences—and the ire of feminists, police, and prosecutors. And all three continue today. More than a thousand dancers have taken it all off in those shows since they opened in January of 1977.

Ultra Room: lesbian bondage under glass. (Then, for a few years, sans glass.) Whips, chains, dildos. Boots and saddles.

Kopenhagen: Live shows in front of (and sometimes on) the audience by a pair of naked women. Done in a small room, with groups of maybe twenty men at a time.

New York Live: cabaret show–style strip act with women usually dancing a three-song set, usually totally nude for the last song. Girls who are not dancing on stage are circulating in the audience, sitting on laps for tips.

The Ultra Room opened January 4, 1977. The twenty- by thirty-foot padded room, surrounded by windows facing into thirty narrow private booths, was finished just hours before the first show at 4 P.M. The shows cost $10, and the first five half-hour shows were sold out before the first one started.

The Mitchells were in New York for the premiere of *Autobiography of a Flea*, leaving Boyer to handle the opening.

C.J. Lang, twenty, who had performed in the porn movie *Anyone but My Husband*, and twenty-two-year-old Ghianina, a player in *CB Mamas*, did the first shows.

According to an account by Ivan Sharpe in the next day's *Examiner*,

Ghianina became angry before the first show when C.J. insisted that she take off her rings. She threw a tantrum and refused to wear the mask that was part of her costume. "I don't like it," she said. "It's a joke."

The patient Boyer tried to soothe her. "The mask is a nice effect. It's not humorous. It's very serious. Besides, we had it tailor-made for you."

"I hate it!"

Boyer caved: "Okay. Okay. Leave it off for the first show."

After the show, which was accompanied by the narration of a weird Japanese "folk tale" of peasant girls being abused by the rich, Boyer told Sharpe, "This should be like looking through the keyhole in your sister's bedroom," adding, "we'll take it as far as we can. There's a market for people who want to see live sex."

There certainly was. The numbers, raw as the shows themselves, told the story: ten bucks a head times thirty, times eight shows a day, seven days a week. At the beginning, the dancers were paid a flat $20 per show.

It didn't take long for the show to be pilloried—and copied. Even as women marched outside holding placards like "Who Says Pain Is Erotic?" and "Ultra Room—A Hazard to Our Health," the competing Sutter Street Theater began planning a live show of its own.

The protesters angrily—and quite accurately—characterized it as a male-conceived, male-defined image: women pretending to hurt other women for men's sexual excitement. And it did not escape notice that, despite the fact the dancers were well paid, the males who ran the joint were paid better.

Jim was equally accurate, however, in his defense. He said he had women clamoring to perform in the room. More subjective was his claim that the performers enjoyed themselves as much as the men watching did, but certainly many of the performers did enjoy it.

The protesters weren't buying that, of course. "It's a choice of doing this or being unemployed," one of the pickets said. "I know. I had to stay with a husband I didn't like for two years because I couldn't get a job."

A more cogent criticism was that the Ultra Room represented an escalation in the world of pornography, and that live depictions of women being violent with other women could convince some men that all women liked such treatment. But protests or not, the shows averaged 90 percent capacity attendance.

Things got really wild when the New York Live opened. This show was the Mitchells' biggest innovation and the one designed to remake their empire. The audience watched raptly as the first dancer performed to Bad Company's "Rock and Roll Fantasy" and later came down into the audience and sat, quite naked, on customers' laps for tips. Obviously, a lot of men thought this was a great advance in the world of entertainment. Lines suddenly appeared outside the door of the theater.

The Mitchells hired dancers as fast as they could to keep up with the demand, and they were off to another huge sex-show success. From that time on, the O'Farrell would be renowned literally worldwide for its live shows. A huge chunk of the business would come from the many Japanese men who took business vacations in San Francisco. Visiting one of America's most expensive cities, and going to places like the O'Farrell, was dirt cheap compared to the prices back home.

They were just like Americans going to Tijuana.

Coddling strippers and helping to develop live sex shows wasn't Bill Boyer's idea of a good time, or a good job. He had come back to write movies, and although the Mitchells would still do movies from time to time, it was clear that role was vastly diminished. So he left again, this time permanently. Others in the original group had left too. Ceccini and Fontana both had developed lucrative businesses for themselves from the technical skills they had learned and honed with the Mitchells.

Jeff Armstrong and Richard Mezzavilla, though, were more and more important. Jeff was functioning as business manager, concentrating on video distribution and sales.

Mezz would take a big role in the brothers' money management. The outside accountant was dismissed after a big chunk of money turned up missing. A woman named Ruby Richardson, who had worked in the dismissed accountant's firm, applied directly to the Mitchells after her erstwhile boss was fired. They liked Ruby; she was a no-nonsense accountant, and they were in dire need of one. She trained Mezzavilla as an in-house controller, where he quickly became invaluable for his low-key efficiency.

Cousin Rocky was solidly entrenched and indispensable—as close as there was to a third Brother. Three other managers were in the inside circle: Charlie Benton, Vince Stanich, and an old army buddy of Artie's, Jimmy Gish. The brothers felt that they had the team they needed to keep the business going well, no matter what.

The Mitchells set about refining what they had, making the shows better. The fairy-tale hokum was dropped from the Ultra Room, and for a while so was the glass. Customers could nuzzle and nibble all sorts of things for the right tip. Eventually, they went to a single admission price—over the years, it fluctuated from $10 to $25—allowing entry to all the shows, which then ran on tips.

The Mitchells even contemplated private booths where performers and patrons would meet one on one, but eventually decided it wouldn't be worth the heat. Besides, what they had was working. The place was crowded day and night, and they were making money like crazy.

The O'Farrell itself was becoming a landmark. The brothers had always treated the brick exterior like a canvas; when it opened, the bricks were painted in pastels and a couple of wispy clouds floated around above the door. Then they hired an artist to turn the entire Polk Street side of the building into a striking ocean scene, with orca whales and giant squid and all manner of aquatic critters floating around in a sea of blue.

Inside, the Mitchell Brothers' office was known to cognoscenti around the city as one of the best places to find a party, just about any time of day. It was certainly designed and decorated with fun in mind.

It was on the second floor of the cavernous old building, along with the strippers' dressing rooms and the lighting and tech areas for the New York Live and cinema stages. The big, bare-raftered office occupied a corner of the old building, offering views down onto O'Farrell Street. Fishing nets from their friends on the Wharf hung from the ceiling. A very good Brunswick pool table occupied the center of the room, and a Wurlitzer juke squatted next to the safe along the back wall.

The brothers used a poker table as a desk, and the pool table as a credenza. In mid-project the surfaces of both would be covered with reels of film, video box design suggestions, schedules, scribbled ideas, rolling papers, phone messages. But they were never so cluttered they couldn't be cleared off for a game of pool or lowball.

And of course, when the real parties were in progress, it wasn't so unusual for the office to be decorated with lingerie-clad women from the New York Live.

Things were coming up aces all around for the brothers.

Even their personal lives seemed to smooth out. Jim had a pleasant but bittersweet romance with Sharon McKnight, a vastly talented some-time cabaret singer who directed some films for the Mitchells. Friends say it did not result in marriage only because she had a hysterectomy, and Jim had his heart set on having kids. They stayed friends, and Jim started seeing a dancer and artist named Mary Jane Whitty, and married her within a year. There were no children from his first marriage, but

Mary Jane would bear him four children in short order: Meta Jane in 1978; James Rafael, "Rafe," in 1982; Justin Samuel in 1983; and Jennifer Skye in 1985.

Artie too had begun a new relationship—one that would change his life forever.

In February 1976, Vince Stanich was looking for someone to cater the set during the shooting of *Autobiography of a Flea*. A friend of his had a girlfriend who ran a catering business, and so he talked to her about it.

Karen Kay Hassall made a good impression when she came to the theater for an interview. She was young—not yet nineteen—slim, and pert, with a cloud of red hair cascading well below her waist. And she had experience as a professional cook.

Her parents had split during her childhood, and as a teenager she had lived for a while in Guatemala with her father, a wandering sailor who traversed the world twice on his trimaran.

There, she said, she had landed a job cooking on a Caribbean charter boat, a fifty-two-foot motor sailer. And she had gone from there to Nantucket, hired as a private cook by a family who had met her aboard ship. She had recently decided to return to San Francisco (she was a Berkeley native), and start this catering business.

All that sounded okay, and she and Vince began to discuss the menu. "What will you all want to drink?" she asked. "You want me to bring Cokes?"

"Fuck the Cokes, we don't need any Cokes," she heard someone say behind her. She says she thought, who is this jerk, and turned around to see a skinny little guy laughing at her.

He may be a jerk, but he's kind of cute, she thought, with his little tweed racing cap. "Karen, meet Artie," Vince said to her, and the guy spent the next few minutes flirting with her in sort of an engaging way.

She got the job, and started work. It was two days into filming before she realized that the brash, skinny, handsome little guy in the cap was Artie *Mitchell*. The desultory flirting continued, and finally he and Bill Boyer made plans to double-date with her and her roommate.

Artie and Bill stood them up.

The next day on the set, Artie saw the dangerous gleam in Karen's eyes, and realized he'd screwed up. He went running downstairs where the prop manager had a huge bouquet of flowers waiting to go on the set. He grabbed them and ran back upstairs to the office and presented them to Karen with a flourish and an apology, and she was charmed.

That afternoon, the prop man came rushing into the office. "Has anybody seen—where did you get those flowers?"

"Artie gave them to me."

"Well, let me borrow them for this scene. I'll bring 'em back."

The next day, Artie and Karen went out, and, as was his way, he impulsively decided that she was the one. Separated from Meredith, he was sleeping mostly at the O'Farrell, and he was ready for a steady girl.

Especially one who could cook.

Karen lived with the woman who was her catering partner in a smart little place on Jackson Street in upscale Pacific Heights. Artie thought that was nice too. To the roommate's chagrin, he started staying there with Karen quite a bit. They would go out to dinner someplace nice, or she would cook.

The brothers were still suffering the effects of *Sodom* and the embezzlement, and neither was taking a paycheck out of the corporation, but both of them had plenty of cash anyway. So he was always ready to go out and have a good time, and Karen liked that a lot.

The way she tells it, Russ Mitchell took her aside one day on the set and asked her out for coffee and a conversation. Whoa, this sounds serious, she thought, and sure enough, Russ wanted to know just what she thought she was doing. Did you know Artie is married and has three kids?" he asked her.

No, she answered. Which was only half true. Artie had told her he was married, but separated. But he hadn't mentioned Liberty, Storm, and Mariah.

"Why didn't you tell me you had kids?" she demanded.

"You never asked," he said. "Does it matter?"

"By that time," she said later, "it didn't."

She had tried to keep him at arm's length for a while. This man is not my dream come true, she thought. A pornographer. Married. And broke.

Or is he? He is funny, and cute, and he does seem to be *making* money, all right.

He started staying at her place, and when her roommate left in disgust, he suggested, "Let's get a place together. Jim's looking for a place too. We can all live together."

What the hell, she thought. Artie was an unusual character. He was fun. He kept her entertained. Why not?

Neither party went into it exactly starry-eyed. For Artie, the relationship was not the first blush of true love. He had always held some-

He had found very early that it made him all the more desirable and allowed him to keep the emotional upper hand. From now on, that trait would be much more pronounced.

His basic view of women had been preternaturally amplified by two things: his experiences in the sex industry, and the hurt he still carried from the relationship with Meredith. The first time he had allowed himself to love deeply, it had ended badly. As a result, he was well on his way to regarding women as interchangeable and replaceable, like cars and Heinekens.

Still, Artie was not yet willing to let failure embitter him. Instead, he vowed to wipe it away with new success. It was important to his masculinity, to his ego, so much modeled after J.R., to prove that he could have a good relationship. He would replicate his family, start all over again. He would show Meredith that he could have a happy family without her.

They found a great short-term rental over in the luxurious Marin County enclave of Tiburon. It was a beautiful place, right on the water, owned by some guy off on sabbatical for a year. It was idyllic; they reveled in the magnificent view, fished for sharks off the dock, and threw party after party.

Then, as she would quite often over the next decade, Karen got pregnant.

She says now that she and Artie decided to get married. His divorce was almost final, and it seemed like the right thing to do, so they got invitations ready, the whole deal.

The way Karen tells it, "Meredith came over and the invitations were sitting on a table waiting to be mailed out and she said, 'You can't get married. We're not divorced. Ha, ha. Give me five grand.' She hadn't signed the divorce agreement yet.

"Artie said, 'I don't have five grand,' and she said, 'Well, you're not getting married then.' She was cold.

"So we canceled the wedding and I had an abortion."

Karen says she wasn't sure for a long time afterward if she wanted to marry Artie or not, because Meredith was so hostile. But they did decide a few months later to have a child anyway.

Karen also decided to do something about their living situation. After the lease on the Tiburon place was up, they had moved to an apartment in Emeryville, but she wasn't satisfied with that. She was only twenty, but she prided herself on her business head and ability to see all the angles. "Start taking paychecks," she told Artie. "We should buy a house." She kept after him about it, and finally they were able to buy a big old house in Oakland for $92,000.

By the time Aaron James Mitchell was born, on August 9, 1978, the situation seemed to have calmed down quite a bit. Artie and Karen were ensconced in their new digs. Meredith was going to law school and raising her kids. Although tension remained, quite naturally, between Meredith and Karen, they managed an outward civility. On holidays, everybody—Meredith included—would get together at Artie and Karen's house.

The older kids loved little Aaron. Liberty was eight, and she was thrilled. "I just adored him. He was my favorite person in the world. I went over every weekend."

She liked Karen too. "We had a lot of good times. Karen would take me shopping, take me out to dinner, make me feel really special. I was the oldest and they would make me feel really grown up."

They bought Liberty a beautiful four-poster canopy bed for when she stayed over on weekends. Storm and Mariah enjoyed visiting their baby half brother too, and of course they looked forward all week to the time they would get to spend with their dad.

On June 17, 1979, Artie and Karen had a huge outdoor wedding in an Oakland park. Artie, resplendent in a gray tuxedo, held Aaron during the ceremony, and then presided over an appropriately wild party. Even Meredith was in attendance. She was out of law school now, working full-time for the theater as an attorney on staff.

But the day was less than perfect for Artie. He would tell friends later that he overheard Karen's father say to another guest, "I guess she must be doing it for the money." Legend has it that Artie, infuriated, left the party, went to the O'Farrell and spent a good part of his wedding night with an Ultra Room performer.

By the end of the 1970s, the brothers, only in their mid-thirties, were venerable institutions in the pornography business. As their father had in his, they had become legends in their arena.

Of course, that status was a blessing and a curse. They had proved that the police couldn't stop them from making and showing their films. But now they had formidable new legal challenges: Could their dancers legally sit on laps in the nude? Could their customers legally do whatever the women were letting them do in the darkened theater for tips? Could they operate without fear of getting their dancers—and patrons— busted every few days?

All of this was complicated by the fact that Dianne Feinstein, always a strident antiporn voice when she was a county supervisor, was now mayor after the Moscone and Milk slayings. She had made it clear that she expected District Attorney Arlo Smith to be aggressive on porn and obscenity cases.

So both sides geared up for what promised to be a tougher, more complex legal battle than before.

This time, the prosecutor was Bernard Walter, a quirky, quixotic, complex assistant D.A. who had inherited the thankless task of vice prosecutor.

"It was the least popular job in the office because it was dangerous," Walter, who is now in private practice, recalls. "You spent your time prosecuting pimps, working with people who were victims of pimps, and victims of porn.

"It's tough to prosecute these cases because the public tends to think you're some right-wing moralistic crusader, some zealot who is out of touch," he says. "But I worked with enough people who were victims of the Mitchell Brothers that I could empirically draw some conclusions about what they did to people. It's very painful to see these women's lives ruined. A lot of them are lovely people."

Walter insists he is not bitter about his epic clashes with the Mitchells a decade ago, but he is still outspoken in his denunciation of the brothers and the empire they created.

"In all my contacts with them, they were charming, they were affable, they were quick-witted, light-footed." Walter likes adjectives. "But I know they had another face, and that other face is cruel. Ruthless. Exploitative. Manipulative. Violent. In ways that exceed polite terminology." Walter *loves* adjectives.

"It is a side they have been very successful in concealing, but a side that has been described to me many many times, by women who worked there. They were afraid to turn state's evidence because they didn't want to die." He pauses, thinking for a moment he may have gone too far, and adds, "They didn't want to die in their prospects for happiness in the future."

Walter is not simply spewing closing-argument demagoguery. He is sincere.

He was not your garden-variety D.A., and it is clear that he has felt the pain of ridicule, from colleagues as well as opponents.

Bernard Walter is a fifth-generation San Franciscan, although he was born in Boston (Dad was getting his Harvard MBA at the time). He is probably about the same age as the Mitchells, and in his own way he is every bit as much a product of the 1960s as they are.

He went to prep school in Portugal, college in France, and then, in what most would consider the very antithesis of being a prosecuting attorney, Bernard Walter spent nine years as a Buddhist monk, mostly in Sri Lanka, although he traveled around the world in the course of his religious study and duty.

He left the monastery, did some graduate work in comparative philosophy, and decided to turn his intellect to the law. He graduated from San Francisco's Hastings College of the Law, then clerked for a time at the state Court of Appeal, First District. He went back to Asia, looking for work in international law, didn't find what he wanted, and returned to San Francisco. He had also clerked in the District Attorney's office there, and a friend from that time told him about an opening, and suddenly the City and County of San Francisco had a well-traveled Buddhist prodigal homeboy assistant D.A.

Zen and the Art of Nailing Dirtbags.

He followed the typical career path in the office, starting by prosecuting traffic cases and petty offenses in Municipal Court, moving on to doing preliminary hearings, then moving up to the Superior Court level. Typical, except most don't stick it out that long, opting instead for more lucrative private practice.

But the life of the prosecuting attorney appealed to Walter on an intellectual level. "The only attorney who has an absolute duty to justice is the prosecutor. He has a duty to society as a whole, a duty to the victim of the crime, and also, uniquely, has a duty to the criminal defendant, to ensure that he or she gets a fair trial.

"And that is very much the spirit in which I attempted to perform my public service. The D.A. is the one who has to stand in front of the jury and tell the truth, presenting all the evidence, exonerating as well as inculpatory, so that twelve people must be able to find, beyond a reasonable doubt, to a moral certainty, unanimously, that the person is guilty."

Putting this nerdish, earnest person in the courtroom against Mickey Kennedy would seem, on the surface, a little like matching Stallone the pretty-boy actor versus Tyson in a *real* twelve-rounder, heavies, nontitle, at the Garden.

Barney Fife vs. Pretty Boy Floyd. Boy Scouts of America vs. the Crips.

It really doesn't help any that Walter's corner man in this fight is none other than the old loser Jerome Benson, now head of the D.A.'s Criminal Division, and an old-timey prosecutor who has absolutely no use for Walter's style or philosophy.

But before it is over, Bernard Walter, practitioner of his own offbeat brand of the sweet science, like a gangly southpaw with an explosive right hand, will manage to put a huge scare into Kennedy and the Mitchells. He will have them hanging on the ropes, in danger of suffering their first significant defeat.

Despite having to deal with Benson, he would have the pendulum of city politics on his side. He had been hired during the anything-goes era of Mayor George Moscone and District Attorney Joe Freitas, who could have cared less what went on inside the O'Farrell Theatre. Freitas had been elected on a platform of "let's stop wasting law enforcement on victimless crimes." Like prostitution and obscenity, for instance.

Although this policy was modified slightly during Freitas's tenure (prostitutes flooded the city from all over the country, milling like a plague of locusts around the posh hotels of Union Square, until some token enforcement thinned their ranks again), it wasn't until the Dianne Feinstein and Arlo Smith era that the prosecutors seriously contemplated a resumption of hostilities against the Mitchell Brothers.

Many of the new City Hall cadre felt it was overdue. The O'Farrell, just a couple of blocks from City Hall, a quick walk from the Federal Building, was an upraised middle finger to law enforcement in the city.

On the night of July 9, 1980, fifteen San Francisco police officers, led by Lieutenant Diarmuid Philpott, raided the O'Farrell after receiving a prearranged signal from undercover cops inside. They arrested fourteen patrons, including one seventy-five years old and another seventy-three, and charged them with being inmates in a house of prostitution and/or engaging in prostitution. They charged six performers with engaging in prostitution. And they charged seven employees, including Charlie Benton, with being keepers of a house of prostitution. To the cops' embarrassment, one of the others charged was a moonlighting transit officer working security for the Mitchells.

Neither Jim nor Art were present, but their office got searched anyway. The police said they found a .45 caliber submachine gun, two rifles and a sawed-off shotgun, two pistols, a leather sap, a pair of lead-filled "sap gloves," brass knuckles, a police baton, $3,000 in cash, a bag of marijuana, and "a white powdery substance that may be cocaine." No drug charges were ever filed.

The theater operated defiantly for the next several days as though nothing had happened. But then the Mitchells saw an angle and struck back. The next week, they closed down the theater, claiming the "police brutality" their employees and patrons suffered during the bust made it too dangerous to operate.

"We're not going to open it until Dianne Feinstein guarantees us safety from the vice squad," Jim said. One dancer was punched in the stomach and kneed by a policewoman, he said, and a manager was struck by police too. "We've been in business here eleven years. We've been arrested 150 times, and we've never been brutalized like this.

"Somebody's going to get hurt, and it's bound to be us or our patrons," Jim said. "We have a reputation for fighting and I'll fight when they arrest me, but I'm not going to sit here and run an operation, sell a ticket and have some guy have a heart attack or get beaten up by a vice cop. It's not worth it."

Of course, he also denied the brothers or their dancers had broken the law. "We believe we have a legally protected show under California laws. Fondling a girl's breast is not prostitution."

He also couldn't resist taking a shot at the city for tiptoeing around gay bathhouses and clubs, and said maybe the theater would reopen with a gay live show.

"Gays don't get bothered because they are a political force," he said. "Heterosexual rights are being trampled because we're a minority group."

In the crowning thrust, the brothers put Feinstein's unlisted home number on their marquee with the message, "For Showtimes Call Mayor Feinstein."

The brothers also charged that the police took employment records, an accusation substantiated by the fact that present and former dancers got calls at home from investigators fishing for stories of wrongdoing by the Mitchells.

One of those who was called was a former dancer named Lisa. "They asked me what kind of employers the Mitchells were, and I said, 'Excellent.' Then I hung up," she said.

That loyalty would bring Lisa Adams back to work at the Mitchells several times over the next few years—which would in turn lead her into Jim's life.

Meanwhile, the District Attorney's office sifted the evidence they got in the bust. Prosecuting the patrons, including the elderly men, seemed neither advisable from a public relations standpoint nor an altogether robust legal prospect, particularly since patrons at the O'Farrell and other theaters had been doing basically the same things every other night for years.

So they proceeded against the women. In the first trial, three dancers—Dana Harper, Rena Hernandez and Dona Bragdon—faced charges of committing lewd acts in public.

A playful story by Jim Wood made the front page of the *Examiner,* and described vice cop Richard Adkins's discomfiture as he testified about being manhandled, as it were, by a dancer in the moments preceding the bust.

The circus of a trial produced one misdemeanor conviction—Bragdon—and mistrials in the other two cases. Dona Bragdon thus became the unluckiest of creatures—the only Mitchell Brothers dancer to earn a rap sheet at the theater over the years. She was given a thirty-day suspended sentence, six months of probation, and thirty-two hours of community service.

The Mitchells, perhaps in an economy move, had not used their usual legal talent in the case, and they lost no time in changing that. For the next series of dancer cases, they went back to Dennis Roberts who was now practicing on his own, and he found a solution that not only took care of those cases, but made it clear it would be fruitless to prosecute such cases in the future.

It was almost by accident. As the jury was being selected, one of his defendants told him, look, I've got to get out of here. I can't stay and deal with this. Plead me guilty.

"What?" he said. "Absolutely not. I refuse."

"Hey, buster, I've got a job up on the pipeline in Alaska and I'm going to make a hell of a lot of money up there. Plead me guilty and I'll pay a fine."

So in desperation he looked at the statute on first-offender diversion programs—designed to lighten court caseloads and give petty offenders a break—and discovered that in the case of some misdemeanors, defendants with no prior convictions could plead guilty, go into the program, and emerge with no criminal record. True, it usually occurred before trial, but the law read anytime before conviction.

"So I go before the judge," Roberts says, "and the D.A.'s there and I say, 'These young ladies want to take advantage of the diversion program' and the D.A. goes nuts and says, 'You can't do that!'

" 'Yes, I can,' I tell him, and the judge starts laughing his ass off, and says to the D.A., 'Not only can he do that but it seems to me that what you're going to have if you keep prosecuting these women is a series of cases that are going to drag on for years toward trial and as soon as they get into trial, Mr. Roberts is going to divert these people.'

"That was the last of those prosecutions."

Enter Bernard Walter.

"I wasn't the vice D.A. when the 1980 bust happened," Walter says. "I took over soon afterward.

"It seemed to me that it was unfair either to victimize the men, who had every reason to believe they weren't going to be arrested, or, similarly, the women. A lot of these women were going through post-adolescent rebelliousness, toward their parents or toward societal values. They are troubled enough, exploited enough, and they don't need a rap sheet to further complicate their lives.

"Especially since many of these women are lured into this behavior on a very slight gradient," Walter says. "They have told me that the brothers told them, 'You don't have to do these things. All you have to do is your stage performance.' That is crazy like a fox.

"The Mitchell Brothers knew from years of experience that the woman faces strong peer pressure, that she won't make any tips if she doesn't allow some liberties in the audience, and if she doesn't make tips she will leave. Plus she will see that the women who are getting the money, the attention, the applause, the good shifts, who are smiled upon by management, are the ones who play the game. The ones who get the short end of the stick in every respect are the ones who are just there for the art of erotic dancing."

Walter pauses for a moment. "It was an intellectual exercise. What do you do? I was concerned about the women being arrested and hurt, knowing that it was only going to give the Mitchell Brothers enormous publicity, public acclaim, give them the sympathy factor, and make the police officers look awful in court. I didn't like any of that, and I thought, there's got to be a better way.

"The red light abatement law provided the answer."

This law, left over from the days of the Barbary Coast, was a civil remedy, designed to close down houses of prostitution. But it was a civil action with criminal teeth: if an abatement order was won, and later found to have been violated, the brothers could face fines and jail terms for contempt of court.

But first, Bernard Walter had to get the order, and he was venturing into the minefield of civil litigation, where he had no experience but would surely be up against the best litigators porn profits could buy.

D.A.'s investigators took pictures of all manner of lurid goings-on in the glassless Ultra Room. The women performed in front of each open booth, on a stage that put their genitals at mouth level for the average man. And the average man took advantage of that.

Al Goldstein wrote luridly about the salad days of the naked Ultra Room in a Mitchells retrospective published in *Penthouse:*

"The mook would ready himself for the typical peep-show experience. But he got something else—the fragrant meatus of a living, liquid pussy, inches from his nose. Hand over enough bills and he could bury his face in it. Or slobber over big California-girl suckems. Or just stare as the girl talked dirty to him, reaming out her body cavities all the while. It was the apotheosis of fast-food sex.''

Little wonder, then, that the D.A.'s infrared camera–toting investigators were able to get pictures of all kinds of salacious activities.

Dirty pictures in hand, Walter went before Superior Court Judge Ira Brown to try to get an injunction.

The Mitchells were represented this time by Paul Halvonik, an accomplished First Amendment lawyer who had first become involved with the brothers when he took their side in an early federal case in an amicus role representing the American Civil Liberties Union. Halvonik, who would later become a state Court of Appeals judge but resign his seat after a pot bust, made a spirited argument.

Walter, in his turn, demanded an injunction.

Brown knew what Walter really wanted, if Walter didn't.

"Bernard, are you telling me that you want me to tell the Mitchell brothers how to run their theater? I think I'll do my job and let them do theirs," he said.

What he did do on December 30, 1980, rather than issuing a mandatory injunction, was to enjoin the Mitchells from "encouraging, allowing or permitting prostitution to occur on the premises."

By enjoining the conduct, Brown gave the order force to persist even in the face of an appeal. A mandatory injunction, which Walter had sought, would be automatically stayed in the event of an appeal, which could have tied up the case with no effect for years. But instead, his prohibition made management responsible to ensure that no illegal acts occurred.

The Mitchells chose to interpret Brown's order quite liberally.

"They laughed at it," Walter says.

Whether they laughed or not, precious little changed inside the theater. The Ultra Room stayed Ultra-hot, and New York Live performers kept sitting on laps and allowing generous patrons to fondle their breasts.

More photos were taken. When negotiations with the Mitchells' counsel proved useless, Walter dropped the other shoe: he sought criminal contempt convictions against the brothers and manager Vince Stanich.

Walter admits that his inexperience in civil matters hurt him. "Criminal law, which I was used to, is very different. I didn't have anybody teaching me civil law, and I made some big mistakes."

But in this bout, he had the referee on his side. The case was heard by Superior Court Judge Frank Shaw, who was a former vice prosecutor himself. The Mitchells' best arguments left him unmoved.

"Judge Shaw did his best to insulate the judgment from my mistakes," Walter said. Shaw also found the Mitchells guilty. And he imposed the maximum fines possible: six months in jail and $62,000 in fines.

Each.

At that point, the Mitchells turned to Tom Steel, former protégé of Michael Kennedy. Steel lived up to his name when it came to taking depositions and arguing in court. He had joined Kennedy and Rhine out of law school, and when the firm split up in 1977, with Kennedy going off to New York, Steel went into practice for himself.

The red light abatement contempt appeal was Tom Steel's first opportunity to work for the Mitchells since he got out on his own. And, in concert with former partners Kennedy and Roberts, he did the Mitchells proud.

As it turned out, Judge Shaw probably made a bigger mistake than any of the errors he saved Bernard Walter from when he denied the Mitchells' request for a jury trial, preferring to keep control of the outcome himself. The Mitchells appealed on that point, and lost at the Court of Appeals.

The case went up to the state Supreme Court, then dominated by Governor Jerry Brown–nominated liberal justices, most nobably Chief Justice Rose Bird, later ousted from the court by a shrewd conservative political campaign.

The Bird court sat on the case for years. It ended up as part of the court's final flurry of decisions, announced January 2, 1987.

Finally, the Mitchells had won. The court ruled 6–1, with only Justice Malcom Lucas dissenting, that since the penalties were consistent with a criminal case, the brothers had been wrongly deprived of a jury trial by Shaw.

The case wasn't over yet. Emboldened by the much more conservative court that succeeded the Bird court, headed by now Chief Justice Lucas, the state asked for and got a rehearing by the new court.

Despite the court's ideological rightward shift, the brothers still prevailed, and the Mitchells had their victory in the bag.

The issues in the case had been settled years before. After the Shaw conviction, the Mitchells' attorneys negotiated in earnest with the D.A.'s office while the case languished on appeal. Walter haggled with his nemesis, Dennis Roberts, and Tom Steel. Finally, a deal was struck. Glass would go up in the Ultra Room. The brothers would promise to actually enforce certain standards, which would include some minimal amount of clothing worn by dancers in the New York Live audience.

Walter and Roberts had their bitterest confrontation during the contempt trial. Dennis Roberts had a trick up his sleeve, and it turned into a supreme embarrassment for Walter.

"He was two-faced as hell," Roberts remembers. "To your face he'd tell you that he was really interested in the First Amendment issues from an intellectual standpoint, that you had some really good legal points, that you'd probably win. Then you'd see him on television, raving about 'lives ruined behind the velvet curtain,' 'the Cadillac of whorehouses,' 'purveyors of gross smut,' all that stuff.

"He was also sort of an obsequious ass-kisser, let's be buddies, really big on the collegiality of brother attorneys, all that rah-rah stuff, he was into that. So I asked him to lunch at a place over on Polk Street."

Uh-oh.

"I was the kind of D.A. who didn't approach litigation as a war with opposing counsel," Walter says. "I truly attempted to keep the focus on the issue, the big picture of what is just. So at the end of the trial, emotions have been aroused, with the deluge of personal insults that Dennis Roberts so graciously colored his trial tactics with before Judge Shaw. I felt as a gentleman and a representative of this state constrained not to respond to him in kind during trial.

"To me we have to be bigger than that. Sometimes there is dramatic license in a trial. Sometimes there are tactics an attorney will use to try to break the spirit of opposing counsel, perpetual barbs and cuts and harassment that could cause a more volatile person to become unhinged.

"But I didn't. I tried to keep a clear mind on justice and truth and not allow these street tactics of Dennis Roberts to bog me down or inflame me or occlude the vision I was trying to present to the court and in fact to the people of San Francisco.

"When the matter is over, I'm also not interested in then letting him have it. I'm interested in saying, at this point we do not know who prevailed in this action. There's still work to be done, but let's do it as gentlemen, as men of good will, with a big enough picture to permit the collegiality of reasonable minds.

"So when he invited me to lunch at a nearby restaurant I thought it was a chance to bury the sword, not in each other, but to put the vicious hostility in which Mr. Roberts seemed to delight during trial behind us.

"I perhaps misinterpreted the graciousness of the invitation, which turned out to be a foul tactic."

After a few drinks over lunch, Roberts had Walter just where he wanted him.

"I said to him, 'You know, Bernard, you've never been inside the Mitchell Brothers' theater, you don't know what goes on there. You've always taken the cops' word for it. Why don't you and I walk down to the theater right now?' "

"It was a judgment call," Walter says. "It was a chance to see the place that had occupied so much of my attention, to see it firsthand. My interest in having firsthand knowledge overstepped the discretion of keeping a distance."

"So we go to the theater," Roberts said. "We walk into the New York Live and sit down. It takes our eyes a few minutes to adjust to the darkness, and then a very attractive young woman is walking down the aisle, and she sort of leans in toward us and then suddenly she sits on Bernard's lap.

"It's dark but I can tell he's turning all sorts of colors so I say to her, 'My friend's shy. Sit on my lap instead.'

"And she does. And I'm telling you, it was a complete refutation of everything the cops said at trial. For one thing, he saw that it was so dark you couldn't see shit in there. And also, this woman must have sat there ten minutes, chatted with us about how we were doing, and when it was very clear she wasn't going to get a tip, she got up and said, very politely, 'I have to go, I have to feed my meter,' or something like that.

"So anyway," Roberts continues, "we went out and I said, 'You know, Bernard, I'm really going to have to call you as a witness now.' "

Walter was absolutely dumbfounded. He ended up having to go to Tom Steel's office and be deposed about just what he saw on the afternoon he visited the O'Farrell.

"Which wasn't much," he admitted.

"Deposing Bernard was a hell of a lot of fun," Steel remembers.

Judge Shaw was beside himself, and so was Walter's boss, D.A. Benson.

"He had some words for me about it," Walter recalls ruefully. "In retrospect, I shouldn't have done it. No doubt about it."

Bernard Walter had learned that there was no free lunch. But that didn't mean the Mitchell Brothers' legal battles were over.

There was the matter of Savings and Loan villain Charlie Keating and the Mitchells' Santa Ana theater. Which happened to be right next to a branch of Keating's Lincoln Savings. Keating's fervor for financial wheeling and dealing was exceeded only by his hatred of all things pornographic. To have a smut house next to his S&L was a constant irritation.

In 1975, after members of a nearby church complained to the City of Santa Ana, the city hired James Clancy, a former Los Angeles prosecutor who was affiliated with Keating's antiporn crusade, Citizens for Decency Through Law.

Clancy began filing lawsuits against the Mitchell Brothers at a staggering pace. Every week, every time they would show a new movie, Clancy would file a new suit.

For *eleven years*.

The cases churned through the legal system. Not one of the cases resulted in an injunction against the theater.

Keating, meanwhile, ordered Lincoln Savings employees to picket the theater, and made a $25,000 donation to the city for legal fees in the thrift's name.

The city even hired an off-duty Los Angeles Police Department vice cop, Robert McGuire, to sneak into the theater and surreptitiously photograph the movies being shown.

Every Wednesday for *eleven years*.

McGuire, whose cover was eventually blown, cost the City of Santa Ana thousands of dollars, and none of the evidence he gathered was ever used to the city's benefit.

For their part, the brothers probably spent in seven figures on the case, but Roberts said he nearly got his head bitten off once when he suggested that the brothers give up and close down the theater, which by that time wasn't making that much money anyway.

"They spent a ton to guard their right to lose money," he said.

Finally, the cases were settled in March 1987, on terms the brothers could be proud of. The City of Santa Ana paid them more than $200,000 in damages, including $80,000 in legal fees. They could keep on showing porn, and in return agreed to remove their gaudy marquees.

The case had several interesting postscripts, including Keating's denouement. Clancy was fired by the City Attorney, who said he was obstructing a settlement in the case. And then, a couple of years later, the theater was quietly closed after the Mitchells lost their lease.

But, as always, they had stayed the course until the other side lost or surrendered.

Tom Steel said, "For the brothers, the 1980s were winning times, times when they made great contributions to constitutional law with their persistence and willingness to fight."

He is justifiably proud of his record as a litigator for the Mitchells. "We had the Midas touch," he recalls. "Everything we did, we won."

Back in San Francisco, Walter would make one more fruitless effort.

Acting on a tip, vice squad officers raided the theater in the early hours of February 2, 1985, stopping a show by none other than Marilyn Chambers herself.

Marilyn's "Feel the Magic" erotic act included altogether too much feeling by some twenty patrons, police said, including "digital penetration of her orifices" and "fondling of breasts and nipples."

But after Walter decided not to press prostitution charges against Chambers, opting instead for another attack on the "corporate pimps," as he termed the brothers, both the police department and the D.A.'s office came under a chorus of protest from politicians, the media, and the public. The police were particularly vulnerable because of a number of recently revealed, controversial sex-related incidents, including a police academy graduation party that involved hiring a prostitute to fellate a blindfolded graduate.

Firebrand *Chronicle* columnist Warren Hinckle wrote several columns critical of the Chambers bust, and then became an instant martyr when he was detained for violating the dog-licensing law with his famous basset-hound sidekick, Bentley.

Walter's anti-Mitchells effort had backfired once again. Even Judge Frank Shaw refused his motion for an injunction shutting down the theater pending a renewed red light abatement action.

Bernard Walter was forced to admit that busting the O'Farrell was not a high-percentage proposition.

The Mitchells continued to come up with one crazy idea after another, and most of them involved puncturing the sanctimony of the establishment. Throughout the 1980s, there would be a constant stream of fullbore zaniness, everything from hiring Hunter S. Thompson as ersatz night manager of the O'Farrell so he could do research on a *Playboy* piece, then a book (neither of which happened), to trying to arrange for Llona Staller, the famous porn star Cicciolina who was also a member of the Italian parliament, to do a five-day gig at the theater. That was forestalled by the federal government, which for some reason wasn't crazy about the idea of giving her a visa.

The brothers loved to sit and talk, with each other and with whoever happened to come by the office, spinning schemes, ideas for practical jokes, for new shows at the theater, for political games, and, always, publicity.

When Thompson first approached, the brothers did what they often did: they told Jeff Armstrong to check it out. He and Hunter spent an afternoon at the posh Waterfront Cafe that ended with the biggest two-person lunch tab in Waterfront annals (well into four figures); a session of hitting golf balls from the pier behind the café into the bay; and a cemented friendship that soon included the brothers. Armstrong told them, "He's for real. Everything he's ever written is true. You'll love him."

Their trusted lieutenant was right. Hunter and the Mitchells were made for one another, sharing a hillbilly background and a well-developed sense of fun in its rawest forms: politics, sex, drugs, golf, gambling, fast cars, *action*.

It wasn't long before Hunter was ensconced at the theater, auditioning dancers, taking target practice with his pellet gun, wrecking the Jeep the Mitchells lent him, on and on.

The Mitchell Brothers understood the gonzo concept, and Hunter certainly appreciated the advantages of running the Carnegie Hall of Public Sex in America.

In 1980, Artie and Karen decided they wanted a bigger house. They had good reason: not only did they have Aaron, as well as Liberty, Storm, and Mariah on the weekends, but Karen was pregnant again.

They had worked really hard on the Oakland house, rehabbing, doing the garden, getting it all gussied up. The real estate market in the Bay Area was exploding. Demand was high, prices were spiraling, and they knew they could get good money for the place.

One afternoon, Karen was watching KQED, San Francisco's PBS station. They had the annual fund drive going, and they were auctioning off a 1953 Morgan, a real beauty, British racing green, in perfect shape. It was her dream car, and Artie told her, "Go ahead, bid on it." So Karen and some guy in Marin County managed to bid the $14,000 car up to $20,000 before she finally got it.

They picked up the car and zipped around in it for a while, Karen nine months pregnant and barely squeezing into the little wood-frame two-seater. They were bumping along back roads in an unincorporated part of Contra Costa County when they saw a for sale sign, and they turned down the lane to take a look.

Artie got out of the car and said, "Kay, this is our new home."

Before they even got in the house they decided to buy it. They loved the location, six acres in the middle of nowhere, two thousand acres of federal reserve land all around it, thirty-five fruit trees, a rose garden, daffodils, a huge vegetable garden, and room for all kinds of wildlife—goats, ducks, pheasants, chickens, peacocks, the works.

So right after Jasmine Monet Mitchell was born, they moved into this bucolic paradise.

Where everything turned to shit in a hurry.

Karen says it was the drugs Artie started doing because of the stress he felt over all the legal battles. "It just tore him up inside," she said. "He hated more than anything to put on suits. When he had to dress up to go to a trial every day, it drove him nuts, and his reaction to it was taking drugs. He started taking psilocybin mushrooms and it didn't bother him to eat them and go to court because he thought it was pretty fucking funny.

"And of course he smoked reefer. He always grew his reefer. It wasn't unusual for him to smoke ten or twenty joints a day, homegrown, best bud.

"But then he got into the coke, and the coke's what really messed him up. Jim was into it too, until he went back east and got cleaned up. They bought it by the ounce and kept it in their filing cabinet under S for stash. They thought it was an elitist drug, that it wasn't addictive, that it didn't cause any problems. They didn't realize about the hostility, the paranoia."

All his friends agree that Artie, never the soul of moderation, started doing way too much of a lot of things after he moved to the farm.

At issue is the reason.

Artie's surviving friends and family say almost to a person that it was his deteriorating relationship with Karen, not the suits, the wearing kind or the court kind, that made Artie go sideways.

Karen is right about one thing: Jim, by his own admission to close friends and family, did go back east in the summer of 1980 to clean up and get off the coke. He bought a house on Cape Cod, a mile or so from the Bradford family's summer place, and he and Mary Jane flew out to get away from the whole San Francisco scene, the O'Farrell and the filming and the cops and lawyers and everything, and Jim, in his methodical, task-oriented way, cleared up his nose problem.

But he couldn't get away completely. While he was on the Cape, another problem surfaced—and he made an enemy for life.

Jim had done his best to ingratiate himself with the Bradfords, upon whose turf he was clearly treading. He had bought several lavish gifts for the family, including an ostentatious oystershell driveway for their summer place.

It was an effort doomed to failure. An Okie pornographer brother of an ex-son-in-law does not mean that much to a Mayflower family on Cape Cod, no matter how much money he has. The Bradfords were polite but reserved if not aloof. They had been charitable about Jim's use of their private beach, but when he came by day after day, and Mary Jane even sunbathed topless, something had to be done. Meredith's father politely told Jim that he was expecting quite a lot of guests for the rest of the summer, and asked him to come less frequently.

Jim was equally polite in his response to the elder Bradford. Fine, he said. Then he drove, grim-faced, to Meredith's house nearby and fired her on the spot.

Liberty and a cousin and a friend were walking toward Jim's house that afternoon, as they often did during that summer when there was nothing to do. Jim saw them as he left, picked them up and said, I'll take you back to your house. He did so without another word, and when he left, Liberty found Meredith in tears. "Jim's just fired me," she said.

And although the firing may have been done on impulse, it stuck. When they returned to San Francisco a few days later, Meredith's Volvo station wagon, leased by the O'Farrell for her as a perk of her job, was summarily repossessed.

"That's what I really remember," Liberty said, "our car being taken. All our baseball mitts were in it, and we couldn't even go to practice that day. My mom had to go out and buy an old Rambler. It was so humiliating. I thought, 'That's my dad and my uncle, doing this.' "

At first, Artie and Karen's place in the country seemed like a wonderland to Liberty, Storm, and Mariah. Soon, though, it would become a symbol of all that was ugly and wrong in their lives, and they would come to dread the weekends they had to spend there.

They still loved being with their dad. But the opulent house and beautiful grounds stood in sharp contrast to the shabby, cramped little tract house they had moved into after Meredith was fired.

It was a symbol of all the money their father was making, that they weren't getting. Their mother was taking them to K-mart for school clothes, teaching them how to fake it in snobbish suburban Lafayette, and their dad was living with his new family in this fairy-tale mansion on a hill.

And then there was Karen.

The sweet, nurturing relationship they had with her at first was turning sour fast.

For one thing, there was the food. Karen was an accomplished cook, but she was also a health food devotee, and Meredith's kids weren't exactly used to a sugarless, meatless diet.

"She used food as a weapon," Liberty says bluntly. "Everything she fed us tasted like sawdust. As the years went on and it got more hostile, the food got more and more barklike. And she loved to tell us at the same time that my mom was trying to poison us with Cheerios and 7-Up. It was so bizarre."

One memorable Sunday morning, some healthy little flat brown grainy pancakes were the offered fare. Artie rebelled. "This stuff tastes like shit!" he howled. "Come on, kids, let's go get some real breakfast!" The kids all yelled with glee and jumped up from the table as Karen glowered. Artie and the kids went to an International House of Pancakes, where they had plump buttery white-flour pancakes with lots of syrup.

But the worst part for the kids was the fighting.

"Artie and my mom's marriage was not a screaming marriage," Liberty, now twenty-one, remembers. "But he and Kay. God. We'd be out there and they'd get into it and I'd look for someplace to hide.

"She's a short little bitch, but she's strong, and she can scream like no one you've ever heard. They would beat the shit out of each other, break things. It was so disturbing to us. We'd just freak out. And the next minute she'd be telling us, 'Oh, I really love your father.' It was an incredibly warped existence."

When the fighting started, Liberty's instinct would be to grab one of the little kids and go into a closet, just hold Aaron or Jasmine close until it was over. Often, the older kids would try to get away before it started. The farm was big enough that there were a lot of places to go. Storm would go hiking in the mountains. Liberty would find a secret place and curl up with a book.

Karen says the fights she remembers are the times Artie beat her up when he came home drunk and coked up, which was often. "He would come home late at night and he had been doing something he felt guilty about, God knows what, but he would come home and rip the sheets off the bed and accuse me of doing something and start beating me with a belt. That was intolerable. Here I am with babies in the next room, getting beaten for something I didn't know I did."

Liberty, who had been so thrilled when Aaron was born, reacted quite differently to the birth of Caleb Robin Mitchell, her father's sixth child and his third with Karen, in September 1982.

"I mean, he's my brother, and I love him dearly now," she says. "But at the time I thought, 'Great. Just what they need. Another kid.' It was like she'd just given birth to another weapon. Against us, against my dad."

For Liberty, the worst humiliation came on Christmas 1982, when Caleb was three months old. Artie called Meredith's house that morning and said, "There are more presents than I've ever seen under this tree. Get over here." So the kids went, and he was right: there was an unbelievable mountain of presents under the tree. Literally hundreds of presents.

But when they started opening them, they all seemed to be for Karen's kids. Soon Aaron, Jasmine, and even tiny Caleb were surrounded by mounds of wrapping paper and new toys.

It turned out there was one present each for Liberty, Storm, and Mariah. "I got a pincushion I'd seen in her sewing basket," Liberty says. "Storm got a jump rope and Mariah got some Smurf underwear.

"That was it.

"Dad had just left buying the presents to her, you know. Mae was there, and she tried to make it better. She had brought presents for us, and she would say, here's one for you, you know. It was so humiliating.

"I was sitting next to Caleb and I tried to open one of his presents for him, and Karen came over and said, 'What are you doing? Get away from his things. Don't touch them.'

"I asked Mae to take me home, and she did. She took me out to lunch and made me feel better.

"Dad came over later that afternoon and gave us each $100, and I thought, great, that really does it, Dad."

After that, Liberty stayed away. More and more, so did Artie. He would stay at the theater, out until all hours. Karen says she never caught him being unfaithful to him, though she sneaked down there a few times and popped in, trying to do just that.

She acknowledges, "I don't know if he would have considered getting head on the pool table in the office being unfaithful," but says she doesn't know if he even did that.

From all accounts, he was doing that and more.

Maybe Artie wasn't having a lot of fun at home, but the marriage wasn't exactly peaches and cream for Karen either. She contends that while he was doing drugs and hosting wild parties, she was dealing with motherhood.

"He suggested some group sex stuff to me a few times, but it wasn't my idea of fun," she says. "I was pregnant and nursing and full of hormones all the time."

Others have different recollections.

Artie had become very close to a San Francisco physician named Donald "Skip" Dossett. Dossett had performed Sharon McKnight's hysterectomy and met Jim in the process, and Jim had introduced him to Art. Dossett liked both brothers, but he and Artie were soulmates. Skip liked to have a good time, he had a great sense of humor, and he loved Artie's wildness, the way he injected excitement and fun into everything he did.

Often, Dossett and his girlfriend, a pretty, sassy blonde hairdresser named Debbie Greaves, would socialize with Artie and Karen. They would go out to dinner together, go out on Skip's boat, whatever was happening.

Once they decided to rent a houseboat on Lake Shasta for the weekend, and the first afternoon they were on the boat Karen came up and handed Debbie a little plastic case that looked like a makeup compact.

"What's this?" Debbie asked.

"It's a diaphragm," Karen said. "We're going to do some switching tonight, and Skip says you don't use any protection."

Greaves says now that she was freaked out, and went to Skip, who told her sternly, "Do whatever they tell you."

So sure enough, the four of them got naked that night, à la Bob and Carol and Ted and Alice, and Debbie quickly discovered that getting it on with Artie was a hell of a lot of fun.

Except that in the middle of what they were doing Karen, who's not thrilled that Skip doesn't seem to be, well, in the mood, notices just how much Artie and Debbie are enjoying themselves, and goes off. "You rotten motherfucker," she yells, and starts beating Artie with her boot.

End of party, but beginning of a funny flirtatious relationship with Skip's friend "Debbie Do" Greaves that would last all of Artie's life.

Liberty's recollection is that Karen was not always a gentle mother. "She spanked those little kids," Liberty says. "I couldn't believe it. I remember her spanking Caleb when he was barely a year old. She picked him up and was about to nail him and I was cringing, and she screamed at me, 'Shut up, get away,' and I said, 'You don't have to hit him, he's just a baby, he's not going to understand, just because he knocked over a plant.'

"Once she showed me a picture of Jasmine as a toddler, she had dumped sugar all over herself and she was laughing. Karen said, 'I came to the pantry and found her like this,' and then she handed me another picture of Jasmine crying and said, 'Here's a picture of her after I spanked her for it.' She not only spanked her, she took pictures to prove it."

Karen denies this, saying, "There's never been any spanking done in my household." She says people who criticize her mothering are just vindictive and have other axes to grind. "Somebody even told Child Protective Services that I lock the twins"—her children after she and Artie split up—"in their room," she says. "The door doesn't even have a lock on it."

But several people say that she frequently ties the door closed to keep them in while she is busy with something else.

Karen says she loves Artie's older kids, even though they remain angry with her to this day. "I took care of those kids four days a week for five years while Meredith went through law school," she says.

Nonsense, Liberty says.

"Toward the end of their marriage we wouldn't even go up there if we could help it. Sometimes we didn't see Dad for weeks. He'd go to Guatemala or someplace and never even tell us until he got back.

"I feel like I was severely mentally abused by her, and my dad was negligent to let her get away with it. Once I went up there and the canopy was gone from my bed. The next time the four posts were gone. Finally, the bed was gone altogether, like I didn't exist.

"She *knew* how much I loved that bed."

In 1983, Karen says, she and Artie went to counseling, to a husband-and-wife psychiatric team in Lafayette.

It is certain that the Mitchells were not one of the team's memorable successes.

"I went alone a few times and they said, 'Look, you've got to bring him in,' so he came and he just went crazy. I started talking about how much cash he was taking out of the O'Farrell and he threatened to break my arms and legs. He was out of control.

"He got up and stormed out and they said, 'You know, Karen, we don't usually say this to people, but considering the circumstances, you have to protect yourself and your children. Because of his attitude he's not helpable. He seems to like being the way he is.'

"I said, 'What do you suggest I do?' and they said, 'We don't usually say this, but you should consider getting a divorce.' "

A few weeks later, in November 1983, Artie wanted to go to Guatemala to help Karen's father launch his new boat. Karen says she was in school, and didn't want to drop out to go, so she told him, go ahead, have fun.

"He took a big entourage, nearly a dozen people," she said. "Rocky, my brother, my grandmother of all people. Apparently they had a pretty wild time down there, got the boat launched, and my brother got a pretty bad case of clap from one of the legal whorehouses.

"Anyway, the day he got back he was sitting up late with Aaron, and he drank a whole bottle of Stoly and smoked a bunch of pot and got really out of it. And Aaron told him about this tennis pro. I was taking tennis lessons at the time, and Artie had met the guy before he left, and he was pretty good looking, so Artie was jealous. And Aaron told him that this tennis pro had come by here and dropped Aaron off when it was dark, and he had come inside.

"Artie just flipped out. He came upstairs and started beating me to death. He got me behind a door and started kicking me in the face, and then he put a gun to my head and threatened to kill me."

A few weeks earlier, at a dinner with Michael Kennedy, Karen had asked him in all innocence, "Michael, who's the best women's divorce lawyer in town these days?" And he had responded to what he thought was an abstract question by saying, "No question about it. Sandra Musser. She's one of the best in the country."

The day after the beating, Karen says, she called Musser, signed divorce papers, then went to the Philippines for two weeks with a girlfriend, leaving the kids with Artie. He was served while she was gone.

Karen says, "When I came back he tried everything possible to get me to change my mind. He offered me all the money he had at the time, which was $30,000, and I said, no, you can't buy my love.

"He bought me a $10,000 fox coat for Christmas and I told him, look, this isn't going to work. You can't buy me back. It's going to take more than presents and money."

Karen says Artie moved into a back bedroom and they agreed to start looking for a house for him.

Around then, Karen says, she was talking with an attractive Korean woman who was her longtime makeup assistant at the fashionable Neiman-Marcus store in San Francisco's Union Square.

"She told me, 'Karen, I've just got to find a wealthy man. I don't care what he looks like, how old he is, nothing. I want a rich man and I need to find him quickly.'

"I said to her, 'Take my husband. I don't want him anymore. You can have him.'

"She said, 'Really?' and I said, 'Sure. I'm done with him. I'll bring him in and introduce you.' "

She and Artie did indeed have an affair. And he did move out of the farmhouse, first to girlfriend Joanne Scott's house, then to a house in Walnut Creek that Karen says she helped him pick out and buy.

But he was not through with Karen Mitchell. His war with her was just beginning.

PART 3

"WOULD YOU LIKE SOME COMPANY?"

Dogs in Lingerie

. . . In my dream, the
strip club where I
work had begun to
hire dogs, pregnant
mongrel bitches with
teats hanging down
to the ground
there were about
five or six of them
sniffing around the lobby
when I came in
I stooped down to
pet a malamute in a
blonde wig and a
green silk negligee and
the desk guy told me
not to mess up her hair
because she had to
dance in ten minutes
the management had
built a separate room
for the dog acts
the walls were all
hot pink chrome and
the stage was a huge
slowly rotating carousel

surrounded by
rows and rows of plush seats
the usual afternoon
porno crowd was there,
about fifteen docile
older guys slumped in
their chairs like
lobotomy patients
clutching flyers with
a picture of a Doberman pinscher
in a black rubber dress
arching her back
beneath the legend
BITCHES IN HEAT as the
lights went down and
sharp teeth
clicked together
behind the curtains.
Danielle Willis,
Ex–Mitchell Brothers dancer
1990

To some, it is sacred ground, the cavernous old building at Polk and O'Farrell: the Gettysburg of the sexual revolution.

And it is much more than that. It is the nexus, the fantasy factory. It is one of the world's renowned marketplaces of sexual energy, the trading pit for humanity's most consistently sought commodity. The men—the old raincoats, the hot young studs, the more prevalent fortyish types in between—are the buyers. The dancers are the brokers, the ones with the seats on the Exchange. Buyers and sellers meet, and the transaction is made, over and over again.

It is also the ultimate male clubhouse.

A marketing expert would probably tell you that one of the primary reasons for the Mitchell Brothers' success is that they were so closely in touch with their market.

The brothers knew what the market wanted, because they *were* their market.

Consider. You're a man who grew up in the 1950s and 1960s in mid-America.

When you were ten, you already knew you wanted more from life than Good Clean Fun, baseball and stamp collecting and the annual trip to the circus. You took the nickels from your paper route and you sneaked down to the bus station to play the pinball machine, maybe the Tropical Isle, or Gottlieb's Slick Chick model. Your mom would have been mortified, and that was part of the fun, and what fun it was: the slightly sleazy atmosphere, the thrill of chance, the delicious high of winning, the youthful ego sated by that great orgasmic gunshotlike crack! of a replay, bringing the mute smiling approval of the big-bosomed, provocatively clad women—*chicks*—painted in salacious poses on the machine's back glass.

When you were fifteen, your prurient instincts led you to matriculate to the pool hall, that wonderful forbidden-fruit bastion of maleness. Drunks and hoodlums slouched in front of the place on Main Street, and old men sat on the benches that lined the walls and chewed and spat and watched the young bucks in their testosterone-on-green-baize battles. You learned to shoot, and if you were lucky, you learned to *hustle* . . . you listened to friends brag about imaginary backseat conquests and you eyed the Pabst tap covetously. Fat billows of stale cigar smoke hung high in the air, authoritatively, like they'd been there since 1929, and maybe they had, and the sour tang of flat spilled beer wafted up to join them. The pinball machine cost a dime now, but it was still there in the corner like an old friend, and the ladies still smiled wickedly on the back glass.

Then there was Vietnam and your big brother dying and Chicago and Bobby Kennedy got shot and *Playboy* started showing pubic hair and a couple more years passed and you discovered marijuana and Electric Ladyland and oral sex and L.A. Woman and the Grateful Dead and Cream and the Haight and everything, and you lost yourself in it all for a few years.

When you went back the pool hall seemed tame to you, not the same. Maybe there was no mother left to disapprove, but you still had that rebellious desire to taste forbidden fruit. After all you'd been through you were expected to grow up now, to be satisfied with Good Clean Fun, or maybe no fun at all, but you weren't.

You couldn't quite hack never being able to leave the postorgiastic, married-with-children, nine-to-five, striving yupster world you found yourself in. You respected real-world women, knew they weren't to be thought of as *chicks*. You understood the issue of sexual harassment, and you believed in treating women as equals, as professionals when they were professional, not patronizing, not belittling or objectifying.

But you lusted.

These were your peak yearning years.

You yearned not just for sex. You yearned to please the painted lady, to gratify that male sportsman ego you inherited from your childhood culture, to throw the touchdown pass, to sink the 9-ball, to make her want you, show her she was smart to want you, because you were *good*.

Women in the real world forever made you want *them* with all the ways they knew to be desirable, but by God you'd better not come on to one, or you'd risk being classified as some hairy-handed hot-breathed lecherous loonball who should be Put Away. Still, something inside you still yearned to show your stuff, get the replay, be a man, be *the* man.

The old-fashioned pool halls are gone now, gone forever, like your youth, except maybe the ones in Worland, Wyoming, or Hemingford, Nebraska, and even those might be gone now too, you don't know, because you've joined the big-city rat race like everybody else.

Only weirdos and crackheads are left at the bus station, and the pinball machines have mostly been replaced by soulless plastic video games. And besides, too often you feel like the *ball* now, careening from bumper to bumper in the inevitable downhill progression toward the final rollover, the big gutter that yawns closer and closer.

How do you make the painted lady smile, make her realize that all the other players can come and go, but you're the man of her dreams, the one to fulfill the promise in her eyes? Where do you go to satisfy that black bottomless angst that fills your head and your pants despite your best intentions, despite your rational denial of needing anything but Good Clean Fun for the rest of your life?

Easy.

You go into the Mitchell Brothers' O'Farrell Theatre, on Polk and O'Farrell streets in San Francisco, California, and you find that the painted lady has come to life and she's taking off her clothes just for you, just the way she promised to on the pinball machine all those years ago, and then she comes and sits in your lap and if you're lucky and you have a twenty she puts her tongue in your ear.

Always gets the replay, never seen him fail.

You are a sport. You are the man, and you know what to do. You play your role faithfully, handing over the twenties you've earned in the real world you have left for a while. Just like the nickels you put in the pinball machine, they are incidental, a necessary prelude to the real thing, just a conveyance. A way to make the Slick Chick come to life.

This is not Sam Keen's Fire in the Belly.

This is Bob Seger's Fire Down Below.

 ho *is* the Slick Chick?

How did she get up there on the back of the pinball machine, on the runway in the New York Live? How did she land in your lap? How did she get to be different from all of those other untouchable women out in the real world?

How did she end up harnessed to the wall in the Ultra Room like the prisoner in the Wizard of Id?

She might have been a rebel, from a little town somewhere in Iowa that was too tame to hold her. Maybe her father beat her, or worse.

Or maybe she's got a master's degree, like Simone, and got bored doing other things. Maybe she's addicted to your money because she can't make nearly as much anywhere else, like Sara. Or maybe she has a stupid drug-addict part-time burglar stiff for a boyfriend and she's supporting him because she's used to abusive relationships, despite the fact that he will eventually kill her, like Sassy.

Maybe she has an expensive guru who has sold her a tantric rap about liberating herself from sexual repression, like Sara and Eva and Robyn and Amy and Susy and Natalie and Fuchsia and Elise and Sahaj and quite a few others.

Or maybe she likes the money, loves sex, loves to nurture, loves to perform, loves adventure, and knows more about what *you're* doing there than you do, like Nina.

Maybe she's making it with the boss, like Karen and Joanne and Krystal and Gigi and Heather and Inge and Mary Jane and Lisa and God knows how many others at the O'Farrell over the years. Or maybe the boss has had his hands all over her too many times and she'd like to strangle him, like dozens of others, including the vicious dominatrix poet Danielle, and including a pretty lesbian named Lady T, who later killed herself instead.

Like Raven did. Like a lot of others have.

Maybe she'll die with a needle in her arm, like Sebastian, and maybe she'll strip until she's 60, like Annie Blanche Banks, aka Tempest Storm. She could be 18 (or conceivably, like Bronwen Morgan, she could be 16 with false ID). She could be 45. She's probably about 24. Chances are about sixty-forty that she's lesbian or bisexual. Chances are about ninety-ten that it makes no difference. She's not there for the sex. She's a performer, and she's there for the money.

Sara grew up middle-class in a small Australian town. Her father was a merchant, her mother a housewife. By her early teens, she was already in full rebellion against her father, whom she despised for the way he treated her mother—and his attitude toward females in general. She is the youngest of three children, and she remembers the feeling all through her childhood that she was never taken seriously. She was the baby, and she was a girl.

She is in her mid-thirties now, and the pain is still evident in her voice as she talks about this. She also has a sense of "something happening" between her and her father, something awful, when she was a young girl.

"I've been through a lot of therapy and I've dealt with this a lot but I'm still not sure what happened," she says quietly. "I worshiped my father to that point, and whatever it was really disappointed me in him, and my whole world was shattered. Whatever it was really destroyed our relationship."

Sara is just over five feet tall, blonde, slim and tightly muscled, small-busted: she has a miniature athlete's body. On the street, she wears simple casual clothing, almost no makeup, and sensible shoes. She could be anywhere between twenty-five and thirtysomething. She has a pleasing but not classically pretty face, enhanced by a ready smile and straight white teeth. If someone who didn't know were pressed to guess her occupation, real estate agent or paralegal would come many guesses before the correct stripper.

The Australian accent is still quite strong as she talks about her childhood. She experimented with drugs very early on. In fact, she decided that she would buy some marijuana and have her friends try it at her thirteenth birthday party. She managed to buy it from an older boy she knew, but made the mistake of telling one of her friends, who freaked out and told her parents, who told the police. A week before her birthday, the police came to the family's home with a search warrant.

They didn't find anything—Sara had cleverly hidden the pot in a stuffed donkey on her bed—but the experience humiliated and enraged her father.

It was only a year later that she had her first sex, which she basically did on a dare, and as another manifestation of her rebellion. "I was petrified, but curious," she remembers. "It was pretty awful, but I wanted to belong, be recognized at school." For the same reason she would deliberately fail classes, despite the fact that she is very bright and articulate. "I couldn't deal with other kids being jealous, and of course it drove my parents crazy."

That was fine with her. She developed a bravado that enabled her to hide her fears, rebel against her parents, and simultaneously earn the respect of her peers. It was a potent mix.

When she was seventeen, she left home and got a house with a bunch of her friends, and then shortly afterward began to travel. After a couple of years rattling around Australia on the back of a boyfriend's motorbike, she took off for Europe with a girlfriend.

At a disco one night, she met a German doctor who was wearing a string of red beads around his neck. He was a disciple of Bhagwan Shree Rajneesh. She fell in love with the German, and with the Bhagwan's way, and a whole new world opened up to her. She is still sannyasin, as followers call themselves, and her devotion to the Rajneesh philosophy has dominated her life for the last fifteen years.

She came to the United States to live at the Bhagwan's Oregon commune, Rajneeshpuram, but she couldn't stay without resolving her immigration status. Which led to a marriage of convenience. Which turned weird. Eventually, she found herself in San Francisco, looking for a job so she could save the money she would need to return to "the ranch." It wasn't cheap. If you wanted to go to Rajneeshpuram, and you weren't invited by someone, you paid $3,000 for three months. That was your accommodation, and you worked for the commune in some job. Part of the reason for being there was to work. But you paid for the privilege.

A friend suggested that she try to find work in one of the traditional sex emporia in the North Beach section of San Francisco, and she did. For one night.

"It was one of those places where you sit in a window with a bunch of other women and the men point out who they want to talk to. And you go in the room, and there's glass between you, and you talk on telephones.

"This was such a scene, I swear.

"I go in there, looking pretty young and innocent, wearing my little pink satin teddy, and all the other women working were real hard-core bitches, and so naturally all the men pick me, and so I get all this heavy stuff from the other women about *that*.

"When I went in for the job they showed me the hustle, which was: The guy points you out, you go into the room, and pretty soon you say to the guy, would you like to meet me in my other room. The guy says how much, and you figure what you can get from him, and name a number, $50, $75, whatever you think, and he puts the money through a slot and then you both move into another room that is exactly the same as the first room. Glass between.

"You can imagine how pissed he is.

"So you have the women laying a trip on you, and you get all the heat from the men, and you get only a *quarter* of whatever you bring in.

"I said, forget it, man. No way am I going to do this shit. I walked out of there that night scared somebody was going to put a knife in my back."

A friend told Sara about a topless bar on Powell Street that was hiring, so she went there, and found out that she enjoyed being a stripper.

That schoolgirl bravado got her past the initial fears of getting onstage almost nude. And Sara loves to dance—"music triggers something inside me," she says—so that part was easy too.

Slowly, the whistle past the graveyard turned into real confidence.

"I got a lot of positive feedback. I began to conquer the body fears I'd had when I was younger: my butt was too big, my tits weren't big enough. You know. I'm not a buxom-type stripper and I was pretty insecure. So the energy I got from being a success at it was nice."

That wasn't all she got. Sara would get tips when she danced—usually dollar bills stuck in the strap of her G-string—and then she would sit with the customers and push the drinks. She got a dollar for each drink they bought.

All those singles and drinks added up, and most nights she took eighty, maybe a hundred bucks home with her. Not bad, she thought.

But a sannyasin girlfriend named Sherry came in one day and told her how to make some real money. Go dance at the Mitchell Brothers, Sherry said. They don't serve alcohol there, and you don't have to hustle drinks.

Then, as now, the way to get hired at the Mitchell Brothers was to show up for amateur night. This ingenious marketing and recruitment event occurred weekly. Any woman who wanted to dance could come on Monday night. The one who "won"—getting the most response from the audience—got a cash prize and, if there were openings, a job offer.

So one Monday evening in early 1983, Sara and a girlfriend, Veet, went down to the O'Farrell to strut their stuff. Entering the womblike darkness of the theater, the two women sat in the back of the New York Live and took in the whole tableau: half-naked women grinding in men's laps, one very naked woman onstage, dancing in a spotlight, other women walking up and down the aisles, talking, laughing, flirting with the customers. She had never seen so many good-looking women, stripped down and ready to hustle, in one place before. It was as intimidating as the first day of school.

"No way can I do this. Let's get out of here," Sara whispered to Veet.

"Relax, let's just watch for a while," her friend replied.

So before long it was time for the amateur contest, and a guy named Vaughn with a pony tail and a Hawaiian shirt herded all the contestants into a dressing room. It had urinals in it and somebody said, wow, we're in the men's head, and everyone laughed nervously.

When it was her turn, Sara went out onstage—Jesus, what a stage! She was used to the tiny little stage in the bar, barely five steps from one side to the other, with mirrors so she could see herself and poles to swing on, nice friendly lighting, everybody yakking while she danced. Now there was just this enormous theater stage with a merciless white spotlight cutting through the gloom and following her everywhere she went, a stage as big as the Australian Outback, with a ramp and wings on each side and beyond it the great blackness of The Audience, the infinity of anonymous men who would decide her fate, who could laugh her off the stage if they didn't think she was sexy enough or graceful enough or pretty enough.

If she didn't make them want her enough.

Big gulp. Schoolgirl bravado. Fuck them if they don't like me, she thought, I'm making a hundred bucks a night keeping my pants on and peddling booze right now and I can keep right on doing it no matter what they think.

She won.

Veet came in second. Vaughn offered them both jobs on the spot. Minimum wage. Keep all the tips you get. Go to it. Have fun.

Sara loved it. The fear evaporated. The positive reinforcement was a steady stream of tips—and a feeling of belonging, of family, of being sexy *and* smart—smarter than the men with the jones who were handing you their paychecks. A feeling of being a key part of the slickest, hippest, classiest, most glamorous sex boutique in America: it was the Gump's of sex, the Abercrombie & Fitch of sex, the Georgio fucking *Armani* of sex.

If you were going to take off your clothes for a living, there was quite simply no better place to do it. This was a hell of a long way from gypping drunks out of their money in a North Beach dive. This was *art,* and style, and glamour. This was the bigs, the major leagues. The Show.

Many of the women became good friends. A lot of them were sannyasins too—maybe a third of the sixty or so regular dancers. It was a special thrill, as you were wiggling on a man's lap, your back to him so you didn't have to deal with his bad breath, taking a fiver from him every few minutes, to look down the aisle and see . . . a *sister,* fellow sannyasin, colleague, another member of the Club, another smart one, pretty, with her shit together, sitting on a guy a few seats down, popping her gum and grinning at you, doing *exactly the same thing!* Oh, what a great joke it was!

Maybe 60 percent of the dancers were lesbian, and although Sara was primarily heterosexual, she became very close to many of the lesbian dancers. They were sisters, and with the shared femaleness of the O'Farrell Theatre experience, it was natural to her to feel a special bond with them. Every so often, while she was onstage, doing her "floor work"—usually the last of a three-song set, when the stripper lies on the floor nude and moves to a slow song—she would feel a mouth, or a hand, *there*. It would be another dancer, moved to join her for some sexy interplay onstage. She welcomed it; the men loved it, of course, and it meant bigger tips, and it was fun. It was sexual play, for her, and the theater was a safe venue for it.

One of the great ironies of the O'Farrell scene is that there is so much lesbian sex—and it is all legal. As long as it isn't heterosexual. It's as though in this male-dominated legal system, two women having sex isn't really considered *sex*. It is an amusing by-product of a chauvinist culture that two women can fuck their brains out in public without violating any laws because there isn't a penis involved.

As if they needed one.

Sara found herself firmly supported by a tremendous sorority at the O'Farrell. The women who danced at the theater came from varied backgrounds, but they shared an undeniable professional bond. They laughed about the tired lines they heard every night. "Let me take you away from this" actually popped up pretty often (take me away from $1,500 a week after taxes?), but the most irksome was probably "I'm a professional photographer, and if you'd agree to a *session* I can give you some wonderful prints." It was amazing how many times Sara heard it. She couldn't believe it. "I mean, I guess it must have worked sometimes, because they kept using it," she said.

They talked about common problems: the Significant Others—of both sexes—in their lives who couldn't deal with what they did for a living; men who grabbed and pinched and hurt, the ones who expected unbridled lust for a buck tip; the ones who didn't think that you wanted *money,* but thought instead that you were just working there to meet someone like *them* to go out with ("Can you meet me later?" was another frequent inanity).

Of course, there was another common problem: Artie.

Artie visited the dressing room like an English duke out for a shooting party in his private game preserve. Especially when he was drunk, or stoned.

Mind you, quite a few of the dancers loved it: if you didn't mind Artie copping a feel, he was absolutely certain to have a joint to share, or, in those days, a bindle of coke. And, of course, some of them—an astonishing number of them—would fall in love with him.

Sara was not one of those. But she certainly did not escape his attention.

One night, as she stepped offstage after the first song in her set and took off a couple of items of clothing, she felt someone grabbing her from behind. It was Artie, and he pinned her on the steps just off stage right. As his hands roamed, he chuckled and told her not to struggle. She screamed, wrestled with him, finally broke away, and raged, "Don't fuck with me ever again." She realized with horror that the exchange had been in full view of a third of the audience. Later, one of her regulars told her he saw the whole thing.

Ah, regulars. They were the dancers' lifeblood. Every dancer coveted them; the lucky ones had several of them. The promise of regulars was always there: if you touched a chord deep inside the guy's psyche, somewhere in the hooded primordial area of the brain where his sexual identity resided, if his gut twisted like a corkscrew and his scrotum tightened to the size and hardness of a walnut when he saw you swiveling down the aisle toward him in your black felt hot pants, spilling out of that leather bustier you bought last week, if you looked like the Holy Grail in the quest that brought him in that door, if you looked like the Slick Chick, if, in fact, *he fell in love with you,* he'd be back.

He might be back every day, as long as the money held out. He might come every two weeks, when he got paid, and give you half of what he made, right off the top, like vigorish to a loan shark. He might keep coming to see you for *years*.

Another great thing about regulars was, you could get past the sex stuff with them. If they were so into you that they kept coming back and coming back, they could end up being companions of a sort, and they'd pay you just to sit with them, and talk with them. Sure, they wanted to fuck you. That was the given. But often, the regulars wanted more. They became friends. Of course, how that went was strictly controlled by the woman. That's the beauty of the relationship, as defined by the theater: as a dancer, you are In Total Control. How much you say, how much you wiggle, when you ask, "Do you want me to stay?"—all that is strictly up to you.

There was no feeling in the world like working a tired audience of one-dollar tippers for a couple of hours and then suddenly seeing a regular come in, blinking and squinting as he got used to the darkness, trying to see if you were there.

Sara would quickly develop an enviable stable of regulars, and she prized them highly, as all the dancers did. Her regulars were nice guys who made decent money, and she grew to be very close with some of them.

Even though she enjoyed the job immediately, Sara felt a little guilty at first: she didn't understand what the men could get out of having her sit on their lap. "I would feel guilty, taking their tips, and I would always say, don't tip me again, I'll stay a while longer anyway."

She remembers, "I was making pretty good money, but after about six months I was talking about it with the guy I was seeing then, this Israeli guy, and he told me, 'You are whatever you decide you are, and you are worth whatever you decide you are worth. It's just like hooking. You can be a low-class street hooker, or you can be a high-priced call girl. It's up to you.'

"I thought about that, and immediately my income doubled. Instead of making $150 on an average night, I made $300. It was a matter of staying focused, thinking, 'You're here for a reason, and that reason is to make money. You are providing a service to these guys, and they should pay you for it.' "

Sara had a harder time with the Kopenhagen room, where two women paraded nude in front of men sitting in the dark, tip money in one hand, a special long red plastic flashlight in the other. The girl would stand with her crotch inches away from the guy's face. Sometimes, the amateur gynecologist would think the flashlight was to be *inserted*.

"You'd think, 'He's getting really close with that,' and then you'd realize what he was thinking and you'd say quickly, 'No, no, don't do that.' "

For some reason, Sara didn't mind the Ultra Room, where she swung on trapezes and had crazy sex with the woman she was working with. "It was sort of like being a monkey in a zoo," she said, "and it was so outrageous it was silly and fun." But the Kopenhagen was her nightmare.

"A lot of drugs were done in that place—but the only time I did anything was when I was going to work in the Kopenhagen," she recalled. "I couldn't dance on cocaine. I would be too stiff, too wooden. I couldn't relax and move. But whenever I did the Kopenhagen, I would eat a Valium just to calm myself down first."

What the dancers did in there was directly in proportion to what the men tipped. If someone gave Sara a single, she would stand in front of him for a few moments, then move on. If he gave her a five, she would play with herself in front of him for a longer while. If it was a ten or a twenty, she might call the other girl over and have oral sex in front of him, or kneel on his lap as she touched herself. The money was supposed to be incidental, according to the law, but the reality was that the Kopenhagen involved conditioned responses, and money was the conditioner.

Sara dealt pretty well with having her sexuality tied to her work life. But sometimes the real world wasn't quite ready for it. Once, on a night off, she sat at a trendy bar, having a drink and chatting with a girlfriend. Suddenly, the other woman's eyes widened. "Sara," she said, "you're playing with your tits." Sara looked down, and sure enough, she was. Oops.

Every so often, she got burned out on it and had to get away for a while. Happily, coming and going was no problem. Leave for a month, fine. Come back, fine. For Sara, that was one of the nicest parts of the job. She would go to the ranch for a while. One time, her parents came to San Francisco from Australia on vacation, and she showed them a great time. Of course, they had no idea what she did for a living. Sara didn't want to tell her mother, even though they were really close, because she didn't want to give her mother a secret she had to keep from her father. And she certainly wasn't interested in him knowing she was a stripper.

It was hard enough for him to accept when Sara put them up at a fancy hotel and took them out for expensive meals. He hated not being in control, and he was always extremely tight with money. But for her, it was a way to announce, "I'm taking care of myself just fine, thank you."

Like many dancers, she struggled a lot with her relationships. She was luckier than some; many of the men she was with dealt pretty well with what she did for a living.

But not all of them.

On one visit to the ranch, she met a man she really liked. Kevin was young, black, in his twenties, and very rough around the edges. He came from Milwaukee, where he had made a living selling drugs, but he had been together enough to be interested in Rajneeshpuram, and to go up to the ranch and clean himself out. He was smart as hell—crazy, funny, really a good time. They lived together for a few weeks on the ranch and then she went back to the theater.

He tried to find work, couldn't. He had no real employment background, no marketable skills. Sara didn't mind supporting him, but Kevin minded, and he had an increasingly hard time coming to terms with being supported not only by a woman, but by a woman who stripped for a living.

He started drinking again, got back into drugs, and Sara saw the fun guy she knew turn into a morose, bitter, closed person. They had been able to communicate so openly about everything, and now they could hardly talk at all.

She got home one night and told him, in her honest way, that her old boyfriend was in town for the evening and she was going to go out for a drink with him, and Kevin took that very badly. He had a dark side that she was just beginning to see, very schizoid when he was drinking, very grim, and she started to get really scared.

She got home, and he had been through her things, and had taken out all of her pictures of this old boyfriend, and spread them all over the house.

In crisis situations like this, what she did for a living took its toll. She was drained of a lot of her emotional energy. Look, she told him, I've been dealing with drunks all night and I don't have energy to keep doing it.

They had a huge fight, but they made up and made love and afterward he kept saying, "I'm going," and finally she said, if you want to go away take some money, take off for a few weeks, get it together, and come back to me. She did love him and it did neither of them any good for him to be this way. He said no, and after a while she said, I love you, good night, and he said, I love you too. Good night.

But he got up in the middle of the night, and took all her money, all her jewelry, her credit cards, everything, and left. Three days later she got a call from the police in Los Angeles: Kevin had hanged himself.

A day later, the letter came in the mail. It was a beautiful letter, saying thank you for all the good things, apologizing for his final act of rage, taking all the stuff.

Saying goodbye.

It shook her to the core. "I've never experienced anything like it. Suicide is . . . there's no undoing it. There's no discussing it, like, 'Let's talk through this.' It's done. He's gone."

She knew that if someone is ill enough to take their own life, another person isn't really the cause. But she knew too how much what she did for a living had grated on him, how it had eaten away at his self-image. The thought haunted her.

• • •

Sara also knew, talking to her friends, that lots of dancers had more of a problem with how their lovers took what they did for a living than they did dealing with it themselves.

Some of them were supportive. Others were horribly jealous. Here they had this beautiful girlfriend, a real knockout, and she spent her days, or nights, letting men paw her.

It was especially insidious if the lover had met the woman at the theater. In one way, you might think it would be better: The person knows, from the start, what you do for a living. They should be able to deal with it.

But human nature defies rationalization.

Because, of course, if they met you at the theater, they knew: it was possible. You could tell them and tell them and tell them: it's just a job, these guys are gross, I just take their money, whatever. But they knew. It happened once, with me. Why couldn't it happen again, with somebody else?

Some women liked their lovers dropping them off and picking them up at the theater, or coming in to see them during the shift. Others hated it, because it brought their professional and private lives into collision even more than they already were, and because it was confining, inhibiting.

But the alternative was often, "Why are you late? Where have you been?" The subliminal question, sometimes not subliminal at all: Who have you been fucking?

It was even more complicated for some of the lesbian women. Of course, the same jealousies existed, but the added layer of gender hostility was often there. Some of the women's women lovers didn't like men all that much, and certainly didn't like men's hands all over their lovers. And there was occasionally some fear too, that some man might actually be attractive, might actually be sexually intriguing. Especially if the dancer was bisexual or had a heterosexual background.

Of course, Artie was a factor. Dancers' lovers of both sexes who understood the dynamics of the theater hated and distrusted him, for good reason. No doubt, sooner or later, he would see their lover perform. If he liked her, he would have sex with her if he could. Period. That was the rule.

Sometimes, a lesbian dancer would stake out a claim on a new girl, start a relationship, and then Artie would swoop down. Sometimes he would hit on both halves of a dancer couple, separately or together.

This caused a lot of tension in the workplace.

So much sexual tension, all over that building. The marketplace of sexual energy. Not all of it emanating from the buyers in the seats. The sellers were not immune to the Fire Down Below.

It was the dancers' dilemma. It was chic to be detached, to act like it was no big deal to strut your stuff, put your sexuality out there for everybody to see, no big thing to reduce men to walking, drooling ATM machines who spit out bills whenever you punched in their particular number. But it was also necessary to be sexual, to have real sexual force, to feel it and breathe it. This was method acting in its rawest form. You were expected to live the wild sexual fantasy life that you projected. If your lover loves you partly because you're very sexy looking, partly because you're a stripper, and that feeds his or her ego even as it breeds weird jealousies, he or she is going to expect you to be pretty hot stuff.

Sara took a couple of extended breaks, including a lengthy trip to India. But whenever she came back, her job—and her regulars—were waiting.

One of them, her favorite really, was a young Asian man. She saw him outside the theater. They would go out for long, chatty lunches, and he became a good friend. But she would never sleep with him, and though he wanted her badly, he was quite gentlemanly about it. It was as though his role and hers were preordained, defined by immutable, irrevocable boundaries. She liked it that way. She could always replace a lover, but replacing a regular would be another matter.

Occasionally, she fretted that she wasn't getting much in the way of transferrable job skills. But not much. She was young, healthy, and making great money.

Eventually, in 1987, she fell in love with another man she met at the ranch. This man was not another Kevin. Jay was in his fifties, and before becoming sannyasin he had been big on Wall Street—the O'Farrell Theatre of the stock market. He invited her to go to Bali with him, and after more than five years of dancing, she quit the theater. For good, she thought.

Why so many sannyasins at the O'Farrell? The answer lay 630 miles north, in the commune of Rajneeshpuram, near the tiny town of Antelope, Oregon. The former Big Muddy Ranch, all 64,000 acres of it, had been turned into a prosperous city with the money and hard labor of thousands of sannyasins. And from 1981 to 1985, if you were into the Bhagwan, it was the place to be.

As the Bhagwan said, everyone (including him!) has their trips around sex and money, and the two are often inextricably linked. And sannyasins, of course, knew from the Bhagwan's teachings that repression of sex is a mechanism of bondage, a major occlusion to the eyes of wisdom, and in order to free yourself from that bondage you had to go through it, experience it, come out on the other side liberated and free. So what was the matter with sexual energy? Nothing! And to get paid for expressing it? Nothing! In the earliest days of the first Rajneesh commune in Poona, India, some sannyasin women worked as prostitutes in Bombay.

Among the Bhagwan's followers, the word spread, as it had spread to Sara: the O'Farrell is a good place to work, and the money is good. So in the early 1980s, more and more women in California who were trying to save money to go live at the ranch would show up at amateur night.

One of them was Bronwen Nicole Morgan—Tika to her fellow sannyasins.

In January 1987, headlines splashed in the San Francisco newspapers: "Woman Sues Mitchell Brothers, Saying They Hired Her at 14."

Morgan, then eighteen, sought $100 million from the brothers, saying that she went to work for them "in or around 1982," shortly after her mother went to the ranch, and that she was employed as "a dancing stripper, a prostitute, a participant in pornographic movies and private parties." She was "coerced, compelled, and required to dance nude, masturbate customers, engage in a variety of sexual acts and acts of prostitution" and "sexually molested, assaulted, battered, and raped."

There is no question the Mitchells hired Morgan when she was underage. According to Jim and Dennis Roberts, Morgan was hired March 23, 1984, after presenting a falsified driver's license and other ID that showed her to be eighteen. Her real age was sixteen.

"If she looks eighteen and tells you she's eighteen, what are you supposed to do past that?" Roberts asked. "Call her mom?"

Jim Mitchell contended that almost two years later a San Francisco vice cop came to the theater to check out a rumor about an underage dancer named Tika. The cop didn't find Morgan, who danced under the name Elise, but theater managers did, and they fired her. The police confirm that an inquiry was made, but say they never had any solid evidence.

Several strippers who worked at the theater at the time agree with the Mitchells' account as to when Morgan was hired.

"She sure as hell didn't look underage," one former stripper said recently. "She had the biggest set of tits to go through that place in a long time." Another former stripper said, "She seemed immature, but a hell of a lot of eighteen-year-olds seem immature. Nobody ever doubted she was old enough to be there."

At the time the story was made public, Morgan, then eighteen, officially offered to settle for a mere $893,000. In rejecting the offer, Jim said, "It would mean the end of live shows . . . the end of an era."

The attorney who filed the suit for Morgan was David Olick, a Contra Costa County litigator who told the press, "There is a certain moral aspect to this case. We don't in our society exploit children like that." He added that it was his understanding that the Rajneesh leaders "send out girls or women to make money for the commune."

Morgan also appeared in the Mitchells' movie *The Grafenberg Spot*. She was fully clothed and only in the film for one five-second sequence, but the Mitchells pulled back all copies and edited her out. (The movie was ill-fated; scenes showing porn superstar Traci Lords also had to be excised when Lords, who had made more than 100 movies—but only one with the Mitchells—admitted she had lied about her age and started making movies at fifteen.)

The Mitchells filed a countersuit seeking damages against Morgan and her parents because she deceived them about her age.

Morgan's ballyhooed case went nowhere. She replaced Olick as her attorney, choosing Angela Nolan of the prestigious San Francisco firm of Pillsbury Madison Sutro—a move Olick opposed bitterly. The case file is filled with arguments, declarations, and exhibits relating to the attorney change but very little on the merits of the case itself.

Olick claimed in a rambling declaration filed at the time of the substitution that Morgan made the change under duress, and that she was very scared of what the Mitchells would do to her if she kept Olick.

He repeated his charge of an "unholy alliance" between Rajneesh and "the porn makers of America," and accused Nolan and the Mitchells of joining forces to discredit him.

"I cannot save the world," Olick wrote. "I cannot do any more to try and save this child. What I have done is a great personal expense. The lies and fabrications and the viscousness [sic] with which they are perpetrated is like nothing I have ever seen. The importance of not only substituting me but thoroughly discrediting me is quite apparent and comprehensible in light of the stakes involved. . . . It's the court's problem now. Do what you will and let it be on your conscience, not mine."

On August 10, 1987, at a hearing on the substitution issue, Judge Robert McGrath ordered that Olick be allowed to speak privately with Morgan to allay his fears regarding her duress. Which it didn't. He said she sounded "frightened and extremely nervous" on the telephone, but admitted to the judge that she did ask him to consent to the substitution.

Shortly afterward, the case was settled quietly and both her suit and the Mitchells' countersuit were dropped. There is no indication in the record whether or not Morgan was paid.

Bernard Walter said recently that Morgan "disappeared" after the suit and said he thinks she is dead, and he makes it clear that he doesn't believe that is a coincidence. He offers no evidence to support this, other than a suggestion to call Olick.

Other dancers who knew Morgan admit they haven't seen her in a while, but say she may be in Bali or elsewhere with other sannyasins, who were dispersed all over the world after Rajneeshpuram ceased to exist.

(That happened in 1985. The Bhagwan was deported and top aide Ma Anand Sheela was charged with wiretapping and attempted murder in connection with bizarre plots to attack Sheela's enemies within the Rajneesh organization. She fled to West Germany but eventually returned, pleaded guilty, served two and a half years of a five-year sentence and was deported to India.

(The city the sannyasins had built with their labor was dismantled and the Bhagwan's fleet of ninety-three Rolls-Royces was auctioned off to meet tax bills. The Bhagwan died in 1990 in India.)

Olick agrees with Walter's theory: he, too, thinks Tika-Elise-Bronwen Morgan is dead. But he has no proof. He speaks cryptically of "things that happened leading up to the attorney substitution that make me think that" but will offer no specifics.

"I wasn't scared of those guys," he says. "But I wouldn't put anything past them."

Sara was lucky in two respects: not only did she have regulars, but hers were pretty normal, as normal as sexually obsessed, lonely men can be.

Other dancers got other kinds of regulars. Pretty, dark-haired Simone became the fantasy object of a paranoid schizophrenic.

She sat with him for months before she realized that he wasn't quite right. One day, he told her about hearing God speak to him through the radio. His conversation got more and more disjointed—she thinks that he quit taking whatever medication he was using—and she began to be concerned about her safety. He came whenever she worked, without fail, and he sent her more than 150 letters. Some were indirectly threatening.

She didn't know what to do. It was her job. She was paid to sit with a man who was clearly delusional and totally obsessed with her. Paid to let his fingers stroke the soft white skin of her flanks as he whispered disturbing weird babble into her ears.

She would avoid him whenever she could, but if she was working for tips in the audience, he would find her. Every day.

Finally she asked the theater management to bar him, but they weren't willing to do so. What's he done? they said. He's into you, he's a little funny, so what?

Jesus, she thought, does he have to bring a knife in here and try to fucking *kill me*, before you guys will protect me? Is the $80 or $100 a week this guy represents to you that important?

She got a stamp made: "Return to sender," just like the song, and for a while she used it on his letters, but later she was advised that no response is the best response, so she quit sending them back.

He sent flowers. He sent a nightie. One day he sent a letter with a package of Rolaids, because his telepathy had told him she was having indigestion (she wasn't).

He even sent two volumes of Proust.

One day, Simone's weirdo told her who his psychiatrist was, and she called the doctor, who promised to try to do something, to tell him that this sort of behavior just wasn't acceptable, get him back on the medication, whatever they could do. These sorts of attachments were very strong, the psychiatrist warned.

Whatever the doctor did seemed to work. He quit coming around for a long time.

And then, one day, she was in the audience and somebody touched her arm and she looked over and he was in the next seat, watching her.

He didn't resume the obsessive stuff, and so to this day she figures she dodged a bullet. But it is perhaps the worst occupational hazard of the job. She'll never be sure he isn't out there, like a time bomb. Watching her. Where she lives. Waiting for the day when God says the wrong thing to him through the radio.

A lot of the time, amateur night really wasn't.

Like Sara, many of the dancers who won were pros, already working at other clubs. In the 1970s and 1980s, certainly, the O'Farrell was by far the most desirable place to work.

The O'Farrell's chief competition for much of that time was the Market Street Cinema, a tremendously funky old house open to this day, specializing in headliners with abnormally large breasts and names like "Heidi Hooters."

One stripper recalled that getting hired away from Market Street to the O'Farrell was a huge relief. The money was much better, there was a microwave and a toaster in the dressing room, and, she added only half in jest, "your feet don't stick to the floor."

In earlier days, a lot of women came to the O'Farrell from the Sutter Street Theater, an old burlesque-type house that had gone to a few nude acts, including peep booths that surrounded a big revolving bed upon which a couple of performers would give the sports a show.

For a while Sutter competed strongly with the Mitchells, but after an obscenity bust that the owners didn't have the energy or money to fight, the place slid into secondary status, then disappeared altogether.

Because the O'Farrell was classier than the other joints, and the women made more money, and their feet didn't stick to the floor, the Mitchells basically had their pick of all the dancers in town. That selection process resulted in the place being known for the best-looking women, which made the competition even more lopsided.

One of the dancers they snagged from the Sutter theater in the early 1980s was a blonde Berkeley nursing student with the stage name Nina Hartley.

Nina just loved her job. She only worked Saturday nights, while she finished school. Nursing and the sex business had a lot in common, she thought. You're taking care of human needs.

Her husband, Dave, encouraged her. He had told Nina about how the women used to lap-dance in the nude at the O'Farrell, and how guys would actually get to touch and kiss the women in the Ultra Room. He used to go down there on his boys' night out, he told her, and it was the best.

That sounded great to her. Amateur night was no contest with her onstage, and she was hired on the spot.

On the round, rotating bed at the Sutter Street Theater, she had had her first lesbian sex, and she loved it. She wanted a welcoming place to work, where she could indulge in live sex shows, have totally casual lesbian relationships, and make some money. The O'Farrell was pure heaven.

Nina Hartley was determined to become a star in the porno business. The Mitchell Brothers' job was a logical step, and it worked. She went on to become a megastar in the porno movie world, having performed in more than 275 films.

It wasn't an altogether natural progression. She grew up in Berkeley, the daughter of liberal, intellectual, spiritual parents. She became, as she puts it, a "Berkeley Birkenstock lesbian hippie chick," deeply feminist, deeply committed to liberal ideals.

But she did love sex. She had been taught that there was nothing dirty about it. She had been taught to believe that curiosity and freedom of thought were healthy things. And the more she got into sexual exploration and experimentation with Dave, the more she decided she wanted to go into the world of sex professionally.

She had to work at it. Nina's feminist ideals had led her to disdain women who wore makeup, much less had sex on stage. She actually felt sorry for women who wore makeup, who felt forced to paint their faces in order to attract a mate. She resented men for needing women to wear makeup. She was much more comfortable in bib overalls, hairy legs, and a plaid shirt. But that look didn't play on the stage in the New York Live.

She *had* always liked costume drama, playing dress-up, old movies. She understood the whole thing on a theoretical level. So she set about learning, at age twenty-one, what most girls learned at thirteen or fourteen.

Now, she can "throw on a face," as she puts it, in two, five, or ten minutes depending on the level of artistry required for what she's about to do. Mastering the external was symbolic for her, and it was the first step in creating a new identity for herself.

She is straightforward about that identity. "Naughty Nina Hartley is a conscious construct of my philosophy, that of my husband, and of our girlfriend Bobby.

"Nina is the persona of the educated feminist sex entertainer.

"It was at the Mitchell Brothers where I really got my start, where that persona really started blooming. She is not a false figure, she is a paragon, something to work toward for me, something to strive toward. I actually find that the more I am Nina, the more her good attributes rub off on the real me and filter into my daily life," she says.

Nina lives with Dave and Bobby in an open, warm, three-cornered relationship that is at the heart of her sexual outlook.

That outlook kept her from feeling a lot of the stress that other dancers felt. This is a woman who felt more stress about putting on makeup than about encountering an exhibitionist in a raincoat.

She always wished she could lap-dance nude, but by the time she got to the O'Farrell, those days were over. Clothes were mandatory, but that didn't mean she couldn't enjoy herself.

"I loved it if the guys I sat with could get off. Because I always thought that for them to be able to have an orgasm with two layers of clothing separating us, they must have really needed it."

With experience at the theater came insight into some of the subtleties of her role playing, and some of her perspectives, while still firmly rooted in feminism, began to change.

She discovered that a lot of what women do in creating their supposedly male-defined "pretty" image was really for other women. That men are a lot easier to fool. At first she'd get mad at men who would say to women wearing wigs—bad wigs—"Oh, your hair is really pretty." They didn't know or care that it was a wig; it looked sexy.

"Then I realized, why am I getting offended? It just makes my job easier. And I realized I still have that female prejudice, of not wanting other women to look at me and write me off as a bimbo.

"It's all very interesting to be inside that persona of floozy, tramp, bimbo, male-defined sex symbol, whatever words you want to use. I know I used to walk around in makeup that would make any other woman look at me and go, yuck. How tacky. And men would think I looked great.

"Nina is a combination of qualities," she says. "She's an intellectual, conscious, self-aware person who examines her life. She's able to analyze the world around her and her place in it. She's trying for the breakthrough level of being aware enough to observe others who are observing her. I'm really working on that.

"And Nina also has the best of traditional female values. I'm a nurturing person. I like to cook and feed people. My nature is that when I like someone, I like to do nice things for them. And that's not a bad trait, because in our society someone has to be the nurturer. It's a very fundamentally valuable energy.

"I try to tap into the goddess archetype of the great mother, who is forgiving and loving but also stern and strong. She knows about death but she also knows about birth and nurturing and feeding and growing and giving birth. The natural balance."

To Nina, working in the sex industry is the most natural thing in the world.

"Sex energy is great healing energy," Nina says. "I try to have a great maternal caring, accepting, open energy around my sexuality. I try to put that energy out strong and sweet, because there's so many negative sexual vibes out there that need to be counteracted.

"There needs to be a role model out there, somebody who can show you, for instance, how you can be sweet and sexy and still strong enough to get what you need from a man without freaking him out and making him lose his erection.

"It can be done. I used to make guys run away because I would ask for what I wanted, like the books told me to, and sure enough, they acted like, you know, men with their fragile egos. As it turns out, after I did porn, I found out there's a positive, encouraging way to ask, and get it, and make him feel terrific."

When Nina started at the O'Farrell, Jim was married, and she almost never saw him because he wasn't down there when she danced, on Saturday nights.

Artie was, of course. She watched him torment other dancers, but they became pretty good friends, and with her he was never a problem. She shrugs this off with, "I'm not his type. Those Okies like skinny-hipped, flat-butted women." But this is patently untrue. Nina Hartley was most certainly Artie's type: she is female, gorgeous, and loves sex.

A little closer to the truth may be that Artie wasn't Nina's type, and he was perceptive enough to see it. This woman had the scene figured out, was already in a great relationship, and wasn't about to come under his spell. So why waste your energy where it isn't going to do any good?

Mind you, he did make a pass or two. He wouldn't have been Artie otherwise. "I had to push him off me a couple of times, but it was no big deal. I never really saw him sober, of course, because I only saw him on Saturday nights. If I had seen him on Wednesday afternoons, it might have been different," she says.

The nights at the theater went along fine, and Nina enjoyed them to the utmost. She got the casual lesbian sex she was looking for, and she had fun with the men in the audience, and she made some money.

"I wanted to be up to my eyeballs in pussy, which is a great place to be," she says, sounding startlingly like a horny male making a locker room comment. Which is not out of character. "That's why I have a little more understanding of male lust than some women. I have it too," she says. The first thing she thinks about when she sees a beautiful woman is what it would be like to be in bed with her, to give her an orgasm. "With women I tend to be active. I like to do them. Sort of, 'Lay back honey, have a good time. How much pleasure can you take here?' But I pride myself on being a sensitive partner, not just doing it for my ego. I really try to tune in and make it a pleasurable experience. I think of it as having a male view of 'doing' women and a female sensibility about not abusing or exploiting them. And that's the best balance.

"Lust is not a bad thing, depending on how you treat somebody once you actually have them naked."

Nina's big break into movies came in early '84, when her husband saw female porno producer Juliette Anderson at the grocery store.

That night, he went down as he usually did to catch Nina's act, say hello, and wait to take her home. When he saw her, he told her about meeting Anderson, and she went nuts. "Did you talk to her? Did you talk to her?" she asked. "He said, no, and I hit him. I said, 'My God, we'll never meet her again.' "

She had already decided she wanted to start making movies with Anderson because her biggest concern was for her physical safety and she thought she could trust this woman, who was older, educated, and, as she puts it, obviously not scum.

"As I found out later, most people in the industry aren't scum, but I didn't know that at the time," she says.

So the next week her husband and Anderson did their grocery shopping at the same time, same place, and he used what they learned was the standard come-on line: "My girlfriend wants to get into the movies," and she said, sure, sure, here's my address, write.

Nina and Dave labored over a typewritten letter, which was a big deal for a couple of hippies, and sent it off with some Polaroids that they had taken with Nina trying her best to look sexy.

They mailed the package, figuring they might hear something in two or three weeks, and four days later there was a phone call saying hi, come over to my house for an interview. And that resulted in Anderson deciding to star Nina in the movie she had just gotten the money together to make.

Clearly, Nina was something out of the ordinary. Not only was she fresh and pretty and sexy, but she was so incredibly *earnest*, about sex, about the business. She was extremely intelligent. And she had a relationship with a man who was accepting, even enthusiastic, about her making porno movies.

Anderson introduced her to other people she could trust in the business. She started making movies once a month, on weekends, while she finished school and worked at the Mitchells' on the other Saturdays in the month.

From the start, the brothers and Vince and the other managers were supportive of her efforts, and arranged her schedule around her movie work. Why not? All they were losing was a dancer one or two shifts a month, and they stood to gain tremendous prestige and publicity in the porno world. Not since Marilyn Chambers had they produced a bona fide star.

Soon, Nina finished nursing school, and her movie-making pace increased. She still enjoyed dancing at the O'Farrell, but she was in production a lot of weekends, so she finally let it go. But she would return often as a headline attraction, now that she was making a name for herself.

By this time Jim was divorced from Mary Jane and seeing Lisa Adams, who was a good friend of Nina's and a former porno movie actress herself, so she got to know Jim a lot better than she had when she was just a part-time house dancer. Jim was the one who booked her as a feature dancer most of the time. So it was always like she was family, and it was great to go back from time to time.

She saw the brothers as an intriguing set of contradictions.

"They were open and liberal in that they created a great working space, and they fought for it in court. Yet they liked the girls to look the way they liked them, and they were very much in the old school in that they wanted party girls. They wanted girls who for a little of this, a little of that, would fuck them and fuck their friends. They approached me a couple of times, but I didn't operate that way.

"So as club owners they were enlightened and regressive at the same time."

She views their movie making in the same way. She was a product of the Mitchell Brothers in more ways than one: the first porno movie Nina Hartley ever saw was the Mitchells' *Autobiography of a Flea.* "I'd read the book, and I wanted to see the movie they made of it. They did pretty well."

Other Mitchell movies get less favorable reviews. "They did a lot of real raincoat stuff. I like hot heavy raunchy sweaty sex as much as anybody, but I like the context to be believable. No, I will not fuck with my head in a toilet, and I won't let men call me bitch on film. There are certain things I won't put up with."

She would make one movie with the Mitchells. She had a bit part in *The Grafenberg Spot,* and she remembers that the brothers were easy to work with, the set was businesslike, everything went without a hitch.

"I had a three-way scene with two experienced pros, Lili Marlene and Harry Reems. Harry directed the scene. He knew exactly what to do and when to do it and how long to do it. So I just followed along and had fun with it. It was only my fourth or fifth movie, so it was still new: how can I do better, how can I learn? It was an afternoon's work, and that was it.

"So moviewise they weren't that great a force in my life, but they created a performance space that was amazing. It made a real difference in my bisexual side, to do live sex, which I always wanted to do, to fuck myself with dildos, fist fuck, eat pussy, have orgies.

"It was fabulous."

Seven years and hundreds of movies and live shows later, Nina retains both her enthusiasm and her intellectual commitment to pornography. She expects to make her debut as a director and producer soon, and she is full of ideas. She wants to market new ideas in the oldest marketplace. She'd like to do more safe sex movies, and movies showing regular-shaped bodies instead of movie star bodies. "I'd like to make movies when I'm forty, fifty, sixty, because people need to see people that age having sex."

She finds herself spending a lot of time defending her profession to other feminists, arguing passionately for her position.

"As much as I understand the feminist argument against explicit sexual material, and I do hear their point, I still think that mainstream widely available commercial adult material—not the kid stuff, not the fetish stuff—is so benign that I really think they need to rethink it.

"Yes, there is ugly material out there, but pictures are not actions and at some point you're responsible for your actions. 'The devil made me do it' is nonsense.

"Most people do know the difference between a fantasy and an action. Because these pictures are so upsetting to some women, it's easiest to focus on them. We're so sex-negative as a culture that it's easy to get people on your side and condemn these icky-nasty pictures instead of the fact that the hierarchical authoritarian monotheistic patriarchy has fucked up everything for two thousand years. These people don't attack the Bible, but that's the root of our cultural differentiation between male and female roles. That's where people get the idea that women are dirt and men are superior, and women are supposed to bow down to men, and bla bla bla, as God is leader of the Church so is man leader of his house, and submit to your husband, bla bla bla, all the pap we've been forced to accept.

"I was raised to examine things. When confronted with an upsetting thing, to examine it: Why am I upset about this? What's going on here? Be analytical. My parents' Buddhism helped teach me that, and so did early feminist writing that said: Take Power. Take responsibility for your own emotional well-being, your own sex life, and don't depend on the man.

"I see certain feminists, out of frustration or whatever, running back to the victim role. 'Ack, we're victims of male lust.' I've been around feminist theory since the 1970s, and it's always been about rising above that status, and becoming powerful, so I'm clueless as to what has happened to these people," she says with some asperity behind the smile.

"The whole thing really got crossed over the issue of objectification. That's where it just split from one end to the other. Objectification became the Great Satan.

"I think a lot of women resented the fact that men's dicks are connected to their eyeballs.

"And instead of trying to get their own clits connected to their eyeballs, they decided that you men can no longer have your dicks connected to your eyeballs.

"Wrong.

"It should be more about making it more okay for women to say, 'Ooh, he's looking good!' instead of slapping her hands for touching her peepee. It's such a sex-negative thing. I do know firsthand from women about the pain and fear and humiliation and objectification they felt as the object of male lust.

"But as a friend told me the other day, never forget how painful it is *not* to be the object of male affection and lust. It's not a bad thing to want to be sexually attractive, to the sex of your choice. That's a positive thing to be striven for. The integration of your adult sexual identity with your intellectual identity is something we all should want as complete human beings. Part of that is sometimes I want to be a sexual object.

"And when a man is tweaking my left nipple I don't want to talk about the deficit. I don't need him to like me for my mind then. I want to look sexy for him, because that's what's going to get *me* off.

"Objectification is not intrinsically bad.

"Where these women do have a point is that once the guy comes up to the woman, too often he still acts like a Neanderthal. He does not treat her as a full human being with likes and dislikes and priorities and prerogatives. It's just, 'Yo, babe, nice melons.' That has to change. What doesn't have to change is trying to be physically fit and moderately attractive in your appearance.

"They messed up the whole equation instead of fixing the bad half of the equation. So for twenty years now, men have been feeling very besieged about liking to look. And certain women have felt very bad about liking to be looked at. And that's very bad. The world of sex is more muddled and befuddled than ever, and we have this huge hue and cry over the red herring of objectification.

"Now the feminist movement has two camps, the anticensorship camp and the antiporn camp, some members of which would resort to censorship because they think that porn is so evil. But that casts women as poor little things who need to be protected from male lust.

"How about more female lust instead? That would be nice."

For every Nina Hartley, seemingly impervious to the pitfalls of the professional sex performer, there are dozens of dancers who do not find the business so hospitable.

For almost all of the dancers, the actual work represents a significant conflict, maybe even a series of conflicts, with privately held values. Of course, there are the traditional values they had been raised with, and even though they often have shed those long ago, their new value systems, some based on feminism, are no less accusatory. Also, there are the specific risks of ostracization by their family, and jealous rage from their lover.

While most dancers develop a protective carapace of sorts, to blunt all of that negativity, it is rare to escape all of it unscathed. The rationale of "It's entertainment, I'm not selling sex" doesn't stand up. What's the difference between an O'Farrell dancer and a prostitute? The prostitute may be selling one thing—penetration—that the dancer isn't selling, but that's really the only distinction, and that can become hard to deal with for some women. Many others, of course, have resolved those issues, and find nothing wrong with working in the sex industry in either role. Their view is that the people who have problems with it should reexamine *their* morals and attitudes.

Still, some women who found their way onto the laps of the New York Live audience did not deal at all well with it. An example cited by several dancers was a young dancer stage-named Nicole, who came to the O'Farrell to shed her life as a suburban housewife with two kids, a husband, and a house in the East Bay. She loved the glitter and the raunch of the place, and she loved the women. The O'Farrell was a hell of a lot more fun than cooking dinner and doing the wash in Concord.

She separated from her family, took another dancer as a lover, and became a central figure in the O'Farrell's lesbian clique for a while.

"She rolled into the O'Farrell and immediately she got divorced and she hooked up with Susie, and they became a couple," one dancer remembers. "They did shows together, and they were around for quite a while.

"But for some reason it began to fall apart. I think in some ways the relationship, for Susie, was taking care of Nicole. She assumed the husband/daddy role. I think she really cared quite a lot about Nicole. I don't know what really triggered their split-up.

"Then Nicole was dancing down at Market Street, having separated from Susie and gotten some sort of lowlife boyfriend. And then I heard she got into some sort of drug hassle, police trouble.

"And then the last couple of years I was working at the theater she was living on the street near the Civic Center. Here's this person who starts out with this classic suburban housewife life and ends up a bag lady in about five years."

It is an extreme example, but one that Bernard Walter loves to cite. He found out about Nicole when her husband came to him and said, my wife's come under the spell of the Mitchell Brothers, I can't do anything about it, I'm losing her and our kids are losing her, do something.

Walter says he was told, but could not confirm, that the brothers lured Nicole into the business with cocaine and the promise of stardom. He investigated, but could prove absolutely nothing prosecutable. "You should have seen the look in that father's eyes when I told him I couldn't do anything," he says. "It was one of the hardest things I ever did."

This little morality play, with all the subtlety of *Pinocchio* or *Reefer Madness,* is society's worst nightmare about pornography—a plot right out of a Baptist pulpit. Lust, avarice, drugs, and dissolute living break up a family, and the sinner ends up as a street beggar. And of course it helps that the *sinner* is a woman, the *victims* a God-fearing family man and helpless children. It's easy to overlook the fact that Nicole's real problems started when she got a drug pusher/pimp boyfriend, not when she started dancing, and of course we aren't privy to what sort of guy her husband really was.

Nevertheless, the life of a house dancer was full of pitfalls. "You had to look over your shoulder all the time," one former dancer said. "It may have seemed laid-back, one long party, but you had to be damn sure you weren't ripped off, that you didn't piss off the bosses, get out of line in some way. The money was good, but there was absolutely no job security."

There was another ugly little fact of life that reared its head often at the Mitchells'. One veteran dancer put it bluntly: "If you're a stripper, sooner or later you're going to feel intense pressure to fuck some male authority figure who can have a huge impact on your career." That impact could be as basic as hiring and firing, or it could be more subtle, like what kind of shifts you were going to be assigned, ergo, how much money you would make. At the O'Farrell, the pressure was often indirect. Someone would approach you to see if you'd like to go to a party with one of the brothers or some friends. The brothers loved to show the women off to friends, and the O'Farrell office was the scene of many such parties.

When the New Century Theater opened in 1990 in a former gay movie house on Larkin, almost in sight of the O'Farrell, its managers unabashedly copied the O'Farrell's recipe for success. They justified the hefty admission price by bringing in top feature talent. They made the theater clean and comfortable, and filled it with lap dancers. They offered more explicit shows in smaller rooms, like the Ultra and Kopenhagen (their versions are the Arena and the Playpen). And they began to do what the O'Farrell had done to the other clubs years before: they began to steal away strippers by offering better working conditions. Like the O'Farrell, it was, by porno standards, palatial. Like the O'Farrell, the money was good. Unlike the O'Farrell, there was no Artie roaming the dressing room, no pressure to party. And no capricious firings.

One slim platinum blonde who now dances at the Century says of working at the O'Farrell, "It was really a drag. I was always getting asked to come to a bachelor party, to do this guy or that guy. And you really got the feeling that you better do it if you wanted to stay around, and get the shifts you wanted.

"This place isn't perfect, but at least they run it like a business, not a petting zoo for the owners."

Once, she remembers, the Mitchells had a party for a member of the San Francisco 49ers football team. "They gave me $100 to come in and squirt him a few times," she said. "I'd go back in the dressing room and put a bunch of water up my . . . you know. And then, just like the Grafenberg girls, I'd go in and squirt him. The first time I knelt on his lap and he was playing with me and I let it go. I have great muscle tone—I can squirt several feet—and I really drenched him. Wow, was he surprised."

Danielle Willis, the poet who went from Market Street Cinema to the O'Farrell, also moved on to the Century.

Willis, whose writing reveals a drug history to rival Hunter Thompson or William Burroughs, was kicked out of Barnard in 1986. Since then, her bio notes in her poetry books will tell you, she has worked as a nanny, poodle groomer, stripper, and dominatrix.

She is a stark, imposing twenty-five-year-old, easily six feet tall in her spikes. Whippet-thin. Flowing black hair and pale white skin. High angular cheekbones, big strong unapologetic nose and a set of teeth like a quarter horse, huge pretty swollen red-painted mouth stretched over them, snarling, laughing, giving you a look at them, big bright white straight ripping teeth that could really do some damage—have done, you get the feeling.

Her working uniform, before she shucks it onstage, is a tiny shiny black leather bikini, nipples on small breasts riding just above the top triangles, black gartered hose on incredibly long legs framing the bottom triangle, washboard belly above it.

One night Artie decided to pinch her as she stood in front of a mirror in the dressing room, preparing to go onstage.

Bad decision.

"Artie was coming through there like he always did, 'Hey, how are you, let's fuck, heyheyhey,' and he pinched the wrong butt. I wasn't into it, and I turned around and smacked him.

"He hit me back, and I just went nuts. I can't stand men hitting me.

"I had this spike heel in my hand, I was getting dressed, and I went after him." She had probably three inches of height and a couple of inches of reach on him, maybe ten pounds of weight too, all muscle. She got a headlock on him and used the spike like a meat tenderizer all up and down his body. He had little pointillist blue spike-heel bruises from his shoulder to his ankle on one side.

And all the women were cheering: "Yeah! Yeah! Right on! Give it to him!"

The cover of Willis's third book of poetry bears the following endorsement: " 'ONE MEAN BITCH!'—Artie Mitchell."

Maybe it was because the theater was spawned in the days of free love. Maybe it was because a few of the managers were not only sort of ex-hippie contemporaries of the brothers, but in the main were also known by the dancers to be friends of the family. But whatever the reason, some women often felt sexual pressure on the job, and it wasn't just from Artie. A couple of the midlevel managers would succumb to the sexual intoxication of working around those women.

"It was the whole atmosphere of the place," one longtime dancer says. "Even if they know you, even if they have some basic respect for you, figure you're smart, there are times when they forget, and you're still a twenty-year-old stripper to them, and it's 'How about a blowjob?' It didn't get talked about much, but it was there."

Still, Artie was always known as "the one to watch out for." And he didn't particularly care for other male managers asserting themselves sexually. He told one horny, frustrated male employee, "You shall not poach the royal deer."

If you were a male and one of the big dogs around the place, you either handled it like Artie, submerging yourself in sex, or you went the other way altogether, like Jeff and Mezz and Rocky and most of the others. You didn't mess around, period. It was a job, you did your job, you went home to your family, and you kept out of the cookie jar.

Of course, if you were male and you weren't one of the honchos, the place could be emasculating as hell.

You probably took the job because it was in your nature to like to be around all those good-looking women. But what torture! You were right there next to their perfumed nakedness. Maybe you were a tech assistant or a DJ. You shone a spotlight on them when they danced. They walked up naked and handed you the cassette they wanted you to play during their act. They might even smile. But ninety-nine times out of 100, maybe 100 times out of 100, you had nothing for them, and so they had nothing for you.

You weren't a customer with a roll of twenties. You weren't Artie, or Jim, who were *cute*, and had wealth and power over their professional lives. You didn't even stand as good a chance as some schmuck off the street. Because the women knew that you were nothing but Hired Help. They made more money than you. You were just there to help them look good, to put more money in their G-strings, to clean their toilets, run the projector, watch the door, call them a cab, whatever. Unless you were really physically attractive (occasionally some handsome young guy would get hired and send a ripple through the dressing room), probably none of them would ever get to know you well enough to fall in love with you for your *personality*.

There were men who worked for years at the theater, pining away, lust twisting their guts every night, and never had sex with a dancer. Not once in all that time, despite the fact that they were ready, willing and able every one of the thousands of shifts they had worked. Not surprisingly, a couple of them became known for being bitter and rude toward the women. "I felt sorry for a couple of those guys. It's just not healthy," one dancer said.

"But of course I sure didn't want to fuck them, either."

For the O'Farrell house dancers, the ground rules were constantly changing. For one thing, the degree of police pressure fluctuated wildly over the years, and so did the theater's response. And for another, Jim and Art would get crazy ideas all the time. They ran the place like a laboratory. Let's try this. How about this. They were forever building new rooms, then tearing them up before they were finished and going on to something else.

The main stage, the New York Live, usually included lap dancing in the audience while lap-dancing rules went from don't do it to anything goes. For a while, dancers would be nude, and any sort of touching was allowed. Then, post–Frank Shaw, came G-strings, and then more substantial clothing, including bras. For a while, women even wore sweat pants or tights, although that didn't last long.

Joanne Scott remembers another change: "Jim had this idea for a Cine Stage show called Pink Video, and he rented a lot of equipment for it. The idea was, you sat pretty still on the stage, maybe rolled around a little but basically you had to stay in the same spot, and they had a camera super-close-up on your pussy, and they projected that image onto the cinema screen behind you while you were onstage. This was going to be really thrilling. Well, the problem was, the camera wouldn't allow you to move around much, and, Jesus, what were you going to do, just sit there?

"So I started bringing some props to the show, and it really improved it a lot, made it a whole lot more fun."

The Pink Video didn't last that long. For one thing, a blurry fifteen-foot-high image of a vagina wasn't quite as much of a turn-on as Jim had apparently thought it would be, despite the "props." For another, the Cine Stage was always darker than the New York Live, and having women sit on laps in there was, at the time, considered risky. "They didn't know what they wanted," Joanne recalls. "They kept switching from 'it's got to be stricter,' to 'loosen up, let it happen.' But at the time they were on a cycle of being really strict, and they were wondering, suspicious—'What are those girls doing with the customers in there in the dark?'—so they stopped it."

For a while they decided to try pulling the dancers out of the audiences altogether. This time it wasn't so much a reaction to heat from the cops as it was an experiment to see what would work. Jim had the idea that more sophisticated shows would bring the customers in regardless of whether they were able to have physical contact with the performers—sort of a throwback to the old burlesque days, but with updated shows. He even hired Judy Rowe, the doyenne of the Sutter and an old burlesque star, as sort of a creative director, to choreograph some shows.

What a bomb. Once again, dancers with little prospect for tips fled in droves, and the customers went with them.

Joanne stayed, again, and weathered the storm. The theater was so short of dancers that the few remaining women were all pulling double shifts, but it was still pretty sparse. "One evening everybody else was at dinner and there were only two of us—me and this Chinese girl, I can't remember her name—to dance in the New York Live. We kept taking turns on the stage."

A full retreat was obviously in order, and it was accomplished with haste. The girls went back on laps, and customers and dancers came back. Rowe departed, her first show lasting only a few days of its scheduled week-long run.

The wacky ideas proliferated.

At one point, the brothers decided to put a live all-girl band in the Cine Stage, and have near-nude taxi dancers. Jim and Artie wanted the band to be totally nude, and the idea fell apart there. They auditioned some good musicians but—surprise, surprise—none of them wanted to play in the buff.

Shortly after the Green Door Room opened in 1988, the brothers launched another ill-fated venture that really pissed off the O'Farrell women: the Topless Shoe Shine.

They bought four fancy shoe shine chairs and equipped them with polish, brushes, rags, the works. Jim asked Joanne Scott to come up with costumes for the girls. He actually suggested a bikini made of shine rags, so the girl could actually *shine the shoes with their bodies*. Horrified, she compromised with little bow ties and cuffs.

For some reason, none of the dancers particularly wanted to shine customers' shoes. So faithful Joanne was put to the task, along with a dancer named Diana Minetti.

It lasted all of three days. The men weren't interested in it either. They weren't coming to the O'Farrell to put a gleam on their Guccis.

Although the house rules and the extent to which they were enforced varied widely during the eighties, one rule was absolute: no sex with customers. And it was rare that someone would break it. After all, the dancers were making good money without taking that step.

Occasionally, though, it happened. In the summer of 1988, a dancer was fired after being caught copulating with a customer. The barely literate note that a guard wrote to management about the incident conveys a soil and sadness far beyond its intent. What a pathetic, ill-starred, joyless, destructive little human transaction:

Saturday July 23rd at 5:35 P.M. one of the dancer's came up to me with a complaint about what one of the other dancer's was doing in the Audience I went to see and she was on this guy's lap I sat down in Back of them about 1 min went By and she saw me She got up quick and said you can't do that after the guy was screwing for the past 5 mins. When Bring the guy to magr. (Lonnie) he said $20 and I could not even finish getting my rocks off. He talk to Lonnie and left. Lonnie thin told her to go home. She then went up the stairs and broke one of the small windows at the top of the stairs.

Until 1988, dancers at the O'Farrell were Mitchell Brothers employees, paid minimum wage and all the tips they could get. But the Mitchells changed the ground rules. Now the dancers not only weren't employees—they *paid a fee* to perform there, for the chance to earn tips. They were now independent contractors. No benefits, no insurance, no job security (although that had been minimal anyway).

Vince Stanich, who had been supervising the dancers, was set up as the head of an entity called Dancers Guild International. Nominally, he was an independent contractor now too, a booking agent. His office was moved a block up the street to a building on Geary.

The dancers' contracts included ironclad language like, "PER-FORMER is an independent contractor and thereby assumes responsibility for payment of all federal, state, and local tax liabilities for fees . . . tips and gratuities." And "PERFORMER, at her sole option, may enter into an audience entertainment situation after her performance whereby she may come into contact with patrons. PER-FORMER explicitly understands that patrons of PRODUCER are under no obligation whatsoever to tender tips or gratuities. Furthermore, PERFORMER shall under no circumstances whatsoever solicit tips or gratuities from said patrons."

One of the most-grumbled-about features of the new contracts was the clause mandating that the women present proof to the theater that they were "free of all venereal diseases." If sexual contact wasn't part of the job, why did it matter? This rule was sometimes described as the "Artie clause," and it meant the dancers were forever having to go down to a clinic for new tests.

Although Vince did the schedule, Artie and Jim couldn't resist pulling the strings, hiring, firing, moving dancers into good shifts and taking the good shifts away.

A constant stream of memos on dancers flowed from the brothers' office to Vince. A variety of reasons were put forward for laying off a dancer. She could be overweight. She could be underweight. She could have an "obvious health problem" (drugs). She could have "reached maximum exposure," a catchall that supposedly meant a dancer had been working so much that the public was tired of her, which rarely actually happened; most customers did not differentiate between dancers, and those who did were regulars seeing a particular woman, and the last thing they wanted was for her to leave. If women were still getting good tips, the customers were obviously satisfied.

But dancers who had fallen from favor with management often showed up on the "maximum exposure" list. Danielle Willis, after the spike-heel tattooing she administered to Artie, suddenly found herself on it. Vince ignored it at first; she was a good dancer and he didn't think it was fair. But she was on the next memo too, so she had to go. She considered suing, but discovered one of the occupational hazards of the business: for a stripper, there is no such thing as sexual harassment. Also, she wasn't even an employee, and there were plenty of other women who had been laid off so she couldn't prove there was any connection between her fight with Artie and her appearance on the list.

For a while, the brothers instituted a subjective "scoring" system based on several factors, including tardiness, absence, drinking and drugs, "hustling," allowing customers excess liberties in violation of house rules. The disc jockeys would also assign points to each dancer based on what he or she thought of the dancer's performance.

"That was a bitch," said one dancer. "If a DJ was pissed at you, because he didn't think you were nice enough to him, or you wouldn't fuck him, or whatever, he could blow you out of the water. It was the only power those poor bastards had, and they sure used it."

Another memo to Vince listing dancers to be fired carried the handwritten shorthand notation "B.U." next to one name.

Vince had to ask what it meant.

"Butt Ugly," he was told.

One dancer who is now at the Century recalls, "You just knew, if you were a little older, a little heavier than they liked, or just unconventional-looking in some way, you were going to get laid off at some point. They said everybody was treated the same but some women were clearly exempt from it. Nobody ever touched them."

When this dancer's turn on the layoff list came, she went to Jim and Artie and complained.

"They told me, 'Your mistake was in thinking this was a regular job. You're not an employee. We don't promise you full-time work. Give us a call in a month or two and we'll see if we can use you.' I did, and they eventually rehired me, but then this job at the Century came up and I quit. On my terms. Before they had a chance to do it to me again.

"I have kids to support and I need to work. Since I've been here, I've been on full-time, no problem."

"This place is worse than the NFL," one O'Farrell manager would say. "If you're twenty-five, you're washed up."

A memo from Jim to Vince dated January 16, 1990, included the following garbled warning:

"Dancers whose monthly average scores are below 2.00, i.e. less than 'good,' and whose poor scores are substantiated by direct comments by O'Farrell management in regards to hustling, drinking, allowing customers to touch sexual body parts, no-shows, repeated tardiness, or other major violations of the 'House Rules' will be a one-month suspension for the first offense.

"That being the case, the O'Farrell will not accept bookings from Dancers Guild International for the followiing dancers for the month of February 1989." (Presumably 1990, given the date of the memo.)

Four names followed, including that of a tall, black-haired dancer named Raven.

"The penalty for a second offense has yet to be determined," the next paragraph said.

Raven didn't wait to find out. She had a fight with her lover and killed herself.

She wasn't the only one.

Another lesbian dancer, Lady T, ran afoul of Artie, and the confrontation certainly changed her life, and may have had something to do with shortening it as well.

One evening toward the end of December 1988, between Christmas and New Year's, Artie was at the theater, late in the evening, doing coke, drinking, quite possibly doing psychedelics. Her shift over, the theater closed, Lady T was leaving when Art spotted her.

"Hey, how about a hug?" he asked.

Lady T was a smart woman, and she knew damn well she couldn't tell her boss to fuck himself. He was her boss and she would be out of there in a flash. She could see too that he was not in any state to be crossed, or put off. His eyes were glazed, his speech slurred. His clothes were ragged and torn; he had had a scuffle with one of his male friends earlier.

Of course, this was the sort of volatile situation the O'Farrell officially tried to prevent from happening with their dancers. Here she was, being menaced by an obvious wacko, leering at her in a sort of electric drunken Charlie Manson way, blocking her path down the stairs. If Artie had been a customer, he would have been hustled out of there in a flash. But the security guys in the lobby couldn't protect her from the boss.

Also, there was an undercurrent of competitive sexual tension between them; they were both chasing a new dancer, a pretty, petite Filipina.

So Lady T decided to vamp her way out of it. The thin, sinuous dancer gave Artie a hug, made a cat growling noise in her throat and ran her fingernails down his chest and back, then slid by.

Artie freaked out. In his state, her playful attack seemed real. He looked down and saw his torn shirt, and thought she had scratched him. He thought he could feel the scratches.

He bellowed in rage and chased her down the stairs. Lady T, scared out of her wits, made it out the door and onto O'Farrell Street with Artie right behind her. As usual at closing time, there was a cab at the curb waiting for dancer fares, and she got into it just before Artie could catch her. He slammed the side of the cab and threatened her as she sped away.

When she got home, there was a series of chilling threats on her answering machine. It was Artie, drunkenly threatening to kill her. The last message was from Artie's girlfriend, Kristal, who was obviously doing his bidding in adding her threat to his.

The following week, Vince Stanich told Lady T she was suspended.

When she asked why, he told her, "Because Jim and Artie own the theater." He said, look, sometimes Artie does some things that we're all embarrassed about. And he thanked her for being a good sport about it.

Two weeks later, she sent a letter to Jim at the theater, explaining her side of the incident, and enclosed the answering machine tape. It worked. Suddenly her name was penciled back onto the schedule, and the next few months passed without incident.

Then, with no warning, her name appeared on one of the lists sent to Vince, and Lady T was out of a job.

She got on at the Century, and danced there for a time—before she took an overdose of sleeping pills and went into a coma. She was hospitalized at Davies Medical Center in San Francisco, and several dancers from the O'Farrell kept a vigil by her side. But she never regained consciousness, and a few days later Lady T died.

The subject of suicide is not painless to Debi Sundahl, aka Fanny Fatale. Sundahl worked at the Mitchells' for five years, and she was a very good, very successful stripper because she enjoyed it. She enjoyed the art of it, the performance. She enjoyed the sex with the other women, because she was enthusiastically bisexual—perhaps more correctly pansexual. And for the same reason, she enjoyed a lot of the sexual play with the customers.

Also, she was good because she was smart, and a tough-minded businesswoman.

Those characteristics led her away from stripping, ultimately, when she and friend/lover Nan Kinney started *On Our Backs,* an erotic magazine for lesbians that became successful on a national level.

For anyone, it is an intensely disturbing experience to lose a friend to suicide, and Sundahl has suffered that loss several times. Each time, she felt the usual range of anger, depression, personal loss, and helplessness.

But she also felt another kind of frustration. She felt angry because dancers committing suicide was *bad for the sex business.* She knew that to outsiders, to antiporn crusaders like Bernard Walter, the deaths confirmed the thesis that selling sexuality is ultimately destructive. At worst, the deaths could be portrayed as karmic retribution for the immorality of stripping.

Sundahl was so moved by the dancers' suicides that she wrote about stripping and suicide in her advice column, "Ask Fanny," in the May/June 1990 issue of *On Our Backs.*

She wrote that some people might think it proves true all the stereotypes about sex performers:

" 'Unstable, lost little girls looking for love, not sex; destined to succumb to abuse, drugs, or an early death. If we got rid of the sex industry, all would be saved.'

"Yeah, right.

". . . Few of us could withstand a daily put-down of what we do for a living, yet this is what strippers face on and off the job, from close friends to acquaintances. More twisted yet is the incredible fascination people have with what strippers do, usually followed by all the problems they have with it.

"Sex is a loaded medium. I know too many people who met and fell in love with strippers because they were strippers and symbolized hard-to-come-by personal freedom and sexual desire. Then, once the lover gives the stripper the promise of love, the rules change. 'I will only love you if you quit working.' 'I am too jealous to let others see what is mine.' 'How can you love me and do THAT?'

"THAT happens to be the stripper's self-expression and her livelihood. To make a stripper, or anyone, choose between love or her self-integrity, is to destroy her trust in intimacy, her self-esteem, and to play on her fears of abandonment. It's a nasty, fucked-up business, and I'm not talking about the sex industry."

Fanny knows what she's talking about. Bitter experience has been the teacher.

She saw the difficulties her fellow strippers had with what they did. "I loved and hated those women," she says. "I loved them for their creativity, their interesting lives, and I just detested them for their shame in what they were doing. And it was there for a lot of them. They put on a good front but it was there."

Jim Mitchell was her role model in the sex business, Sundahl says, but that doesn't mean she approved of the way he and his brother ran the theater.

Just as the Mitchells were pioneers in the business, different from the rest, they soon became the old guard, and in many ways not different at all. They did fall prey to the stereotypes, what with Artie in the dressing room, abusing alcohol and drugs, putting sexual trips on the dancers, and with both brothers using their power to hire and fire for all the wrong reasons.

"They let a lot of excellent performers go for personal reasons, and then they hired women who couldn't dance for shit," she says, "women right off the street. They brought in a lot of beauty queen types who either had no idea how to dance or had terrible attitudes, or both. I really hated dancers who had shitty attitudes toward the men. It's so destructive. What the hell were they there for?

"The O'Farrell really lost its creative edge," she says, "because there weren't enough controls. There are so many good dancers, especially in this city, women with heads on their shoulders, women they could have nurtured."

Sundahl's connection to the Mitchells has not always been comfortable for her in her role as publisher. The contingent of women who would inevitably be against her magazine's eroticism, considering it antifeminist, seized upon her association with Jim and Artie and accused the magazine of being male-dominated, male-defined, even secretly bankrolled by the Mitchells. None of which was true. The Mitchells offered nothing more than words of support to her enterprise.

It is an especially galling charge to lay against someone who has the ambition of creating a whole new, enlightened power structure in the sex business, dominated by women. "All those old fuckers are dying off," Sundahl says of traditional male pornographers. "We will run the industry someday."

Sara, who left the O'Farrell to follow her heart, was to find out the toughest thing about the job was not having it anymore.

She hadn't trained herself to do much of anything else. And it was really hard to work a week at a straight job and earn less than she made in a good night at the theater.

Her relationship with Jay, the older sannyasin, lasted several years. She invested a lot of time and effort in it. They went to therapy together, and they had the bond of Rajneesh. But it wasn't enough, and part of the problem was his inability to deal with what she *used* to do for a living.

She tried waitressing, and it didn't pay enough, and it was too damned hard. If I have to fake a smile at an obnoxious customer, Sara thought, I might as well get paid for it like I did at the Mitchell Brothers', instead of, if I'm lucky, a couple of bucks after half an hour of work.

Besides, she needed money. She was taking flying lessons, and wanted to take more. She wanted to be able to buy new clothes, and a better car, and all the rest.

So, in the summer of '91, four years after she had quit and a few months after Artie's death, Sara went back to the Mitchell Brothers'.

It was not altogether an easy reentry, although her old pals, managers Vince Stanich and Nancy Harrison, an ex-dancer, were very welcoming. The theater was a different place. She didn't miss getting groped by Artie, but she did miss the party atmosphere that used to prevail. The place seemed colder, more businesslike. The dancers were now independent contractors who paid the theater for the right to perform there—$10 for a day shift, $15 for a night shift. No more minimum wage, health benefits. Just tips. And those weren't the same either.

Sara called a couple of her old regulars. One of them came up on her first day back. "He was so sweet. He took me out to dinner, and I get to the table and here's this huge, beautiful bouquet, one of those art things, just gorgeous. Unbelievable. He told me, you know, I've dropped this whole sexual obsession but it's really important for me to remain friends. It was great."

Another old regular came in, and it was a harbinger of the chill she was to feel over the next week or so. It was the young Asian guy, the one she used to go to lunch with. The one who used to give her half his paycheck each week.

"It was very strange, seeing him. I mean, it was different. Of course it was. He used to be in love with me, and now he's not, and that's the difference."

She says he told her he wasn't coming to the theater regularly anymore. But in the dressing room, another dancer told Sara that he was sitting with someone steadily at the New Century.

For Sara, the stuff that used to come automatically when she started out at the theater became forced and difficult now. Her years of therapy didn't make the acting any easier. "My feelings are more to the surface now," she says. "Before, when negative feelings came up, as they will at the theater, I'd push them away, just say, 'Don't give that any energy. Push ahead.' Now I tend to deal with things instead of pushing them down or away. It's cash on delivery now. Deal with the feelings as you have them. It makes you more vulnerable."

Shortly after Sara returned, a woman who danced under the name Sebastian died at her home of a heroin overdose.

Nancy called a mandatory meeting of the dancers to talk about it, which was a real departure from past years, when there would have been no official reaction to such an event.

"It was a chance to talk about things if you wanted, and it seemed to me that it took the important step of acknowledging the shared difficulties, the importance of talking," Sara recounts.

"We never have meetings. It was the first time I'd ever seen that many dancers in one room. It was great really. I just sat next to the door and watched them all come in with a smile on my face because it was such a visual treat, all these good-looking women together with the trappings of their outside lives . . . their different outfits. The whole variation. It was quite wonderful.

"Some looked very straight. Cassie, from the street, I mean, she dresses straight, like an accountant, a little old-fashioned. Then there's the amazing stuff . . . like black bicycle shorts under cutoff jeans, pulled up to the crotch, big old thick black boots, trench boots, baggy black leather jacket, bright red hair. . . . Then there's these young, fresh eighteen-year-olds with a lot of the bright colors, retro punk 1960s, sort of Carnaby Street, with their cute bodies in these little leggings and flounces and stuff. And then some really conservative power dressing, bow ties, and some classy casual, suede boots, gray silk stockings."

About eighty women attended the meeting. But when somebody suggested that they should start a sisterhood group, to meet regularly to talk about problems, a support group of, by, and for strippers, one of the veteran dancers squelched it.

"Michelle's real cynical and she always had been. There's a toughness and an aloofness about her. You don't want to get on the wrong side of Michelle. But I didn't expect her reaction. She said, 'Get real, I mean get real. This is not going to happen. This is not a safe place. You don't bring your home stuff here. You get your support system outside. You come here to work. It is competitive.' Everybody applauded, and that was that. She killed it."

In fact, in her first couple of weeks back, Sara found the atmosphere much more aggressive and competitive all the way around. Of course, only a couple of her friends were still there, and only a handful of sannyasins. She found herself suddenly one of the oldest dancers at the theater, and some of her old doubts returned.

"It's hard. I'd forgotten that there's a lot of rejection to deal with. A lot of the guys either don't want company, or they don't want company yet, or they're waiting for their regulars, or they don't like the look of you somehow. Either you're not blonde enough or you don't have big boobs or whatever they're looking for, you're not it.

"You blow it off at the moment, but later, on some level, to be honest, you flash on it. You go back upstairs and you look in the mirror and you think, wow, I'm getting older, and you look at the girl next to you that's making money, she's got a couple of regulars down there today, and you look at her and you compare. You do these things. You think, I'd rather be me now, how I am inside, than what I was ten years ago, but unfortunately this business is all visual, and there's a lot of tit jobs in there now. A lot. It's become the craze. It's amazing. A lot of guys love them. Some don't but a lot of them do."

Sara sighs.

"The other thing that makes it hard is just the whole play, you know, you're sitting for money, and the guy you're sitting with knows you're sitting for money. You pretend that that's just by the way, and you can kind of convince yourself. You shut down the visuals because some of these guys, I mean, you would never go and sit on their laps in a bra and panties if the lights were on. You just wouldn't. So that's hard . . . like yesterday, the classic.

"I got this guy in the movie theater. That's new, dancers in the movie theater. You sit on laps in there now. In fact, that's where you make most of the money. It's darker in there, more gross. The movie's going, it's much sleazier and the guys expect you to do more. It used to be in the New York Live it was a party atmosphere, nightclub energy, it was rare for somebody to really get out of line.

"So yesterday I go in the movie theater and this guy hands me five dollars. I take it, and I sit down on his lap and he says, 'So am I going to get laid for that?'

"Five bucks.

"This is the mentality of some of the guys you're dealing with.

"So I look back at him and say, 'Don't be a jerk,' and I went to sit down, right, on his lap, and he whips his dick out.

"Yeah, it happened before, in the old days, but only a very few times.

"There was one guy, you'd be on the stage, dancing, and you'd look down . . . he'd be sitting usually on the right-hand side of the stage, right up close, and he'd sit there, and you'd dance around, and you'd go down into that corner, and look down, and you'd see this huge dick, sticking out of his pants and you'd be like dancing and see that and you'd freak.

"He was a real raincoat guy. I can't remember his face but I'll never forget his dick.

"Actually, you know what? It happened twice to me yesterday. Another guy, a really normal-looking, reasonably good-looking guy, maybe in his thirties. He hadn't sat with anyone all day but he seemed quite shy, and kind of nice, and I went over and sat with him, and I was rubbing him, and something felt strange, like something was poking, like a zipper, and I had a look and he had his dick out. Twice in one day. I couldn't believe it. It happened maybe three or four times in five years, other than the raincoat guy, and now twice in one day.

"Also, I've never seen it as slow. It was maybe the same ten guys all day. Maybe twenty. After a while, they've been hustled to death, and nobody's making any money. One girl walked out of there with $40.

"I've never seen it like that. It must be the recession. Maybe it's the competition, the New Century. I don't know."

Bad days, good days. The following Saturday morning, the theater was busy, just like old times, and so was she. The inevitability of aging, the cruelty of youth and plastic surgery, the tyranny of desire, the ugliness of the audience mouthing words of rejection like a disapproving chorus in a Greek tragedy, all faded to the background, and she felt much better. Sara the Slick Chick cruised through the New York Live, her brave little body sparkling in a white spandex bikini and heels, the timeless hard beauty of her smile beckoning the sports to get out their money and play the game, one more time.

PART 4

"I'M A HELL OF A FUN GUY"

"You are my sex slave."
—Artie Mitchell, to Joanne Scott, Bana Witt, and Missy Manners.

"You're the best dancer I've ever seen!"
—Artie Mitchell, to Joanne Scott, Missy Manners, *and* Kristal Rose Lee

"When I met him he seemed like the guy next door who was really fun to be around at a party."
—Missy Manners

"My job is to mess with your mind and torture you and fuck you. I'm a hell of a fun guy."
—Artie Mitchell, to Joanne Scott

"It was either abuse or wonderful sex, sometimes both in the same night."
—Missy Manners

"It was sick but it was wonderful too."
—Bana Witt

"Artie was the best fuck of my life."
—Kristal Rose Lee

"I controlled his drug use."
—Missy Manners

"I got him off coke."
—Kristal Rose Lee

"He didn't do drugs as much when he was with me."
—Joanne Scott

"He knew more about women than anyone on the planet."
—Bana Witt

                                            half
"You're only as good as your last second."
—Kristal Rose Lee, as amended by Ârtie Mitchell

Sometimes in our society, we can see a train wreck about to happen, and actually attempt to *do* something about it, before it's too late. For instance: convicted child molesters are prohibited by law from driving ice cream trucks.

But when it comes to consenting adults, there's only so much our government can do.

There's no law to keep a skinny little Okie, impossibly charismatic and hornier than most of his customers, from co-owning a strip joint. In the case of Artie Mitchell and the O'Farrell Theatre, we're talking about maybe the most successful strip joint of all time, and one of the most successful skinny little Okies of all time too, especially when it came to diddling the help.

Masters and Johnson and any number of honest men and merciless women tell us that a man reaches his priapic peak at age nineteen, and it's all a decreasing acute angle from there.

Maybe in the strictest physiological sense, Artie Mitchell was no exception. But his sexual maturation—his metamorphosis from fun-loving hippie boy to frenzied, satyric sex freak—took a little longer. By the time he was forty, he had grazed in the fertile fields of the O'Farrell dressing room for more than fifteen years—several sexual lifetimes for most men.

All of this made for a complicated existence, to say the least, but that didn't bother Artie. He relished the complications. He thrived on them, built on them, slathered layer after layer of sex-related angst, ecstasy, jealousy, and rage on his life like a baker trying to replicate the World Trade Center with buttercream frosting.

As the mid-1980s arrived, events had pretty much defined the parameters of his existence: Two divorces. Six kids. Seven grand a month in alimony and child support, and a continuing vicious battle with one ex. An unquenchable thirst for alcohol and a taste for damn near any other drug. Hundreds of porn-related arrests. A mythic reputation to uphold. A troubled, complex relationship with his brother. And a mental state that left him constantly needing not only the next groping rendezvous, but the simultaneous outraged love, submission, and forgiveness of multiple women. By this time, Artie was not only an alcoholic. In today's talk show pop-psych patois, he was a sex addict.

In that respect, Artie Mitchell was no different than the customers of the O'Farrell, the men whose loneliness and psychosexual need had made him a millionaire.

Even though he clearly loved several of his girfriends in different ways, on different levels, after his second marriage collapsed he was way too far down the road to do a U-turn, to commit to the classic societal image of boy-girl love. He was utterly incapable of a simple, linear, monogamous relationship. He craved the complication, gamesmanship, competition, and above all the ego gratification that multiple relationships brought. All the insecurities of being the little brother, of being the little guy in a class full of bigger, stronger athletes, of being the Johnny Concho figure that lived on the edge of disaster, of being considered a crazy Okie outlaw pornographer who loved to party and was just along for the ride while his smarter big brother took care of business, of being the sucker taken for a ride in divorce court—all of those subtle belittling forces cried out for compensation, for some sort of emotional accounts payable that would bring his psyche into balance.

Artie needed to dominate, to cast a big, dark shadow across his own psychosexual landscape, to tower over a group of women who loved him on their terms and lost him on his, who submitted totally in order to keep whatever part of him he allocated them.

Sex was Artie's great equalizer, his way of living up to his father, living up to his universally admired big brother, his way of regaining control. Wherever he lost it elsewhere in his life, with Jim, with Meredith, with Karen, with booze and drugs, he got it back with his women, negating all of his real and perceived shortcomings with conquest after conquest. Artie saw each subtle difference in each woman, and played that knowledge to his advantage.

He created an intricate network of dominance, of worshipful women competing to give him master-slave sex. It was almost a cult: the Church of Artie Triumphant. Occasionally, to boast and to confirm his power over this woman or that, he would invite friends in for a sample, and force this woman or that to go along.

He demanded unconditional acceptance of his wildly eccentric behavior, and total forgiveness for the sexual, emotional, or physical violence he had committed in order to assert his dominance in the first place. And he knew just how to get that acceptance. Sometimes it required contrition, humor, tenderness, and promises of change; other times new outrages piled atop the old worked just as well.

And he had a devilish sense of humor about it all. He loved to pit two women against each other; to watch both of them suffer the consequences and work all the harder to win a larger share of him, or even to keep the stake in him they had.

To this fearsome admixture of sexual rage, paranoia, machismo, and cunning, he added cocaine, vodka, beer, marijuana, mushrooms, acid. When Artie got really drunk, Mr. Hyde surfaced. He pushed himself onto women at the theater. He threatened. And he lashed out at the women who loved him. Just as the traumatic struggle with Karen was both a symptom and an excuse for other excesses, so was the booze.

By the late 1980s, his web of relationships was incredibly complicated. Four of these overlapping liaisons bring his personality into sharp focus: those with Bana Witt, Joanne Scott, Missy Manners, and Kristal Rose Lee. All four were professionals in the sex industry during at least some of their time with Artie. All four admit that he was the love of their life, and all four acknowledge being deftly manipulated, but in the main do not regret it.

Of the four, Missy lived with him the longest, and was by far the most public girlfriend. They were a couple on national TV and in magazines because of the safe sex movie they would make and Missy's public relations acumen. Kristal lived with him for several shorter stretches. Joanne always wanted to live with him, but did only briefly, although they were lovers for nine years. And Bana was completely in the background during the seventeen years of their relationship—at least partly because she never really wanted to be Artie's public woman, his main person, a mother figure to his kids. She just wanted to have sex with him, and she got to, every once in a while.

Bana had no maternal instincts whatsoever, and in fact actively disliked Artie's younger kids, whom she thought were obnoxious and jealous of the time she and other women spent with their father.

Missy recognizes that her relationship with Artie was co-dependent, and that he abused her physically and mentally, but despite her subsequent marriage and two children, she says she's never had a love like she had with him. Kristal says she's never met a man like Artie, and she's met a lot of men. Bana says she was the "classic battered woman," but adds, "I've never had sex like that." And there is no doubt that Joanne, in her heart, will always be Artie's woman.

Joanne and Missy have a deep and vicious hatred for each other, perhaps because they each sensed the threat that the other represented.

Each was far more dangerous to the other than were any of Artie's other girlfriends. Missy was probably the closest thing Artie had to a complete, multifaceted relationship. And Joanne was the deeply ingrained, constant sexual presence in Artie's life, the place he turned for reinforcement, for worshipful adoration, for kinky sex. She was his refuge, the emotional and physical place he could go and find unconditional acceptance at all times. And she was the only one who didn't do drugs with him. Bana's relationship covered more years, but it was much more sporadic and one-dimensional.

Also, Kristal and Joanne strongly dislike each other. One reason is that they worked at the theater together while both were seeing Artie. Competing for tips (and Artie's attention) at work, competing for him in every way the rest of the time.

Perhaps because their relationships with Artie didn't quite overlap, Kristal and Missy get along, at least superficially, although they are not close. Both are polite in wishing each other good fortune and happiness now.

Each of these relationships is a story in its own right:

"Artie and Missy" is a spectacular, deeply kinked postmodern love story with unrivaled intensity, sort of *Romeo and Juliet* meets *Blue Velvet*.

"Artie and Joanne" is a nonfiction reprise of *The Story of O*.

"Artie and Kristal" should be told in an X-rated country-rock song, preferably by the Grateful Dead: Trouble Ahead, Trouble Behind. Let's Get Drunk and Fuck.

"Artie and Bana"? Bana, a poet and lyricist, tells it best herself, in the many lines she has written about the relationship, including:

> *The breeders you married get your money*
> *your children get your time*
> *I get your dick*
> *when you're too drunk to drive home*

("That's not true," Joanne Scott says. "I did, most of the time.")

Which goes to show the central truth: These are not discrete, neatly compartmentalized stories. They are messy, interwoven, in conflict and in collision. Just like Artie's life.

If it weren't for the accident with the amyl nitrate, Bana and Artie might never have happened.

It was 1974, and Bana was the prototypical hippie chick. She had grown up in Fresno, the daughter of an artist, sort of a counterculture child anyway, and the arrival of her hormones and the Summer of Love were terribly, fatefully synchronized. "When I was fourteen, suddenly I gained forty pounds, I started smoking pot, dropping acid, shooting up, and I got heavily into kinky sex with my boyfriend, who was running LSD from San Francisco down into Visalia," she says. "He'd call me up on a Friday and tell me there was a plane ticket waiting. I'd hitchhike to the Fresno airport, fly to San Francisco and spend the weekend with my boyfriend in the Haight, then head back to school in Fresno on Monday.

"The other girls would ask me for advice on how to avoid getting pregnant. I told them, 'Anal sex.' How I graduated from high school I'll never know. I thought I was Tim Leary or somebody."

She spent a couple of years in Santa Cruz, then hit the city on her own in '74. She heard about the Mitchell Brothers from a girl on the Haight Street bus, and she went down and got hired.

The Mitchells had just started the "Ultra Core" loop series, and Bana made three of them: *Hot Nazis, Southern Belles,* and *Ringmasters.*

During the filming of *Hot Nazis,* one of the other women had an open bottle of amyl nitrate, "poppers," that some people thought went with sex like popcorn went with the movies.

Somebody jostled the woman's arm, and the whole bottle went into Bana's eyes and nose. For some reason, Jim Mitchell had a gallon of water next to him, and he probably saved Bana's life. Lightning-fast, he took the water and started flushing her face.

Now she says, "You know, I don't think they would have called an ambulance under any circumstances. No matter how bad it was, they would have toughed it out somehow. An ambulance would have been too heavy. And it didn't matter who I was. I think they realized I was a disposable person."

Bana, sputtering and retching and high as three monkeys from the amyl, went into the next room to lie down.

Enter Artie, unzipping his pants.

He had been attracted to her during the filming because she had a great attitude. She was not a classic beauty, but she obviously just loved sex. The rest of the women were sour, like they were tricking, doing it for money. She was doing it because she liked it. "I should be paying you guys," she said at one point. "This is so much fun."

One day at the O'Farrell, she says, Artie came in and said, "My brother wants to fuck you."

"Okay."

She says that Jim took her up to the loft, where one brother or the other often slept during marital breakups. "He wasn't like Artie," she said. "Either we didn't sync up, or he just didn't have what Artie had. Nobody else did."

At the time, she was enraptured with this gritty male-dominated world. She went over to Art's house when he and Meredith were living in the East Bay. There was a poker game going on, men she knew from the theater, and she was surprised to see they were all wearing guns.

Then Artie offered her to the winner of the next hand.

Sure enough, the victor took her upstairs and had sex with her—with his gun to her head. She loved it.

"I can't believe all the macho posturing, all the stuff I put up with then," she says. "But I had sort of a bad-boy complex. I was sexually attracted to men and situations that intellectually I couldn't deal with."

Artie would be the perfect solution.

He saw her intelligence, her passion, and her vulnerability, and they maintained a sexual relationship for the next seventeen years.

She soon soured on the porn scene. "I did the three ten-minute loops plus some extra footage for *Sodom and Gomorrah,* just some insertion shots. My face was never shown and I never got credit. Then I did one other porno movie in Tahoe for somebody else," she says.

"I auditioned for a lot more. They always wanted to screw me but they never wanted to give me the job. I was so erotic tactilely but not what they wanted visually. I didn't have the prototype body.

"It was so horrible for your self-esteem, so destroying," she recalls. "Doing porn really triggered a total lack of self-worth."

When the Ultra Room opened, she came down and tried it, but she got a bad yeast infection after four days and had to quit.

A few years later, she danced for one night, made $300, and was totally turned off. "The films and even the Ultra Room were one thing," she said, "but having the public contact, the hands on you, was too close to tricking. I couldn't handle it."

Still, her relationship with Artie endured. He would call her up, all hours of the night, and come over. After he split up with Karen, she would often go to his house.

"It was heavily sadomasochistic," she said. "He would show total coldness in the early years. He actually called me Eva [Braun] after we made *Hot Nazis.*

"It was sick but it was wonderful too. The sex was totally, inhumanly good. No one on the planet could have sex like he could. He would fuse his mind with yours. We could change roles, female-male, completely, lose our sexual identity together. He would allow me to be the total aggressor.

"I had done a lot of sex on LSD and I was totally tuned up, able to really grok out, and I was always horny back then. But he was unlike anyone I'd ever been with. 'God, I've met my match,' I thought after first being with him.

"Artie was capable of manifesting energy during sex that was unbelievable. Drugs, no drugs, it didn't matter, he was the drug."

For all of her adult life, Bana has wrestled with huge black periods of depression, and her physical health has always been precarious. She is asthmatic, and the combination of physical and mental illness has divided her life into stark segments. Most of her relationships have not survived the wrenching periods of illness.

The only one that did was Artie.

But he was not the only interesting part of her life. She was heavily involved in the early days of Apple Computer. "I became a genius junkie," she said. "At one point I went from really kinky pretty boys with no brains to hard-core computer types." She was employee Number 49 at Apple, and in 1979 she married a top programmer.

"I was really rich," she said. "It was so much fun. I never stopped seeing Artie. I would send him bottles of Perrier-Jouët, show him my new sports car. He was so proud of me for marrying well, and my husband was so proud that I had Artie Mitchell as a lover."

Sounds idyllic, but it was not to last. Her husband became sick with cancer, and then had a mental breakdown, and the marriage ended in 1983.

By this time, Bana had decided to pursue a career in rock music, as a singer and lyricist. For a year and a half, she performed with East Bay Ray, a guitarist from the Dead Kennedys, in a group called the Kage, but they never made any money. People told her she couldn't sing, and she *was* pretty pitch deaf, but she sang with incredible emotion and intensity—good for the club scene, but not for commercial success. The lyrics, though, were acclaimed, and she kept writing poetry all the time.

The biggest impetus for her creativity was her relationship with Artie. The weirdness, the bad treatment, the incredible sex, all made for an intensity that rewarded her in her writing. "It wasn't safe and comfortable, but it was better than not having an edge," she says. Artie taught me that if you're not offending anyone, you're probably doing something wrong." She began doing more and more readings and performances, using the stage name Bana LaTour.

Artie would never come to her performances. "He would call and say he was coming an hour before, then he wouldn't come. His ego just couldn't handle it."

But that was okay with Bana. She didn't really want to be with him in public anyway. He felt compelled to behave like a pig in public, for his persona. She liked him a lot better in bed, even though he was often abusive there too.

Even so, he had a code of conduct that she appreciated. "He had a lot of self-worth. He was fastidiously clean. Even when he was drunk, he would never do male things. He never came over without calling first, would never have bad breath, he would never leave the toilet seat up.

"And he never came before I did. Not once."

The relationship may have been weird, but it was as convenient for her as it was for him. "I never really wanted to have an old man. But if I wanted to I could say I had Artie. If I didn't want to go home with somebody I could say, 'No, sorry, the porno guy Artie Mitchell is my boyfriend.' "

Bana's place—as Joanne's would be—was a refuge for Artie, a cut-out, a place to shut out the rest of the world. "One time I remember him coming over after a big fight with Jim," she recalls. "The Mitchells had sold one of their theaters downtown. They thought they had sold it to some guy from L.A., but he turned out to be a shill for one of their in-town competitors, someone they hated.

"On this day he told me he and somebody else—maybe Rocky [Davidson]—had gone over there and trashed the place. They took sledgehammers to the screen, really ripped it apart.

"Then when he got back to the O'Farrell, Jim was pissed, and told him, 'Boy, you really fucked up this time. Fifty thousand damage, easy.' And Artie told him, 'Hey, we didn't do anything, we went over there and just as we got there we saw some Mexican guys run out.' And then he came over to my place."

She remembers Artie's quirky nature. "He never drank anything but alcohol and water," she said. "He would poison himself with alcohol, but he was really concerned about the water. I always lived in old places, and he was really worried about lead from the old pipes. He would be sitting in my kitchen, totally whacked, and ask for water. He'd say, 'Let the water run for a while. Doc Dossett says let it run, because there's lead in those old pipes.'

"He was pretty healthy, other than the alcohol. He almost never ate junk food. But he did have this sentimental thing for chili dogs, from growing up I guess. He would come over and be totally drunk and he'd want some chili dogs. 'Artie, you'll throw up, you're too drunk,' I'd say, but he'd insist. So I'd have to go out and get the chili, get the hot dogs—I didn't eat meat—and I'd cook them up and he'd eat them and throw up and pass out."

But the sex made up for the chili dogs.

"Teenagers didn't have the sexual energy he did," she said. "It was so incredible that when I was younger I'd just think about him and I'd come.

"You could tell him about any kinks you had, anything you wanted to do, and he would never laugh, and he would never be grossed out.

"He was so good at conceptual S & M. He could suggest a scene, a fantasy, and totally visualize it, live it, without any props.

"He could take over your brain."

They didn't ever know it. They never really knew each other, although they have met. But Bana Witt and Joanne Scott have a lot in common.

The incredible passionate adventure that was Artie Mitchell would consume Joanne Scott's existence, but it was not as if her life had been devoid of excitement before they met.

She was born in Sacramento. Her father was in the army, and she grew up all over the place, with early childhood stops in Japan, New York, Tacoma, Las Vegas, on and on. Finally, as so many wanderers do, she ended up back in California. High school in Sacramento, college at UC Davis. In 1968, she married, but it turned out wrong. Her husband "proceeded to go really crazy," she remembers. "He got totally into religion, antisex, antieverything." They split, and she went back to UC Davis, got a master's in English and a teaching credential, then spent some time in the Ph.D. program.

Her ex-husband kept bugging her, following her around, and she had to get out of town. She did, but her luck with men stayed bad. Her new boyfriend turned out to be a drug smuggler; and even worse, he got busted on a federal conspiracy rap—smuggling arms into Mexico, drugs back into California—which meant a long stretch at Terminal Island.

She moved down to San Francisco, and for quite a while she was a street artist on Fisherman's Wharf. Despite her considerable classical education, she wasn't into becoming an upwardly mobile professional. She had grown up in the hippie generation, and her definition of fulfillment went beyond a nine-to-five job.

She did try a couple of teaching jobs, one at a Catholic girls' school and one at Soledad Prison. The prison work fascinated her, but any hopes of a career there ended when one of the frequent riots at the facility caused the cancellation of the program in which she taught.

So in 1981, at age thirty-two, with some rough miles behind her, with a lot of enthusiasm and more than a little trepidation, Joanne Scott started taking off her clothes at the Mitchell Brothers' O'Farrell Theatre.

From the start, her age made her a bit of a maverick. There were certainly women dancing who were her age and older, but most of them had been in the life for years. She did develop a tight friendship with a dancer named Rita Ricardo, who would soon be a headliner in her own right, and eventually would succeed Carol Doda as the name on the famous blinking-nipple Condor Club sign at Broadway and Columbus.

For a newcomer like Joanne, there was a lot to learn and a lot to keep track of. For one thing, just what you could and couldn't do while you were perched on the customers' laps kept changing. It depended on the level of police pressure, and to some degree the whim of management. At first, it was certainly looser than it is now; customers were allowed to touch the fabric covering the women's breasts, which is now off-limits. A lot of women, Joanne included, wore padded bras to protect sensitive nipples from groping, tweaking hands.

The customers paid well for the privilege of those kinds of liberties, and suddenly Joanne was making quite a bit more money than she ever had before.

One day, a couple of weeks after she started, she met someone interesting in the tech area upstairs. "I had no idea who he was. I just knew he worked there. He was funny and he smiled at me a lot, flirted really. I said to myself, 'If I ever get a chance to fuck this guy, I'm going to.' "

She soon found out he was Artie Mitchell, one of the brothers, and one of her bosses. The chance she was looking for didn't come for a while, and when it did, the San Francisco vice squad was responsible.

For weeks the vice cops had been sending in people with little James Bond cameras to photograph hanky-panky in the New York Live and the various show rooms. And they found some. They mailed Jim and Art a bunch of photos of acts they considered illegal, and threatened to prosecute unless the place was cleaned up pronto.

The first Joanne or any of the dancers knew about this was one night in 1982 when a Mitchell security guard shone a flashlight on Joanne as she sat in the New York Live audience and told her, "Don't get so friendly with the customers."

This was news to her. After all, she knew the importance of giving the customer enough, giving him something to remember the place by.

"If a guy actually got to feel some pussy, he'd think, that happens here? Wow! And he'd tell people, and he'd come back." And, of course, he might tip better. Naturally, the onus was on the women when the heat came down, but the feeling was generally, if you didn't get caught you hadn't done anything wrong.

Suddenly, all that was out. The heat was on, and the Mitchells decreed: Stop all contact with the customers. Dance, and that's it. No sitting on laps. No contact.

No tips.

"Everybody was freaked out. A whole bunch of dancers left immediately. There had been about eighty girls working, and within a week, half were gone. Some of them went to another place to dance, some did other things. At the time they were still having live sex shows in Japan, and a few women went over and did that. Some had some money saved, and took a vacation.

"Nobody knew how long it would last, or if it would always be this way. Or even if the place would close up. But it only lasted about a month," she remembers. "I stayed through it. By that time I cared about the place, and I wanted to see what was going to happen."

With no hustling the audience between shows, Joanne had lots of time on her hands during that month, lots of time to be backstage and bored. And on one of those nights, when she was just sitting in the dressing room, not doing much of anything, Artie walked in.

"I think he just said, 'How are you doing, how about a kiss?' And I kissed him, but I didn't just give him a peck on the cheek. He asked me into the office, and I was very mindful of the sign on the wall by the door to the office, you remember it, I think it's still there. It says, 'All dancers beyond this point must be clothed—Jim Mitchell.' So I remember getting dressed and then going into the office." She didn't know if it was against the rules to be naked when you were going into the office to have sex with the boss.

Turns out, it would have been fine.

That night—first in the office and then a couple of hours later in the film editing room off the dressing room—Joanne Scott and Artie Mitchell "got it on," as she remembers.

"It was so great. He just had this instinctive sense of what you wanted. He was so sexual. I just knew then that this was somebody that would be very special to me. I mean, it sounds cornball, but really from that time I started to fall in love with him."

So began the love affair of Joanne Scott's life, her consuming passion.

"Over the next nine years," she says, "I don't think I ever said no to him. There was never any reason to, I never wanted to, it never entered my mind."

At the time, Artie was still married to Karen, but Joanne says she didn't know it. "He was messing around with other people up there at the theater, and I never dreamed he was married. After a while, of course, I found out, but by then it was too late. I was in love with him."

Joanne insists that she had nothing to do with the marriage breakup. It was so acrimonious between Artie and Karen in the ensuing years, Joanne reasons, they would have parted anyway. Karen, of course, simply says she got tired of being abused and left him.

At the time, Joanne didn't know that the dalliance with Artie would develop into a long-term thing. But she liked it. They were easy together; they had quite a bit in common, including ancestry: both of their families had given them Oklahoma roots and Cherokee blood.

Joanne also liked working at the theater. She wanted to see how the legal hassles played out, and she found out along the way that she really cared about the place. It was an identity, a cause, and a good-paying job all in one, and with Artie in the mix, she suddenly had a lot of reasons to stick around.

When Artie moved out of Karen's house and stayed with Joanne for six weeks in January and February of 1983, she was overjoyed. But he certainly wasn't ready for monogamy, or anything approaching it. He moved into the Walnut Creek house, and Joanne's reign as lover-in-waiting began in earnest.

Although her affair with the boss often increased her isolation at the theater, she soon became a fixture. One of the reasons was the energy and inventiveness she brought to her work, and even that was because of Artie.

Like any worker eager to please her boss, Joanne found new outlets for her industriousness. Tired of the old bump-and-grind, take-it-off routine of the New York Live, she began doing highly theatrical themed shows. And others followed her lead.

It wasn't necessarily the path to better tips. As the brothers had just discovered, most of the patrons didn't come through the door for the special effects, the social satire, or the choreography. They assumed that the hefty admission price paid for the "shows," whatever they were. They tipped for the privilege of having women on their laps, or nude in front of their faces. Not for the privilege of watching avant-garde performance art.

But the shows were a way of getting Artie's attention. "It was a way of flirting with Art," she recalls. "More than that. It was one way of making love to him."

In one of her special shows, Joanne came out looking like the image of the theater's nemesis, Dianne Feinstein. Her personal resemblance to Feinstein is considerable, and with the businesswoman's suit, white blouse with trademark bow tie and collar, black sensible shoes, and briefcase, the look was complete.

When "Dianne" strode purposefully out onto the O'Farrell stage and sat in an office chair, things happened that you wouldn't expect to see in City Hall. Up hiked the suit skirt, out of the briefcase came a black dildo, and the show went from there.

Joanne also became a regular performer in the Ultra Room, where Artie would make occasional visits after the regular show was over.

"Artie always liked to think that, man, if I was in the Ultra Room, I was having hot sex. To me, I mean, it was just an exercise, something you did for money. So many head trips were tied up in it that it was not sex to me. But he always liked to imagine that it was real, and it made him excited to think of all that sex I was having.

"The Ultra Room *is* interesting, as a phenomenon. I mean, even though it wasn't sexual to me, it was intriguing."

So was Artie Mitchell. Not too many men like to fantasize about their girlfriends having hot sex with someone else—right before they go on a date.

"Artie did. And you know, similarly, if he had been with someone else before he saw me, it was much more exciting for him. That's just the way he was wired up. He demanded a lot of variety, a lot of complication. He got bored easily. That's why he liked my imagination."

And indulgence. There was never a time during their nine-year relationship that Artie wasn't also seeing someone else. Most of that time, there was another woman who was anointed as his serious "girlfriend" and was living with him—à la Missy, Kristal, and another toward the end, Julie Bajo. Of course, there were also constantly other recreational sex partners, including old girlfriends, new dancers at the theater, women he'd meet in restaurants. Sometimes, he'd bring them over and stage-manage a group sex encounter. But they didn't bother Joanne as much as the "girlfriends." They infuriated her.

For one thing, they monopolized his time to a great degree, knowing as they did that Artie off the leash meant Artie with somebody else. And they spent time with him when he was doing what he loved so much to do—be daddy to his kids. They got to take trips with him, of course, but it was more than all that. It was that they were publicly acknowledged in Artie's world, which was also Joanne's world, to be his woman.

Joanne started the relationship being the Other Woman in a mar-

riage, but she could never have expected to have that status prolonged
in such an embarrassing way. Not only was she the O.W. when he was
legally bound by marriage—but even when he wasn't.

Not that she wanted marriage, necessarily. "I think at the theater
there was this not very sophisticated attitude that if I managed to chain
him down or get married or get a two-car garage in the suburbs, then
I would have achieved the pinnacle. That wasn't Art's nature and that
wasn't what I wanted.

"There are just a lot of different kinds of love. It doesn't have to be
marriage," she adds. "Artie had about three weeks of monogamy in
him, max. Ever. And then, it didn't matter if it was some girl he'd just
met or an old friend, he had to back up his reputation. He sort of made
this public persona, and I think he felt that he had to keep proving that
he was Artie Mitchell. That meant picking up the waitress, drinking
everybody under the table, and he was afraid that if he didn't do that,
something bad would happen to the business, his children would go
hungry."

All of this is not to say that Joanne didn't harbor dreams of being
the Number One Girl, the one who shared his house and his kids and
the lion's share of his life. Nursing those dreams over the years, she
had to settle for being the woman who was on call, night and day, for
"some easy fucking," as he said once in a note to her. "It would be so
hard," she says, and the tears spring fresh. "Everyone would think he
was with just this other person, but he was still seeing me, in private,
all the time."

Joanne survived by taking the long view, vowing that no fresh fling
would force her to give up the one thing she wanted—Artie. After a
while, she always knew they would break up, and he would keep seeing
her. "Most of them were younger. They came from a different generation than I did, and they wanted different things—money, marriage,
gifts. I just wanted him.

"I viewed it as a continuum, and I knew he would always come back,
and I would have him in the end." Artie told her as much: "He said,
'I'll always be with you, Joanne. I'll be fucking you when you're eighty.
And there will be times when you won't see me for a long time, and
think I'm never coming back to you, but I always will, because I love
you. I just want to experience all the angles.' "

Thinking that, and living it, were two different things. Jesus! Agony,
pain, humiliation, loneliness. Hostility to and from the other women.
Sitting on a hundred laps, enduring bad breath, roaming hands, and
clumsy lines, not more than a hundred feet from the one lap she wanted
to be sitting on, knowing that someone else was probably on it instead!

Could anybody devise a more fiendish torture, a more hellish hell?

For fifteen minutes here, for a night there, Artie would turn his white-hot beam of sexual energy toward her, and she would swell and flower like a desert plant after a rainstorm. Then he was gone, for a day, for a month, and she would wilt back into shades of gray, survival mode, waiting for the next sweep of the beam to hit her.

God, it was tantalizing, the prospect of living in the sunshine of his love always, having that high beam turned directly on her in all its intensity, having him inside her, having his cawing laugh in her ears and his skinny little butt in her bed when she woke in the morning. Auuugh! She wanted all that so badly, and so often it seemed like the endgame was near, that she was finally going to get it.

There would be periods of time when she thought one of the other women Art had been with a lot would be gone from his life. It would be so great. Then, suddenly, she'd be back.

Especially Missy, oh, God, there were so many times when she thought her hated rival was out of the picture, but she would always turn up, like a recurring illness in Joanne's life.

When she did, Artie would be watching, to see what would happen. He'd play the relationships against each other, figuring out what reactions he could cause.

Artie loved that. He loved to shuffle the status, call up someone from the minors, put them on the roster, change the lineup card. The sheer perversity of it thrilled him beyond measure.

"Having someone come back—letting someone come back—was always so exciting for him," she remembers. "He knew exactly what he was doing. With me, with the others. It was an elaborate game."

In an article she wrote for *Spectator,* a Bay Area sex weekly, she expanded on this: "He was a brilliant, intuitive game player, not only with cards but with people, especially women. With the last several girlfriends it was as though Art stood back directing the action and walked away when he'd had enough. With me it was different. The game was: 'How much do you love me? Will you take me back even though I starred some bimbo in a movie or took one on a trip?' It heated him up to stir up some anger or jealousy and have me get past it and show him that I wanted him. I loved Art and I always wanted him no matter what he'd been up to or what he would be up to tomorrow."

Artie told her, "I've never seen a woman so in love as you. And it tears you up when you know your daddy's fucking some other girl, because you know I'm fucking her a hundred different ways and she's falling in love with me. Every girl I fuck falls in love with me, Joanne, because I'm a man. There's only a few men and a lot of boys out there. And the boys don't know how to fuck."

If it was a game, it was a byzantine, convoluted, cruel one. But Joanne believed firmly that it was not without purpose. The whole Story of O idea—through having your lover act out sexual trips with other people, and seeing you do the same thing, you and your lover become closer—was at the heart of it for both of them, she thought.

In the 1980s, the theme of Artie as director recurs. And if he was talented at manipulating the characters to fit the script, he was nothing short of a genius when it came to casting for the roles. He chose the women with whom he had longer-term relationships shrewdly, and he developed them in their roles with masterful ease.

He had a poker player's instinct for finding weakness, and incomparable finesse in exploiting it once he had laid it bare. The soft spots in a woman's character, the bruises and attitudes and needs created by past relationships, with men, with parents, all came into play, and he found a way to turn them to his advantage.

In Joanne, he found the perfect player for the role of long-term love slave. He found her able to give him the unconditional love he craved. She needed to give it as much as he needed to take it. And each indignity she suffered, each seeming cruelty he inflicted, seemed to strengthen their bond. "I grew more and more in love with him over time, in spite of or maybe because of a lot of the stuff that happened. He told me it would be that way, and it was."

For Artie, it was just right. He needed the excitement, but he also needed to do the unthinkable, the outrageous, the cruel, and then be forgiven, to realize that Joanne loved him no matter what, that she would take him back no matter what. And that was the underlying theme of their long-running drama.

"Most people don't crave that sort of love, but he needed it. He needed to have the sort of complications that he delighted in, all running along at the same time. Most guys never have that life experience, but he needed it, and he needed to be told that it was okay."

Joanne Scott is bitter about the way she was viewed at the O'Farrell, about the lack of recognition of her importance to Artie. "Nobody at the theater really understood what we had," she says. "They often had the perception that I was just someone he fucked over. But I don't see it that way at all. I loved him so very much, and I always felt that he really loved me."

One of the managers at the O'Farrell said to her, "I don't know why you're with him. You don't even get high." Joanne was astounded. As if the only reason a woman would want to be with him was for his drugs. She got plenty high just being with him, thank you. She loved him.

Another midlevel manager watched the ebb and flow of the relationship, and when it was ebbing—when Artie was living with someone else—he could be counted on to make a pass at Joanne. "It was sort of like, 'Come on, he's fucking around, why don't you?' " she remembers. She wriggled out of it each time, and tried hard never to be alone with the man, but that just wasn't possible all the time, and so the clumsy passes continued over the years.

Not that she wouldn't have sex with another man. She would, but only if Artie ordered her to. Which he did, occasionally.

That was just one of the travails she put up with in exchange for the time she got Artie to herself. One of many. None of them, though, would be as painful for Joanne as the one named Missy.

Elisa Florez grew up repressed, in Utah. That may be redundant, but it is certainly true.

The daughter of a Republican honcho father—Undersecretary of Education in the Bush Administration—and a fashion model mother, she was raised with the strict moral values of the conservative religious right wing. She was also the "ugly duckling" in a houseful of beautiful women. Her mother and her sisters, who also modeled, kept telling her that she would never be a classic beauty. Her boobs were just too big.

She compensated by being an intellectual and an overachiever. By her early twenties, her educational successes and her dad's GOP connections had landed her a job as Senate page, and then a series of other Republican posts. She worked for Senator Orrin Hatch, and later held a staff job for the Republican National Committee, where she found that politics had a hell of a lot to do with sex.

But within ugly-duckling, super-straight, Republican Elisa Florez, behind her personal Green Door, just waiting to be discovered, lurked not just a beautiful swan, but a sex bomb. She started the metamorphosis herself, moving to California, bleaching her hair, dieting, exercising, getting a tan, getting a boyfriend in the sex business—*Spectator* editor and photographer Dave Patrick—and deciding to compete in the Miss Nude America contest.

Not a bad start. It was to be Artie's job to finish the transformation, and he was most certainly up to the task. He was her Henry Higgins, and he filled the role to perfection.

Patrick had been telling Missy about the O'Farrell and the Mitchells, how wild it was and they were, and about amateur night, the dance contest from which they drew their onstage talent. So she allowed Patrick to whisk her off to amateur night—something he has regretted ever since.

That night in 1985, the contestants changed in a deserted side room that would in a year or so go through a transformation of its own and become the Green Door Room, the place where Elisa Florez, stage-named first Missy Manners, then, after newspaper columnist Miss Manners filed suit, just Missy, would change her life forever by starring in *Behind the Green Door: The Sequel.*

On this night, though, it was just a dark, dusty, cavernous pit adjacent to the New York Live stage, where the contest was being held. Missy remembers nervousness when she met her fellow contestants. "Some of them were real biker-chick types, big tattoos, scary."

After her inevitable victory in the contest, Artie came down to meet her and invited her and Patrick upstairs to party. She remembers that as they followed him upstairs, he dropped a little paper bindle on the stairs. They picked it up and found two grams of coke inside.

Missy had been just as nervous about meeting the Mitchells as she was about the contest. She had expected two fat old disgusting men, sort of sinister types, smoking cigars and giving women the fish eye. The pornographer stereotype.

What she found was infinitely more dangerous.

And more fun. Artie immediately put her at ease, and she spent much of the evening "drinking and partying," in the office with Dave Patrick, Artie, and another girl from the contest. "We were up there all night. We just drank and did coke and laughed. Artie said, 'You're one of the best dancers I've ever seen in all my time here. . . . You *are* the best dancer I've ever seen. You should work here.' And I said, 'What, are you crazy?' It just did not seem like the kind of place where I would work."

Patrick took her home, and she didn't think that much about Artie. "I was impressed with him. He seemed like a really nice person. My first impressions were, you know, party Artie, fun, normal, sexually open in a refreshing way, hip, happy, upbeat, not too weird or off the wall, just the guy next door who was really fun to be around at a party."

In about a week, she got a call from Vince Stanich, who supervised the dancers, asking her again if she'd like to work at the O'Farrell. "I said, well, I'd consider it, and took his number, and that was that."

But she continued to think about Artie, and since she was in the Miss Nude America pageant at the Civic Center, just around the corner from the theater, she stopped in one evening, early, to see if he wanted to have a drink.

"He said yes, so we went down to the Blue Light, Boz Scaggs's place in Cow Hollow, and we had drinks, and that was nice, and I drove him back to the theater. We kissed each other goodbye, and it was still pretty early so I said, 'Do you want to do something else?' And as he was kissing me goodbye, he said, 'No, I have another date tonight . . . but I could be persuaded to cancel it.' And I said, 'Okay fine, have a good time,' and I drove away."

This was not a woman who was going to beg him to break a date, and fall into that dependent little trap, the implication: "I could have had somebody else tonight, baby, so it better be good." At least, not yet she wasn't.

He called a couple of days later, and invited her to play a game of tennis, which never happened, because they stopped instead at a little café in Walnut Creek and had cappuccino and gelato, the 1980s version of vanilla Coke with coffee cream at Hazel's in Antioch, and went to his house, and rutted like crazed animals on the floor.

That night, he told her he loved her.

"It was wild and fun and crazy," she recalls. "His house was not fancy at all; he was there kind of on the rebound from Karen. It was sparsely furnished, very tracty and middle-class. I had to wonder why he was living there." Later, of course, she would find out. One, it was close to the kids. It had a swimming pool and was a nice place for them to come on weekends. Two, it was simple, and Artie wasn't into fancy. Those two reasons would later motivate him to get the place in Corte Madera where he died. But he had a few stops to make in between, and quite a few of them with this raucous, witty, perceptive, sexy, newly blonde Republican with the big brown eyes and the enormous breasts.

That date was the beginning of their sexual relationship. Now Artie would set the hook, begin to change the ground rules, and it didn't take long for him to start. Their very next date would go a long way toward defining the relationship.

It was to be a casual thing, dinner with a few friends, Artie said. Come by the house for a drink first. So she did.

The first thing she saw was two naked women. They were dancers from the O'Farrell, Sara and one of her sannyasin friends, Sahaj. Sara was always a little on edge around Artie, after the groping incident just offstage during one of her performances, but Sahaj, one of her best friends, was madly in love with him. Dave Hassall, Karen's brother, was there too.

Missy went for a swim, got a little loose, got into the party mode.

She didn't really have a tight thing going with Artie. They'd had their initial frolic, but that was it, and when she showed up at his house there were two naked women wandering around, so she didn't really think of him in terms of a monogamous relationship or anything. She was just there to have fun.

She liked the other girls. Their whole Rajneesh trip seemed a little quirky, but interesting. She appreciated the way they were so into being meticulous, putting energy into what they did, taking joy from each little thing, making everything just right.

She assumed they'd been intimate with Artie before she arrived (Sara denies this). But then, she thought, they walk around naked all day at work, why shouldn't they do it here too?

Soon it was time to leave for dinner. Missy rode with Dave Hassall on his motorcycle, Artie took the two strippers in his car, and they met at the theater.

Where Artie turned surly fast.

"I think Artie suspected that there was something, some energy between me and Dave," Missy recalls. "He did not like that one bit." It was okay for him to be cavorting with two strippers, of course, when she showed up, but he didn't want her so much as to take a ride on the back of some guy's motorcycle. This, on their second date.

They all got into Artie's car. "He was drunk and doing coke and he suddenly got real weird and domineering and possessive. Really verbally abusive, I couldn't believe it. I said, let's go to the Buena Vista for a drink, and he said, 'Well that's a good fucking place for a goddamned little yuppie like you to go. You'd like that, wouldn't you?' I was stunned, and said something else, and he said, 'Shut up before I turn around and grab you out of the backseat by your hair, you little slut!' "

"I was just floored. I started crying, and Dave and the other girls tried to reassure me, saying, it's okay, it's okay.

"That just pissed him off more, that someone was showing sympathy for me. When we got to the restaurant—it was Maxwell's Plum—I was still crying and both girls came up and put their arms around me and said something like, 'It's okay, it's just the drugs and alcohol, he didn't really mean it.' "

Where was the "nice, normal, fun guy" that she had met? Was it the drugs, or was it something else too? Was he beginning the initiation? Was it her first test?

If so, she responded beautifully.

"I just resolved that I wasn't going to let it bother me, and I was going to show him just how much of a good time I could have."

They went into the restaurant, where the maitre d' told them somewhat brusquely that there was nothing available.

Missy took him aside and asked him, are you sure, no room anywhere
for us? Sara recalls that he couldn't take his eyes off Missy's bosom,
but Missy thinks her success was due to the fact there were still tears
in her eyes from the hassle with Artie.

For whatever reason, he magically produced not only a table, but a
private room. Where Missy proceeded to get smashed.

Sara remembers, "We were eating our salad course, and everybody
was pretty tipsy, and I remember looking over and seeing her and saying
to myself, 'Jesus, she's got her tits in the salad!' "

Missy doesn't recall that, but she does remember deciding that she
wanted to give everybody oral sex.

"So I got under the table and gave Artie a blowjob, he really loved
it, and then I had oral sex with the girls too, and I think I jacked Dave
Hassall off as well.

"Everybody thought it was great, and it turned out to be a real funny
evening. At the end of the dinner the waiter asked if there would be
anything else, and we said, yes, strip and get butt naked on the table
for dessert!"

Missy laughs. "It was one of those nights, the first of a lot of those
nights. After dinner Sahaj wanted Artie to drop us off and come home
with her, but he said no, he had to go home with Missy, and he did.
And we were together just about every night after that, for more than
four years. We wouldn't always go home alone, but we'd go home
together."

Missy had learned a lot: When Artie turned ugly, forgive him. Get
outrageous, appeal to his sense of fun. Get under the table and give
him oral sex.

She had passed her first test with flying colors.

She had also come to the shocking realization that she wanted to
cross all the barriers with this man, to allow him to exploit her sexual
submissiveness like no one ever had.

The next night they were together, she left a pair of handcuffs on
Artie's pillow.

He knew, then, that she was giving herself to him, to their relationship, without reservation, which was the ultimate erotic charge for him.
Soon, he would introduce her publicly as "my sex slave."

In her submission, though, Missy knew that this Mephistophelean
sexual bargain was not as one-sided as it seemed. Not only were her
own needs being met, but there would come a time, in the primal depths
of their passion, that the slave would become the master.

Artie and Missy were having a lot of fun out of bed too. Like a couple of teenagers going steady, they became inseparable. "Things were pretty intimate," she remembers. "We liked each other beyond having sex. He was a person that I could play tennis with, or talk to, or bike-ride, whatever. We played racquetball and squash at the Bay Club. We became really good friends. We were just always together. Not just always in bed together. Always together."

That meant some changes in Artie's life. He had the remnants of his relationship with the Korean beauty from Neiman-Marcus to deal with, but saying goodbye was not one of Artie's problems. He did it all the time.

"One night she called the house about midnight, really pissed, and she told him, 'When you fuck Missy you think of me, and you tell her you're thinking of me' and hung up," Missy recounts.

"I think he blew off most of the other girls too. I don't think he really had that many other girls at the theater when he was with me, because we were basically together every night."

Joanne Scott remembers those days well.

"Oh, that was heartbreak time, 1985, when he was beginning to be with Missy so much," she says. She had sensed the thing with the Korean girl was about over, and she'd never really worried about it that much, because Artie was seeing her often anyway.

"I went to Europe that summer, and when I got back he was over at my house every night for three weeks. I was so in love. And so much thinking that this was going to be our time.

"Well, unbeknownst to me Missy had done the amateur contest, and he'd met her, and I think started thinking Green Door. And so he disappeared for maybe ten days. I didn't think too much about that. It just happened occasionally.

"And then they started getting tight. After she found out about me, found out that Art had a relationship with me, she did everything to get rid of me. It was weird having someone else coming in there acting like she was Missy Mitchell. Really weird."

Missy realizes now that it wasn't long before Artie began to be abusive, but she didn't see it that way at the time. "I just thought, oh, this is kinky, or oh, this is fun."

One night, two or three weeks after she started going out with Artie, they went to a birthday party at one of the pier restaurants. They showed up in the brothers' big fishing boat, the *Graciosa,* which was so big it would barely fit into the pier. "We made a grand entrance, me in this little white dress, with a bouquet of balloons, everything just tra-la-la.

"People were looking, who's this new girl Artie's with, and I made this picture of pristine innocence, I know, to a lot of people around him.

"Of course we were doing up a lot of coke, and drinking, and I know sometime during the evening he called and arranged this. We were really fucked up, and he took me to this woman's house, one of the women that he could always call up and go fuck. She answered the door wearing a gorilla costume. I know he told her to. Then she carried me off into her bedroom, where Artie went too, and he told her what to do. It was all planned. She threw me onto the bed and tore off my clothes, and started fucking me wildly with this dildo and hurting me. I was really drunk, and really submissive, and willing to go along with this little thing because it was what Artie wanted.

"God, she must have hated me. With a passion. Here I am Miss Sweet and Innocent, maybe ten or fifteen years younger than she was, and a whole lot prettier. He didn't let me see her face or know who she was. She had to wear this gorilla mask. How completely denigrating. But she was so denigrated that she would do whatever he asked.

"So she was really violent and vicious with me, and she made me cry. She said, 'Are you having your menstrual cycle?' and I said, 'No, why?' and she said, 'Because you're bleeding.' I was so coked up and drunk I didn't know what I was doing and I said, 'What, I'm bleeding?' She showed me that bloody dildo and I was so sickened, I started crying. Artie got really upset that I was crying and really upset that she had hurt me so much, so he told her to go into the bathroom and take off her clothes, and he whipped her violently until she was almost bleeding. And then he said, 'This is what you get for crying' and he whipped me too. Then he fucked her, and afterward he told her, 'I'm not going to fuck you ever again. This is my girl and you've hurt her, and you're a fucking bitch.'

"Then he fucked me until he had an orgasm, and told her she was just nothing, she was an outcast, a reject, and she couldn't even get him off anymore. And then we left."

Afterward, he was contrite, and solicitous, and sweet, and Missy forgave him totally. "It didn't even cross my mind that this was abuse," she said. "It was just one more wild and crazy night with Artie. It was early and I didn't really see what I was in for."

She had passed another test.

Looking back on it now, Missy sees that it was just one step in his plan to dominate her totally. "He was trying to throw me every fastball he could, to see what I could take, what he could get away with. And he could get away with a lot."

One reason is that he did it skillfully. There were so many great times, so many wonderful in-love nights with just the two of them, so many wild and wonderful parties, so many weekend trips and good times with his kids and all the rest, that the bad times didn't really amount to that much, at least at first.

Again, he had found someone with needs that matched his own. Missy really needed to cut free from her puritanical upbringing, to get loose and crazy and fornicate wildly and do drugs and drink. It was part of her personal empowerment, her new identity.

Plus—and what could be better!—Missy had alcoholism in her family, and she was used to people acting out when they were drunk, making allowances for them, helping them deal with life on their terms.

Perfect.

Joanne, of course, tells a different story, but it was almost certainly the same evening. "Once right after he started seeing her, I guess, he brought her over to my house," Joanne said. "For a few days he'd been sort of suggesting that there was somebody he wanted us to have a three-way with. I didn't really want to, of course, but I thought, 'It'll please him. He's into this stuff. Think of it as a show you're doing at the theater.'

"It's interesting. When you're in the sex industry, what you begin to feel that sex is making love to somebody that you love, but all other sex is not sex, it's just something that you do for work or for whatever reason. And over time I got so enmeshed with Art that I couldn't relate to other people sexually. We just got closer and closer, until he *was* sex for me.

"So anyway at this time I thought, you know, do a little show, make him happy, she'll go home, that'll be it. What the hell. I had no idea at the time who she was. As far as I was concerned I thought she was just somebody he picked up in a bar.

"Now, I don't know what he told her about me. Obviously, he didn't let her know that I was somebody important to him, that he had keys to my house, that I was somebody who loved him.

"So he brought her over, and we both fucked him. And he wanted her to see my gorilla costume, so I put it on at some point. I remember she was kind of whimpering. I think it was kind of offensive for her to see him fuck me. He was really coked up that night, so coked up that he couldn't even get off. But it was such a power trip, because I think he foresaw how this could play out between the three of us, down the road.

"So he was acting dissatisfied and decided to leave. I was upset because he left and she went with him.

"But I talked to her for a minute or two, and I told her that I'd been seeing him for three years and I really loved him. I was pissed off at the time, and I told her I didn't think he was capable of love.

"She wanted to know, did I work at the theater. So I think she found out enough about me to know I loved him, and cared about him, and worked close to him, and I was a threat. And I think that had a lot to do with her trying to get rid of me."

As she began to realize that this person was someone Artie cared about on some level, Joanne became more and more upset.

"I didn't completely know what was going on, because he still came over several times, when it was just beginning. But I could tell that she was teasing me. Like one night, I was dancing and she was up there, and she goes up to the tech area and props her feet up on the rail like she's Jim Mitchell watching the show, critiquing my performance. And I get off and she says, 'Jo,' using his nickname for me, 'Jo, that was really a good job.'

"I think Art was letting her play out the fantasy that she was going to be in some position of power. Of course she wasn't, it was always him calling the shots, and he would have always withheld her sense of security about it, as he could. But he would let her think for a while that she was powerful."

Artie and Karen, meanwhile, were playing out a truly nasty divorce. Nearly two years after their separation, no divorce had been granted and the legal wrangling continued.

Sandra Musser tore into Artie with gusto. In a scathing, sarcastic "factual background" filed with the court, she charged:

"Respondent, his brother, and mother own Cinema 7 Inc. and various wholly owned subsidiaries. Cinema 7 runs a number of movie theaters, the Mitchell Brothers' O'Farrell Theatre and produces movies. The corporation also owns the Manteca Fish Co., which is a corporation whose main purpose is to purchase fishing equipment so the brothers can play.

"The company is treated as the alter ego of the brothers. Pension plans are created and terminated to suit their whims and/or fears of taxes or divorce. The company owns numerous luxury cars that are mainly used by the brothers for pleasure. Family employees are hired at substantial and excessive salaries. Skimming is rampant."

When Artie had divorced Meredith, Cinema 7 was worth very little on paper, having absorbed the twin calamities of *Sodom and Gomorrah* and the embezzling accountant. That had served Artie well in the divorce, and in exchange for assuming any corporate liabilities had been allowed to keep his entire share of the company.

("My mother didn't press for a huge settlement," Liberty remembers bitterly, "because she knew he'd be fair with her once he got back on his feet. And then after he was with Karen, even those payments wouldn't come for months. Here they were living in luxury. She would write the checks and she'd put the decimal point in the wrong place, like it was supposed to be $450 and she'd make it for $4.50 and here it was already two weeks late.")

Now, though, the company's lack of value at the time of his first divorce would come back to haunt Artie. Musser was poised to argue that the company was worth almost $1 million more than it was when he and Karen first started living together—and, naturally, that Artie's share of that appreciation was community property. (Each of the brothers owned 45 percent of Cinema 7, with Georgia Mae owning the remaining 10 percent.)

Artie tried desperately to lower the book value of the O'Farrell. But Musser was ready for him. "Respondent contends that since separation, Cinema 7 Inc. has been reduced in book value by approximately $500,000—or more than one-half. This was the exact modus operandi of respondent in conjunction with the dissolution of his first marriage.

"It is interesting to note that although affairs are so dismal, respondent and his brother and the manager (Vince Stanich) each received a new leased Mercedes-Benz in 1984. In 1985, a new luxury fishing boat was acquired by the company and the brothers purchased car telephones for their automobiles."

The skimming charge was a particularly sensitive one for Artie. The O'Farrell generated large amounts of cash, and the brothers could count on being audited every year. In court documents, Karen repeatedly charged that Artie was taking from $4,000 to $8,000 a month in unreported cash from the theater.

(Certainly, the brothers were never short of cash, but just how much was not reported before it found its way into their ubiquitous Levi's is not known. Artie told one of his girlfriends, "If you've got your own business, you've got to steal. The government assumes that you're stealing 10 percent. We take 25 percent." Of course, Artie was given to hyperbole, but if that was true, the skim was a lot more than even Karen and Sandra Musser charged.)

At any rate, Artie had a lot to lose—not just the farm, a bunch of cash, and a big chunk of the business. He was worried about losing his kids. And things were not looking good. Musser was regarded as one of the best women's lawyers in the country. Karen saw the divorce as a chance to get enough money to take care of her and her kids for a long time.

For the first seven months of the separation, Artie "loaned" Karen $5,000 per month. On July 26, 1984, the court ordered that the loan payment obligation be released and recognized the $35,000 as family support. It further ordered Artie to pay $5,800 per month from August through the end of the year. In December, he was ordered to continue payments at the same rate until the time of a trial or settlement. He also was ordered to pay Karen's state and federal taxes on the first $35,000 he had paid.

Karen had dropped out of high school, but she had resumed her studies in the later years of her relationship with Artie. After the divorce, she got her high school diploma and started taking health and chemistry classes, and Musser told the court that Karen planned to enroll in medical school in about two years.

Because of her client's lofty educational goals, Musser asked for six years of spousal support in addition to child support.

"Respondent's gross reported income is $139,000 a year, or $11,160 per month. In addition, petitioner has proof of the following income respondent receives: Cash $4,333.33 per month [God knows how that number was determined], the benefit of automobile lease payments, gas, insurance and repairs and car telephone with a value in excess of $1,200 per month, other perks with an estimated value of $5,000 per month including company-paid trips to Mexico with entourages, fishing boats, supplies and equipment and other toys." Musser estimated Artie's total income at "over $17,000 per month," acknowledging that he paid $1,250 a month to Meredith for child support.

Musser asked for a total family support payment of $8,000, which was more than Artie's declared income after taxes.

Things were looking bad for Artie, but the game wasn't over yet. Karen was about to take a tumble.

In the fall of 1985, acting on a tip, Contra Costa County Sheriff's deputies raided the farm at Canyon. They found a stand of marijuana under cultivation, and they found cocaine and psilocybin mushrooms.

Karen will always believe she was set up. There is no way to know for sure, but there is some evidence to indicate she is right.

She says that after Artie moved out, he came to her and asked her to grow him some marijuana. He had always grown pot at the farm; what was the use of having an isolated acreage if you weren't going to grow some smoke? Karen says he told her, "Kay, you know I have to have my smoke. I can't grow it here in Walnut Creek. There are too many people around and I don't have the space. You know I'm going to give you the farm; can't you do this for me? I'll even pay for you to hire somebody to tend it."

She agreed, she says, and hired somebody to take care of the plants.

She says they were doing nicely, with the buds just ready for harvest, when she went out one morning to find that they had been cut back drastically. Someone had come into the place and ripped off the buds, she says—someone who was known to her dogs, because they hadn't raised a fuss at all, as they would with a stranger.

She believes Artie sent Rocky over to harvest the buds. Again, she has no proof.

The next afternoon, she was out in the yard, feeding her chickens, when the cops came. "Here come twelve guys in SWAT uniforms and machine guns. I just about peed my pants. I just froze. 'Oh, no,' I thought. 'This is the nightmare I thought would never happen.'

"They went through the house and apparently Artie had left some coke and some mushrooms in a closet. I didn't even know it was there. Apparently he didn't know it was there either, at least he says he didn't."

But Karen believes Artie did plant the other drugs in the house. A few days earlier, he had come to the house—broken in, she says—and had taken some rugs, the fox coat he had given her just before the breakup, and some artwork, including an Erté lithograph that would become the subject of another dispute in years to come. The burglar alarm went off, she said, and when officers responded, Artie said, hi, we're getting a divorce and I'm just getting some of my stuff out of the house, and they said, fine, Mr. Mitchell, and left. (Karen says now, "I let it slide. There was no way I was going to get into another battle with him over a few objects." That is difficult to reconcile with later events, since she battled with Artie over "objects" for seven years and is still fighting with his estate.)

Karen raises the possibility that Artie planted the coke and mushrooms at that time, but there is no evidence to support or to dispute that allegation.

After they searched the house, the deputies took Karen to jail.

She called the theater, looking for Artie. "He had always promised that if anything happened to me he'd bail me out," she says, and here was a perfect opportunity.

Artie wasn't there, but she got Jim.

She says that Jim told her that day, "Kay, my brother's a fucking asshole. I hate his fucking guts. He knew what happened to you. He knew before it happened, and he's out getting drunk with Rocky and they're laughing about it. They think it's funny." She says Jim told her, "Don't worry about it, I'll take care of it." Karen Mitchell says Jim paid Dennis Roberts $5,000 to defend her—although in papers filed the following January in the divorce case, she listed an outstanding $5,000 debt to Dennis Roberts.

Karen says the police tried to get her to inform on Artie so he could be busted for tax evasion. "They told me he turned me in," she says. "The narc told me, 'He wants to put you in prison for the rest of your life so he can have the kids.' "

But Karen says she wasn't interested in squealing on Artie, just because he had stabbed her in the back. For one thing, she says, she was scared to. And even though she says the cops threatened to take her house under asset forfeiture, she refused to do so. "Go for it, boys," she says she told them. "I know the law. You can't take it."

Despite the evidence, Karen managed to avoid total disaster. Whoever paid his bill, Roberts was effective. "Dennis went to the D.A. and said, 'Look, Artie's torturing this girl. It was his stuff. Drop the charges,' " Karen said.

"And they did. So I got off, and Artie got his smoke."

Did Artie set Karen up?

One of his girlfriends at the time thinks he did. "He said Karen was growing way too much pot, that it was too risky, and that she was greedy about it," she says. "He said she was refusing to give him enough of it." She says Artie told her that he had someone report that they had seen marijuana on the property as they had walked by the place. She said he didn't say anything about the other drugs.

Karen contends Artie had a financial motive for getting her busted. "His attorney went before the judge in the divorce and said, 'This woman's a drug dealer and she doesn't deserve anything from us.' And the judge believed him."

Whether or not that happened, she did suffer some reversals in court. The divorce was finally granted in December 1985, but the other financial issues weren't decided until July 1986. In the order, Judge William O'Malley ruled that:

- Karen would not get a share of the brothers' business, as she had sought;
- the farm must be sold, with the proceeds to be split evenly between the two parties;
- Karen's palimony complaint against Artie, stemming from the period of their cohabitation before marriage, was dismissed;
- Karen was not entitled to replacement or payment for the Mercedes;
- the Morgan belonged to Artie and had not been a gift to Karen, as she had alleged;
- Artie was not entitled to the refund of money paid to Karen before the trial;
- Artie had improperly taken back the fur coat he had given Karen, and she had improperly failed to pay three monthly mortgage payments on the farm despite receiving his half of the payments and his support payments. These two claims were found to be offsetting; Artie kept the coat and Karen did not have to repay him for the mortgage;
- Artie must pay $4,000 in unpaid fees to Sandra Musser and up to $4,500 to Karen's subsequent attorney, Carol O'Connell.

"I told them, 'That's all right, take the money and shove it, boys. I've got my kids and I'm happy and I'm not immoral and I'm not an asshole,' " Karen says now.

She also was awarded $3,800 a month in family support, and for the next seven years, she and Artie would fight constantly and bitterly about the support payments and about the child custody arrangements. Despite Artie's protestations, the family support order was steadily increased over the years.

In the late 1980s, when Karen was in her early thirties, living in a $750,000 house on top of Redwood Avenue in Corte Madera, Artie was fond of saying he had in effect paid for that house and everything in it. "I've supported Karen Mitchell all of her adult life," he would say, with equal parts of pride and bitterness.

It was substantially true.

Soon, Missy adjusted her life to the schizoid schedule of Artie Mitchell: party all week, daddy all weekend. She came to love both roles as much as he did.

The wilder and more uninhibited she got sexually, the more he liked it. She would also party with him, seriously party, egg him on, take acid, mushrooms, Ecstasy, drink with him, coke with him. She never smoked much pot, but that was okay. He smoked enough for both of them.

Also, he liked her attitude.

It was much more than rebellion. It was a repudiation of her parents, of the rules she suffered under all her life, of the hypocrisy she found in politics. It was a celebration of freedom from all restraint.At the same time, she served as a message from Artie to the straight world. That was the essence of the O'Farrell, of course, squatting evilly just a couple of blocks from the mayor's office. It was a message, and so was Missy. She became a way for Artie to drive home his point even more, and he loved that: *To all you Republican prosecuting pigs who have been after me for so long, from Bernie Walter to Ed Meese and all the rest, here I am with Missy Manners, one of your own, and, in case you didn't understand my message clearly, here it is again: Fuck you.*

He loved to shock San Francisco's elite, and the wannabes too, the yupsters with their conservative politics and secret carnal urges. Well, there was nothing secret about Artie and Missy.

When the Fog City Diner, famed restaurateur Cindy Pawlcyn's grand creation, opened on the Embarcadero at the edge of the financial district, everybody who was anybody in town showed up. Artie and Missy were there and in fine form.

"It was such a nice bar, they really did a good job. The food was good too, and we were having a blast," Missy remembers. "The place was jammed, hundreds of people, and Artie and I were sitting at the bar, doing our usual, drinking, Artie laying down lines at the bar. He'd just pick up a menu and lay the coke out on the bar behind it. Soon a lot of women were swarming around the coke, and he took a bunch of them into the rest room, and was making out with them in there, and I was talking to the men at the bar, having a great time. Artie comes back and he sees the guys and says, 'You guys like seafood?' And they say, yeah, sure, not knowing where he's going with it, and he says, 'You want to see my girl's pussy?' They just gaped at him, and I took off my underwear at the bar in front of everybody. I just had this short little dress on. Artie had shaved my pussy so it was bare, and I just leaned back from my chair and put it right up on the bar.

"People were just going crazy, dropping their glasses as they stared, glasses broke all over the place, and then after that all night the joke was somebody would come up and look at me and deliberately drop their glass, and the bartenders were getting a little mad, like, come on, too many glasses being broken.

"Artie just loved it.

"And so they put my panties up on the wall near the rest rooms, where they have all the framed autographed pictures from the celebrities. It was a great night, and then we met this great older lady who was all turned on by me and by Artie. And she came home with us and was just totally wild, let Artie fuck her every which way. It was amazing. That sort of thing happened all the time. People were so excited by our sexuality."

Nights partying at the theater, so many nights. One night the party pair were holding forth in the office, getting bombed, playing pool and partying with whoever showed up. At one in the morning, on the way out the door, Missy decided she did not want the party to be over. She was wearing her uniform of the day, a see-through lace body stocking. (Artie loved her to dress that way. Sometimes she'd go out for the evening wearing nothing but a Dior slip and a fuck-you attitude.)

And what could a drunken woman in a strip joint wearing a see-through lace body stocking be expected to do at one in the morning? Right. She lay down on the floor of the lobby and said, 'I'm not leaving until I fuck every man in this theater.'

"I was so drunk, so ridiculous," she said. "I can't remember what manager it was, maybe Charlie Benton or maybe Jim Gish, but they thought it was funny as hell, and Artie did too.

"It wasn't like I was some hooker. They knew I was just turning it loose. It was my time to kick up my heels, and I couldn't have had a better place or a better partner.

"Artie told me to get up, and I didn't, so he grabbed the body stocking and started ripping it off in all the pertinent places. He just ripped it to shreds, so I just stood up and walked out the door of the O'Farrell, into the Tenderloin, absolutely naked.

"I got into the front seat of his car, I sort of sat on the thing in the middle, sticking my head out the sunroof as we went over the Bay Bridge, with Artie finger-fucking me as he drove and my friends in the backseat getting blowjobs. And we all went home and had riotous sex. Crazy crazy nights, all the time."

Despite the in-flight entertainment, it got tougher and tougher for the two oft-inebriated lovers to schlepp all the way out to Walnut Creek in the East Bay after a night of partying. One night Missy remembers: She is driving, toasted on Ecstasy and magic mushrooms, and the lights of the Bay Bridge blur into one glowing waving golden tracer. She can't see the road, and she tries to pull over on the bridge, and Artie, just as loaded but alert to the inevitable run-in with the law that a stop on the bridge would bring, talks her into continuing, like an air traffic controller bringing in a sick plane, until she can safely exit and he can take the wheel the rest of the way.

On another occasion, there was absolutely no question of Artie driving. He was smashed beyond control. So Missy, looped herself, tried to get them home and got pulled over instead out in the East Bay, somewhere around Lafayette.

She didn't know what to do. She was definitely over the limit. She almost fell down as she got out of the car to take the sobriety test.

"The cop said to me, 'You are drunk. You can't even walk a straight line.' I said, 'Officer, I'm not drunk, I'm just so in love, and we're having such a great time, that I lost my head and I forgot what I was doing when I was driving.'

"He says, 'You're going to have to walk this line before I'm going to believe you're not drunk,' and I said, 'It's these heels. I can't walk in these high heels.' And he told me to take them off and I said, 'And ruin my silk stockings? You must be nuts.' But I took off my shoes and I still couldn't walk straight. I could see where this was going so I said, 'Couldn't you just give us a ride home?' and he said, 'No, but I'll follow you.' But then he said, 'What about the person in the passenger seat, can he drive?' "

The cop came up to the window and peered in. Artie had a bottle of tequila and a Heineken in his lap, following his usual practice of straight-shooting tequila and chasing it with the Heineken. Which he proceeded to do as the cop watched.

"He was totally loaded, drinking in front of the cop. The guy must have been able to smell the pot, everything. I just said, 'Oh, God, no, no, just leave him alone. He's way too drunk to do anything.' The cop just shook his head and followed us all the way to our driveway."

And these were the good nights. When they were really fucked up, they wouldn't even leave the O'Farrell. They'd just get under the pool table in the office and roll up in the table cover. Rocky or whoever was cleaning the theater would turn out the lights and leave them there until morning.

In every way, Missy began to fit herself into Artie's life. Each sex-soaked, drug-laced week would dissolve into Leave It to Beaver weekends, eating pizza with the kids, dealing with homework, shopping, Little League, cooking and cleaning, camping in the backyard. Missy loved all of it, and it made her realize just how much she wanted kids of her own someday. But for the present, she treated Artie's kids like they were hers.

Now Missy has a husband and two children of her own, but she is still close to Artie's kids, and she wishes she could see them more often.

"There was a real bond from the beginning," Missy says. "There was always a feeling of love, like we were all a family, and I still feel like I'm part of their family. Those kids will always mean a lot to me. We had a real loving feeling between all of us, and that just doesn't go away," she says, the emotion cracking her voice.

Missy says she'll never forget the first time she met the three littlest kids. They came over on Friday night of the first week she was with Artie. She was wary and nervous at first, but it went fine. They all sat down on the floor, around the coffee table, and talked. "We played games and colored and just chitchatted. We had a really nice time. I traded watches with little Jasmine. We were just friends immediately. We had instant good energy, nothing unnatural or uncomfortable. They weren't the least bit apprehensive and I tried not to put them off, to be loving. It was easy because I really liked them right away.

"We had a lot of good times out in that Walnut Creek house. At first I didn't want to involve myself too seriously in that relationship, with his kids, but the feeling I always had just couldn't be overlooked as time went on. I grew to love those children a lot. The littlest boy, Caleb, was maybe a little over a year old, still in diapers, and he would sleep with us when he was there. We had a special relationship, perhaps because he was so little, and later he would call me Mom."

She was probably closest to Jasmine. "A lot of people would think that I was Jasmine's mom because she looked like me. She had brown hair and big brown eyes, and we had the same coloring. We were just inseparable."

It turned out that Missy and Jasmine were both fond of a little Japanese cartoon character named Hello Kitty. Both of them had Hello Kitty trinkets and pictures, and that cemented the bond between them. Artie and the kids often called Missy Hello Kitty or just Kitty, and he was forever buying Hello Kitty items for his two girls.

For Artie, Missy's relationship with his kids was a huge plus. He simply couldn't be with someone as much as he was with Missy if the relationship with the kids wasn't there. It made everything easier, and it pulled the two of them closer, because he adored his kids.

Also, for Missy, it normalized the relationship in some basic way. She was enjoying the hell out of the bizarre nights at the theater and wearing nothing but a slip when they went club-hopping and giving Artie blowjobs as they hurtled across the Bay Bridge. But being the equivalent of a suburban housewife on weekends grounded the relationship in reality, in a context that was comparatively prosaic, but somehow reassuring.

Even that was a way for Artie to draw the net tighter. The revolution in Missy's life had been caused in part by disillusionment with her parents and the values they taught her. But it also served to isolate her from what had been a very close-knit family. More and more, Artie and his family became her only family, her only source of support and love. Which made her all the more vulnerable to his moods and his demands.

But at this point, Missy didn't give a damn about that. She was too busy falling in love with this crazy, mercurial, sexy man, who could be so sweet, so caring and loving, and so aware of who she was and who she wanted to be. He made her feel so good, so special, so loved.

And as she fell more deeply in love with him, she began more and more to understand the frustrations that she felt led to his drinking and occasional weird behavior. She began to see firsthand the horror of his fight with Karen. He opened up to her about his complicated relationship with Jim. He felt as though nobody took his ideas seriously enough. Jim was widely viewed as "the brains behind the operation," and that grated on him. This would be a recurring theme in the years ahead, as he became more and more detached from the operations at the theater.

So there were more and more reasons to be accepting of whatever might happen in the relationship. She hated the booze-soaked, screaming, crockery-throwing fights that would punctuate the good times, but she was holding her own. One night in Walnut Creek, he pushed her against the garage door, hit her, swore at her, and she ran inside, picked up a lamp with a big heavy base and broke it over his head. It knocked him down and stunned him, and he shouted in drunken outrage: "You fucker, I'm bleeding, look what you've done to me now!"

Still, at that point, those days were few and far between, and one of the best things about fighting with Artie was making up. It was another excuse for more of the great, groaning shuddering screaming sex that was the Super Glue of their relationship. Some of the sex was violent, some was sweet and tender. But for Artie and Missy, everything was an excuse for more sex. "We'd fuck when we were happy, we'd fuck when we were sad, when we were angry, when we were ecstatic."

That simplified a lot of things.

"One thing about it was, you always knew where you were with Artie. You didn't have to take his temperature to figure out where you stood. That was kind of nice, and the sexuality was so appealing.

"But it was painful, always, to go through all the hell he put me through, because we were both so intense. I'm not so on the surface, but when things do come to the surface with me, I can get very angry. There were times when he was choking me and hitting me that I would come walking down the hall with a knife in my hand and hell in my eyes, and he knew I could use it."

Through it all, she loved him, understood him, and depended on him more and more each day.

For Liberty Grace used-to-be-Mitchell, now officially Bradford, her father was a source of love, and confusion, and pain. She had never totally recovered from the six-year-old desolation produced by her parents' divorce, but she had learned to handle it with the toughness that was characteristic of both sides of her family.

Almost equally challenging was learning to deal with what her father did for a living.

"As a little kid I pretty much always knew that my dad made 'naked films,' and I never thought that much about it. I always walked around naked when I was two or three, so as I grew older I thought, what's the big deal?"

The first time it was a big deal came in the fourth grade, when her teacher asked her, "Is your dad one of the Mitchell Brothers?" When she said yes, her teacher responded disapprovingly, "Oh, well, I don't go to that kind of movie."

Suddenly Liberty was ashamed, and she didn't really know why. She was a sensitive child, and she began to feel alienated by whatever went on downtown in that big building her daddy always went to.

By the time she was in the sixth grade, things were getting worse with Karen, and she missed her dad terribly. He was the master of the grandiose gesture. When she had a school play, he would fill her dressing room with flowers, take out a big ad in the playbill, be a hero. In the process, pissing off her mother, who was the one to take her to lessons and rehearsals every day, doing the grunt work of parenting.

She would go to the theater to meet her father, and she would see the signs, nobody under twenty-one allowed, and she would think nervously, am I going to get arrested? She knew that her dad got arrested every once in a while. People would explain the First Amendment stuff to her so she wouldn't think her dad was a hard-core criminal, but it was still weird.

Meanwhile, when her friends would ask her what her daddy did, she would say he made documentaries, or he had a fishing boat, which was true enough as far as it went. Later, at boarding school, she would meet girls from Mafia families, and they would have the shame of their father's business in common.

Finally, at her mother's urging, she had her name legally changed to Bradford, along with Storm and Mariah. Which broke Artie's heart. It would always be a point of bitter contention between them.

At least in high school, her male friends thought what Art did was cool, but even that didn't help much. As Liberty began to develop feminist views and sensibilities, her conflict over her father grew worse. She was proud of him for what he had accomplished, but the issue of women and pornography was tough for her to handle.

In college, she continued to keep her father's identity under wraps for the most part. It was hard, because family is a big part of her life, but it was just too much of a hassle to start explaining and defending. The issue did serve one purpose: it became a litmus test for friendship. Was a person uptight and judgmental, or could they deal? Still, it was pretty tough to come down on other people for the way they handled it when she wasn't even sure herself.

"It was hard for me to compare how he could have feelings from the strippers, and then could have feelings for me, and mom, and everything, like there are good girls and bad girls."

She thought, "I wonder if my dad hates me, because it's obvious he hates women." She knew he loved her on one level, but how could he say those things about women, when she was one, and expect her to ignore it?

Being a pornographer's daughter wasn't easy under any circumstances, but it certainly made her tough and self-reliant. Her clear-eyed, youthful freshness and appeal belie the fact that she has experienced more emotional upheaval than most women twice her age.

Finally, Liberty would decide that pornography had its place. "I think it serves a strong societal purpose," she says. "There are a lot of people who will never have any more warmth than that in their lives. It's really sad, but they have to have someplace to go."

Still, the issue certainly complicated her own sexuality. During her college years, she would attend parties at the O'Farrell. Sometimes, the men there would mistake her for one of the employees, and their leering looks astonished her. "I would be dressed in jeans and a coat, nothing provocative, and it was like, 'I've got the right to look at you like a piece of meat,' " she says. "I would say, 'I'm Artie's daughter,' and they would jump back three feet.

"I was disgusted. It was like, 'Are all men such total pigs?' It disturbed me immensely."

· · ·

Artie kept asking Missy, when are you going to move in with me?

Well, it made sense. The relationship had been going on for almost a year, and they had been together almost every night. She was paying rent on an Emeryville condo that she almost never used.

But she didn't want to move into the Walnut Creek house, even though she was spending a lot of nights there. There were a lot of reasons for this.

For one, it really was getting ridiculous, she thought, driving all the way out there from the theater late at night when they were always smashed. There had been a few close calls, and it was just insane to keep doing it. If they had a place in San Francisco, at least they could take a cab home instead of sleeping under the pool table. "Looking back on it, it was so stupid," Missy says. "Here we were trying to manipulate our lives to fit our addictions."

But there were other, deeper reasons for not moving into the Walnut Creek place. She felt that to do so would be total surrender. Why should she move into an inconvenient, boxy little tract house that she didn't even like? If they were going to live together, she wanted it to be in a house more appropriate to their lives. Someplace with some style and class. Someplace that would be their place, not just his place that she had moved into.

Also, she felt that Karen was really dictating Artie's situation too much. She was still living in the palatial house she and Art had shared and here he was in a dowdy little crackerbox house. Karen liked that just fine, Missy suspected. But she was damned if she was going to live in a house that was inferior, just because *Karen Mitchell* wanted it that way. "I wasn't with him for the money but if we were going to be together I wanted our lifestyle to improve," Missy says.

So she and Artie began to look for a place in the city, probably in Pacific Heights or the Marina, they thought, someplace that would be close by, but would really be someplace they'd like to live, a refuge from the world, someplace where they could have the kids, sure, but a place Missy would feel comfortable with. Their place.

As most people do when they house-hunt in San Francisco, they became depressed. For most people, that happens because everything is ungodly expensive. But that wasn't the problem for Artie and Missy. They just couldn't find a place they both liked.

They went down to one of San Francisco's most beloved greasy spoons, Clown Alley on Lombard, ordered hamburgers and milkshakes,

and glumly perused the classified ads. They'd already checked out everything that sounded any good at all.

So they decided to cruise through the Marina and see if they could
spot any for-rent signs on promising buildings. That, and word of mouth,
were the two best ways to find a place in the city. By the time it hit the
newspaper, if it was any good, it was already spoken for.

And sure enough, on Marina Boulevard at Scott Street, right across
the street from the Golden Gate Yacht Club, was a sign. They looked,
and they loved it. It was horribly expensive, of course, but it was one
of the most desirable addresses in the city, and what a view! The bay
in one direction, the lights of Pacific Heights in the other. It was magnificent.

It seemed like Missy and Artie had been dealt a handful of aces.
They had been going out for a year, and that relationship had survived some tough times. Now the relationship was entering a positive
new phase. They had found a beautiful place to live, and Artie
seemed to be nearing resolution in the vicious divorce fight with
Karen.

But something that happened on moving day gave evidence that they
weren't exactly riding off into the sunset just yet.

Karen was enraged by Artie's move, and somehow she got the address
of the new place, and that first night she drove around and around the
block, honking the horn and screaming.

"I couldn't believe her," Missy says. "It went on and on. 'Nice fucking
house, Mitchell,' she'd scream, and lay on the horn, and go around
again. 'Nice fucking way to spend your money, asshole,' she'd yell, and
hit the horn again."

Missy was mortified. What their new neighbors must think! Everybody had their bedroom on the bay side, for the view, so they all must
have heard Karen, going bug-nuts outside, and wondered just who the
hell had moved in?—bikers?—rich but tacky royalty, like the Saudi
prince who painted the statuary green in Bel Air?—the Beverly Hill-
billies on dope?

Nope. Just a down-home Delta boy who made good in the "beaver
business," as he called it, with a nice Republican girlfriend and a horribly pissed off ex-wife.

The conflict with Karen worsened. She was openly hostile when
the kids were picked up or dropped off. "I think she was angry
because Artie and I were doing so well," Missy says. "We were
happy, we had a nice house, a nice car, everything was going okay,
and here she was having trouble. It was just getting uglier and
uglier."

Not long after Missy and Artie moved to the Marina, Karen moved too—to a place on Pine Street in the city.

From then on, Artie called it Swine Street.

The crazed partying continued. Missy would go down to the theater to be with Artie, and inevitably opportunities to be wild and crazy would present themselves.

One evening she stripped and got on the New York Live stage with Pepper, a popular dancer, who was in the midst of a relatively tame S & M routine. She told Pepper to whip her, but Pepper, seeing how drunk she was, declined. So Missy took the whip and started dancing, and Artie stood up onstage and pulled down his pants and demanded to be whipped.

Missy obliged with relish, earning applause not only from the paying customers but from a group of strippers who watched with delight from the upstairs balcony. They'd had their share of Artie in his role as the Dressing Room Groper Who Happened to Be the Boss, and just like the Danielle Willis incident, seeing lusty, busty Missy lay into him with the whip was sweetness itself.

They both loved to travel, and they took wonderful trips together: Cabo San Lucas in Mexico, Lake Powell, Las Vegas, L.A., the Cayman Islands. They'd take the kids if they had them; otherwise, they'd blast off by themselves. Sometimes they'd jump in the car with no idea where they might end up. Sometimes they tripped on their trips. Missy remembers one time they bombed down the coast in the white Mercedes, both of them with a headful of acid, Artie white-knuckling the wheel like Neal Cassady, music blaring, the night wind blasting them as they traveled that sacred highway, the path of so many zonked fun-seekers before them, down past La Honda, Monterey, Big Sur, looking for their own immortality, settling for a picnic lunch on the famed nude Black's Beach eight hours later, acid still amping through their neurons, yeeeee-hah!

"I remember this squirrel coming over and trying to eat our lunch, and we didn't give a damn about lunch anyway so we were feeding it to the squirrel, and he was heavily vibing purple for both of us. One of us said, look at that squirrel, he's got a purple head, and we kept calling him little Purplehead.

"The next weekend we went to the Humane Society with Jasmine, and we ended up becoming a foster family for the society, and we'd take care of the animals who were too young or sick or had something else wrong with them so other people wouldn't adopt them. The only thing was, I loved the animals so much that we'd never turn them back in after we'd fostered them, we'd just keep 'em. So we got these cats that weekend, and we called one of them Purplehead, and he was always with us."

Also, Artie bought her the little white teacup-sized poodle puppy, whom they christened Mr. T. Missy adored him from the first day, and she carried him with her wherever she went.

Those early days at 515 Marina Boulevard were suffused with fun. Whatever else happened, there was fun, and it overshadowed everything else. "Artie always used to say it's damned difficult to find people you can get along with well in this world, and I believe he was right. We did get along well, it's true."

Sometimes when they got home, around midnight, they'd take scissors and brown paper grocery bags and head out across the lush gardens of the Marina on a guerrilla mission.

"We'd call ourselves the Snippers and we'd go out and cut flowers in the middle of the night, all through the neighbors' yards, and we'd come home and have beautiful bouquets all through the house and laugh like little kids."

No matter how well things were going, Artie couldn't get too relaxed, too happy.

Karen would see to that.

She used the custody agreement like a cudgel, constantly jabbing and clubbing. Once Artie took the kids for a weekend trip to Mexico, and Karen called the police and the FBI, alleging he had taken them out of the country illegally. Artie showed the cops his divorce papers, and that was that, but it was yet another nasty jab to the gonads from the bitter redhead.

Karen had no compunction about calling in the law. The agreement specified that Artie was not to have the children's hair cut while they were in his custody. So when Georgia Mae trimmed Jasmine's bangs one weekend, Karen called the police.

Every weekend, picking the kids up on Fridays and dropping them off on Sundays were the dangerous times. Artie never knew what Karen would do. One night, he and Missy returned the kids only to find Karen's front gate locked. Artie unlocked it and took the kids in, but Karen wasn't there. She was down the road at a phone booth, calling the police to tell them Artie was trespassing.

During the latter stages of the divorce fight, Karen actually sued *Missy* for $40,000. She contended that since Missy worked for the corporation, and lived with Artie, a percentage of her earnings really belonged to Karen.

Right.

The suit went nowhere, but it cost Missy and Artie some money to get Gene Seltzer, Artie's divorce lawyer, to get rid of it.

It was just another little Karen reminder. I'm out here, don't get too comfortable.

Missy's outrageous defiance of her parents and their values was beginning to have an effect. They came out to see her, and the whole scene left them aghast. "Of course, they never went inside the O'Farrell or anything like that," Missy said. "But it really hit them when they saw what it was all about. I don't think they understood what was going on until then."

Her father had come out once before, and had gone out to dinner with Missy and her new boyfriend. Amazingly, Artie was on his best behavior, and didn't even get drunk. But Daddy wasn't buying it. Although her description of Artie had not been completely forthcoming, she suspected that Dad's GOP and, ergo, government sources had told him plenty about the brothers.

They went out for sushi, and Florez bitched about the raw fish, refused to eat anything, and made it very clear he was disgusted to be in a pornographer's presence at all, especially in public, especially a pornographer who was sleeping with his daughter.

"He just drank tea and looked at us like, 'This is really fucked,' Missy remembered.

Which was, in a way, exactly what she was after, but still, the experience itself was a bit disquieting.

So were the occasions when all the bubbly fun stopped, when the dark side Artie had revealed so early in the relationship came back to plague Missy.

There was, of course, Artie's continuing interest in other women. And, in spite of her best rationalizations, it did bother her a little. Even though they were together almost constantly, and even though a lot of his sexual experiments and adventures involved her and other people, Missy knew that he slept with other people occasionally. "Of course, he had Joanne, although I don't think he saw her that much while I was with him, and he had others like her, women who would just do anything for him, women he could call up and take two or three of his friends over and do whatever they wanted to her."

Also, there were the nights when Artie would turn ugly, as he had on their second date. Always, it happened when he'd been drinking a lot, and almost always, it happened after some blowup with Karen.

Missy would say something Artie didn't like, and he would just go off. "All women are the same. You're all greedy money-grubbing sluts," he would rage, and sometimes with the words came blows. One night, really late, they got into an argument as he was driving them home. They were on Scott Street, just a block or so from the house, when Artie exploded.

He pushed Missy and Mr. T out of the moving Mercedes and kept on going.

Missy fell, suffering cuts and scrapes, and Mr. T almost got hit by a car. "He just ran around and around on the street. He couldn't stand it when we fought. He'd go and hide for days after we had a fight," she says.

Another car stopped, and the driver asked if she was all right. Embarrassedly, she told them to go on, it's okay, and she dragged herself home.

On another evening, they had just left the theater when the rage struck, and on this occasion, about 2 A.M., he forced Missy out of the car in the Tenderloin.

"Fuck you, bitch, find your own way home. I don't care if I never see you again!" Artie raged, and there was Missy, deep in the worst part of downtown San Francisco, at an hour when hookers and pimps clustered on each corner. Missy, wearing a dress and heels, must have looked like she was in the market too, and she had to walk for fifteen blocks or so until she got out of the 'Loin and a cab would stop and pick her up.

Meanwhile, the animus between Missy and Joanne continued to grow. One night in October 1985, she went down to the theater with some friends, including Dave Hassall, Artie's ex-brother-in-law, and took her whole party into the Ultra Room area where Joanne was working.

When Joanne saw Missy, peering at her from the other side of the glass in one of the booths, she lost it.

"She started screaming and pounding on the glass. She yelled, 'You've already taken the man I've loved for all these years, you wench, you've already fucked me over, what more do you want?' She started whipping the glass with her black belt.

"So I went around to the door where the girls go in and out, and said, 'What the fuck is your problem?' She said, 'I love Artie and he loves me, and what the fuck do you think you're doing with him?' and she threw me up against the wall and dislocated my shoulder.

"I was standing there screaming, and Dave came up to me to see if I was okay, and he took me up to the office. I told Artie what happened and he went nuts. I told him I was going to press charges, that now she'd gone too far. I told him to fire her right away, and he did. I think he beat her. I mean, I wasn't there, but I'm positive he did. And he told her she was fired, and she wasn't going to get any attention from him ever again."

Bana Witt remembers those Missy days with distaste.

"She threatened to kill me," Bana says. "She called me up at home and told me, 'My name is Missy Manners and I'm Artie Mitchell's fiancée and I don't want him with you. If you see him again I'll kill you.' "

"You bet I did," Missy says. "She had called Artie at our house, over a coke deal. And anybody who did that with Artie, when I had to pay the price, when I was home taking care of his kids and he was out fucking that bitch and doing coke with her, and then coming home and beating the shit out of me, was going to hear from me. I told her if she called again, I would be her Worst Fucking Nightmare.

"I told her it would be the last call she ever made."

"The bovine slut, I called her," Bana says. "She was so patently offensive."

Hunter Thompson, who had been around for several months doing his night manager research, loved Joanne's creativity, and praised her shows highly. He particularly liked her gorilla act, in which she would put on the suit, complete with attachments, and, in a bestial mixed metaphor, would copulate with a stripper named Bambi.

"His praise meant a lot to Jim and Artie, and I began to get booked into better times, which of course meant more success, more money. They were both very impressionable that way. Input from famous people like Hunter meant a lot to them, and if he said my shows were great, they thought they were great."

But all of her new success came crashing down after the confrontation with Missy. Joanne, who denied assaulting Missy, was devastated.

"When she had me fired, God, it was awful. I thought I'd not only lost my job, I'd lost Artie, and I'd lost any chance to see him." For three months—from October 1985 until January 1986—she lost contact with Art. She was jobless and miserable. She had a grim Christmas.

Fortunately for her, Hunter took up the cudgel for her with Jim, writing a memo urging her rehiring and calling her "The most creative girl act in the theater" and "The spirit of the O'Farrell."

One day, she got a phone call from Vince, asking her what she was doing, if she wanted to come back. She came down to the theater next day, went into the office and saw Jim—and Artie! She was ecstatic at seeing him. After a couple of minutes of conversation, he took her into the bathroom and they had a wonderful reunion.

Artie later told friends that he wanted her back, and having Jim do it avoided a shootout with Missy.

But nothing was ever the same at the theater for Joanne. "When I came back, I knew I had to watch my back, constantly," she says. "Even though I'd worked there for years, I felt like I couldn't do anything wrong, period. And that was hard, because I had this horrendous situation with her and Artie going on, but I had to ignore it, and be absolutely perfect.

"What that did was take all the pleasure out of my shows. It just changed the whole dynamic for me. I was defensive, and worried all the time.

"I just kept thinking she'd eventually hang herself, by being such a bitch."

Artie brought Bana Witt down to Tosca one night to read her poetry for Hunter. Artie adored Hunter's writing and Bana's too, and he thought Hunter would appreciate her. And, of course, he would. But it was too weird, and Hunter was speeding and too busy dealing with other things to get into this bizarre, stark woman with the darkest similes this side of Richard Brautigan.

Thompson kept asking Artie agitatedly, "Who is this woman?" Artie would say, "Chill out, she's an old girlfriend, Bana, listen to her, she's great." Then Missy showed up and dragged Artie out of there. Bana thought, that's sick.

She went into the bathroom where she ran into a woman in a gorilla suit. She had the head off, and she was crying.

It was during the time the brothers were filming *The Crazy Never Die,* an abortive movie they made about Hunter, but never released, and they had been doing some filming with Joanne and the gorilla suit at the North Beach bar.

Bana did not know any of this. She just knew that here was somebody in a gorilla suit who claimed to be Artie's lover.

"My name's Joanne and I've been in love with Artie for five years, and I just can't stand this," the gorilla woman said. Bana thought to herself, my God, I hope I never look so pathetic, I hope he never makes me look this bad.

To her knowledge, it is the only time she and Joanne Scott ever met.

Albee couldn't produce scenes as bizarre as this: one girlfriend reading her poetry to a bemused, irritable literary lion; another bursting in like an angry housewife with a rolling pin; and yet another, dressed in a gorilla suit, crying in the bathroom, off stage right.

Of course, Missy *was* furious that Joanne was rehired, and in particular, furious at Hunter for engineering it.

Hunter took a clear position on the Joanne-Missy issue. He went to Hollywood with the Mitchells to attend the 10th Annual Erotic Film Awards, and the *Examiner* column he wrote on the event contained the following volley: "There was no public sex, and the only violence was a deranged outburst by rookie sex starlet Missy Manners, who wore a body stocking all night and screeched relentlessly at her patron, Artie Mitchell. She was quickly subdued by security specialists."

That struck a nerve, really pissed her off. So did the *Chronicle*'s Herb Caen, when he tagged her in his column with the sobriquet Bossy. She didn't know if he meant Bossy the Cow, because of her endowment, or whether he meant bossy, as in bossy.

She *was* bossy. She *did* screech at Artie sometimes. But she thought she had to. That was her role.

She had to be the one to make sure his drug and alcohol abuse didn't prevent him from functioning. She was basically the moderating influence that kept him from going clear off the rails, so to speak, and that sometimes meant being, well, a bitch.

"Sometimes the evening would reach the point that I knew, if we weren't going to sleep at the O'Farrell, we'd have to go right then. Most of the time he'd say, 'You're right, we have too many children, we have to go,' and then he'd make his goodbyes and then we'd leave.

"But everybody thought I was the bitch, the bossy one saying, 'Break it up, the party's over,' because usually it was over if Artie left. I would be the one at a restaurant to say, 'We have to quiet down, Artie, get off the table, we'll get kicked out.'

"That happened. One night he and Liberty and I went to the Billboard Cafe, and he stood up on the table and yelled and screamed: 'This place sucks, why can't I get a fucking waitress, all these sluts are back there fucking each other instead of waiting on us.' We left, I think, and sometimes I would just let that happen, let him go, but sometimes I would say, no, we can't do this, so I would be the bitch."

Before long, Missy had other concerns, other factors to deal with that would make her fears of getting a reputation as bossy seem almost insignificant: she decided she wanted to star in a pornographic movie.

But not just in any skinflick.

The Mitchell Brothers had decided to try to repeat what they had done fifteen years before: to shake the porno industry to the tips of its bare toes. Once again, they aspired to make a film of lasting value, a film that would change the way people thought about pornography. It would be another grandstand play for the brothers from Antioch. In these dark days of the Inquisition, when a presidential commission headed by Attorney General Ed Meese had issued a report excoriating pornography's effect on society, when AIDS horribly but undeniably equated sex with death, when some feminist advocacy groups eloquently decried the degradation, exploitation, and objectification of women that they saw in pornography, it would be a movie that would make it *all right* to watch pornography again. In sum, a politically correct sex film, a one-eighty from porn's dubious image, a bold foray into public service pornography.

A safe sex movie.

Always in the past, defenders of porn had tried to advance the argument that the films were instructive, that they helped people's sex lives, that they relieved tensions instead of creating rapists and murderers.

This argument, while put forward with passion and eloquence by proponents, including "expert" witnesses hired by the defense at their many trials, had always been a relatively weak reed. It was all right to say that watching pornography was your First Amendment right, but a hell of a lot of otherwise open-minded folks had trouble with the idea that watching improbably good-looking women act out male-defined fantasy roles was aiding anyone's understanding of sexual reality.

But now! With this movie, the Mitchells would have an argument the size of Long Dong Silver to back up the thesis that porn is educational. With apology to Erica Jong, this film could be subtitled How to Save Your Own Life. They would make a film that showed how to protect yourself, protect your lover, from sexually transmitted disease— and still enjoy yourself! Ah, that was the key! This would not be an instructional video on How to Put on a Rubber. This would be clever, imaginative, steamy, riveting, wall-to-wall Sex.

Safe Sex.

The Mitchells so believed in this project that they decided to confer the mantle of greatness on it from the beginning. They would do what they had resisted doing all these years—invoke the Green Door name. This film would be titled: *Behind the Green Door: The Sequel.*

This was more than a shrewd marketing move—it was an article of faith. Not only did it exploit the tremendous name identification of the Marilyn Chambers classic, but it sent a signal to the cognoscenti. This will be another epic, a blockbuster. The Mitchells are serious about this.

Of course, the name, combined with the safe sex hook, guaranteed a major media play for the film.

But Missy, who was just as excited about the idea as Jim and Art were, had yet another hook in mind. What if this safe sex epic, this *Green Door* epic of a movie, starred a hitherto respectable card-carrying conservative, a former Republican National Committee staffer, someone who believed in safe sex and had the aggressiveness, media savvy, intelligence, and articulateness to become a leading spokesperson for the issue—and for the movie?

Jim and Art were both, above all, unfailingly intuitive about the media. They knew Missy was right. They knew that she would give the movie a tremendous head start, that the combination of ingredients was explosive.

But both were initially set against the idea. Missy was family. Artie, used to orchestrating, hadn't come to terms with being dragged along like a caboose on the train of progress, of being upstaged in his own business and his own relationship all at once.

Jim, no neophyte in these matters, was concerned about on-set emotional dynamics inherent in having his brother's living companion fucking under the lights. He was concerned with Missy's total lack of film experience. And he just wasn't convinced that she could pull it off.

Moreover, on an altruistic level, neither Artie nor Jim were sure Missy knew what she was letting herself in for. Yes, she had been systematically flouting the conventions she grew up with. Yes, she was alienated from her parents. Yes, she reveled in being a rebel, and she was good at it. Yes, she'd had more wild sex in a year with Artie than a lot of people ever experience. But making a porno movie—*starring* in it—is a whole other level of rebellion. Example: How many people saw her display at the Fog City Diner? Maybe a hundred?

Well, maybe a *million* would see her in this movie. Maybe more. Doing a lot more than not wearing any underwear.

Missy wasn't the only one contemplating risks. For the Mitchells, the stakes were huge. This was not just another movie. They weren't like some L.A. porno producers who knock out two or three movies a week. Another Mitchell Brothers movie was an event. There weren't that many. It was a big-budget, big-time deal. It was taking a big risk using the *Green Door* name, putting it all on the line. If it was a flop, the Mitchell Brothers' reputation would be reduced immeasurably. People might start saying they were washed up, that the business had overtaken them.

They ran an ad to start casting, and it was a masterpiece of hype and Jim and Artie humor. The ad ran in *Premiere,* and read: "Mitchell Brothers' Film Group casting for a very important adult feature film. Wanted: Midgets, Fat Ladies, and Geeks. Geeks must provide their own chickens. Contact Chico, O'Farrell Theatre."

The ad not only pulled a huge response, but it was also a way of telling the rest of the industry, look out, here come the Brothers. We are back in the arena, and we're ready to kick ass.

J.R. always used to tell Artie and Jim, there's only one way out, and that's over the top. And that's the way they did business. They weren't afraid to tell the world, hey, we're making this film, because they were confident they could back up the words with another blockbuster.

But they didn't have a female lead.

They didn't want to use someone who'd starred in dozens of films, like Barbara Dare or Nina Hartley, or even Marilyn, who'd rocketed to fame in the first *Green Door*. They wanted to recapture the excitement of a fresh star that Marilyn had given them, back in 1971.

Like Prince Charming with his glass slipper, they auditioned dozens of women. Nobody seemed just right.

Missy grew frustrated. She knew she was right for it. She met every need. She was young, fresh, with the same sort of shocking gimmick that Ivory Snow had provided for Marilyn Chambers. Why couldn't Jim and Artie see it?

"It never seemed like Artie was pimping me or grooming me for it, like many people thought. Really, the reverse was true. But I could see that it just wasn't working with the people they were interviewing," she says.

Jim had refused when Missy said she wanted to audition. But she went ahead and auditioned anyway. They had a video cam set up on the stage at the New York Live, so when nobody else was around, she produced her own video.

"I had the whole thing set up, where I was going to masturbate to the point of orgasm. I mean, what else are you going to do by yourself?

"So I had sex with my favorite person. Me.

"I had one of those long scarves, really lots of them tied together, like a magician's prop, you just keep pulling and pulling and more and more come out. So I had it stuffed inside me, and on the video I just kept pulling these scarves out, dozens of them.

"Artie just loved it. And Sharon McKnight, who was going to co-direct the movie, was in the office and saw it, and she did too. She said, 'This is a first-class, grade fucking A New York quality audition. You could get a job anywhere with this. You're sexy, you're fun and bubbly, it's hot.'

"When Sharon likes something, I think Jim tends to like it, because they are such good friends. She was a respected person, she knew what she was talking about, and so he put aside his bias against me."

Jim still had his reservations. On top of everything else, he knew how powerful Missy's family was, and he was afraid they'd try to make trouble in some way. That could be a really heavy scene, enraging the big shots in the Republican Party.

But everybody responded so well to the tape, and they *did* need a fresh person, and she *did* carry an automatic publicity bonanza, and she *was* smart and tough enough to handle it, and nobody else they looked at was right. It was decided. *Behind the Green Door: The Sequel* would star Missy, and it would be the prequel to the rest of her life.

Missy negotiated a deal with Jim Mitchell. It was agreed that Artie wouldn't take part in those discussions, since the money would be flowing into his household. Jim was a tough negotiator—his poker-playing skills always came in handy in these situations—but Missy came away from it feeling she had been treated very fairly. After they arrived at a money deal, she also got informal assurances that her wishes regarding the shooting would be honored: no anal sex, no super-close-ups, etc.

Production details were worked out. It was a pretty tight-knit core group: Artie, Missy, Jim. Sharon McKnight, the talented former dancer, cabaret singer, former flame of Jim's, sex-positive feminist icon, would co-direct. Artie, who had, after all, come up with the original *Green Door* concept, contributed lots of creative ideas for the film. Jim did too, and as usual, managed to take all these synergistic sparks and use his technical knowledge to turn them into reality, to figure out what would work and what wouldn't.

As the first day of shooting approached, the pressure mounted within the group. Performance anxiety was never like this. Each of them felt a tremendous amount of personal investment in the project. For the brothers, their continuing reputation as creative geniuses was on the line, and so was a hell of a lot of money. As usual, as it had been with the original *Green Door,* the Mitchells spared no expense.

A team of artists, including famed cartoonist and Mitchell Brothers' habitue and sometimes screenwriter Dan O'Neill and Jim's wife, Mary Jane, transformed the vacant room next to the New York Live into the Green Door Room, the showplace of the O'Farrell, and the scene of the massive, mystical cabaret show/orgy that would comprise most of the film. Scores of extras had been hired. State-of-the-art cameras, booms, lighting, and sound equipment had been brought in, along with the crews to run them. That included former Mitchell core group member Jon Fontana and Antioch classmate of Jim's, who brought in his crew to run the cameras. Dana Fuller, who was close with Jim and had worked with the Mitchells extensively before, did the lighting.

Makeup artists, hair stylists, costumers, caterers—everything had been laid on. And the meter was running.

For Missy, of course, the pressure was different, but in a way much greater. Not only was she facing the realization that she was going to have wild, multiple-partner sex *in front of the whole world,* but also she had to put up with the whispers around the theater that she only got the starring role because she was fucking Artie. Or because of her bankable personal background. Or both.

The plan was to shoot the entire club scene, the guts of the movie, in one day, while the whole crew was available and in one place. It would start at the decidedly unpornographic hour of 6 A.M.

That day, Missy woke up knowing that her life would never be the same.

"It's like when you're having a baby," she says. "You know in advance that you're going to have it, but you don't really know, until you're in labor and you're driving to the hospital frantically, what it's going to be like.

"I mean, you can get the script and get the idea and everything but until the day you're going to the set, you can't really know. The game was over and it was time to count the chips. Some people get cold feet and burn you on movies, don't even show because of that feeling."

Artie knew what she would be going through, and did everything he could to help. "I went into my dressing room that morning— in our Marina apartment we had separate dressing rooms off the bathroom, really nice big rooms. And Artie had filled that dressing room with gifts for me, little gifts, everywhere. Jewelry, clothes, nice little presents.

"And he had written me a wonderful little note that said, 'Dear Hello Kitty, Today you're going to start a new adventure, a new chapter in your life, and it will never be the same. Hang on because it's going to be a wild ride.'

"And I knew exactly what he meant by that note. Everything would change from that moment. With my family. With my friends. Once you take that step to make a porno movie, you're not going to get a job as a secretary somewhere, you're not going to go to work at IBM. Because if anybody knows who you are, they're never going to look at you the same. It excludes you from a lot of things.

"I could never go back to the Republican National Committee."

And she knew that wasn't all.

"When my kids grow up they're going to know their mom made a porno movie. If my neighbors find out, they'll never treat me the same way they did before. If you're going to marry somebody else ten years down the road, they're going to have to accept it. Some men might say, 'I think you're a wonderful person, I think you're really great, but if my mother ever found out about this I couldn't be married to you.' It's not like even being a prostitute. You can't say you weren't there, you didn't do that. Your picture's right there.

"The only thing you could possibly do to blot out that past is to do what Linda Lovelace did, renounce everything, say you were exploited and forced to do it. You wouldn't really change anything but you might be able to redirect your path of destiny back toward what it was before.

"But I would never do that.

"I'm not saying now that I'm ashamed and I'm sorry I did it, because I'm not. It did change my life. I'm not sure I would do it again, but I probably would. It was a hard path to choose and it made a lot of decisions for me.

"And I knew all of that on that morning. I knew I had just gone off one road and onto another."

Missy and Artie arrived at the theater well before the first cast call at 6 A.M. Everyone knew this day would be a marathon.

McKnight was a real top sergeant. She made damn sure everything was set to go. She had a memorable clash with a celebrity extra—Huey Newton. Newton, who was friendly with both brothers, had been doing some weightlifting, and he was excited about the chance to show off his newly buffed-out physique. But he made the mistake of showing up around 8 A.M.

Just as Artie greeted him with a friendly, "Hi, Huey, howya doin'?" McKnight roared, "You're late. Cast was told to be here at 6 A.M." Newton started mumbling an excuse, hey, sorry lady, I got here as early as— "Too bad," she yelled. "Nobody can walk in here two hours late. There's the door, buster. I can't use you." Newton exited meekly.

From the start, Missy was as taut as a violin string tuned an octave too sharp. She was a professional; everyone was watching, waiting for a misstep, a sign of weakness from her. Equipment that cost thousands per day and crew being paid top dollar and all those extras were on hand. Mitchell old-timers Alex Benton and Russ Mitchell were positioned high above the set, shooting stills of the movie being shot. And it all came down to her. Most of the shooting that day revolved around her, and she knew it.

"It was really stressful and tense and I was shaking, trying to get it together. I would categorize it as an out-of-body experience. It was like I was floating up there in the lights, looking down upon myself doing the scenes."

But in another way, she was very much there. It was extremely hard physical labor, and she didn't get much help.

From the first, the safe sex element of the shooting had been emphasized. It was for real. It was probably the first—maybe the only—porno film where safe sex techniques were mandated. McKnight met with the entire cast, and everyone was given instructions on how to use the condoms, the dental dams—pieces of latex stretched over a woman's genitals to avoid fluid exchange during oral sex—and the spermicidal liquid Nonoxynol-9. "This is a safe sex movie," McKnight bellowed. "If you have a question or need help with any of this during the filming, raise your hand and someone will come over. Ask before you do something wrong because if it isn't done right we won't use it. This is what we're here for and if you have a problem with that, leave."

All that was fine, but it increased the pressure on Missy. Usually, in porno movies, "fluff girls" are used to get the male stars aroused and ready for the leading lady and the camera. But that technique wouldn't have been safe, and so the responsibility of keeping her male partners at attention fell entirely to Missy. And in one pivotal scene, a trapeze scene in which she had sex almost non-stop with three men, it wasn't easy.

In the movie, most of the sex scenes take place in a cabaret with people watching. So during the filming, there was a built-in audience watching every move, and that was hard for Missy. It was the first time she'd ever done sex on film, and here was this crowd of people taking in every move, every groan.

"I think anyone would have been nervous with all the pressure riding on that day, and then to have all those people watching, well, it was really difficult. I felt like everyone was looking at me because they were jealous.

"I mean, a lot of things were said and done that always hurt me. Someone said, 'Oh, that was really hard for Missy, she just wasn't sexual enough, she just couldn't do it, the guys always had to go backstage and jack off.' I'd like to see anybody else do it better, with the camera and the lights and that many people staring at us, with some guys who'd never performed before, weren't accustomed to doing it either. In L.A. they have some guys who can just come on the money, on demand, they are told when and what to do and they can do it, but these guys were aerobics instructors or weightlifters or boat drivers or whatever and their performance was on the line."

In an early scene, Missy was ravished by six vibrator-wielding women. In one of her *Playboy* interviews, Missy remembered the pleasurable aspect of the scene: "I had a screaming orgasm. I mean, if you can't get off with six people using vibrators on you, then there's something wrong with you."

But she remembers it differently today. "They were actually sort of bull-dyke lesbians in real life. They were dressed up as these beautiful nymphs, but they were really rough and mean to me. I remember thinking, I'm really going to be bruised after this, because they were hurting me and grabbing me. There was a lot of animosity there. In the scene it looks like everything is fine, but the way they'd grab me was not nice and sexy, it was mean. They would be holding me and when they'd cut or go to a different shot they'd just drop me and go. They were really ruthless. Every cut it was like, 'Oh, did I step on your hand?'

"They knew I wasn't one of them. I wasn't a lesbian. I wasn't even bi. I wasn't having sex with them all the time in their little group. Plus they were jealous like a lot of people at the theater because I was so close to Artie, and I had this starring role, and I was getting the TV talk show interviews and the spots in *Playboy,* and who were they? Just some little lesbian strippers. Maybe a lot of them had been used by Artie, but they knew I meant something more to him. We lived together, and we had a nice life together, and I was the one who would go to nice dinners and things. They were jealous of my life, and they took it out on me that day."

It got harder and harder as the day wore on. Jim and Artie and Sharon felt the tension. Artie left the set for a lot of the sexual parts, repairing to the office to smoke a joint rather than watch Missy. "He said it didn't bother him, that he knew it was just work, but I think it did," Missy said. "He said it would have been weird for the guys if he had stayed, but I think it bothered him."

Jim tried to make it as easy as he could for Missy. He got things for her to stand on, got her cold drinks, asked her, "Are you too hot? Are you okay?"

Missy wasn't okay. During one of the sex scenes, she had a bit of a breakdown. She had stayed on the set for hours, not taking a break, and they had brought her food, new makeup, costume changes right on the set instead of in her dressing room so they could keep shooting. But finally, it got to be a little too much.

About that time, they needed to start shooting the audience anyway. At the start of the shooting, everyone had been drinking soda water in the champagne glasses in the cabaret scenes, but Jim thought everybody needed loosening up, so he had the caterers bring out real champagne, and it did the trick. People started getting loose for real, and the sex was heating up in the audience, so while the cameras roamed the audience looking for the best action, Missy fled to her dressing room.

"I started crying and getting sort of generally weird, shaking and sobbing. I said, 'This is just too hard. I don't know if I can do it.' Sharon McKnight and the hairdressers were saying, 'That's all right. You're going to be fine. You're doing great. Don't worry.' But I was having serious doubts about going through with the rest of it, and I couldn't stop shaking. Part of it was I hadn't really eaten, either. So a couple of my friends who were in the audience asked if they could go check on me, to see if I was okay. They came and said, 'Come on, Missy, you're a real pro, you can do it.' And it made me feel better, and I went back down."

So the filming ground on, and Missy kept her emotions under control. During one scene, she was to be ravished by a satyr creature, half man, half goat. So this guy with his genitals hanging incongruously between weird fake goat legs, sort of chaps that were in actuality made out of yak hair, mounted her as the audience watched. "I don't know if he really liked me or was just a good performer or what, but he was really getting into it, overly enthused, and he was really pulling at me and hurting me, tearing my clothes off. I still have the costume and it's all torn. When he started doing that, Jim came running over and yelled, cut, cut. He knew that my shoulder could be dislocated really easily, and he said, 'Lighten up, you're hurting her.' The funny thing was I never spoke up for myself like that in sexual situations. I mean, if it was hot and erotic, I just let it happen, let people get away with it, and I was used to getting victimized, so I didn't say anything even when he was ripping my bra and my garter, but thank goodness Jim did. That was really hard."

Jim's wife, Mary Jane, helped too, bringing Missy a blanket between scenes, offering her something to drink. "People were really concerned about me because I was going through so much," Missy remembers. "Like in the scene where the statues come to life, I was really getting into it, screaming, doing my part, and I screamed so much that I lost my voice."

About 11 P.M., seventeen hours after the start of filming, Missy decided to take a break and get something to eat. The Mitchells had set up an elaborate catering service, and there was lots of food, but she hadn't eaten much all day. She took some food down to the Kopenhagen Room and sat and ate with some friends. It was her first real break, and it was a good release. They had some of the male performers come in and dance for the women, which was probably a first in the Kopenhagen Room, and cranked the music up high.

Too high, apparently, because it could be heard on the set, and Jim stormed down the hall and threw open the doors and said, "We're trying to shoot a fucking movie here, does anybody fucking mind?"

Missy remembers, "He just looked at me like, 'What the fuck are you doing?' and stalked out. We were all sitting there laughing. It wasn't really that funny. They were trying to have quiet on the set and here we were playing the loud music, but we were all sort of punchy.

"So we went back in for the rest of the big scene that everybody was in, and Artie came back on the set and told me, 'Okay, come on, really get into this, act like you're really enjoying it.' He was really good at getting people psyched up about what they were doing, and comfortable. He went around to the people in the audience too, doing the same thing, getting them going, and then the camera would come over."

By now, the cameramen were getting antsy, and their boss, Fontana, began taking it out on Missy.

"That's okay, Missy," he yelled. "Don't worry about the fucking time. Take all the time in the world. We don't have homes to go to, we don't have beds to sleep in."

"I was trying to get the guys ready for the scene," Missy remembers. "I didn't need him yelling that shit, in front of everyone on the set. 'It's okay, we don't have wives, Missy, we don't have girlfriends.' I mean, who is he? He's not the director, he's just a fucking contract cameraman. He should be pleased, he's getting paid a good daily rate. He should have been glad the meter was running. He was having fights with Jim and Artie. He was going up, saying, 'My men and I are leaving. This crew's off this job.' And Jim would say, 'What the fuck are you talking about?' And he would say, 'You and your men from the theater are smoking too much pot. We don't want to be around pot when we're working. We're professionals.' And Jim would say, 'Hey, who's paying you to be here? Shut up.' And Fontana kept up a running stream of bitching, saying, 'I'm never going to work with the Mitchell Brothers again. You smoke pot constantly. You're getting my men stoned, we don't work like that.' "

Probably nobody else could have gotten away with his act, but Fontana was trading on his background as an insider, someone who graduated with Jim, who was with the brothers almost from the beginning.

As she recalls the incident, Missy's anger returns. "There was a lot of tension going on already, but the Fontana thing was just too much. It was so fucked. He was just doing everything he could to piss me off, and it was late, and I didn't need it. I've never liked him since then."

But for Missy, the worst was, so to speak, yet to come.

"We were shooting the finale, the last big scene. Joanne Scott was up on the corner bar seat, dressed in some little weird cowboy costume, and it was just disgusting what these men were doing to her. Typical Artie sex only in front of everybody. She's bending over on this barstool, and she's got her butt up in the air, and I think they were doing anal sex, taking turns on her, and they're slapping her and hitting her, and she starts screaming, 'Faster, faster, more, oh, Artie, Artie, Artie, I love you' while these other guys are fucking her and fisting her and everything.

"I was sipping on some ginseng tea. They gave it to everybody to keep their energy up. You know, it's supposed to be an aphrodisiac, and it does give you a rush. So I'm having my ginseng, watching Joanne get fucked in the ass, and listening to her yell, 'Artie, Artie, Artie' while these guys are taking turns doing her. I just couldn't believe it."

Later, during the editing of the film, Missy pulled out all the stops in an effort to get those words and a lot of Joanne's scene cut from the movie.

"When we were looking at the final cut, I said, 'I will not be in that scene,' and they said why, and I said, 'Because it's clearly violence against women.' Funny coming from me, right? But I would often speak out on women's issues, protecting women's rights.

"I mean, here they were, showing her getting slapped, knocked around. She's into it, which is why she could be one of Artie's little sex slaves. (That's what he called a lot of women he was with, including me. I mean, he wouldn't introduce me to you, here's Missy Manners, my sex slave, but if the three of us were having sex on the pool table he would say, 'Missy is my sex slave and she'll do whatever I want her to.')

"Anyway, I said, 'You can't show this, it's disgusting, and if you put it in the movie I will sue you because I don't want to be in any movie that promotes violence against women.' "

McKnight agreed with her, and most of the scene was taken out.

Joanne was having a tough time dealing with it all. It infuriated her that not only did Missy have Artie, but she was the star of the movie, the center of attention.

Although she had survived Missy's attempt to get rid of her by having her fired, and she had been reinstated, she felt like she was still walking around on eggshells.

"Nobody really wanted to do the sex in that movie. Despite the precautions everybody was scared to death of AIDS at the time, and they weren't paying the extras much, just $125 for that whole grueling day.

"But I knew I should do it. There were several factors. I knew it might mean I got a better work schedule at the theater, and also I wanted to get back at Missy if I could.

"I'd really had it with her. She crank-called me through seven phone numbers. I kept changing it and she kept getting it.

"And she was being such a prima donna about everything. I heard that when they went to the airport to shoot some of those fill-in scenes at the front, she demanded to go in her own minivan because she was the star.

"I felt the only way I could win in this intolerable situation was to overact and upstage her that day. Having done so many Ultra Room shows, I kind of knew what to do to get attention. If you're doing the show alone and you're down at one end you can't be silent because the guys at the other end won't get into it at all. So you have to scream, and when it came to this movie, I knew screaming would work. I started messing with a couple of different guys, and I started screaming my head off and the cameras came over to me. I didn't have any makeup on, and I was wearing a mask because you didn't know what sort of weirdos would be there, you know, and by the time I got down to it, ripping my mask off, I knew I didn't look that good, but I was one hell of a distraction, and she froze right up.

"I was screaming, 'Faster, faster,' and stuff like that, but I think she thought I was screaming Artie's name, and he thought I was too, so it worked, she totally freaked.

"It was the only way I could deal with the whole damn thing."

• • •

After the Kopenhagen embarrassment, after the Fontana sarcasm, after the Joanne debacle, after the last cup of ginseng tea, after the last trapeze had swung, after the last hands had mauled her nipples, after the last latex-covered penis had been sucked, it was 6 A.M. Twenty-four hours of safe sex. Safe sex with goat-men, vicious vibrator-wielding nymphs, painted men on trapezes. Twenty-four hours of masturbating condom-clad actors, trying to keep them hard until the camera got there and she could do them for posterity. Twenty-four hours of bruises and squeezes and pinches and penetration. Her adrenaline began to run down, and Missy was more tired than she had ever been in her life. She went and took a shower, put on her white terry bathrobe, put a towel around her head. Artie had to stay a while longer, but he called a taxi for her, then went out with her, out on the sidewalk in front of the theater, and gave her a hug as the sun came up. And he said, again: "Your life will never be the same, Kitty. Never."

She said, simply, "I know." And she added, "My God. What a day."

Missy was so tired she could barely move. "There I was, practically naked, wearing just my robe and a towel, in the middle of the Tenderloin at dawn. I just got into the cab and said, 515 Marina Boulevard. I didn't have a purse, keys, anything. I went home and rang the doorbell so my housekeeper could let me in. Thank God she was there.

"When I talked to other people, they said it was just as bizarre for them when they finally left. We'd been in there twenty-four hours and hadn't seen the light of day. We'd been immersed in this weird reality, nothing but nonstop sex. Everybody said the same thing: God, what a day."

Missy recovered quickly. Although it had been arduous, she was really glad she had made the movie. To her, it was a metaphor for her own transformation.

She did believe that people all have a Green Door in their brains where their sexuality lies, their fantasies, the essence of their sexual identity. And she knew that Artie helped her open her own Green Door, to allow her own sexuality to come to fruition.

"For a change I wasn't hearing, 'This is bad, don't ever say fuck, don't ever actually fuck, don't ever talk about it.' Artie was just so enthusiastic, we're making this great movie, it's all out there. It was sort of a Gestalt sex therapy for me because that's what the movie was all about. If you really look at the movie, it was like my life. I mean, here's this nice girl next door, first Marilyn and then me, and the girl is taken behind the Green Door, into the club, and led through all these sexual things. And that's really, in all honesty, what my life was like with Artie.

"That openness was really great. Being open is what making a movie is all about, and Artie and I really liked each other's openness, raw sexuality. We both liked sex a lot, and we had a lot of sex, and we were very sexually open.

"It was a gigantic rite of passage."

Of course, there was the predictable fallout. Her parents had come out to visit again, and she broke the news to them. If they were shocked at her living with a pornographer, they were shocked to the point of near insensibility at the news that she had acted—no, *starred*—in a porno movie. The nobility of the safe sex cause was lost on them. All they knew was, now there existed a movie, about to be released, of their daughter, presumably doing unimaginably lewd things with God knows who. What if the neighbors got it? Imagine, being a fine upstanding religious Republican, and discovering that your daughter's pornographer boyfriend has filmed her, not just for his own perverted pleasure but for the world to see! Doing deviant, weird, lesbian sex! Fucking and sucking crazily! Vibrating! Screaming! Coming! With a rope of fake pearls clenched in her teeth and her tits flopping wildly and her ass jammed up against some sleazy porno actor's yak fur–covered flanks as he rams his condom-coated member into her time and again! All in the name of safe sex? What happened to her Traditional Republican Values?

Missy's parents asked Artie if there was not something they could do, something to keep this movie from being released.

"If he'd said, yeah, $50,000, or $500,000, or a million, or whatever, they'd have immediately said, okay, let's talk about this, we can do something. But we both told them, no, there's nothing.

"And they were like, 'Why did you have to do this to us?' They were horrified. And they never talked to me after that, never called, never sent a birthday card, for years. All the time I was with Artie, even afterward. I really did think I would never be able to speak with my family again. Now, now that I'm respectably married, now that I've given them grandchildren, they are really nice to me again, but I didn't know that would happen. I thought that was that.

"And of course it hurt me, and it also put me even more under Artie's control. Suddenly he was my only source of affection and love. That total connection to the person, without any recourse, without the safety net of others, makes you even more of a co-dependent. It's like the battered wife who has no friends, no support system."

But Missy didn't have much time to dwell on the dissolution of her relationship with her parents. The next few months were a whirl of activity. She promoted herself, and the movie, with persistence and skill. Soon, she was on the big talk shows—Oprah, Donahue, Letterman. She spoke out articulately and forcefully for safe sex, handed out the safe sex kits featured in the movie, and of course managed to get in a plug for the film. She tangled with right-to-lifers, Moral Majority types, every conservative, anticontraceptive, antiporn group around. And she knocked their socks off.

Artie accompanied her to the shows. In the Oprah segment, he could be seen, sitting in the audience quietly, applauding Missy's sallies and listening intently.

She had a total of three *Playboy* interviews, including a major feature article and pictorial in the January 1987 issue. The movie itself, after an initial sales rush, was only a moderate success, receiving mixed reviews. But the publicity was a bonanza for the Mitchells, and for the cause of safe sex. And it made Missy somewhat of a household word.

The trip to Chicago for *Playboy* was a memorable one in many ways. Journalist David Talbot, a friend of Missy and Artie's, had pitched the story. *Playboy* was interested, and wanted to meet the couple and hear some more. So they went back to Chicago and talked to G. Barry Golson, then the magazine's executive editor, and others, including photo editor Gary Cole.

"Artie was very happy that they wanted to talk to us, and they were really very nice people. I really liked all the people at *Playboy* a lot, and they treated us wonderfully. Gary Cole said to me, 'Obviously we like you a lot, and we'd like to use you. Would you take your clothes off?' Well, yeah, I would. So they said, 'Would you do a test shoot?' and I did, so then they said, 'What are you doing the rest of the week? Could you just stay here and finish the shoot for the magazine?' And I said, I don't know, so we talked about money, and worked it out.

"They were really good to me, and it seemed like working for *Playboy* was one of the best gigs anybody could get in the business. I probably learned more about modeling in working for *Playboy* than I ever could at a modeling school. I asked a photographer once if I could come and watch him shoot professional models sometime, maybe when they were in L.A., and he said, 'We don't use professionals. You're as professional as we get. We go for the girl next door, the girl off the street, the average person.'

"So Artie and I spent the week in Chicago, and we had to go out and buy all these new clothes because we just came with an overnight bag and we had to stay a week. And while I was working Artie went out and bought all these nice clothes for me."

But it didn't take long for Artie to begin to feel threatened. He wasn't the center of attention here. Sure, the star was his girl, but he was used to being the boss, being in control. So he used the only weapon he had to regain the upper hand.

Artie met a woman in Chicago who really wanted a career in porn, and so he used his position and his charm to do what he did so often.

"They had provided us with a wonderful penthouse suite, with free fruit and wine, beautiful, great big bathrooms, it was wonderful, and I needed it. I was absolutely exhausted each night when I came back from the shooting.

"So this one evening I came back and Artie and this woman had left underwear, condoms, sex stuff spread all over, a burning joint, the bed unmade, everything. It was like a slap in the face, and I was hysterical.

"I called a friend in San Francisco, and she said, 'Missy, you know Artie always competes with you, and right now he's jealous of you. You're the center of attention, and he knows that thousands of men are going to be looking at you, you're going to be the beautiful girl in *Playboy*, and here he is stuck waiting around for you. He had to put you in your place, to put you down one more time, show you who's in control.' And I thought, that's exactly right. But I was still devastated by it. It was so denigrating to me. I mean, if he'd wanted to fuck he could have gone and got his own hotel room. It was a deliberate message to me."

And it worked perfectly, just as Artie had known it would.

"When the movie came out I thought she'd be content with the publicity," Joanne says. "The movie opening, the TV shows, the whole nine yards. But no, she had to torment me at the same time, as if I didn't feel like shit anyway, and she started crank-calling me around the clock. I know Artie made her feel insecure too, laid the same trip on her I was getting, and that's why she was doing it, but it was ugly.

"It did take them forever to finish that movie. I got the feeling at the time that maybe Missy felt that when they were finished, Artie would be finished with her. But Artie was so funny, so unpredictable.

He'd get bored so easily that sometimes, just for the hell of it, he'd sabotage his own plans.

"I remember once a few days before they were supposed to finish the movie, he ran into the Ultra Room, really high, while it was open. The manager closed it up quickly, made sure there weren't any people watching, and he fucked me in there. He'd probably had a fight with her, and of course I egged him on. It was just what I needed. It was a confirmation that in spite of her, in spite of the movie, in spite of his firing me, in spite of everything, I was still in his life. Even though everyone was acting like I wasn't."

That part was really torture for Joanne. Everyone viewed her as just some slut Artie used every now and then. She knew she meant more to him than that. He told her so. But she was still the outcast in public, and Missy was the star, living with Artie.

In June 1986, right before the last day of shooting, Missy refused to be in the scene they had left to do if Joanne was in it. Her reason was chilling: she charged that Joanne and a friend, porn headliner Rita Ricardo, were planning to slit Missy's throat.

Joanne remembers getting a call from Jim, at home, that night. "Joanne, are you and Rita planning to cut Missy's throat?" he asked bluntly.

"Could you repeat that?" said Joanne, aghast.

Finally, the situation was resolved: they didn't need Missy in the scene; they were able to shoot around her. Of course, Artie used the crisis to test Joanne's loyalty, the depth of her love.

"There was one time, the only time he really did something like this, around the time of the movie. Some fisherman friend of his was having a birthday, and he told me I had to go out with this guy and a couple of his friends. I was so furious.

"This guy and his buddies had all been doing crank, which Artie knew, and of course guys really can't do a whole lot when they've been doing a lot of that stuff, and that was part of the joke for Artie.

"So I ended up doing a little stuff with Artie and these guys, and then he basically sent me with them. It was weird, but in that Story of O way, it was another way for me to show how much I loved him. It's very much involving power, having your lover do things with others as a sign of love for you. So what I decided is, wow, so you want me to go with these guys, well, I'll be so wild that you'll hear about it. And I was."

But what happened a couple of weeks later was awful.

The fishermen came back. They wanted a repeat, an encore.

"Artie wasn't around, and Jim made me feel like I'd better fucking well go if I wanted to keep my job. At the time Art was living with Missy, and work was my only contact with him. I just wasn't sure enough of our relationship to choose to leave, and that's the way he wanted it. I didn't know if I could continue to reach him if I left the theater environment, with Missy and the movie and everything, and I was so in love with him.

"Plus I was getting booked so well, making such good money, that I hated to give that up. So I had to do it again, and it was awful. I mean, they couldn't have cared less if it was me or some other person, maybe they would have liked a blonde this time, you know, this wasn't romance, it was sexual sport.

"Before I went with them, I had to do my stage shows, with them watching me, knowing all the time I had to leave with them. Awful.

"Of course, this sort of thing happens to women in the business. At one time or another, it happens. So I ended up going with them and just feeling terrible about it."

Artie wasn't pleased when he heard about it. After all, he wasn't doing the choreographing, and he didn't like his brother ordering his girfriend to fuck somebody else. It was his own power being misused, usurped. But he didn't make an issue of it.

"He was still into the thing with Missy, and he couldn't really go nuts about it," Joanne says.

"I think the whole situation we were in was kind of exciting for Artie at the time. I mean, he had Missy, the star of the movie, soon to be the national porno figure, and he had me, in the background, still dancing at the theater, and there whenever he wanted. And we both loved him so much. It was really a high point for him, I think. He loved that constant interplay.

"And I don't regret any of it."

Missy kept making her public appearances, preaching the gospel about safe sex and feminism and pornography the way she saw it. Through her own efforts, through her skill at media promotion and the controversial message she put forward, she became a national spokesperson for safe sex, and for pornography as an attractive alternative for women. In a feature story on the cover of the Life section of *USA Today*, she was quoted as saying that pornography was for women as sports had been for minorities: a way to get ahead, become financially successful, become empowered. Not, as the old stereotype would have it, a way to be repressed and exploited. (She makes the same argument today. "That's not to say that women can't get ahead in college or other careers, but it does provide an opportunity," Missy says. "I can tell you that Nina Hartley is making more money than a secretary somewhere, and more money than a lot of women who are lawyers.")

At the time, she was voicing ideas that just had not been given much of an airing in the mainstream, and that made her a pioneer of sorts. Also, at the theater, she spoke out, and not just about Joanne in *Green Door.* She got after Jim and Art for making—and selling—a Marilyn Chambers film called *Never a Tender Moment,* in which the Ivory Soap Girl is in the Ultra Room on a leash, being whipped and fisted and having objects of all sorts rammed into her body cavities.

"Of course this is everything the Meese Commission wants people to believe that pornography is, and if we're out there saying they're wrong, we'd better think again," she told them. "If this place were raided and they found that, that's all they would have to show in court. That's enough to take the Mitchell Brothers down." And the Mitchells did pull the film off the market and take it out of the theater.

But there was a great irony too in her fighting for the feminist viewpoint in pornography, in campaigning against movies that showed abusive behavior toward women. Because, of course, she was living through her own abusive relationship with *her* pornographer.

The good times were still really good. There were still the wonderful evenings, wonderful parties with friends at some of San Francisco's best restaurants and clubs: at Scott's, at Fog City Diner, at Izzy's, at Stars. There were still the great pulsing tidal waves of sex. There were still the weekends with the kids, and there were still the spontaneous getaway vacations that the two of them would take.

"Karen would be throwing a fit, keeping Artie from picking up the kids, or something had happened at work, you know, that was upsetting. And instead of staying and being really negative and fighting, we'd just head for the airport and go someplace. Those were really great times."

Missy will always remember one of those weekends, above all.

"We needed to get away. We'd had the kids for weeks, and we finally had some time alone. We drove down into the desert, and it was pouring rain, and we were on acid, and we wanted to get out and be on this mesa in the rain, on top of this beautiful mesa. You could see the whole world from up there.

"So we did, we went up there in the rain, and pitched a tent, and we told each other we would always be with each other spiritually. He told me that he knew we'd been together on that mesa before, and we both felt that. We talked about how we felt, like we were really united, and did have a marriage on the highest level, and we said things to each other that were promises.

"And I do think at that time we had a very spiritual marriage, a spiritual bond. His Indian name was Tenclaw. He called me Rolling Thunder and I called him Tenclaw.

"We felt like we had past lives together. We felt like we had been together before, and I'm sure we had. It was the most powerful and intense feeling. I always had that with him. It wasn't a relationship where I had to go and get a lawyer and divorce myself from him when it got ugly. It was just something that was between me and Artie, and that was our whole relationship."

Never had Missy had such a relationship, with such intensity, such intricacy, with so many levels and subplots, such currents of emotion. Neither, perhaps, had Artie. But more and more, Missy found herself trapped in the vise of Artie's anger and alcohol.

Everyone who was around Artie, from his brother to his lovers to his mother to the dancers at the theater, had to deal with the central fact that he was an alcoholic. For Missy, that was easy to do, because she had done it before.

"I think I accepted the relationship because after all those years of dealing with my mother, who was an alcoholic, I became used to thinking that was the norm," Missy says. "So when I cut off my relationship with her, I replaced her with another alcoholic, and that was Artie.

"He was my first major relationship as an adult. That was somewhat typical in that the people he had relationships with were mostly fairly young, less-experienced, less-mature women. Control is usually an issue with alcoholics, and Artie wanted total control. I think that he found one way to get that was to find someone who was younger and a little naive. Especially someone like me, who was young and naive, and also was willing to accept abuse, because I was used to it.

"I mean, my mother never hit me or pushed me down the stairs or did any of the sort of physical things Artie did, but what she did is still classified as abuse, and I was still willing to accept that in a relationship early on and fall into that pattern with him. I was always a co-dependent. He was co-dependent on me and on Jim, and in all of his relationships. Artie was a functional alcoholic, who was able for a long time to go to work and keep his life together, after a fashion, but in order for that to happen somebody else had to keep other things together for him. It's like sailing a boat, you have to have help keeping everything straight, and I took care of it. I was helpful with his kids, with his ex-wives, I helped him work. I was willing to pick up the slack."

At the same time, she was dealing with her own drinking and drug use, but despite their spates of wild partying, she was definitely the moderating influence.

"I really didn't consume as much of anything as he did, ever, and then after the first year of our being together, I had to slow down and we had to start taking things more seriously. Because then I not only worked with him, but I often had the added responsibility of caring for his kids. And you can't be out there doing coke when you have that responsibility.

"So when we started living together my consumption really tapered off. I'm not saying that we didn't drop acid on vacation, or we didn't go and do Ecstasy. A lot of nights we'd do it and stay under the pool table at the O'Farrell. But on more and more nights, I'd be sober. I was the co-dependent who had to keep it more together. And since I don't smoke pot, and never did coke or drank on a steady basis, it was easy for me to do that. But at that time, of course, I was drinking a lot more than I ever had. I'm very straight and sober now, of course, because I have kids. I want to be that way. It's my choice; I look back and there were things about that time that aren't clear to me because I was too drunk to recall the situation. And I think Artie was that way almost all the time. He did so many drugs, smoked so much pot, that his whole life was in a fog."

But not so much in a fog that he wasn't able to play skillfully on Missy's willingness to accept a victim's role in the relationship. Artie was always in control, and he let Missy call just as many of the shots *as he wanted her to*. For one thing, it was very useful for him to make sure people could extricate him from the threatening situations he created.

Johnny Concho.

If he got abusive in public, in a bar or a restaurant, it was great to have somebody there, like Jim or Missy, to hush it up, settle things down, mollify people before somebody beat the hell out of him, before the police came. Like Missy did the night he stood on the table and screamed at the waitresses at the Billboard Cafe. Like she did the night at sleek, expensive Harry's American Bar, when he overturned a table in the middle of dinner because Missy answered a question he thought he should have answered.

Somebody to drive him home, to clean up the litter he left behind, to make everything all right so he could do it again tomorrow. So often, that role fell to Jim, or the woman who happened to be with him.

Like many abused or victimized women, Missy was extremely together and in control of her business and public life. She had to make
public appearances, and be perceived as a very strong person, doing
combative interviews on national TV and carrying them off articulately
and with intellect. But privately, Artie was always in control, and she
was always submissive.

It was a double victory for him that she did so well in public. First,
it made it all the more significant and satisfying to dominate her in
private; and second, all of her efforts were, after all, bringing money
into the company, and into his household.

As time went on, the violence became more frequent and more
disturbing.

"Our fights were so bad. I remember once he took a photo of me
that I really liked, a large boudoir sort of photo in a glass frame, and
he broke the frame all over the bathroom and then threw the picture
out the back window and said, 'This is what I think of you.'

"He was always so contrite, we'd have wonderful, sweet sex, and
he'd be so apologetic. We'd both say, 'I'm sorry, I'm really sorry.' And
we were. But toward the end there were just so many times when it
was just so intense, you can only take so much and you just say, no
more, that's got to be it."

As often as she said it, she would take it back, because she loved
him so much, and so much of what they had was so good.

"I think the good times were wearing thin, because I was not always
so happy as time went on. I had been hit so many times, thrown across
the room. My cats had been thrown against the wall, my dog and I had
been pushed out of the car.

"One time we were going to go to Thanksgiving at Jim and Mary
Jane's house, and he was really angry because he'd had a fight with
Karen about getting the kids for the holiday. And I took too long in
the shower, or something, and when I came out of the shower he said,
'You know you're such a vicious bitch, all women are vicious bitches.'
And I said, 'What are you talking about?' And he scratched my face
really badly. It was all bloody and furrowed on one side. I tried to get
it together, cover it with makeup, hold my hair to one side over it so
people wouldn't notice. It wasn't much of a Thanksgiving.

"One of my friends said, 'That's it, now he's going to ruin the way
you look, Missy. That's one of the signs they're going too far, when
they try to ruin your face.' "

Some would say that one of the signs they're going too far is when
they slap you around, knock you down the stairs, and order you to have
sex with someone in a gorilla suit. But Missy's own submissiveness had

made her a partner in Artie's domination—to a point that she didn't recognize abuse when it occurred.

A lot of the abuse was sexual, she realizes now. Artie liked violent sex, at least when he was the one being violent. He would slap, whip, pull hair, push Missy to the floor.

"Once he had sex with a friend of mine and she told another one of my friends, who came to me and said, 'Missy, is this what your sex life is always like?' I said, 'Yes, I don't think there's anything wrong with it, do you?'

" 'Do you like it?'

" 'Yes, I do.'

" 'You know it's what Artie likes, right?'

" 'Yes.' "

Years afterward, the friend asks Missy if sex with her husband is violent like that too. Missy says no, and the friend says, "I couldn't believe that you let Artie do that stuff, that you put up with him being violent. If a man were on top of me, whipping me, I would turn on him, butt fuck him with a dildo, make sure he never forgot it."

And Missy says simply, "That was then, this is now. I would never tolerate that again, but it was normal with Artie."

That violent expression of sexual dominance was at the heart of their relationship. Even when Missy was in control on the surface, using her power as a woman, a film star, a spokesperson, a businesswoman, all it did was sharpen his pleasure, make it hotter, knowing he could take this smart, beautiful, self-assured, successful woman and bend her to his will.

Obviously, it all fit with some needs Missy had, with the submissive nature that kept her coming back for more. But that outlook would not last forever. Slowly, painfully, from the darkest depths of the relationship, she began to swim toward the surface.

Missy's friends were beginning to see bruises on her face, fingermarks on her arms. They would say to her, Missy, we know what's going on. It's better that you come out with it. How can we help? *Why are you with him?*

It was taking a heavy toll, both physically and mentally. Missy was becoming more and more miserable, losing the bouncy, happy-go-lucky spirit that had been her trademark—and, ironically, had so attracted Artie in the first place. Once Missy went to a holiday dinner at Warren Hinckle's mother's house, and she was constantly bitching at Artie, stop breaking the glasses, don't lean against that stove, it's on. It was just like being with a kid. A drunken, violent kid.

Mrs. Hinckle said, "Look at that girl. She's so miserable. Such a pretty girl, but I've never seen anybody who looked so unhappy." Missy told her, I just get so tired of being with him sometimes.

So Mrs. Hinckle said, *"Why are you with him?"* And all of a sudden things started clicking in Missy's head.

"I thought, okay, I *am* miserable. That's true. And I went home and thought some more. Why am I with him? He totally abuses me, he calls me names, he treats me like shit, he denigrates me, he makes me *feel* like shit, and I'm staying with him?"

A few weeks later he dislocated her shoulder, and she was in horrible pain, couldn't get to the phone, couldn't get her shoulder back in, didn't know what to do. Finally, she dragged herself to the emergency room, where a doctor treated her, put it back, put it in a sling, gave her painkillers, then asked, *"Why are you in this relationship?"*

Oh, God, a million reasons. Because she loved him, because he had cut her off from every other source of love and support, because it was all she knew, because she was used to abuse, she could take it, but God, why did it have to be this bad? Why couldn't he accept her love? Why did he have to be such a *bastard?* Loving him was so addictive, and she craved his approval, and wanted to help him, felt so sorry for him, for his kids, wanted to help them too. She knew he really loved her, and he had all this trouble with alcohol, and with his anger, that he never really got help for. It wasn't his fault. When he hurt her, somehow she always felt she'd been responsible for making him angry, or she could see how he was under so much pressure, with Karen and the theater and everything. And then he was so nice, so sorry, and there would be lavish gifts, great, sweet sex, a nice trip somewhere, Oh please God, let the nightmare be over.

She remembers, "It got to where I was feeling so tired. It does drain you, after so many of these fights and scenes. Also, the responsibilities of being a co-dependent are so overwhelming. And I was growing up too, seeing things a little differently. With the abuse, you always want to believe it's going to stop. And he was always really, really sorry."

But it didn't stop. The nightmare wasn't over. It just went on and on like a Mitchell Brothers loop. Flesh Factory. You keep feeding quarters in and they just keep fucking. You keep being around Artie and he just keeps fucking you up.

At last, she sought some therapy, but even that was a perfect metaphor for the control Artie had on her life. When her appointment came, she was taking care of Caleb, and so she took him to therapy with her.

"Why do you have this child with you?" asked the doctor.

Good question. Followed by a bunch more good questions.

Everything had turned weird. The wonder and beauty of the relationship, Tenclaw and Rolling Thunder, was receding, breaking up like a
desert mirage, and she began to see that this was it, things would never
really change, even though she loved him and, she knew, he loved her.

Life on Marina Boulevard was a pale shadow of what it once was.
Jim was breaking up with Mary Jane, and he had no place to live, so
he slept some nights on the fishing boat and some nights at Artie and
Missy's house.

That made things even harder. Jim couldn't really live there with
them, because when he had his four kids, and Artie had his kids, that
would have meant ten kids in the apartment, along with Jim, Artie,
Missy, and the housekeepers, and that was just nuts. For a while, Mary
Jane just left on weekends so Jim could spend time with the kids at
their house, but that wouldn't last forever, and Missy felt that Jim was
pressuring Artie to get a house with him, so that together they could
finance something really nice.

Jim would come home to Artie and Missy's place, and he would
bitch about Missy's cats, clawing the curtains, crapping in the house
plants, usual cat stuff. "It's disgusting that you live this way," he would
say. "This place smells like cat piss."

New tensions were building on top of old tensions. Missy couldn't
take it much longer. It wasn't working between her and Artie, it wasn't
working to have Jim around. The end had come, she thought.

One day she had to go down to do a talk show in Los Angeles, and
she told her housekeepers, I might decide to stay down there for a
while, and if I call you—they had their own private line—please send
my clothes down for me. So she flew down to L.A., did the show, and
just stayed. She didn't call Artie, because she knew it would be too
hard.

"I was scheduled to take an afternoon flight back home," she says,
"and I just never took it."

For three months, Missy lived in a sterile little furnished apartment
in West Hollywood, the kind companies rent for employees on temporary assignment, with crummy pots and pans and cheap towels and
yellow shag carpeting with a matching bedspread. Trying to figure out
what the hell to do with herself now that she had torn herself away
from the taproot, the center of her existence. She had few friends down
there, no close ones, and nothing but the pain of being alone and
remembering the pain of being together.

Then Artie came down, and saw where she was and how adrift she was.

"He lay on my bed and said, 'Kitty, this is terrible, I can't believe you've been living this way.' And I said, 'I can't either.' And he said, 'Why don't you just come home and live with us.'

"I said, 'Who's us?' and he said, 'Me and Uncle Jim. You can live with us in Moraga.' "

They had bought a huge house out in the East Bay, sort of a ranchette really, a pretty nice acreage, rolling hills, and an absolutely enormous house, big enough for all the kids.

Missy was tempted, but she didn't want to live with Artie *and* Jim. She wasn't sure she could even handle living with Artie. I'd rather stay here with the yellow shag carpeting, she thought.

So after they talked for a while, Artie tried another tack. He suggested that they leave right away on a trip to Mexico, take a trip and get away. He knew a trip would remind her of all the good times, and of course it did. They went to Cabo San Lucas, that favored refuge of gringo honeymooners and let's-get-back-togetherers, and they lay on the beach and read books together and took long walks and talked and it was great.

And then they went to the airport and Artie said, now, are you coming home with me, and she said no, and he was drunk, and he said, "You fucking slut, you're just a bitch," and he punched her savagely.

Even now, she makes excuses: "He was drinking a lot, and vacations were always sort of hard for us to end, it's so depressing to be going back to work.

"But I told him, 'No, I want to go back to L.A.,' and he went nuts, hit me with his fist a few times, slapped me once or twice too, and the Mexican police saw it. I was crying. They don't take kindly to men hitting women, and they were going to arrest him, and I had to talk them out of it, saying no, he wasn't really hurting me.

"And there it was. I looked like some kind of nut, defending this drunkard after he hit me. Again."

After she went back to Los Angeles, she was really depressed, nearly suicidal as she remembers it, and it was nearly Christmas, so finally she did decide, okay, I'll go try it, I'll go and live with him and Uncle Jim in Moraga.

So many times, Joanne had thought Missy was history. This time, she had been all but sure. The bitch had moved out, left town, gone. And now, right before Christmas, she was back with him, and word was they'd gone to Mexico together.

Oh, God. Christmas ruined. But at least she knew he hadn't forgotten her. When he wasn't coming by all the time, often he would pick up the phone and dial her number, let it ring just a fraction of a ring, and then hang up.

"It was, 'Jo, I'm thinking about you,' " she remembers. It kept that lifeline there, kept her focused on him at all times. A little blip of a ring, less than a second. Then silence. Oh, well. It wasn't much, but it was something.

Meanwhile, Jim had hired her to sew beautiful satin and velvet Christmas stockings for everyone in the Moraga house. He ordered one for everybody: himself, Artie, Liberty, Storm, Mariah, Aaron, Jasmine, Caleb, Meta, Rafe, Justin, Jennifer. And Hello Kitty.

She did all but the last one. She just couldn't.

Merry Christmas.

Well, it wasn't really so hot for Missy, either. As she had feared, living with both brothers wasn't any picnic, although Jim seemed to know what she was going through, and did try to be nice to her. But the fights with Artie continued, and a new layer of stress—trying to keep track of ten kids—was laid on. The simplest things—going out for a pizza—became complex logistical exercises.

"It was so tough to try to govern them all, to keep a semblance of order, keep them from writing on the walls and such. It was difficult."

So Missy tried a little behavior modification experiment. She bought a bunch of toys and if the kids were good, they got one. If they weren't, they didn't.

"Fuck you," Aaron Mitchell said. "That's not fair."

Missy said to Artie, "You're not going to let him talk to me like that," and Artie said, "Fuck you, he's right, it isn't fair making them compete."

Missy was furious. "Aaron had a lot of resentment toward me. He was real close to Artie, and he was sort of angry and hostile, and he'd try to manipulate Artie because that's the only way he knew how to deal with the situation.

"I just went walking off, and Jim came and picked me up in his car and said, 'Come on, Missy, come on home and let's talk about it.' He really was decent to me out there."

The Brazilian housekeepers they had in the Marina had moved out to Moraga, and they were helpful with the kids, but one night they caused a bizarre incident with the police, full of slapstick comedy.

The entire household had settled in for the night, and finally all was quiet. It was maybe 2 A.M. when the police surrounded the house.

Missy and Art could see lights flashing everywhere, and the cops rang the doorbell and shouted on their loudspeaker, "Come out with your hands up."

Artie, of course, was convinced it was a huge drug bust, or maybe even some trumped-up obscenity search, but whatever it was he knew it was bad. Missy told him to stay in bed, and she answered the door in her long flannel nightgown and asked, in her sternest, most Republican voice, "What the hell is going on here?"

The cops asked, did you call 911? And she said no, and they said, well, we got a 911 call and we traced it to this address, and we're going to search your house. They were irritated from the start because the house was remote as hell, not on their map, really isolated, and it took them forever to get there. They were convinced something serious was happening, because the caller had hung up, and they really did have the place surrounded. There were men on the roof.

So Missy said, shocked, "Search our house? I tell you I didn't call 911," and the captain told her that he had to make sure no one was being held against their will, and added that somebody could even have ordered her to come to the door and say everything was okay. We'll have to come in and make sure everyone is all right, he said.

So they made their way through the 6,000-square-foot house, and when they got to Sylvia, one of the housekeepers, they asked her if she called 911 and she said, no, I dialed 011, which is the access code for international calls. She was trying to call home to Brazil, and she was calling in the middle of the night because of the time difference. Apparently she had misdialed, which she vigorously denied, and the cop said, look, you shouldn't hang up when you call 911, and she said, no, I called 011, and that was that.

In the next few years, the 911 line would hold the key to the brothers' fate on more than one occasion.

Missy was drawn into the inevitable friction between Jim and Artie that ensued from living in the same house. Artie privately derided Jim's parenting style; although Jim was a good, loving father, Art thought all he did was spend money on the kids. Every weekend he would take them to the Imaginarium, or Toys "R" Us, or wherever they wanted to go and buy toys.

Artie called him Uncle Jim, the Toy Man.

Again, Jim and Missy clashed over pets. He didn't want Mr. T in the house, although he relented and said, okay, he can be in your room, but I don't want him in the living room. And then Jim went out and bought cocker spaniel puppies for his kids and gave them the run of the house.

It was always something.

Once Jim hired a cook that Artie and Missy just hated. "She was a New Yorker and she walked around in her pajamas and drank coffee and read the *New York Times* all morning like some pseudointellectual," Missy says. "She used to drive Artie and me nuts, but Jim really liked her. We wanted to fire her, but Jim said no.

"Artie said, of course, if we liked somebody, Jim would hate her, if he likes her, we wouldn't like her. We can't agree on anything. I guess those little altercations just come from living together."

After a time, they were only out there on weekends, when they had the kids. The old commuting problem had cropped up again, so Artie and Missy rented a condo on Jefferson Street, around the corner from their old place in the Marina.

But the whole relationship had changed, and Missy knew it had to end. She had altered the situation irrevocably by taking things into her own hands, leaving of her own volition, refusing to play the game, recognizing herself as a victim, holding out and refusing to come back for a while. But it hadn't really helped anything. Despite all the promises, all the contrition, Artie continued to treat her the same. Like sand through an hourglass, the good times waned, leaving her miserable more and more of the time.

Often, others watched as they went through horrible times. Some nights, he would be at the theater, refusing to come home, and they would be fighting on the phone, and Missy would drive down to the theater in her pajamas to get him. She'd park on Polk Street over by the side door and wait for him. Or, if she was really furious, she would march right in to get him. She would call him on the car phone and tell him she was coming. "I want your ass out here," she would rage, and he wouldn't come, so she would go in after him. He would be in the office, wasted drunk. ("God knows who he'd fucked or what he'd done," she says.) Sometimes he would be so out of it that one of the managers would help Missy get him to the car.

I just can't do this anymore, she thought.

Missy's first escape hadn't worked because she had no friends, no support in L.A. So she came up with a better bolt hole: Stinson Beach.

The tiny beach village in Marin County, just north of San Franciso, seemed just right. For one thing, she loved it there. For another, she had friends who lived there. For another, to get there you had to drive an incredibly narrow, winding road, full of hairpin curves and steep drop-offs. Even Artie knew he couldn't drive that road drunk too often, she thought. He had just had to go to traffic school and pay some fines, and his insurance had soared, and she thought it would be hard for him to come out and see her whenever he wanted to.

The clincher was getting a good place to stay, and that was hard because Stinson is so small. For the first little while, she stayed with friends, but before long, she found it: a little one-bedroom house, just up from Stinson's only grocery, Ed's Superette. It had a beautiful yard and a nice deck. Missy painted it pink, which was her trademark, and settled in with her cats. She had left Purplehead for Artie, but she still had her mother cat Bitsy and her kitten, Little Bits. This is my sanctuary, she thought. This is where I will heal.

She tried to do it right. She went to a therapist, who started her going to an evening group session with other women experiencing similar problems, sort of a women-who-love-too-much group. She also went to one Alcoholics Anonymous meeting a week, and one Al-Anon meeting.

It was just so damned *hard*. Missy would be trying desperately to get her head together, and Artie would call or come out, road or no road, and inevitably they would fight.

She was working it out in therapy, how abusive the relationship was, and how she shouldn't let herself be near him. But she would want him so badly at the same time.

She put notes on her phone. Do Not Call Artie. She wrapped masking tape around the phone so she couldn't pick it up and call. She ripped the phone out by the roots.

She threw the phone through the front window.

The suicidal urges would come. She would decide to take all her animals and put them in her car and drive it off the cliff into the Pacific. She would have to take her animals, she thought. Who would take care of Mr. T and the cats if she were gone?

She would take the car keys then, and try to hide them from herself so she wouldn't really do it.

But still, Artie would come out. Sometimes, he would bring the kids, and they'd all stay at Missy's house. For a few hours, it would be great. They'd all go out to dinner, watch TV, go for walks on the beach. But it wouldn't stay great. It would revert to ugliness and violence.

One night they all came out and the kids went to sleep in sleeping bags in Missy's living room and she and Artie decided to go down the street to the Sand Dollar and have a quick bite of dinner. Artie had been drinking, and the waitress came to take their order and he said, what's your name and how well do you give head?

Missy was horrified. Everything she had been hearing in her therapy came rushing back to her, and she realized how denigrating to women he was, and especially to her, and how he was treating her disrespectfully, and how terrible it was to be out on a date with this guy who was trying to convince you to come back with him, whose kids were asleep on your floor, for God's sake, and have him pull this.

So she got up and walked out of the restaurant without a word. She just went home. That was something she'd never done when he had embarrassed her in public before. This was not like going to a porno theater in your pajamas after your man, or talking the Mexican police out of arresting him when he beat you in public. This was a normal, nonsubmissive reaction. Get up and leave.

He came raging into her house and said, "What the fuck do you think you're doing, you bitch?"

And she said, "Get the fuck out, I'm through with you." The kids hearing the whole thing now, Missy really letting it out, screaming, "I'm sick of you and your shit, I'm sick of the way you treat women, I'm sick of the way you talk to me, I'm sick of you, I HATE YOU!"

Then he hit her. Again and again, knowing it was finally over and he had lost her, and then she was down on the deck, and he kicked her, and bent over in his alcoholic defeated frenzy and grabbed a handful of blonde hair and lifted her head up and wham! banged it into the deck. Again and again and again.

And he gathered the horrified kids up and left her, unconscious and bleeding, on the deck.

When she came to, Missy didn't know what to do. She was still ashamed, wanting to keep it all a secret, and in her muzzy-headed sadness didn't want to call 911, call an ambulance, didn't want the neighbors to know, there are only two hundred people in town and they would all know he beat her, God. So she called a friend who was a volunteer emergency medical guy for the fire department and he and a friend came right over and treated her. They were worried that she might have a concussion or subcranial bleeding and so they called Missy's sister who lived there, and asked her to come over and spend the night with her, keep her awake through the night so she wouldn't slip into a coma.

The next morning, Karen Mitchell called, and asked, are you all right? Because Artie had brought the kids over and left them and Aaron had told her that Artie had beaten Missy up because she deserved it.

Missy said, I'm okay, and Karen asked her to call when she was feeling better because she'd like to help Missy press charges, help her go to the police and prove that Artie is an abuser of women. My kids witnessed this, she said.

Thanks, Karen, Missy said. I can't really talk to you, I'm really not okay.

She was dazed and hurt. And the beating had torn something final loose in her. He had beaten her unconscious and left her for dead. And he was carrying a gun. She realized that one of them was going to be killed, probably her, if she saw him anymore.

It had dragged out over so much time. She moved, he moved, she moved. It was ridiculous. She promised herself, this is the last time he is going to beat me.

But that didn't mean the pain was over. She still missed him like a body part that had been amputated, and she was bitter and sad and miserable, and she drank too much. One night in May, she went to a birthday party for her friend the San Francisco political consultant Jack Davis, and got smashed, and started thinking about Artie, and drove all the way out to Moraga from San Francisco.

And when she got there, Joanne Scott's car was in the driveway.

She was drunk and damned disgusted. She tried the front door and it was locked, and so she went around and beat on the bedroom windows and saw that Joanne was in there, and she went in the back door and opened the bedroom door and saw them in bed together, which enraged her all the more.

"Artie yelled, 'Missy, if you come in here I've got a gun and I'll call the police.' And I said, 'Which are you going to do, use the gun or call the police? I can't believe you're fucking that swine in there.'

"And he locked the door and I started kicking the door, and I hit the door so hard with my little pink high heel that I got it stuck in the door, and I left it there and walked out."

So she had to go sheepishly to group therapy that week and tell them: "I had sort of an attack, I couldn't take it, I'd been drinking and lost my sense of judgment, gave in to my gutter senses, and I left my high heel stuck in the door."

• • •

Joanne had known there was a lot of tension between Artie and Missy. You could see it after a while. Art seemed really unhappy.

"It wasn't like he wasn't still into it, he was, all the games and everything, but there was this hostility. When they would come to the theater together, you could tell that he knew he couldn't flirt with the girls right in front of her, and that was hard for him to deal with.

"He wanted me to be there, but he wanted her too. You know, it was like the time we did the three-way. You would think he would want that kind of sex with women who were at least on cordial terms, but I think part of the excitement for him was the drama and tension between the women.

"He encouraged us to hate each other, and we did."

He was always trying to make Joanne jealous, because he thought it would make the sex even hotter. He loved to get his women completely emotionally engaged in fucking him, so that each one was trying to prove to him every time that she, not that other slut, was the best woman for him.

Also, like a stage actor, he knew how to time his entrances and exits for maximum effect.

"He loved for me to actually believe I'd lost him, and then be so happy when he'd suddenly turn up," Joanne says. "After a few years, I could almost tell the timing of it perfectly. I'd kind of know that, no, he wasn't gone, he was just around the corner, ready to show up, teasing me, making those little quick phone calls to me.

"And it did make it very erotic."

Even today, Joanne marvels at his mastery over her, how he masterminded the whole effort, balancing people against one another, making it all work to his advantage.

"Even wanting to do that is incredible. I mean, I'm not somebody who thinks in terms of, 'What if I had five boyfriends and I kept them all begging for me, insanely jealous of each other?' But he not only wanted it, thought it all out, but he did it, pulled it off. Unbelievable."

After *Behind the Green Door: The Sequel,* the Mitchells pretty much abandoned the safe sex shtick and went right back to the old reliable, raunchy, nonstop sex.

Their next big movie, and the last full-length feature they produced, was another sequel of a sort, this one *Grafenberg Girls Go Fishing.* It starred a superheated Brazilian porno queen, Ellie Rio, and despite a few obligatory squirts of Nonoxynol 9 here and there, the sex was unfettered by safety concerns. There was anal sex. Quite remarkably, there were two men penetrating the same woman's vagina at the same time, neither wearing condoms. And there were some scenes that, at least metaphorically, were evocative of abusive situations, like Ellie Rio having sex with her head in the toilet.

Much of it was filmed out on the *Graciosa,* the Mitchells' big boat, and Joanne would play an important role.

First of all, Jim wanted a messenger boy to deliver a telegram to Ellie and her "Grafenberg Girls" at the beginning (and, of course, stay for some high-jinks with them in the opening orgy scene). But he needed a messenger boy costume, something like the old Philip Morris look, with the organ grinder monkey hat and everything. So again he turned to Joanne the seamstress, and asked her to make one for the show. He gave her all of two days, but she did it. And she took it down to the theater to deliver it. And deliver Artie some oral sex.

Then she went out with Artie to the *Graciosa* so the costume could be fitted, and to watch the filming of the major sex scenes. And who should show up but Missy.

"She was boat-hopping, calling out at the top of her lungs, "Artie! Artie!" In her little pink sweats. I couldn't believe how loud she was.

"Of course she was really pissed off that I was there, and she kept walking past me muttering things like 'Trash! Slut! Whore!' you know. Then when they started filming, she was down in the cabin watching, and saying, 'Artie! This isn't safe sex! You can't do this! They've got to be wearing condoms!'

"And one of the male stars went over to Jim and said, who the hell is this, get her out of here or we're gone, or something like that, and they finally got her above decks again, away from it."

But Joanne didn't know yet about her starring role in the movie.

When the film was in the can and the brothers started editing, they discovered, as they so often did, that somehow, unaccountably, despite all the money they spent and all the precautions they took, that almost all the sound was screwed up. They had an incredibly hot movie with no sound. For some reason, despite all their fanaticism about production values, sound problems were almost a Mitchell Brothers trademark.

So they decided to mix in new sound. For part of it, they got girls from the theater to sit around the office with the tape running, making moaning, screaming, groaning, sucking sounds. But for some of it, that wasn't enough. They wanted something better. So Artie nobly volunteered to produce a lot of the new sound. With Joanne.

So they had some, well, screaming sex, in the office, with the tape rolling. Joanne had never done audio for a porno movie before, but she sure enjoyed the assignment, and she gave it her all. Her frenzied cries of pleasure and Artie's low-pitched commands (Suck it! Take it!) certainly add some energy to the production, although Joanne offers a critical note: "I'm so in love with him that you can hear my emotions when we're making love. When I screamed, it was coming from some special place inside me, and it doesn't go well with all the casual sex on the screen."

After they finished the movie, the brothers played it at the theater, and the first time they turned the sound way up. Joanne heard it and freaked out. "Missy was still around then," she said. "I often wondered if she heard it and knew it was us.

"I hoped she did."

Joanne remembers the night Missy showed up at the Moraga house quite vividly. "I couldn't resist showing her I was there," she said. "I didn't know if she recognized my car or not because I'd just gotten it. So I was glad when she saw me with him.

"After that, I think she kind of gave up her dream of marrying him," Joanne said.

Just before Thanksgiving 1987, Artie jumped up on the pool table, slipped and landed on the 8 ball, cracking a rib. A typical Artie injury. He was in considerable pain, which made him drink more.

At the annual Thanksgiving weekend lowball tournament, which he had won the year before, he came in to find all the other players wearing baseball caps with the logo, "Beat Art."

Fat chance.

He was loaded up with painkillers, and drunk, and very tough, and soon he had hundreds of chips in front of him.

Still, the craziness was taking its toll. About a week later, Artie was reaching a pressure point. Too many drugs, too many drinks, too many hassles with Karen. He and Jim were at each other's throats, Jim getting on him for his coking and drinking and being crazy. And his side hurt like hell.

One day he called the theater and said, "Tell Jim I want $10,000 in a bag or I'll Molotov cocktail the lobby!" Whoever received this message saw the wisdom in putting Jim on the line, and Art repeated, "I want ten thousand in a paper bag. I'm sending Joanne down to get it."

Jim replied, "Five thousand now, five thousand later."

Joanne went down to get the money. As Jim gave it to her, he shook his head and said, "Artie's a cokehead. If you need more money, call."

Joanne had rarely seen Artie so tense and miserable. Confrontations with his brother were the worst.

They got in his car and headed south. Slowly, as they made their way down the coast toward Mexico, he began to relax. The farther south they went, the calmer he got. By the time they got to Cabo San Lucas, Artie was his old self again, and they had a great time. They went deep-sea fishing and Artie caught a 100-pound striped marlin.

"God, I'm tired of living up there in all that fog," Artie told Joanne. "Maybe I don't need to anymore. Maybe we could live down here in Mexico, get a big house." Artie's flair for the grandiose started kicking in. "Maybe it could be big enough so that Karen and the kids could live there."

"Right," said Joanne dryly. "But on one condition. Missy has to move in too."

As idyllic as it was, Artie began to get edgy after two weeks. He couldn't wait to get back. To his kids. And to the O'Farrell. By the time they got back to San Francisco, he made a beeline for the place. He needed to know that despite his crazy antics, it was still there for him, his playground, his security, his life.

As always, Jim welcomed him back, repressing his anger about the threats, the money, the deterioration of his little brother.

Tightening the screw another quarter turn.

Slowly, Missy recovered. The therapy sessions were helpful. She began to find out that she wasn't so different from a lot of people who had similar problems with alcoholic, abusive men. She met other people who had grown up with alcohol in their families, and had been used to needing an alcoholic, and to an alcoholic needing them.

She found that she wasn't the only one who kept going back. She met a woman who kept going back to her coke dealer husband, another who kept returning to her crazy ex-husband even though he'd thrown her through a window. She was told that a relationship can be an addiction, just like alcohol or cocaine, that you feel you need that chaos, you need to be needed, and you can sort of feel it coming and have a big burst and then come down from it.

Like a junkie and a fix.

Then, for a while, she tried to cover the pain up by drinking a lot herself. Screw it, she thought, I'm just going to drink and party and have fun. In the month after the Moraga high-heel incident, she was arrested for DUI three times. She came back to earth with a bang.

That month of craziness was expensive. The three DUIs cost her more than $7,000, and the court ordered her to do a year-long drug and alcohol rehabilitation. Also, she had to do hundreds of hours in a community service work program.

"That was totally humiliating. I had to do all my work at the beach, and all my friends saw me. I had to paint the curbs, paint the bathrooms, pick up cigarette butts, the works.

"Artie thought it was so funny."

Then came one of the cruelest things he ever did to her.

"One day I was on my hands and knees, painting curbs, and I look up and there was Artie and his new girlfriend, Kristal, and they were sitting on a bench making out in front of me, kissing and hugging and groping. It looked like he was trying to remove her tonsils. It was so awful, so mean. He was trying to reassert his dominance over me, make me jealous, take advantage of a denigrating situation. It hurt me a lot, and I was crying when they left."

Kristal Rose Lee is a red-haired Nebraska-born Norwegian hippie chick with freckles, a twenty-six-year-old body and a fourteen-year-old face, and when he saw her, Artie did *not* want to let her get away.

The occasion of their acquaintance was—surprise—the night she entered and won an amateur night contest at the O'Farrell.

"This wild character comes running up to me and starts babbling, 'You're the best dancer I've ever seen you've got to come work here right away my home number's on this card call me anytime when can you start?' I didn't know who the fuck he was, but I thought, 'This guy's a fucking crazy man, I've got to get out of here.' "

Vaughn, who was running the amateur night as usual, had given her a card with Vince's number on it. She kept that and threw Artie's card away. A week later, on August 12, 1988, she called Vince and got hired. She started right away.

"At first I was petrified," she said. "The only time I'd had to dance totally nude was at the Lusty Lady, and that was all behind glass."

A few days later, she was standing in the back of the theater, screwing up her courage to go trolling for tips, when the same weirdo she'd seen that first night ambled up to her. "How'd you like to smoke this with me?" he said, and showed her an enormous joint.

Still thinking he was some loony sex freak, which of course he *was*, she eyed the joint longingly but said, "You can't do that here, sir. It's a public place and there are laws against it."

"You can do it if you're the boss," he said, and dug a lighter out of his jeans and fired it up. Astounded, she took the joint as he handed it to her, a smile dawning on her face. "Let's finish it up in my office," Artie said, and she was his.

Later she would say, "It sounds hokey but I think I fell in love with him right then."

Again, Artie had been shrewd about both the woman and his approach to her. Kristal would walk a mile for a good joint, and she loved sex. That gave her two important things in common with him.

Their first date was less than auspicious. A couple of days later he invited her to a party at Charlie Benton's house, and she went, but she'd done a lot of drugs, and she was nodding out, couldn't stay conscious. "He was really ticked off. He put me in a cab and said, 'Call me when you wake up.' "

She did call, and apologized to him, and then the fun began. They started going out every night, having sex brazenly and constantly, all over town.

By the fall of 1988, Artie was getting sick of living out in Moraga. Karen had moved from her house on Pine Street in the city to Corte Madera, a village in Marin County, and he hated having the kids so far away. For one thing, the drive back and forth took too much of his precious time with them on the weekends.

So he had Joanne Scott scout around for a place in Marin, and in September, she found one. It was the only house with a for-rent sign that Joanne found that day in Corte Madera.

They went and looked at it together. It was nothing fancy, but the house at 23 Mohawk had just what he wanted—three bedrooms, a pool, and proximity to his children. The rent was modest by Artie's standards—$1,500 a month.

Artie had Joanne, whom he had introduced to the landlord as his wife, deliver a check for the first month's rent plus deposit. But he delayed moving in until October, because he still had a nice pot crop to harvest in Moraga.

When he did move in, he found he was really comfortable in the place. It was a 1950s-vintage tract house, pleasantly updated. And it was just a few blocks from the kids' school. Karen's house was about a mile away.

He particularly liked the large main bathroom, remodeled from a bedroom. It was big enough to stroll around in, and it had a huge skylight. He put a TV in it so the kids could play Nintendo while they were taking their baths. The den had bunk beds—perfect if the kids wanted to have friends sleep over—and he put two huge fish tanks in the foyer. He even hung the pictures on the wall at kid level.

"This place is for the little people," he said.

Martha Rauber was looking for a job that fall. The slim redheaded divorcee needed something that would pay better than her current waitressing job. She had a five-year-old daughter, and Marin County was not an inexpensive place to live.

A girlfriend, Claudia Schimmer, told her about the guy who had moved into 23 Mohawk. He's really cool, Schimmer said. He's got plenty of money, and he has his kids on the weekends. He's bound to need a housekeeper. Maybe we could both keep house for him.

To Martha it sounded sort of doubtful, but, she thought, what the hell, it might work. So when she and Claudia were walking past the Mohawk house on Halloween night, she agreed to go up and meet Artie.

As if she had a choice. Artie loved Halloween, and just happened to be hanging out in his front yard.

Wearing a Zorro costume with a big black cape.

He came up on the two women like a vampire, the cape billowing around him, and started joking around with them. He took an immediate liking to Martha, with her eye-catching figure and friendly smile. When they talked, he could see right away how much she loved her daughter, and that was something he could relate to. When the subject of housekeeping came up, he said, "All right!"

She started work the next day.

Claudia started work too, but there wasn't enough for both of them to do and Artie soon jettisoned her when it was apparent she was spending a lot of time with Karen.

There was certainly plenty for Martha to do. The kids would come over on the weekends, and often before or after school, despite the fact that they weren't supposed to. Afterward, the house would be destroyed, every dish dirty, junk all over everywhere. Artie couldn't stand that, but he hated doing housework even more, so Martha was a lifesaver. Soon she was going over seven days a week.

For a while she would go up and babysit for Karen, but Artie demanded that she make a choice. Either stay away from her or get out, he said. I can't have you both places. Karen is too devious and she'll use you to get to me somehow.

"She's a vicious cunt swine and she'll get you in the end," he raged.

Martha quickly made her choice. She worshiped Artie and she wanted to be with him, and that was that.

He did pay her generously. He appreciated loyalty and hard work, and she gave him both in great measure. Soon, he came to depend on her for a variety of help. Not only would she clean the house, but she would run errands for him, even come back in the evening and cook dinner for him and Kristal or Joanne or whoever was with him.

Of course, he made a few passes. They necked a little, and he would say, "Come on, let's go smoke a joint in the bedroom," and she knew him well enough to figure out what that meant. She did think he was sexy, and it was hard to say no to him about anything. But she didn't want to jeopardize the rest of her relationship with him, or her job, and so she passed.

A little regretfully.

Kristal Rose is a little chubby, but somehow it doesn't detract. It reinforces her little-girl look, as if she had a little bit of residual baby fat, and looking like a little girl is a marketable asset in the sexual circus of the Mitchell Brothers. She also has lovely carrot-red hair, freckles, and wild memories of her time with Artie.

"Of course I knew when he was screwing around with Joanne down at the theater," she says. "I mean, I was fucking him six times a day. It was pretty obvious when he wasn't, you know, up for it.

"I just said, 'Go have your fun, dude, but come back to me. I loved him so much. We'd get so stoned and so into each other that we didn't care who was around when we did it. He'd lick my pussy for *hours*."

Kristal elaborates: "I had this fantasy about doing it in a limo, so we used to take limos around town often when we went out. Once we ordered one to take us from the Waterfront Restaurant down to Slim's. As the guy drove us, my legs were sticking out the sunroof, and Artie was sucking me like there was nothing else in the world. My legs were kicking back and forth up there as we drove through the city and the driver was so embarrassed that when we got to Slim's he didn't have the balls to say anything, and we didn't notice that the limo had stopped until we heard the crowd outside Slim's. They were applauding."

But the doorman didn't approve, and he wouldn't let them into the club, which enraged Artie. "He tried the 'Don't you know who I am' trip, but I could see it wasn't working, so I talked him into leaving, getting back in the limo, and pretty soon my legs were kicking back and forth again."

That was part of a studied pattern. "We loved to fuck in public," Kristal said. "Artie was always testing people's reactions. He'd want to see how they reacted to us. We would fuck on the drop of a hat, just to see what people would do. And I loved it. I'd just say, go for it, dude. You've got balls, I've got just as much as you."

A few weeks after they started seeing each other, Artie and Kristal showed up at the theater with wedding rings on. It was a trademark Artie goof, but of course it wasn't really that funny. Joanne was mortified. And even for Kristal, it wasn't too neat to have to keep telling people, no, she really didn't marry Artie.

"He told the whole world we were married. It took over two years to live that down. Everybody thought we were married. I'd say, I'm not married to him, and girls would say, you're lying, you're totally lying. He said you were and he wouldn't lie to us. And I'd say, 'God, you guys are total fools. I wouldn't believe a fucking word he said.' "

Joanne knew he was seeing Kristal, of course. He wasn't coming over as often, and she had heard things down at the theater. But the wedding thing really upset her. She knows it was just like Artie to do it, but she blames Kristal too.

"Fallon, another dancer my age, had told Kristal at the theater one day that Artie and I had a thing going, that I really loved him, had been seeing him for years, and he always came back to me. I think it made her really jealous.

"Then a few days later, he showed up at my apartment wearing a cheap gold-braided wire gold ring, like you'd buy from a street vendor.

"I asked him, 'What's that, did you get married?' And he said, 'No, would it matter?' "

That brought nothing but a glare in response, so he said, "Well, you can take it off with your teeth and throw it down the toilet if you want."

Joanne took it off the way he told her to, but she kept it. She has it today.

Then, a few days later, both of them showed up at the theater wearing wedding rings, and Artie told everyone they were married. Joanne was stunned. She was half done putting shelf paper in Artie's kitchen, for God's sake. She thought she would be moving back into the house at 23 Mohawk that she had found for him. Instead, this!

Now she realizes that it was just another little device of Artie's to increase the tension in both relationships, to inspire jealousy and test loyalties, but she blames Kristal too. "It was a really mean thing for her to play along with. Very low-class. I'm sure she went into a pawnshop and bought the rings. He could never bring himself to do that, I don't think, because the idea of marriage was actually really abhorrent to him after the Karen fiasco."

Joanne says, "I imagine that from her perspective, she thought, 'Here's this older woman, she'll be so humiliated by thinking he got married that she'll just drop it and go away.' " She sure wasn't going to do that, but it was a bitter, bitter pill to swallow. Here was the man she loved forever and always, her soulmate, scuffling around with a little hippie chick fifteen years younger than he was. And she was prancing around the theater wearing his ring.

Mrs. Art Mitchell.

Joanne had been through a lot with Artie, and she knew all she could do was grit her teeth and ride it out. "I tried to ignore it, and basically I did, but it wasn't long before Christmas, and it sure screwed up my fucking holiday," she says.

Another Christmas, shot to hell, by another girlfriend. She was getting used to it.

No, they weren't really married, but the relationship between Kristal and Artie *was* clicking along nicely. Her own drinking and drug use was prodigious, but she was often still able to get him out of threatening situations. And her substance abuse was a useful bit of protective coloration. When they talked about a drinking problem, it was *her* problem they discussed. Not his.

She was sexually voracious. He swore that she was going to wear him out. "You've got to ease up on me," he would complain good-naturedly.

"Shut up," Kristal would say. "How many guys get to complain, 'My old lady's fucking me to death?' You love it."

God, did he love it. She would make love with him at the theater, in the bathroom, in the office, backstage. She would jump on him at home, first thing in the morning. She used to hate it when he'd sneak out for an early game of golf because she would have to get up in the morning without sex.

"I practically raped him a few times when he was too tired," she remembers fondly. "It got so that he took to sneaking up on me, trying to fuck me in my sleep. He'd say it was safer that way, that I was killing him, and if I woke up I'd wear him out. I'd pretend to get mad and say, don't you want me to remember it? And he'd say, 'You'll have enough to remember for a lifetime, honey.' "

Also, she had a great attitude about him playing around.

"Everybody else was always clinging to him, like, you're mine. I didn't want to be head-tripped so why head-trip him, you know? But I knew every time. I mean, we were together like glue, and he'd make some weird excuse. He used to tell me that he had to fuck the headliners when they came in to the theater, like it was business, it was expected of him, it was in their contract or something. He was such a riot. Such a bad boy. It would totally crack me up, he's so full of shit. He knew I was hip to him. I would just say, 'Okay, dude, when are you picking me up after, when are we going out?'

"Sometimes he'd fuck them with me at the theater, and it wouldn't bother me at all. I'd say, 'You're not doing it right, dude, you're boring me,' and he'd get all wild.

"I would tell him, 'Right on, go ahead. I know what you are, Artie. Just come back to me.' I mean, why not? Sex was his life. I wasn't there to tie him down. He couldn't understand it because he'd never gone out with anybody like that before."

Actually, Kristal says, she learned a lot from Artie about loving someone, or several someones. "He was the one who taught me that you could love a lot of people at the same time," she says. "I knew he was with Joanne the whole time he was with me, and that was never an issue."

Of course, the old double standard came into play. Artie didn't like her going off on acid-soaked weekends when the Grateful Dead had a gig somewhere.

"I really didn't fuck around at the Dead shows much, but I did when I went home, I fucked all my old boyfriends, and he'd know it. He'd bust me for it. But I would just cop to it, admit it, tell the truth, and that would blow him away. How mad could he get when I told him the truth?"

As much fun as they had, she wasn't totally into his domination games.

"I used to say, 'Artie, I love you, I'll fuck you silly, I don't give a fuck about your money, just as long as you love me and don't boss me around.' I wasn't into that slave stuff, like 'Come here and suck my balls right now.' "

Kristal claims he was never abusive with her, although she admits that he hit her "a few times." But, she is quick to add, she deserved it. "I would usually hit him first. We would have fights all the time. We kind of enjoyed it. He loved to argue.

"But when we really would fight, I would start it, say to him, 'Come on, let me see some of your shit, I want to know what's going on, why you're being such a dick,' and I would hit him.

"And he would hit me back, and then he'd be sorry, and then he'd come out with it: Karen's doing this to me, whatever. Usually that's what it would be, her fucking with him over the kids.

"God, he was sick of that. He'd gone through so much. He didn't want to give up his cubs. His cubs were his world. Little Jasmine, Aaron, and Caleb were just his world. He would go sometimes three times a week to play ball with his boys. It was like, you didn't mess with him those times. That was his thing. He'd say, 'These are my boys and we're going to have fun. You can either come with us or if you're tired you can stay here, take Jasmine shopping, whatever, but we're going.' You never messed with that time with his boys."

She contends that the others who say he was abusive provoked him. "Missy, I like her, but I think she caused a lot of it. And Karen. God. She says, he used to beat the shit out of me, but God, she deserved it.

"I was with him for all that time, more than two years, and he never hurt me," she says. "Sometimes he would show me who was boss. I can understand that. But he never beat the hell out of me. He treated me so good damn near all the time that I got spoiled, and when he wasn't like that I complained."

Of course, the best part of their fights was making up. "He was so good at it," she remembers. "He was just the best. He'd had so much practice."

Sometimes the sex was rough, but she liked it. "He would get me down on the floor, just like I wanted him to. Artie was a man. I respected his strength." Kristal pauses, then says, in her bad-girl way, still trying to act tough, but with the betrayal of tears forming in her eyes: "What can I say? Artie was the best fuck of my life. No doubt about it."

In the summer of 1988, Karen announced that she was pregnant. With twins.

At various times, she would claim that they were fathered by:

- Artie, one night when they got together for old times' sake;
- a well-to-do (and married) San Francisco businessman;
- an Australian "handyman" who briefly rented a room in her Corte Madera home;
- an anonymous "ship in the night."

Almost from their conception, Austin and Karlan would be footballs in various vicious scrimmages over money.

On December 12, Karen gave birth. That event may have had something to do with Artie's behavior that month, which was crazed even by his standard. His drinking and drugging had hit another peak.

There was the wedding ring joke with Kristal. Then the scene at the O'Farrell with Lady T. And then, just a couple of days later, New Year's Eve.

This time, even Kristal would get her fill of it. She had been after him to go to a Grateful Dead concert with her. They were playing a New Year's Eve gig in Berkeley, and he said, okay, we'll go. So he did a huge load of acid and they headed into San Francisco for dinner at Izzy's steak house, one of his favorite haunts.

But there were too many bare wires sizzling and popping in Artie's head this night. He ran around the restaurant with an open beer bottle, doing one of his trademark stunts, cawing like a crow, at top volume. Kristal watched him as he waltzed around, holding the bottle to his mouth, and shouting: "Caw! Caw! Caw!" into it. The other customers looked at him with nervous disgust.

And for good reason. He came back over to Kristal at the bar, and said to her matter-of-factly, "I was just trying to bottle my Caw," then looked at the neatly coiffed, ample, sixty-ish matron who was next to her at the bar, eyeing them with haughty disfavor. The woman was dressed in a fur and an evening dress.

Artie said, "Breasts! God, I love them!" And bit the woman on one of hers.

She screamed, really came unglued, and the manager did too. "Get him out of here before I call the fucking police!" he yelled, the woman still screaming, as Kristal got Artie, protesting, out the door.

"Fuck you, I'm going to the theater," he said.

"Okay, dude, but I'm going to the concert," Kristal replied.

"Go ahead," he said, and she did. He took a cab to the O'Farrell.

He reeled into the dressing room, pinching butts, ordering this dancer or that to go with him to Berkeley. When he got no takers, he tried to choke one dancer. Another woman who was relatively friendly to him pulled him off and told him, "Remember lawsuits, Artie. Be cool."

He took a marker and started scrawling on the dressing room walls, things like "SLUTS" and "BITCHES." Then he decided he'd liven up the stage show in the New York Live. He went out and joined one dancer onstage—with a garbage can over his head and body. As she tried to dance, he staggered blindly around the stage.

He went out when another woman was on and started singing loudly during her act. Finally, to get him out of there, the night manager agreed to drive him over to the concert, but Kristal had taken the tickets. At the gate, he tried the usual: "I'm Artie Mitchell, let me in!" But

Grateful Dead security is used to weird acidheads, and he got nowhere, so he returned to the theater, then went to Joanne's.

"I was really worried about him around that time," she remembers. "He and Kristal were drinking so much, and he was doing so much coke and other drugs. He would come over and pass out and I'd be so scared for him."

New Year's Eve was too much, but on most occasions, Kristal matched him stride for stride. She was a full and happy collaborator.

Once, when they were with one of Artie's friends, the talented saxophonist Tony Pérez, going out to dinner in North Beach, he stopped at the busy corner of Grant and Green, and made Kristal lie down right on the sidewalk, the busiest time of the day, and got down on his knees and rubbed her crotch with his bald head.

He looked up and said to Pérez, "Now isn't that the best head you've ever seen?"

One of the weapons Artie loved to use for punishment was to withhold vacation trips from his women. He would dangle the trips as incentive, then sometimes snatch them away at the last minute and—worst of all—award them to a rival.

He did this repeatedly to both Joanne and Kristal, and he played them off against each other mercilessly on the issue. On one trip, to Mexico, he promised each of them the trip, then ended up taking neither.

Traveling with him was such a coup—to be able to relax with him, to have him all to yourself for an extended period. Both women longed to take the trips, as Missy had.

Joanne had taken quite a few. She wrote about one of them in her *Spectator* piece.

One night, she wrote, he called her and asked her, "Do you still want that certain something in your mouth?"

She did, of course, so he came over. He had to go to New York in the morning, he said, to go to Al Goldstein's party for the twentieth anniversary of *Screw* magazine. Her neighbors were noisy, and they couldn't sleep, she writes, so they "fucked and talked all night."

At six in the morning, two hours before the flight, he told her, "You know, I think I'll take you."

Joanne was stunned and incredibly happy. When they got to the airport, she found that he had already reserved two first-class seats under the names "Mr. and Mrs. Artie Mitchell," and realized he had probably been planning to take her all along, but had decided to surprise her at the last minute.

On the plane, she reports, Artie pointed to a stewardess and told Joanne, "She wants to suck your daddy's dick," to which Joanne replied, "I know." Then, she writes, they "went upstairs into the lounge to scout the bathroom for possible fucking—too many people around" and had to settle for some skilled groping in their first-class seats. Artie, she reports, "spread my fox coat over my lap . . . and fingered me to orgasm. Neither of us cared if we were noticed." She remembers that he said to her, "Scary, isn't it, how I know more about your pussy than you do?"

Of course, a limo met them at La Guardia, and although Joanne hadn't seen New York City since 1964, she wasn't destined to see much on the trip into Manhattan. Artie demanded oral sex in the back of the limo, and demanded that Joanne call him "Master," to impress, arouse, and "educate" the driver.

So of course she complied. "I began to get a bit carsick sucking with my head down as we entered Manhattan," Joanne says. Artie told her, "I want to fuck a girl with black pubic hair tonight," thus limiting the field to probably four million New Yorkers. "Will you find one for me?" Joanne promised him she would.

They got to Elaine's for dinner at five, and not surprisingly, the place was nearly empty. So they sat in the back and—yes—never mind the fact that they "fucked and talked" all night without sleep, never mind the high jinks on the plane, in the limo—they had sex, right there in Elaine's. "We held hands, Artie unzipped his pants and I gave him a hand job the whole time we were sitting there. The waiters knew it and it was making them crazy." No doubt. "When they came close, we went back to just holding hands," she wrote. "And twice, while they were over by the kitchen, I bent lower and sucked his dick."

We get a further glimpse into Artie's sexuality when we join the tourist couple atop the Empire State Building. Joanne has some fear of heights, and she was terrified. Artie realized it, and they left, but later he told her, "You were creeping around like a mouse up there. It made my dick hard."

At the Goldstein party, Artie told Al, "Well, you made it. You lasted twenty goddamn years. Despite the pigs, despite everything, you lasted. I take my hat off to you, Al. Anybody who lasts twenty goddamn years has to be pretty tough, and pretty special, in this business."

Just like Artie.

. . .

After she had been out of the relationship for more than a year, Missy met the man she would marry, with whom she would have her two children.

Occasionally, they would see Artie socially, and usually it came off okay, but one night Artie got all negative and weird, and on the way to dinner at the Waterfront, another favorite Mitchell hangout, he took off on one of his wild antiwoman diatribes, telling her fiancé, "If I was ever going to marry anybody it would have been Manners, but she's a real nutcracker, I'll tell you that much. And any guy who wants to get married is just fucking himself anyway. I tell you, I had my nuts cut off (apparently a reference to his vasectomy, which would become a matter of great controversy after his death) because I didn't want to marry another one of those bitches because all they do is take you to the fucking cleaners with their thief lawyers."

And Missy turned around and said, "If you're quite finished we can go to dinner."

At the restaurant, Artie put the eye on two women at a table nearby. ("He thought they were twins, but they weren't," Missy remembers. "Just a couple of hookers dressed alike.") Kristal was zonked too, and she stood on top of the table in her black leather boots and miniskirt, and yelled, "Twins, twins, come over here, the ones Artie's looking at, that's right, you're looking at him too, come over here."

For Missy, it must have been an evening of conflicting emotions. She used to be the one who was out being crazy with Artie, dressed in nothing but a slip, taking off her underwear at the bar, going home with strangers for wild sex. Now here she was, a bemused spectator, starting on a new, more stable life, without the abuse and the weirdness. Without some of the excitement too.

"Come over here, twins," Kristal yelled again. "Artie wants a twin fuck."

They came.

In so many ways, Kristal was a surprisingly good fit with Artie. She loved spending time with his kids. Her youth, and her looks, made her seem like one herself—after all, she's only five years older than his oldest daughter, Liberty—and, indeed, he used to introduce her as "Kristal, my seventh kid."

Like Missy, she became really attached to Artie's kids, particularly the three little ones.

"I treated those kids like they were my own," she says. "Little Jasmine really related to me, and I think she really needed me, still does. Not as a substitute mom or anything, just as a big sister, to tell stuff to, to ventilate."

Also, Kristal was really easygoing, and most of the time managed to keep him that way. Like Martha Rauber, she knew how to calm Artie down. Of course, Kristal employed some tactics to keep him calm that went beyond Martha's diplomacy and calm nature. If sex is a drug, Kristal kept him dosed all the time.

Sometimes he would treat her more like a male friend than a girlfriend. He would take her golfing. He would trade dirty jokes with her. He would laughingly tell her about all the reasons women had to sleep with someone. "There's pity pussy, where they're really sorry for you. There's revenge pussy, where they're getting back at somebody else by fucking you. There's courtesy pussy, where they think it's the civilized thing to do under the circumstances." He went on and on. He had a long list.

"It's all good," he would say with a leer and a laugh.

She matched his sense of humor about sexual matters. When Artie's landlord, working on the swimming pool one day, was obviously embarrassed by the fact that Kristal was sunbathing nude in the yard, she made a pretense—at Artie's behest—of going over to look for something near the pool, bending over about six inches from the landlord's nose. Artie choked with laughter as Arnold the landlord turned purple.

Still, Artie and Kristal did fight a lot. They had several long-term conflicts, and they grew over time. For starters, she and Martha would talk incessantly about the Grateful Dead, about how cute Bob Weir was, didn't he look great now his hair was longer, Bobby this, Bobby that, on and on, playing the Dead on the stereo all the time. Finally, Artie instituted a rule: No Grateful Dead Before 9 A.M. Music or discussions. To torment him, they would wait until 9:01 and crank the stereo. Artie took this relatively good-naturedly. Both Martha and Kristal were good souls, and they both treated him like a king. They could be suffered this indulgence.

But there were more substantive issues.

He hated Kristal's smoking. "You'll be the first girl who breaks up with me over smoking, choosing cigarettes over me," he predicted darkly. (Occasionally, he would confuse Bana and Kristal, and bitch at Bana about smoking. "Wrong girl, Artie, I've never smoked," Bana would say.)

Also, he wanted Kristal there on weekends. Weekends were family time. He wanted her there with the kids, and with him. But Kristal rebelled. Most of her beloved Dead concerts were on the week-ends. Jesus, I'm twenty-three years old, and all I do is look after his kids on the weekends, she thought. I'm too young to be tied down this way.

Now she is full of self-recrimination. "He was right, totally right. I should have done what he wanted. I was too damned selfish and bull-headed," she says.

Of course, Kristal's captivation with the Dead bothered Artie in a larger sense. If anyone was going to have groupies, if anyone was going to be the object of slavish romantic obsession, by God, it was going to be him.

He made this point rather emphatically one day. Debbie Do, Dossett's old girlfriend with whom Artie had maintained an easy, friendly, occasionally sexual relationship over the years, had come over to see Artie. He and Kristal were having a fight, and in the middle of it Artie and Debbie ended up in the garage.

There was a peephole out of the garage that looked out on the front of the house, and Artie asked Debbie to look at it to see if Kristal was coming to the door. When she bent over to do that, he mounted her from behind—just as Kristal opened the door to the garage.

"What the hell is going on?" she stormed, and Debbie said coolly, "Honey, we've been doing this since you were in grade school, and we're going to keep on doing it whenever we like." Kristal left the house in tears.

It just wasn't in the cards for Artie to settle down with Kristal. She was fun for him, and they were really close for a while, but it wasn't a forever trip, and she knew it too. She was just a baby, and she had a lot of life to live, learning to play guitar, going to her concerts, all that stuff. She wasn't really ready to give him the total submission he de-manded, and if she had he would have found some other excuse to break it off. He gently kicked her out of his house in the summer of 1989, although he continued to see her often.

Finally, after seven years of frenzied sex and competition and worry and anger and ups and downs, it was to be Joanne's turn to sit on the throne.

In typical Artie fashion, it started weirdly. Joanne had been thinking for some time about trying to do something besides dancing. She had been helping Vince Stanich, doing the complicated scheduling for the dancers, as a side job for a while. Now she was nearing forty, and dancing was getting to be more and more of a grind.

But she was unprepared and shocked when Artie suddenly fired her that same summer.

She was crushed, again, and then two days later he called and left a message on her machine: "You know I love you. Call me. We're going to Guatemala. I'm not going to say I'm sorry because I'm not. I love you."

So she called, and he told her to come to the office, and there he told her, "Never let anybody tell you you didn't have an illustrious career. But now I need you with me."

She was thrilled, and she really believed this was it, their time was now, he was ready to settle down and he had chosen her, and she began staying with him at the Corte Madera house. It was only right, she thought. A couple of years before, she had picked the place out for him.

And now, her long suffering had paid off, and she would get to share it with him. She had picked this house out with just this day in mind.

Although they didn't go to Guatemala, they did take a nice trip to Mexico, to Zihuatanejo this time, and then settled into the rhythm of life at 23 Mohawk. But if anything was constant in Artie's life, it was change, and Joanne was about to get swept up in it again.

Living with Artie wasn't exactly a breeze for Joanne. He craved action of all kinds, and there were always people dropping by. Kids were a constant presence—Artie's own kids and their friends from all over the neighborhood. Artie loved that. And having Martha come in every morning at 8:30, with her noisy vacuum, the stereo, and her friendly chatter drove Joanne crazy. But that was the way Artie wanted it. Martha had become a really close friend, invaluable to him, and he knew that her schedule worked best if she came right after she dropped her daughter, Hilary, off at school in the morning.

Of course the pressure of Karen was always there. She delighted in calling the cops on Artie, and it bothered Joanne to see it. She was just torturing him, Joanne felt, and it made him crazy with anger. Nothing ever got him as upset as Karen.

And the phone. God, the phone. It was always ringing, and usually it was another bimbo. Artie kept giving his number to new dancers, and they were forever calling, infuriating Joanne. It was hardly the restful, romantic refuge she had fantasized about for so long.

Artie was getting restless too. He wanted more freedom. In a way, it was a compliment to Joanne, in that he didn't want to embarrass her by doing his crazy act with her at home. He preferred to insulate her from it, and of course it had worked just fine for him over the years to have her stashed away in her apartment just a few minutes from the theater.

"I think what happened was, he would get bored and he would want more complication, more involvement. He just wasn't ready for a simple kind of deal. He decided that he wanted to see me, but he wanted to have more freedom."

Joanne hadn't given up the apartment she had had throughout their relationship, so with sadness and resignation, she moved back to it, relinquishing the throne, resuming her role as senior courtesan.

Artie had his breathing room back and he continued to make the most of it. Among the women he saw around that time was porno headliner Heather Hunter, a beautiful young black starlet from Los Angeles who also was having an affair with Magic Johnson.

After Joanne left, Kristal, who had her own place too, started coming over again. When she wasn't going to concerts, her weekends would often be spent with Artie and the kids at 23 Mohawk.

To soften the blow, Artie gave Joanne a good chunk of cash to ease her transition from the O'Farrell economy to the real world. It took her a while to find a straight job (eventually, she landed a position as a legal secretary, the same sort of work she was doing before she went to the theater) but she continued the scheduling thing with Vince, which helped.

A little.

Karen wasted no time in using the twins in an effort to lever more money from Artie. In court papers filed in January 1990, Karen sought to increase the monthly family support she was receiving from Artie from $4,500 to $6,500.

In a supporting declaration, she told the court, "Since entry of the last support order, I have given birth to twins following an exremely difficult pregnancy. I now have five children in my custody. The father of the twins is an Australian national whose whereabouts is uncertain.

"Since the birth of the twins, I have had to refinance my home, all of my credit cards have been used to their limit and the children's needs are not being met satisfactorily. . . . The Court can understand that I have to use the family support for our entire family, and not just . . . the children of our marriage.

"Respondent has orally agreed that he would share the responsibility for the support of the twins. This statement was first made when I was six weeks pregnant and was reaffirmed on numerous occasions."

Karen's statement showed her to be unemployed, and estimated her monthly household expenses to be $8,880. She also claimed that Artie received "unreported business income of $4,000–$8,000 per month which is not taxed."

In his reply brief, Artie's attorney, Eugene Seltzer, denied that Artie had agreed to support the twins. He added that Karen "has not shown a reasonable and realistic regard for her financial circumstances. She has done nothing of significance to advance her own earning potential or her career, contrary to her stated intentions at the time of the original trial. . . . She spends money irresponsibly: she has two cars, one with a car telephone; has recently remodeled her home; and has recently come back from a two-week vacation to Hawaii."

It took several hearings and another six months, but in June Karen was awarded a family support increase to $5,247 per month.

Bana Witt couldn't believe the war with Karen. Over all the years after the divorce, just about every time she went to Artie's house there was a ranting message from Karen on the machine.

"She wants more," Artie would say to Bana, and show her the latest court papers. "Jesus, can you believe it, she wants more."

"You need a divorce from your divorce," Bana Witt told him. But there was none to be had. No escape. No way out.

One of the services Martha performed for Artie was to introduce him to a cop he could trust.

Sergeant Ray DeLeon had been with the Twin Cities Police Department (Corte Madera and Larkspur) and its predecessor, the Corte Madera Police Department, for more than twenty-five years. He was a respected, veteran cop who knew southern Marin as well as anyone in law enforcement.

For several years, he had served as the department's juvenile officer, and he had met Martha in the course of investigating a crime in which a child in her family had been victimized. They became good friends. Just how good would later become an item of hot dispute.

Martha told several friends at the time, and repeated privately after Artie's death, that she had a long-running affair with Ray DeLeon— something he has always vehemently denied.

At any rate, she desperately wanted to get Artie and Ray together. She knew they would like each other, and certainly Artie was all for it. Thanks to Karen, he had already had several run-ins with the Twin Cities Police Department. She would call the cops on him at the drop of a hat. So knowing a senior officer could do nothing but help.

Martha kept asking Ray to come over and meet Artie. Finally, on New Year's Day 1990, Martha saw Ray in his patrol car as she was heading over to Artie's house and flagged him down. "Come on over and meet him," she said in her excited way, and finally he acquiesced. "Okay, okay. I'll stop by in a few minutes."

Martha rushed over to 23 Mohawk. "Quick, put out the joint, Ray DeLeon's coming over!" she said to Art. ("As if he couldn't smell it anyway," she recalls with a laugh.)

Martha was right about one thing: the two men did get along well.

Ray would say later, "Artie Mitchell was funny and honest and smart. He loved his kids, and I respected that. Cops had always been his enemies, and I think he was happy to find a cop that wasn't trying to bust him."

"He's a stud, he's cool, I love him," Artie told Martha. "When things get really bad again with Karen, I'm going to see if he can help."

It didn't take long for him to ask, and Ray DeLeon came through.

Almost immediately after her victory in her request for increased support, Karen went back into court in an effort to modify the custody arrangement in her favor, accusing Artie of drunkenness around the children and a host of other parental transgressions. She also renewed her request for change of venue, urging that the marathon divorce case be transferred from Contra Costa County, where it was filed more than five years earlier, to Marin, where both she and Artie now lived.

Artie had always vigorously and successfully opposed a venue change. Karen claimed that this was because the Contra Costa court unfairly favored him, intimating but never outright charging Artie with paying off a judge. For his part, Art thought the Contra Costa court simply understood what a wacko Karen was, and a new court, without firsthand knowledge of all the things Karen had pulled during the case, might be more easily swayed in her direction.

Now was a perfect time for Artie to play his trump card. He called DeLeon. Ray, he said, the bitch is trying to take my kids away from me. I need your help. Can you write something for me to give to the court? Ray could. In a declaration dated October 12, 1990, he swore to the following:

1. I am a sergeant of the Twin Cities Police Department assigned to the Child Protection Agency.

2. In my employment capacity, I have become familiar with both of the parties in this litigation.

3. In my dealings with Respondent Artie Mitchell, I have seen no evidence of parental neglect or irresponsibility nor any inclination on his part to become intoxicated when he is caring for his children. I have further observed nothing to indicate that the Respondent is becoming progressively more involved in any kind of substance abuse.

4. There have been a number of contacts from Petitioner Karen Mitchell with my agency over the past several years. She has made numerous accusations regarding the respondent, but, to my knowledge, none of them have resulted in any kind of action on behalf of my agency.

Just a week earlier, Aaron had run away from her house and gone to 23 Mohawk, where he told his father that Karen had "beaten him up." Police were called—it is unclear by whom—and Aaron told them Karen had hit him with her fist in the face and stomach. Karen told police she had slapped the twelve-year-old to get him to stop hitting her.

Twin Cities Police Officer Odetto wrote in conclusion, "I noted a great deal of ill will between the two parents, and Aaron against his mother. I also noticed his father was intoxicated. I was unable to determine the validity of the abuse claim. No evidence exists to support either side."

Despite his pleas to stay with Artie, Aaron went home with his mother.

DeLeon's statement, while an admirable example of loyalty and friendship, did stretch credibility a tad. It also infuriated Karen Mitchell. But it was effective: Karen's requests for restraining orders, custody modification, and venue change were denied—only to be refiled in a few weeks.

DeLeon had earned Karen's everlasting enmity. She accused him repeatedly and publicly of being on Artie Mitchell's payroll, and perjuring himself in the declaration to earn his money.

Artie knew better than to put himself at risk by paying DeLeon. He told Martha, "Look, I can't give Ray money. But I do want him to know how much I appreciate this. Do me a favor. Call him up and get him over here one day when I'm not here.

"Take him out to the hot tub and fuck his brains out."

Martha told Artie she would, but she didn't. She says now that her affair with Ray DeLeon was over, and she didn't want to get that started again. DeLeon, of course, maintains to this day that it never started in the first place.

Every once in a while, Artie would talk to Bana about moving in with him. But she knew it wouldn't work, and she knew he didn't really mean it. "Artie, I know what you're doing," she would tell him. "You're in between girlfriends right now and you're just chicken to be alone."

She was right, and he knew it. And appreciated her honesty. "The more brutally honest you were, the better he liked it," she said. "I used to send him poems, seething, vicious lines. And he would call and say, "LaTour, you're great. There's no one like you.""

She was forever sending him poetry. She would send him poems written on her underwear.

As the years passed, Bana realized what a toll the fighting with Karen was taking on him. Artie grew more violent, more misogynistic. He viewed himself as a victim of women, which was a laugh. "He knew more about women than anyone on the planet, and he used it all to his advantage," Bana said.

One night, all coked up, he tried to strangle her. "Back off, motherfucker," she yelled at him, and it worked. "I was the classic battered woman," Bana says. "He would treat me like shit and then he would kiss me and my pulse would accelerate and it would all be forgotten.

"He was merciless."

The 1989 spike heel incident with Danielle Willis was disturbing. Bana knew her because of her poetry, and when Willis wanted to work at the theater, Bana had told Artie, "I've got a fellow poet named Danielle, she's really pretty and she needs a job."

The night of the fight, Artie called Bana in a rage. "You better get down here right away, goddamn it. Your fucking friend just beat the shit out of me."

She went down to the theater, and as she approached the office she could hear Artie screaming. The manager told her, "You better not go in there, he's real drunk."

"Oh, I'm worried," she said, and went in. He started for her with violence in his eyes, and she screamed at him, just as before. It was one of the defining moments in their relationship. He crumpled before her, sat in her lap, and started babbling about Danielle. Then he pulled a gun out of his back pocket, and at the same time started crying. "I could have shot the bitch," he said, the tears running down his face. "I want you to find her and get her not to press charges." She looked at him and saw the incredible sadness of what he had become.

She promised she would find Danielle, and told him, come on, let's get out of here. "No, I won't go, I can't go, I've got work to do here," he said, which was ludicrous because he was totally zonked. "Just find her." So Bana found Willis, who told her, "Hey, I've got too many friends who work down there. I'm not going to cause any shit."

As 1990 began, Joanne found herself in the same weird psychosexual swamp in which she spent much of the 1980s.

He loves me, he loves me not.

Or rather, he loves me, but he doesn't want me around right now because he's busy getting high and fucking somebody else, but just for a while, and he might stop by later, and he might not.

She had refused to go to the O'Farrell Christmas party unless she could go as his girlfriend. She didn't want to go as an employee of the O'Farrell, now that she wasn't dancing anymore, just doing Vince's scheduling. But Artie wanted to go alone. He always wanted to project a "boss on the loose" image, just in case.

But he did come over to her place afterward, about 2 A.M. She ended up, for a change, spending Christmas with him in Corte Madera, and it was nice, although Kristal kept calling all the time.

Early in January he picked a fight with her, and she didn't see him for a while. He'll be back in about ten days, she thought, and sure enough, he turned up at her place in the wee hours one morning.

But then, he got mad again. Joanne, in an effort to improve her job skills, which had gone undeveloped all those years she was dancing, signed up for a computer lesson.

Art wanted to see her that night, and she said, sure, I'll come after my lesson. It's good to let him know there are some limits, she thought, that I have to lead my own life. But it was a sensitive issue. Her working somewhere else threatened him, left him unable to control her entire life as he had for so long.

On this night, the guy who gave her the lesson was late, and by the time she got done with it, Artie was furious. "Don't come now," he told her when she called.

All right, she thought. Another ten-day freeze. And sure enough, she didn't hear from him. No contact for precisely ten days.

The routine. She could see it was just the same as it always was, but she knew too, deep inside, that someday he would be ready. Really ready. Ready to settle down with her and live quietly and peacefully.

•   •   •

The routine was certainly about to change for Artie Mitchell, but not in the direction of quiet or peace. Two things happened in early 1990 that would have a dramatic impact on his life.

One, he nearly drowned, and two, he picked another "girlfriend" from the ranks of the dancers at the O'Farrell.

On Sunday, March 18, 1990, the brothers and their kids were picnicking on San Francisco's Ocean Beach, near Jim's house. Artie's youngest son Caleb, seven, and Jim's son Rafe, nine, were playing in the shallows, where the breakers hit the shoreline. Suddenly, the two boys were swept out into the ocean by a freakish riptide.

Artie's son Storm, now a burly seventeen-year-old and a strong swimmer, grabbed his "boogie board," a small hand-held surfboard, and plunged into the surf after his cousins. He got hold of little Caleb, who was closer, and took him safely to shore. Then he struck out into the ocean after Rafe. He reached the older boy and, fighting the tow, put him on his boogie board and set out for shore.

Storm got Rafe to the beach, but at the last minute was sucked back into the sea by the vicious riptide. Artie, seeing his son in distress, took a board and swam after him. Then Jim, realizing how dangerous the situation was, grabbed a fiberglass surfboard, tied it to his ankle with a leash, and headed out after the pair of them.

As he dashed toward the water, Jim yelled to Liberty, "Call 911!" She went screaming down the beach as she looked for a phone, and someone heard her and called. The San Francisco Fire Department's Surf Rescue Vehicle and Rescue Squad 2 both responded.

Liberty ran to Jim's house, about a block away, and told Lisa Adams, Jim's girlfriend, what was happening. "I don't think she really understood it was that big a deal," Liberty said. "She was busy preparing for [Jim's daughter] Meta's birthday party. She said, go back down there and if they're still not out, come back and get me."

The surf had turned extremely ugly. Waves were unusually large, averaging six to eight feet, and followed no usual pattern, crashing and boiling, breaking at odd angles to the coastline and then occasionally re-forming and crashing down again as strong opposing currents pushed them along. Three Coast Guard boats waited helplessly beyond the breakers, some three hundred yards further offshore, unable to approach because of the treacherous surf conditions. The Coast Guard dispatched a helicopter, but it would be some time before it would arrive. If the three men were to be saved, the firefighters would have to do it. (One Coast Guard sailor jumped from one of the vessels and swam toward the victims in an effort to assist, coming ashore later with firefighters, who had no idea he was even in the water until he showed up near shore, some seven hundred yards from the boat he had left behind.)

Fire Department Captain Steve Freeman and firefighters Mark Evanoff and Ralph Blanchard immediately donned wetsuits. Freeman and Blanchard, carrying flotation devices, struck out into the surf after the three Mitchells, with Evanoff following.

Blanchard, a former surfer, was awed by the conditions. No surfers were in the water—a most unusual occurrence at Ocean Beach—and he knew that meant trouble.

He was the first to reach Storm and Jim, who were hanging on to Jim's surfboard, unable to make any headway against the currents. Blanchard calmed them, and exhorted them to hold tight to the board so they wouldn't be separated when the waves swept over them. Then he told them to help him kick as he tried to swim toward shore with them and the surfboard.

Shortly afterward, Freeman reached Artie, who was slumped face-down across his boogie board about twenty yards away from the others, with the surf washing over him. Freeman asked Artie how he was doing, and got no response.

Just then, firefighters watching the drama from shore were horrified to see a "monster" set of re-formed breakers that they estimated to be fifteen feet high crash down on the three victims and the three rescuers. The huge waves pulled the six men upward, over the crest of the breakers, and down into the surf and out of sight.

When the men finally surfaced, there were four victims. Steve Freeman had been smashed on the head by the heavy fiberglass surfboard that was lashed to Jim's ankle. He told Evanoff that he was "seeing double and seeing stars." Later he would find out he was lucky to survive his injuries: a severe concussion, brain stem contusion, and a broken vertebra.

Evanoff wrestled Artie, vomiting and moaning and nearly unconscious, into a flotation buoy, and asked Freeman if they should head toward shore, four hundred yards away, or out toward the Coast Guard ships, a hundred yards closer.

Freeman said, "Yes."

Evanoff realized then just how massive a problem he had. He had total responsibility for getting himself and two others, one unconscious and the other injured and impaired, out of this perilous situation.

He took another look at the Coast Guard vessels. The water looked very rough out where they were, and boarding a ship would be hazardous even if all were healthy. Evanoff, fortunately the youngest and strongest of the three firefighters, decided quickly that salvation lay shoreward—almost a quarter of a mile away. He began swimming through the surf, pulling Artie along and exhorting Freeman to keep up.

Meanwhile, Ralph Blanchard was herding Storm and Jim shoreward. He had done a lot of surfing, and so he knew about riptides, and he could feel the savage currents changing direction as they pulled at his body. He directed his two exhausted charges in shifting directions to take advantage of the currents instead of fighting them. Slowly, they zigzagged toward the shore.

Finally, firefighters waiting in chest-high surf met Blanchard, Jim, and Storm, directing them to stand up and walk. They didn't know they were in shallow enough water to touch bottom. Storm was then able to walk unassisted onto the beach.

The heavy surfboard was still attached to Jim's ankle, and the leash was tangled around his legs. Every time he took a step, the board would come back and slam him in the legs. He had been in the water for forty-five minutes, and he was like a zombie, plodding straight forward in an excruciating "death march" toward the beach. Blanchard and the other firefighters tried to stop him to untangle the leash from his legs, but he would not stop. Short of tackling him, which would have been foolhardy in the surf, they could do nothing more, so they let him walk on, getting battered all the way. Once he got to shore, Blanchard was able to stop him, disconnect the leash and get him to paramedics.

A while later, Evanoff, Freeman, and Artie reached waist-high water. Freeman, still dazed, managed to walk to the beach on his own. Artie was unconscious and tangled in his boogie board leash, but Evanoff got him to shore, where paramedics and blankets waited.

When Liberty got back, Storm was on the beach, and she was so happy to see him she sank to her knees and started crying. Then a friend came up and told her, "Your father's unconscious but they got him out of the water. Jim's conscious, but they're both going to the hospital."

The firemen had been in the water for about forty-five minutes, Artie for about an hour. His body temperature was eighty-six degrees, an amazing 12.6 degrees below normal, and he very nearly died.

Jim was released from the hospital in a few hours, but Artie and Freeman both spent three days there.

Jim's clearheadedness and Liberty's quick action probably saved several lives. For his rescue of the little kids, Storm would later receive several lifesaving honors. Evanoff, Freeman, and Blanchard would all receive multiple awards for valor.

Of course, Jim also had faced death doing what he had done so often: trying to take care of his brother.

Bana Witt was living out on the Great Highway by Ocean Beach at the time, and as she was coming home from the Safeway that afternoon, she saw a couple of ambulances, saw somebody being loaded into one of them.

"Somebody just bought it down at the beach," she told her roommate when she got home.

Artie hadn't bought it, but he had come perilously close. For a while, his kidneys weren't functioning well, and he was very susceptible to colds and flu. Still, before long, he was doing his best to party the way he always had before.

After a time Artie's doctor friend Skip Dossett recognized in him signs of severe thyroid function loss because of his hypothermia. He gave him thyroid pills to get his metabolism back into balance, and they helped him some, but Joanne Scott, who had been with him so long, knew he wasn't the same.

"He was always pretty sick after that, even though he didn't talk about it. He didn't have nearly as much endurance, and his breath always sounded liquidy. The booze hit him a lot harder, and he always wanted to sleep later in the morning."

The booze hit him harder, he hit the booze harder. It may have been the thyroid, it may have been the cumulative psychological damage. It could have been both. But after the near drowning, after getting his life back, Artie began to lose a little more of it each day.

He had gone on binges before. He had ridden alcohol and cocaine and marijuana right to the edge of sanity, like a crazed moonshine runner driving the ridge roads of life at top speed in a '64 Ford with bald tires and bad U-joints. He had always survived, always come back from the edge, always lived to take on the next load. But now it seemed like he was intent on gunning that 390 V-8 right on over the cliff, end over end, in one final fireball.

Every few days he would head across the Golden Gate, down to the theater, showing up to do nothing. Perpetuating the myth that he could still function. Filling his cup three-quarters full of vodka, adding a dribble of coffee, getting drunk by 10 A.M. Feeling helpless and useless and angry about it.

For years, the theater had been Artie's most faithful lover. He and this place he had built with his brother into one of San Francisco's cultural landmarks—and a perfect expression of his own sexual ego—

had been locked in a psychosexual union of mythic proportions. When all of his women had disappointed him or left him or betrayed him or given up on him, it was to the O'Farrell that he would return. Like a benevolent goddess, she would give him succor, make him whole again, reinstall him upon the seat of personal power that his cream-colored leather office chair represented.

And, of course, provide him with another woman.

But now even that relationship was in peril. His role was gone. If Jim had been the brains of the O'Farrell Theatre, as everyone said, Artie had been its genitals. But now he was nothing more than its appendix, a shriveled, vestigial organ whose only possible action was to inflame or rupture, causing fever and consternation and crisis.

The alcohol was destroying him, and he knew it. It was as though an old friend had turned on him, a friend that went back as far as Armstrong and Boyer, back to surreptitious six-packs and cruising Second Street. It was a friend that had seen him through all of it, through cops and courts and kids and even Karen.

It looked the same. Tequila and Stoly and Heineken. But it wasn't the same. It tortured him with its nearness to hand. It was always there, and he always needed it and he always had it. But it came and went and brought no relief. It no longer dulled the pain.

Instead, it was making everything worse. He was no longer known as Artie Mitchell, the famous pornographer. He was known as Artie Mitchell, the famous degenerate drunk.

It used to be fun, a real charge for the ego, to be the craziest, most outrageous person that any of his friends knew. (It was what he and Hunter Thompson had in common, and what Artie admired in Hunter. But Thompson actually preferred Jim's company; Artie made him edgy. He was, in some ways, too much like Hunter for Hunter to like him very much.) But now, his friends just looked at him nervously.

One night, drinking with Skip Dossett at the theater, Artie fell into an alcoholic stupor on the floor of the office. Dossett, alarmed, went to him and cradled his head in his arms. "Come on, Artie, come out of it, come out of it," he implored, as Charlie Benton looked on with concern.

Artie's eyes fluttered, and he focused on Dossett. Suddenly he laughed, and tottered to his feet. Benton had seen enough. He was responsible for the theater at night, and he didn't want any trouble. He tried to get Dossett out of there so he could break up the party, get Artie shipped off home, or sleeping it off under the pool table, or whatever.

But Artie wasn't ready to go quietly. He lurched into a corner where his golf clubs were resting and took out an iron. He went back over toward Benton and suddenly swung the club like a baseball bat. Benton ducked and the club just missed his head and slammed into the wall, breaking and making a hole the size of a basketball in the Sheetrock.

Another night, playing pool in the office with Jack Davis, the corpulent, savvy political consultant who was one of the heavyweight gays in San Francisco, in more ways than one, and a close friend of Art's. As they played, sirens sounded; there was a fire in a nearby building and O'Farrell Street was suddenly full of firemen.

For some reason, this triggered in Artie the need to take his expensive inlaid Joss pool cue over to the window and hurl it like a javelin at the firemen in the street below. Which he did.

"What the hell's the matter with you?" Davis stormed at him. "You could have killed somebody. That's very uncool. You think the cops won't know where that came from?" No one was hurt, and somehow nothing came of it. Art had escaped again.

The next day, he called Jack Davis and implored him: don't tell Jim.

Another night. Benton heard a tremendous commotion in the tech area above the New York Live. He ran down the hall, past the dressing room, to see Artie hurling pieces of furniture around in the balcony area above the audience. If any item had gone over the balcony into the crowded audience, the Mitchells would have had badly hurt or dead customers and/or dancers, and, of course, incalculable lawsuits.

Charlie Benton loved Artie Mitchell every bit as much as his own brother. But the sight of his friend destroying himself, and in the process putting everyone in the theater at risk, was more than he could stand. And now, Artie was getting physically abusive, pulling Charlie's hair, wrestling around with him. Charlie sure as hell didn't like to complain, and he didn't like to "snitch" on Artie. But he had to do something, and he did what everyone always did when there was a problem about Artie.

He went to Jim.

Do something about your brother, Jim was told for the zillionth time. It was the most galling thing imaginable for him. Ever since grade school, Jim had always been at his best when he was working on a problem. Give him a problem and the tools to deal with it, and Jim was in his element. But how to deal with this? Over the years, the solution had most often been for Artie to take a vacation—go cool out, if not dry out, in Mexico or Hawaii or somewhere. Get away from the immediate source of the stress (Karen) and the most usual setting for the result (the O'Farrell.) Catch fish, lie in the sun, play with the kids or with the latest companion—Joanne, or Missy, or Kristal, or "the flavor of the month," as Artie's more ephemeral liaisons were snidely referred to by some of his friends.

But Jim knew that it was different now. What ailed Artie wouldn't get fixed on the beach at Cabo San Lucas.

By May, Artie was ready to do some traveling of a different sort. This wasn't just any trip. It was the soon-to-be-famous caravan to Woody Creek, Colorado, to come to Hunter Thompson's defense.

It was partly a clever publicity stunt, partly an excuse to party. Jim and Art had bought and restored a "Red Shark," in the tradition of *Fear and Loathing in Las Vegas*. It was a '71 Chevrolet Caprice 454 convertible, bright red with white top and interior. It had been Jim's idea for a long time to present the car to Thompson, and now, in May 1990, the timing was perfect. The good doctor was under attack in his hometown. He had been accused of sex and drug transgressions by a woman named Gail Palmer Slater, who had made a small stir in porno circles a few years before when, as an undergraduate at the University of Michigan, she had decided to make some porno films.

She had become a producer, and she had sent Hunter a couple of her videos *(Shape Up for Sensational Sex!)* and an enticing note. Then she came to Aspen (unbeknownst to Hunter, along with her new husband) and had asked to come over and meet him. She wanted to interview him, she said, and get his ideas on a new mail-order marital aids and lingerie business she was starting.

The visit ended in hysteria, and she went home and told her husband that Hunter had tried to get her into his hot tub, then tweaked her breast, pushed her on the floor, and, among other things, inhaled from a huge bowl of cocaine.

Her husband demanded that she call the law, and power-hungry prosecutors, eager for a shot at being the first to bust the notorious Thompson, had taken her story and used it as an excuse to search Hunter's house for eleven hours. Now he faced third-degree sexual assault and drug possession charges.

Later, red-faced prosecutors would admit they had no case against the legendary doctor, and an irritated judge would dismiss all charges. But for the moment, the brothers' friend was in extremis, and they wanted to help.

So they decided to schedule the trip to coincide with Thompson's preliminary hearing. They would drive in a caravan with the Chevy and a couple of motor homes, with some dancers from the theater, to make a maximum impact with their arrival in Aspen. Hunter would love it, the publicity would be great, and it would be a hell of a lot of fun.

Artie was still not feeling great. He had been really sick a couple of weeks before the trip, and Joanne had taken a week off work at her new job to look after him. She was infuriated that Kristal kept calling the house, collect, sometimes two or three times a day. She just won't leave him alone, she thought. Artie, grateful for Joanne's loving care, made it clear to her that he wanted her back. "I want you to live with me," he told her one night. "Will you sign a cohabitation agreement?" Joanne would sign anything if it meant living with Artie again, and she told him so.

Wait a little while, he said.

I've got to go on this trip, he told her. Jim and I have been at each other again, and this trip is a lot his idea, but it'll be good for us to do something together, to cement our relationship all over again.

Wait until I get back from Colorado, and we'll do it then.

Kristal had reason to call. Artie had been telling her all about the plans, and it had been agreed from the first that she would go, as one of the dancers, and as Artie's girlfriend. It would be a great vacation for them, he said. They needed a break.

Except at the last minute, the day before the trip, he met somebody interesting. Her name was Julie Bajo—Gigi on the O'Farrell stage. She was a pretty, sexy dancer from Miami, and she thought Artie was the greatest man she had ever met. To hear her tell it, she fell in love with him the day they met, as he showed her the motor home in which he would travel to Colorado the next day.

Suddenly, Artie had a very hot prospect, and he decided that taking Julie to Aspen might be more fun than taking Kristal. (Or Bana, whom he had also invited.)

So he told Kristal she wasn't going, and then offered her $500 to babysit his kids for the weekend. It was a bitter, bitter blow. Once again, he had pulled the rug out from under her on a coveted trip at the last minute.

When Artie came back, it was clear that he and Julie were going to be an item, and Kristal realized her situation was growing weirder by the minute.

"He was very good to me, and I saw him be very good to other people. He was incredibly generous. I was spoiled, though, and I told him, 'You aren't treating me good enough, I want to see you more,' and now I understand what he meant when he said, 'You're just acting like another greedy bitch.'

J.R. and Georgia Mitchell
posed in 1944 with their
first son, James Lloyd,
born November 30, 1943.

Jim and Art were as close as brothers could be, and Artie
kept a copy of this photograph in his home as a remembrance
of that happy childhood.

3

The brothers' senior pictures offered glimpses into their personalities: Jim (above) already looked serious and responsible; and a hint of Artie's mischief can be seen. Jim had signed this print of himself to Artie: "Your loving brother, Jim."

4

5

The brothers, shown here in a film editing lab in the early 1970s, collaborated every step of the way on their films, engendering both legendary disputes and enormous successes.

Marilyn Chambers's appearance on the Ivory Snow box created a publicity bonanza for the Mitchell Brothers as *Behind the Green Door* opened.

Nina Hartley danced at the O'Farrell before she became one of porn's biggest movie stars.

Jim (left) and Artie were gleeful about their court victories over the City of Santa Ana. The city's unsuccessful eleven-year battle with the Mitchells was bankrolled in part by convicted S&L criminal Charles Keating, then owner of Lincoln Savings. Their Santa Ana theater was near this Lincoln Savings branch.

Although she suffered wrenching pain and abuse during their relationship, Missy Manners still treasures the "spiritual marriage" she had with Artie.

For years, Joanne Scott lived to get the next phone call, the next visit from Artie Mitchell, and she is vocal in her bitterness toward Jim.

After Artie threatened to "Molotov cocktail" the O'Farrell in December 1987, Jim gave Joanne Scott $5,000 cash to pay for Artie to go on vacation. Artie and Joanne then went to Cabo San Lucas, where Artie caught this marlin.

When Kristal Rose lived with Artie, he imposed a rule: no Grateful Dead music before 9 A.M.

12

13

Bana Witt first had sex with Artie Mitchell on the set of a porn movie in 1974, and their occasional relationship continued for the next seventeen years.

Gonzo journalist Hunter Thompson, shown here with Joanne
Scott (right) and another dancer in the O'Farrell dressing
room was nominally night manager of the O'Farrell while he
did research for a writing project. He and the Mitchells became close friends.

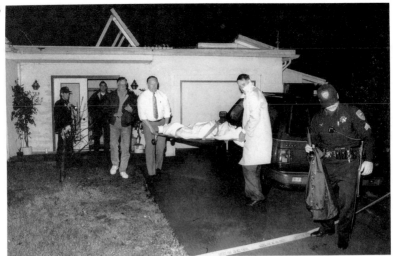

15

Artie Mitchell's body was removed from his home at
23 Mohawk in Corte Madera early on the morning of
February 28, 1991.

Michael Kennedy flew
from New York to be at
Jim Mitchell's side at the
arraignment two days after
Artie's killing, and he told
the judge his client was
"profoundly disturbed at
this time."

16

Karen Mitchell, Artie's ex-wife, appeared at the arraignment
in widow's garb, angering some other members of the family.

Prosecutor John Posey built a formidable case based on expert testimony and high-tech innovation, but the human element kept creeping in.

Marin County Superior Court Judge Richard Breiner agonized over the prosecution's computerized representation of the killing, but finally allowed a modified version of it to be shown to the jury.

Defense attorneys considered Julie Bajo's self-contradictory prosecution testimony about the final hours of Artie's life so beneficial to Jim that they twice declined to cross-examine.

Despite misgivings about testifying, Artie's daughter Liberty Bradford made a powerful witness for the defense.

Jim's emotional testimony highlighted the trial. When
Kennedy asked him if he had intended to kill his brother,
he blurted, "I wish it could have been me!"

Michael Kennedy and Jim Mitchell huddled nose-to-nose as attorney Nanci Clarence and Eleanore Kennedy hovered over them just before the verdict was announced.

"I *was* greedy, but I was greedy with his emotions, not with his money.

"He didn't know how to handle that, and I didn't either, at the end. I mean, we were both starting to be really mean to each other and we didn't want to be. We both said it, 'I don't want to fight with you.' But he was going through so much shit, and now he had this other girl fucking hanging on him and wouldn't let him go, so I just said, 'Whatever. You just take care of your shit and I'm out of here. Just let me keep working.' "

And so it went. Julie knew about her, though, and she was a real bitch to her at the theater. Although she probably didn't see it that way, Kristal had now assumed the Joanne role at the theater, with Artie's new girlfriend trying to push her out.

"If I had an affair with the boss, and it ended, I'd leave," Julie told her superciliously.

"Well I don't have to fucking leave," Kristal retorted. "Because whether you like it or not we're still good friends. I suppose in your situation, you're right, you'd have to leave. But we're tight, we weren't together that long for nothing."

Kristal tried hard to keep her cool. She got both Artie and Julie stoned all the time at the office. She just acted like nothing was wrong. "I didn't try to stir up any shit. I didn't try to get her back for it or anything. I just sat and waited. I knew what she was after. She was just another hustle, and he figured that out way fast. He could see it. He knew. We would have been back together before long, I thought, because I knew how much he missed fucking me."

But Kristal's waiting game ended a few months later when she got in trouble for violating the house rules while she sat on laps.

"It was an accident, I hard-hustled. I didn't realize what I did was against the law. This guy gave me a five and I asked him after a while, 'Do you have another one of those?' And, see, that was hard-hustling. I thought it was okay because I wasn't precisely asking for money.

"I still think she might have had something to do with it. But anyway this guy wrote a letter complaining about me and Artie got all pissed off and they fired me."

Joanne all over again. Kristal lost contact with Artie, and it really upset her. "I knew that if we talked that we'd work things out and he'd fucking fall in love with me again. It was always just that easy because we were so tight. Whenever we'd sit down to work something out we'd end up fucking."

•   •   •

Bana was furious. She fantasized about driving her truck through the front of Artie's house. He had been at her house two days before, and had told her to come over on Friday. She called to let him know she was on her way, and he told her, "There's somebody over here. And it looks like she'll be here for quite a while."

It was Julie.

Joanne was ready to sign a cohabitation agreement, eager to move back into 23 Mohawk. Sure, it was crazy over there, she thought, with women calling and kids always running in and out. But that was Artie's life, and she wanted to be there. She wanted to be his queen, the high priestess in the Church of Artie. Not just one of the girls in the choir, even if she was the most favored soloist.

But for the umpteenth time, her hopes were dashed. She too realized when Art came back from Aspen that there was yet another somebody else.

It never failed. There was always Another Somebody Else.

He kept seeing her, occasionally, spending a few nights at her apartment. During the winter of 1990, he came over a few times—"He must have been fighting with Julie," Joanne says with bitter realism—but she knew that was all she could expect for the time being. She waited, and worried about him, and waited some more.

The last time Bana Witt saw Artie Mitchell was on New Year's Day 1991. He called her in the morning, from the O'Farrell.

"He sounded crazier than ever. *So* crazy. 'I need to get out of here. Come get me.' " She jumped into her old Ford pickup and picked him up.

She couldn't believe how he looked. He was emaciated. She had seen him the day after his birthday in mid-December, and he looked like he had lost fifteen pounds since then. He was also drunk and out of control. Bana had never seen him so crazed.

He got in her truck and immediately took off his pants. Naked from the waist down. "Rub my ass," he commanded.

"Artie, I'm trying to drive."

"Rub my ass!" The tone of voice, the look in his eye, left no doubt. He was long past being playful. "All right, Artie, I'll rub your ass."

Then he tried to rip her clothes off as she was driving, and she lost it. One of the few times she really went off on him, maybe four times in seventeen years, the time he tried to strangle her, the time after the Danielle Willis incident, maybe one other time, and this. She pulled over. "Art, calm down or get the fuck out of the truck," she screamed. "Do you want to come over or do you want me to leave you here?"

He got a grip, and relaxed until they got to her place. After they had sex, for what would be the last time, she looked at him and said, "Do you want something to eat?" He looked like he'd been on a month-long fast.

He looked at her, and his eyes got big. "Food!" he said, as if the idea had not occurred to him before. "Food!"

He sat butt-naked in her kitchen, eating vegetable soup, and eating and eating. Her roommate came in and he said, "I hope you don't mind a naked pornographer in your kitchen."

The next morning, Bana had a message on her machine. It was Julie, and she said, "Bana, if Artie's there tell him to call home."

Oh, fuck, he said, and in a little while he was gone. She figured he went back there, but he didn't.

He went to Joanne's place.

It was almost like he was making the rounds. Saying goodbye without realizing it.

The following two days, January 2 and 3, 1991, were the last that Joanne Scott spent with Artie Mitchell.

They had a nice, placid time together. She remembers that Artie kept telling her, "I love you so much, I've always loved you, I'll always love you."

As he left for what would be the last time, Joanne said, "You're not going back to Gigi [Julie Bajo], are you?" and Artie replied, "Oh, God, no. Give me a break." But after a few days, with no contact, she knew that he had done just that.

He had, and he wasn't that happy about it. When he had left Julie at the theater that New Year's morning, he had told her he was going to Bana's for three days. "He told me that he wanted me to make up my mind whether I was in love with him or not, and whether I was really going to give him all my love and all my attention," she recalled.

She decided she was—"I found out that I didn't want to be away from him, that I loved him, and . . . I was going to try to help him," she remembers, and so she moved in. With her nine-year-old nephew and her mother.

Julie, for all her vivacity and adoration of Artie, was a little more of a hustler than he had thought at first. Some of his friends saw her as calculating and self-centered.

On her application to work at the O'Farrell, she had written, "Currently, Coors Lite commercial running in Canada," but of course didn't mention the hot water she had gotten into down in Miami.

One hot August night in 1989, she had been arrested at a rather inauspicious time and place: the parking lot of the Quality Inn Motel on the South Dixie Highway, in the middle of a Miami-Dade Vice Squad sting operation.

An undercover officer had checked into the motel, called the Companions Escort Service, and asked for some company. When Julie Bajo showed up, the officer reported, he paid her the requested $175 and she sat down, made three phone calls, complained to him about her personal problems, then got up suddenly and left the room. She was arrested outside and charged with petty theft and possession of marijuana, and officers discovered she had another outstanding petty theft warrant.

For Julie Bajo, Artie represented a quantum leap from those days, and she decided to stake out her turf for real.

All of a sudden, life at 23 Mohawk got very tense indeed.

First of all, Julie decided that Martha had to go. Julie's mother started following Martha around the house, taking notes on her cleaning technique, which understandably angered Martha. She had always kept everything neat and spotless. "Do I have to ask you to clean out my closet, or will you just do it for me?" he had asked her, and of course she had done it right away. Now the closets were jammed to bursting with Julie's things and her family's.

The situation was getting really difficult. One day on the phone with Georgia Mae, Artie said exasperatedly, "Mother, why is my luck with women so lousy?" He complained bitterly about Julie—how she had moved in with her mother and her little nephew, and how she had hurt her knee dancing at the theater, and he was going to have to pay for her surgery.

And of course Karen was keeping up the pressure. A hearing was set for early February over custody terms, and Artie was scared to death he would lose his precious time with Aaron, Jasmine, and Caleb.

Julie stepped up her complaints about Martha, insisting that she had to go. Artie would probably rather have tossed Julie, but he wasn't ready to do that. He had too many other hassles to deal with. Stress was everywhere for him now. So one morning in January he called Martha into the bedroom, and unhappily told her he no longer needed her services.

Martha started crying. Other than her daughter, working for Artie was the highlight of her life. "You told me I'd be your housekeeper forever!" she said.

"Who said forever?" he asked.

"You did!" she raged back at him.

Artie went into the bathroom, and she followed, tears streaming down her face. "What did I do wrong?" she asked. "It's her, isn't it? She wants me out. Is she going to clean your house for you? She can't do it like I did."

Artie gave her $1,000 as a severance bonus to soften the blow.

Then, of course, he was left with Julie, and her mom, and nephew little Cesar. As much as Artie liked kids, he didn't need one he didn't even know, living in his house while he was going through a horrible crisis.

So he gave Julie's mother $1,000 too, and she and Cesar went off to Florida.

Artie in extremis, Artie unraveling, a drunken caricature, tortured at every turn, trying fruitlessly to get a grip, trying to *buy* a grip, get rid of people, give them money, maybe they'll go away, throwing out the good with the bad, pissing $100 bills in all directions, unable to control any part of his life.

For Artie, who had always insisted, almost always falsely, "Money's not one of my hassles," this was his pathetic effort at crisis management. Go to the safe, pull out a thousand dollars, and pay a problem to go away. But he couldn't even get that right. Martha wasn't part of the problem, she was part of the solution. She made things work around the house, and after she left he was, in his diminished state, totally dependent on Julie to do things for him. Her mother and nephew were intolerable; that probably was $1,000 well spent. But he missed Martha sorely.

Ultimately, though, who was around him didn't matter. His life was being destroyed by the calculating redhead who lived up the hill at 653 Redwood Avenue in Corte Madera, by the Stoly bottle that lived in his freezer, and by the dark twisted mass of psychoses that lived in his own brain.

The ultimate horror was in *knowing* what he'd become: an obnoxious, dangerous drunk. He could see the fear and disgust and decaying re-spect in the eyes of his oldest friends as he weaved around the office, grabbing Armstrong by the hair and pissing him off, swearing at Mezz or Charlie or whoever happened to be in his face. People at the O'Farrell used to be charmed by his bad-boy behavior; he was respected, and he was loved almost like a team mascot around the place. But no more. Now they couldn't stand him.

Art knew what he was like. He was too smart not to.

He just couldn't do anything about it. And of course his reaction to any kind of criticism, spoken or not, was to be even more outrageous. Nobody was going to tell Artie Mitchell what to do.

In late January a gun-brandishing incident, the first of several in the last few weeks of Artie's life, put into sharp focus the danger that he posed to his friends and everyone else around him in his deteriorated state.

Jack Davis was hosting a lunch for friend Warren Hinckle, flamboyant tippling crusading eye-patched columnist and editor, formerly of *Ramparts,* the *San Francisco Chronicle* and soon to be formerly of the *San Francisco Examiner.*

The locale was Maye's Oyster House, a venerable seafood restaurant about three blocks from the O'Farrell. As the group of about fifteen friends gathered in the back dining room, Artie Mitchell walked in. Davis could see right away that despite the fact he was wearing an expensive suit, he was a wreck—hair greasy and disheveled, eyes blood-shot, gait staggering, words slurred. Artie soon confided to Davis that he had been up all night, drinking, for the past three nights.

Suddenly, for no apparent reason, Artie unzipped the little black bag he had taken to carrying with him everywhere, pulled out a small .38 revolver, and began waving it over his head.

Horrified, Davis and Hinckle both barked at him: Artie, put the gun away, what the hell are you doing?

Like a child chastened by his parents, Artie slipped the gun back in the bag. In a few minutes, when he left for the rest room, Jack Davis opened the bag and removed the gun. He was shocked to see that it was loaded. He put it under his coat, walked across the street to his car and locked the gun in his trunk.

The lunch quickly turned riotous. Artie threw a piece of crab cake at someone, and soon crab cakes were flying all over the room. Glasses and dishes were broken and food was everywhere.

Toward the end of the meal, Artie had cause to open his bag (Davis would later testify that he had seen both marijuana and cocaine in it) and noticed that the gun was gone. "Hey, I know one of you fuckers took my gun," he bellowed. "I want it back."

Nobody said a word, and the lunch broke up. A few hours later,

Davis decided that he should—of course—*tell Jim* about what had happened, and drop off the gun.

So he went down to the theater. As he stood in the lobby, by the big oak door to the stairs up to the office, waiting for it to be buzzed open for him, Artie jumped him from behind.

Artie probably weighed a hundred pounds less than Davis, but his wiry strength and the surprise factor made this no contest. He put his knee in Davis's back and shoved him against the door, at the same time reaching around Davis's neck with his right arm, choking him.

"I know you took that fucking gun. I want that fucking gun back, and I'm not kidding around," he snarled. Only after Davis promised to give him the gun did he release him.

They went across to the parking lot, and Davis took the gun from his trunk and handed it back to Artie.

Davis left, but Artie wasn't finished for the day. He had wanted his gun back for a reason. He went back into the O'Farrell, walked upstairs to the office and found Jim and Charlie Benton talking in the office.

For over a year, ever since the first time Charlie had said something to Jim about Art's behavior, Artie had been angry with him, demanding an apology, accusing him of disloyalty, of "ratting me off" to Jim.

On this day, he meant to get his apology.

When he walked in, Charlie looked at him in amazement. His brand-new suit was covered with grease spots and stains. Food was still falling from the suit, hours after the lunch.

But Artie didn't want to talk about a food fight. He wanted to know why Charlie had told on him again, this time about an incident around New Year's.

Benton had been on vacation around New Year's, and he told Artie so, but it didn't do any good. "I want an apology," he demanded. Then he took out the pistol and pointed it at Charlie Benton's head.

This was no employer-employee spat. Charlie Benton was family. He had been with the Mitchells for nearly twenty years. And Artie was holding a gun to his head.

Big brother to the rescue.

Jim stepped between Charlie and the gun. Benton would testify later that Jim said, "Hey, hey, Art, what are you doing? What is this gangster punk type of move you're pulling on this guy? He's one of the people who helped make you a millionaire."

Charlie, uncomfortable and embarrassed, had his back to the brothers, looking at the door and figuring how he could get out of there, when he heard the gun go off.

The noise in the enclosed room was deafening. Stunned, Charlie looked first at himself, to see if he'd been hit. Then he turned slowly and looked at Jim, who was still standing and looked okay. Then he looked at Artie, who was grinning. Plaster dust was drifting down from a new hole in the ceiling.

Jim Mitchell was not having a good month.

The Gulf War angered and depressed him, and he found the media coverage to be biased and pro-war. So, in a characteristically Quixotic radical move, he went out and started a newspaper.

It was called the *War News,* and it was a noble effort at presenting the antiwar side of things. He gathered his media allies, including Warren Hinckle and the cartoonist Dan O'Neill, leased an old building in San Francisco's North Beach, and started to put the newspaper together.

All of that was fun, but it was a full-time job, and he already had one. And, on top of that, there was Artie.

He saw his little brother wasting away before his eyes.

Artie was looking scragglier and scragglier. He was thin, almost emaciated, and he had let the fringe of hair that ringed his bald pate grow longer and longer in a weird reprise of his hippie days. He had always been a jokester, happy-go-lucky, but lately his stories had grown more rambling and nonsensical, and he had affected a little *tee-hee* of a giggle that grated on Jim's nerves. He thought it was deranged.

He had heard plenty of horror stories, from Armstrong, from Charlie, from Rocky. Now, he had seen with his own eyes just how bad Artie was.

What the hell am I going to do with him, Jim wondered.

The pressure from Karen was stronger than ever. She was again trying to limit Artie's custody of the children severely. And she was still pressing for a change of venue, from Contra Costa to Marin County, where they both now lived.

Artie had yet another trick up his sleeve, though. He retained Meredith to represent him against Karen.

It was a classic Artie move. Pitting one ex-wife against the other. Who could have a better motivation for acting against Karen, who was getting more than $60,000 in family support from him, than Meredith, who got less than $24,000?

After years of almost total estrangement, he and Meredith were actually friends again. It would be one of the few positive developments in his relations with those around him in the last weeks of his life.

He even told Liberty, somewhat in jest, that he and her mother might get married again.

She didn't think it was funny. If you do that, she told him, I'll never speak to either one of you. What would that say about the way you ruined our family when we were kids?

Meanwhile, one Sunday in January, the fight between Artie and Karen very nearly resulted in Artie's death at the hands of the police.

On this night she came to pick up the kids early, and Artie said, I'm cooking dinner, wait. She started screaming and called the police, but Artie was used to that. She had called the Twin Cities police on him so many times that he was on a first-name basis with some of the patrolmen. They would show up, and take the kids out to show them the inside of the patrol car, then stand by as Karen picked up the kids. No big deal. He just kept on with dinner.

But this time, when the doorbell rang, Artie answered it holding the steak knife he'd been using. The cop very nearly shot him, but decided to try talking him out of the weapon. Before anything else, the cop said, put down the knife.

Which of course Artie did, but the cop was not amused, and Artie was scared he'd write a report that would help Karen.

Artie's cute little legal stratagem of hiring Meredith was ill-fated. Soon, Karen's sustained legal assault and his own bizarre behavior would turn Artie's worst nightmare into reality.

On the night of Saturday, February 16, he had Aaron, Jasmine, and Caleb with him at 23 Mohawk. Never mind that he had been trying desperately to quit drinking because of upcoming hearings in his custody battle, never mind Ray DeLeon's declaration that he had never seen Artie drunk around his kids. On that night, Artie Mitchell was hammered.

At about 9 P.M., Artie somehow got it into his head that Caleb, eight at the time, had broken his finger earlier while in Karen's care, and she had done nothing about it. It is possible that Caleb, who is double-jointed, told him as a joke that his finger was broken. But however Artie got the idea, he came unglued.

Possibly seeing a chance to reveal Karen as a neglectful, abusive mother, he hustled Caleb into the car and drove drunkenly to the Kaiser Hospital in San Rafael, where he and Caleb went into the emergency room.

When the triage nurse decided that Caleb's finger wasn't the most pressing case in the emergency room, Artie started offering $100 bills. When that didn't work, and he was told to shut up and sit down, he became furious and abusive. His mood did not improve when a doctor told him there was nothing wrong with Caleb.

By this time, emergency room staff had called police, and San Rafael Officer Jim Strong responded. By this time, Artie had sensed danger, and had demanded to take Caleb and leave.

The first thing Strong noticed about Artie was that he was drunk: staggering, slurring, and smelling of alcohol. He denied being drunk, but seemed to be very worried about a DUI charge, insisting that he and Caleb had taken a cab to the hospital.

That dog wouldn't hunt. Emergency room staff had seen him getting out of his Dodge Colt station wagon with Caleb, and pointed the car out to Strong. "It was obvious he posed a threat to himself and his son due to his intoxication," Strong wrote in his report. "He refused to go anywhere without his son."

After arresting Artie for public intoxication, he found the Colt's keys in Artie's pocket. Karen was called, and she immediately informed Strong that, by Contra Costa County court order Number 255036-256829, Artie Mitchell was prohibited from consuming alcohol while having his visitation with his children. She also mentioned to Strong that she was seeking a change of venue to Marin County, and that a hearing on the matter was set for the following week.

Karen came and took Caleb home, and Artie was booked into the county jail for the night.

"Suspect expressed confidence that charge would be dismissed, due to his notoriety and wealth," Strong wrote. "Prosecution is appropriate."

Artie's foolishness had given Karen the opening she needed. While she waited for the February 19 hearing in Contra Costa County on the change of venue and her motion to disqualify Meredith as Art's attorney, she attacked on another front. This time, Karen filed an action in Marin under the Domestic Violence Prevention Act, seeking a temporary restraining order limiting Artie's visitation to one eight-hour session per week, supervised by a court-appointed monitor.

Meredith desperately tried to stave off disqualification. In a statement to the court, she wrote, "I was married and divorced from Respondent before I met Petitioner. We never socialized or became friends, and I never either represented or sued Petitioner in any capacity. I have not laid eyes on Petitioner since at least 1982. Petitioner is merely seeking to deprive Respondent of the attorney of his choice."

It was to no avail. On February 19, 1991, more than seven years after Karen and Artie split up, Judge Sandra Sepulveda granted Karen's request for Meredith's disqualification, and for a change of venue to Marin County.

Meanwhile, a hearing on Karen's request for a temporary restraining order had been set for the next day—leaving Artie without an attorney in the legal struggle of his life.

Artie represented himself. He had no choice. He did the best he could, but by this time, in his condition, he made a pitiful figure in court.

Officer Strong's police report from the incident four days earlier had been entered into the court file, and Artie knew he had to combat it. He pulled a bottle of Sharp's nonalcoholic beer from his fanny pack and waved it at Judge Lynn Taylor, who had seen this sort of thing from drunken fathers before, and wasn't having any.

"This is all I was drinking that night, Your Honor," he said.

"That does have some alcohol in it," Taylor responded.

"You'd have to drink dozens of these before you got drunk," Artie said.

"I'm sure you could do that, Mr. Mitchell," Taylor replied coldly.

Taylor signed Judicial Council Form 1296.10, Order to Show Cause and Temporary Restraining Order, with box Number 10 (Other Orders) checked, followed by the words: "Defendant shall be allowed up to eight hours visitation per weekend only if supervised by a qualified visitation supervisor."

"I'm finished," Artie moaned afterward, holding his head in his hands. Finally, he had lost access to the children. He was ordered to court on March 12 to present any possible legal reason why the order should not be made permanent.

For Liberty, now almost twenty-one, it was excruciating to see her father in such rough shape. It had only been in the last year that she and her father had developed a really close relationship, and now she was seeing the booze take him away again.

An aspiring actress, she had been living in Los Angeles, attending the University of Southern California. A month earlier, she had visited him at the O'Farrell, inadvertently walking in on a discussion between him and Jim.

Jim had said to Liberty that day, "Stick around, you're a family member—this involves you too. I'm saying this in front of you because you need to know.

"This is a really tough business. We've both been in it more than twenty years. We've each been arrested, what, Artie, 180 times? It just burns you out. Your dad has to kick back, take some time away. I had a coke problem a few years back, and I got the place at the Cape, got over it, dried out.

"Take six months or a year off," he said to Artie. "We'll send your monthly check, whatever. Just dry out, mellow out, go to Mexico or wherever you want."

Liberty remembers her dad saying, "Yeah, yeah, you're right, that's a good idea." But he couldn't leave then. He had the court thing coming up.

Liberty had talked to him on the phone since then, and she had been encouraged. He sounded pretty good, more sober than she could remember. So when Liberty saw him on the Saturday before he died, she was shocked when he said, "Let's get a drink," and the drink turned out to be not a Sharp's or a mineral water but a Heineken and a shot of tequila.

"I told him, 'Here you are saying you'd like to get custody of Aaron, and look what you're doing.' He said, 'It's finished, it's over, she got me.' "

The lunch was not destined to be pleasant for Liberty. Artie had set her up in a business she didn't really want—selling T-shirts in Los Angeles. The shirts were mostly designs by Robert Crumb and Artie's other artist friends, sort of hippie stuff, more San Francisco than L.A. And during the jingoistic fervor of the Gulf War, they weren't moving at all.

She had come up to give him that report, tell him she couldn't do it anymore, and borrow some money.

First he criticized her for not trying hard enough on the T-shirt business, but then made her an offer: I'll pay off your debts if you come back here, live in San Francisco. You can work on the *War News* and live with your mom.

Liberty was not about to go home and live with her mother—or take a patronage Mitchell Brothers job. She had inherited her father's stubbornness and fierce independence. She didn't want him holding it over her: I gave you your start, you owe me.

She just wanted to borrow some money so she could get out of the hole his stupid T-shirt idea had gotten her into.

So Artie said forget it. I'm the one with the money. Just forget it.

It was a down day anyway. All six kids had planned to go on a fishing trip with Artie, but the court couldn't find a monitor who was athletic enough to go on the trip, so it had to be canceled, and everybody was depressed.

Liberty didn't want to argue with him anymore. He was drunk and she could see he'd just given up. So she said fuck you, and drove to her mother's place, where she was staying for the weekend.

She told her mother and her brother and sister, "He looks so bad. I really don't think I'm ever going to see him again."

Storm retorted, "That's real nice. What if he died tomorrow?"

Liberty said, "I wouldn't be guilty for saying it, because I feel he's just gone so far over the edge."

But she called him the next day, not to ask for money again, but to ask him to go into rehabilitation. "Look, you're going to die otherwise," she told him. "I don't want to see you die."

Artie said to his daughter, "You don't have to worry about me if I die. When people mourn when somebody dies it's because they've lost them. They don't mourn for the people who die, they mourn for them-selves."

He said to her, "Come back when you're thirty. You'll be better then."

Liberty said, "Dad, you're not going to be alive when I'm thirty."

She was so upset that on Monday the twenty-fifth, before she went back to Los Angeles, she went down to the O'Farrell to see Jim. She and Jim had not been close; she had always found him intimidating and of course she still carried a lot of bad feeling about his firing Meredith.

But she remembered the conversation she had walked in on a month earlier, and she thought she should tell Jim about her fears.

Jim wasn't at the O'Farrell, but she did see Jeff Armstrong there, and Armstrong told her that her father had been scaring the shit out of everyone at the theater, waving guns around, firing them. It had happened again over the weekend. Jim had told Artie, stay away from the theater until you can control yourself. Infuriated, Artie had gone down Saturday night and, during a wild party with Julie and O'Farrell employees Richard Freeman and a couple of others, he had pulled the gun out again, and fired into the ceiling again. Finally, Julie had man-aged to get him out of there.

Even more concerned now, Liberty went over to the *War News* and found Jim.

"I told Jim that I asked Artie to go into rehab, and Jim said, 'He'll never do it.' "

Liberty said, "I'm going to have to cut myself off from him. I can't keep taking this mental abuse."

"We all love your dad," Jim said, "but I think I'm going to have to cut myself off from him too. Maybe that way he'll get help."

Jim told Liberty, "We all really care about you and we ought to keep in touch."

Liberty felt better. She knew that whatever happened with Artie, Jim would be there for everyone in the family.

Joanne Scott was home for lunch from her secretarial job on that Monday when the phone rang. She picked it up on impulse instead of letting it ring through to her answering machine, as she had started to do.

It was Artie, and Joanne was thrilled. She hadn't seen him since early January. She wanted him, and she told him so in no uncertain terms.

He was telling about the night of the sixteenth, about taking Caleb to Kaiser, getting arrested, going to jail. "The other prisoners lined up to shake my hand," he said proudly.

When he finished the story, she said, "Do you know how much I love you?" And then, "Do you know how much I want to suck your dick?" She knew that explicit sexual talk often got him to come over.

"How long will you be there?" he asked.

"I'm supposed to go back to work after lunch," she admitted.

"Will you move to Mexico with me?" he demanded.

"Yes," came the immediate answer.

"That's more like it," he said. "Hold on. You'll get your chance."

Even as he asked Joanne to move to Mexico with him, he was making plans to take Julie.

He also called Bana that Monday.

"I'm moving to Mexico," he said.

"Who with?" Bana asked.

"Barbara . . . Janet . . . they're all the same aren't they?" Artie responded teasingly.

"That's right, Art, they're all interchangeable," Bana said wearily. "You know, Art, I'm old and tired. If you don't want me just leave me alone."

"I'm old and tired too," Artie said. "Hey, at least come visit us down there."

"Art, I'm not going to visit you with some slut in Mexico. Just leave me alone. I can't do this anymore. If you don't want me just go away."

Actually, Artie wasn't prepared to chuck it all and head to Mexico with any of them. For one thing, he had his eye on a new prospect— Debbie Milligan, a sexy brunette friend of Martha's that he had just met.

"He wanted to get rid of Julie," Martha said.

He did not get the chance.

Wednesday, the twenty-seventh of February, started out normally enough at Artie's place, but it wasn't long before it turned weird and ugly.

Julie Bajo had a morning of errands to run— a visit to the chiropractor, a trip to see a friend. She had some phone calls to make, but Artie wouldn't get off the phone. He was complaining to somebody— she didn't know who—about the fact that his life was turning to shit before his eyes.

Jim had barred him from the theater, and a couple of days before Dennis Roberts had called him with a message from Jim: If Art didn't straighten up, get help, the brothers would have to split up the business and go their separate ways. "I'll take the O'Farrell," Art had said to Roberts. "Jim can have the *War News*."

The more he thought about that phone call, the angrier Artie had gotten. This morning, he was telling whoever he was on the phone with that Jim hadn't had the guts to call himself. He was going on and on about it, the way he did, and about his other problems too. His ex-wife from hell was keeping him from his kids. The Gulf War was out of control. Julie had heard it all before. She just shook her head, and went out to make her calls elsewhere.

Turned out Artie was talking to Nancy Harrison, a secretary at the O'Farrell and the best friend of Jim's longtime girlfriend, Lisa Adams. Nancy would say later that after Artie went through his litany of problems, he turned nasty, and threatened Lisa: "If I find out she had anything to do with breaking up this business I'll blow her fucking brains out."

Lisa, as it happened, was sitting a few feet away from Nancy, in another office at the O'Farrell. She and Nancy were planning to go to lunch.

So Nancy, shocked at Artie's violent threat, told Lisa right away, and Lisa, naturally, freaked out. Jim was across town in North Beach at the office of the *War News,* and she called him there. Lisa says she told him, I want to call the police. It's a very real threat to me, I'm scared to death, and if something happens there should be a record of this.

She says Jim asked her not to call the cops. Give me some time, he said. A few hours. I need to talk to a couple of lawyers about intervening, getting him some help.

Artie needs help.

When Julie returned to 23 Mohawk after running her errands, eight-year-old Caleb was there. "You're not supposed to be here until Saturday," his father reminded him, but Caleb ignored him and went into his room, where he searched fruitlessly for his baseball glove. "Dad, I can't find my mitt and I've got tryouts," he said.

Artie gave Julie some cash and told her, go buy Caleb a mitt and take him to baseball. She did, but baseball was rained out, so she took him home to Karen's big house at 653 Redwood Avenue, up the hill about a mile from Art's.

When she got back home, she found Aaron, who had just come in from the rain and was drying himself off, getting something to eat, just like normal. Aaron—Ace, as Artie called him—didn't give a damn what had happened in court. No judge was going to keep him away from his dad.

The whole thing was taking on a slapstick, Marx Brothers quality. Take one kid home, another one shows up, like the old carny game, Whack-a-Mole. Whack one mole on the head and another pops up.

Artie whacked his own head with both hands and said, "God, if they catch one picture of them in here, I go straight to jail. Get that kid home." So for the second time in half an hour, Julie headed up the hill with a Mitchell boy.

The humor was about to leave the situation for good.

Redwood was narrow, allowing only one car to pass at a time. Julie was on the way back down the hill when she encountered Karen's Jaguar coming up the hill toward her. And Karen wouldn't move out of the road to let Julie pass.

Julie backed up and parked behind another car so Karen could go by, but she didn't. She slammed her car into park and jumped out. Julie could tell something not too great was going to happen. She locked both car doors, leaving the driver's side window cracked, and huddled fearfully in the seat as Karen stormed toward her.

"She started saying, 'If you ever come near my children I will kill you. Do you understand me? I will kill you, you slut, do you understand me?' "

Julie looked up at her—to see a pistol pointed at her face, Karen clutching the handle with both hands, trembling, eyes watering, face red and contorted.

I'm dead, Julie thought. At least they'll know it was her because of where the car is, and it's Artie's car.

Karen smacked the window with the gun and backed off for a moment, and Julie breathed. But then Karen shouted again, "Do you hear me, you slut? I WILL KILL YOU!" And she banged the window again.

Karen Mitchell turned away and walked back to her car, and drove up to her house.

Julie thought, God, I'm alive, and then, she can't get away with this. So she headed down the hill to Artie's house to call the cops, walked in the front door and found her glass living room table, that she'd just moved into the house a month ago, exploded in little pieces all over the room.

She left again, in shock, turned around and got back into the car, thought, I've got to find a cop.

She flagged down Patrol Officer Bonnie Page of the Twin Cities Police Department, who calmed her down long enough to figure out that a madwoman had threatened her with a gun on Redwood Avenue. Page went to find Karen. Which wasn't hard.

Karen had marched into the police station at Larkspur, demanding to file a complaint against *Julie*.

Unmoved, Officer Page read Karen her Miranda rights and asked to see her gun, which turned out to be a .380 silver Beretta automatic, sans clip, which Karen fished out from under the front seat of the Jag.

Bonnie Page was Ray DeLeon's girlfriend, and it wasn't long before the detective heard Karen Mitchell was in the station.

He came into the station and saw a woman sitting in one of the offices. He asked the dispatcher, "Is that Karen Mitchell?"

"It sure is," came the reply, and Ray DeLeon walked in and said, "Do you know who I am?" Karen said, "No." And he said, "I'm Ray DeLeon. And if you don't know who I am, I'd sure appreciate it if you wouldn't spread lies about me all over town." He turned and left.

After the smoke cleared and the yelling stopped, Page issued Karen a misdemeanor citation for brandishing a weapon, and let her go.

Julie went home, stepped around the glass shards and told Artie what had happened with Karen. Artie immediately demanded that she call Nancy at the theater, tell her what happened, so everyone there would know what he was going through. Julie did as he asked.

Artie was vague about just how Julie's table got broken—he muttered something about dropping something on it—but he gave her some money to replace it.

He was feeling terrible physically. He was still bothered by the aftereffects of his severe bout with hypothermia a year before at Ocean Beach. He caught colds easily, and he had one now, along with a nasty sinus infection. Skip Dossett had prescribed antibiotics, but they were making him sick to his stomach. He had called Dossett at his San Francisco office and asked if he could come in for a shot instead, but he didn't feel up to driving across the bridge and into town, so he called Dossett back and asked him to come by the house instead. Dossett demurred, saying he had plans, and Artie went off on him.

"After all the years we've been friends, you can't come over here?" he raged. He called the doctor every name he could think of, kept shouting invective for several minutes. Finally, Skip Dossett had enough.

"Art, listen—"

"You son of a bitch!" Artie screamed. "Either come over here or I'll never speak to you again!"

Dossett said, look, I can't talk to you anymore right now, I have patients to see, and hung up.

God, Dossett thought, he's in bad shape. He considered Artie his best friend, and he was hurt and shocked. He'd seen him rip into other people, but Artie had never talked to him like that before. On Sunday, he had been over there, given Artie a shot and the prescription for antibiotics, and Artie had given his daughter Mary Joy a $100 bill. Just a present from sweet old Uncle Artie. And now sweet old Uncle Artie had turned into a vicious threatening incoherent bastard.

A little while later, Artie called back, and apologized, and said, "Look, I'm sorry, but I'm just upset, and Karen pulled a gun on Julie, and the cops are here, I have to make a statement. Could you please come up here later, buddy, and give me a shot?"

Dossett relented, and said he would visit Art after work.

Meanwhile, Artie called up Martha Rauber, who still absolutely worshiped him, even though she was upset at having been fired a month before. She was glad to hear his voice.

"Martha, the cunt pulled a gun on Julie."

"You're kidding me!"

Artie rambled on about what had happened, and about how scared he was for his kids, "up there with that crazy bitch with a gun." Martha sympathized, and they talked for a few more minutes.

When the conversation ended, Martha was left with growing concern. Artie was drunk, and he sounded bad, and she was really worried about him. She fretted about it for a while. Somebody just had to do something.

So she called Georgia Mae.

She said, "Mae, I'm calling you because I'm really upset about Artie. He is very sick."

Mae asked, "Physically sick, or mentally?"

"Both, I think," said Martha. "But I'm sure mentally. You're his mother, Mae, and I don't like saying this to you, but I'm afraid he's going to die."

That got Mae's attention in a hurry. She called an alcohol treatment center near her home, and they told her what everyone had been told: there's nothing you can do if they don't want help.

By then, it was about 8 P.M. She called Artie's house, and got Julie. Art was taking a nap, Julie said. Mae told her she was really concerned about Art, that she had gotten a call that made her think he could be having some serious problems.

Julie says she told Mae that Artie needed everybody's love and help right now, and he wasn't getting it, and he was getting more and more drunk and aggressive and difficult.

Then Art got up and took the phone.

"Mom, I want you to do something about Jim," he yelled. "I want you to tell Jim that he's killing himself with those cigarettes. He's smoking two or three packs a day. Tell him to stop it, Mother!" He was screaming now, and he repeated the whole thing.

Finally, Mae would testify, she got a word in. "Art, I'm not concerned about Jim, I'm concerned about you."

That set Art off all over again. "Yes, I know how it is," he screamed. "I can go out and drink a beer and everyone is on my case, but Jim, he can smoke two or three packs a day, and nobody says anything to him."

Artie got more and more hysterical about Jim, how Jim was always so perfect and nobody ever got after him for anything.

He stopped screaming for just a moment, to catch his breath, and then he growled, "I'd like to take my gun, put it between his eyes, and pull the trigger."

Mae was stunned. She could say nothing. The silence lengthened.

Finally, Artie said, "Bye, Mom. I love you. I'll call soon."

When Skip Dossett came by 23 Mohawk, a little while before Mae's call, Art was in bed, and he seemed pretty calm. And pretty sick. "Oh, I'm so glad you're here, buddy," he said, knowing he'd been out of line earlier on the phone. "Thank you so much for coming. I'm really sick. I can't take these medicines. They're making me puke."

"Okay, okay, buddy," Dossett said. "You're going to be okay." He checked Artie's vital signs, then gave him two shots—one of Rocephin, a cephalosporin antibiotic, and one vitamin B_{12}.

Artie was grateful, and said it was a big load off his mind, not having to take those pills and puke all night, and now he could rest, and Dossett said, "Artie, one more thing. Whenever you talk to me on the phone like you did today, when you were yelling at me—"

"I'm sorry about—"

"I know, I know, but whenever you talk to me like that, I know you've been drinking."

Artie, cringing like a little kid caught with a pilfered cookie, said yeah, I know.

Dossett paused. "I want to get together with you when you're feeling better and talk about getting you into a rehab program."

Artie raised up and looked at Dossett, eyes suddenly sharp as steel blades, and said what he always said when people suggested this course of action: "No one is going to come in here and take me to a program.

"Through a hail of bullets I'll go into a program."

Lisa Adams left the house she and Jim shared, out near the Cliff House at San Francisco's Ocean Beach, at about 7 P.M. that night to pick Jim up in North Beach at the *War News* office.

They had talked again on the telephone late in the afternoon. Again, she asked him for permission to call the police. Again, he told her to wait, that he needed more time.

When she got to the *War News,* he wasn't there, and she waited impatiently for about an hour before he showed up. He had been around the corner at Tosca, a famous North Beach bar that had been one of Jim's favorite spots for years, having a couple of margaritas with the *War News* staff. He wanted to stick around—they had ordered a pizza from the bar and it would be delivered shortly—but she didn't want any pizza, thank you. She wanted to get the hell out of there, and get straight with Jim about his crazy fucking brother and how he had threatened to kill her.

She was driving when they left North Beach, but she was so upset that she couldn't continue, and they stopped and changed places.

Lisa would say that on the way home Jim told her that he had talked to his cousin Rocky Davidson and to Skip Dossett, and that they were going to meet at Artie's, to see what they could do. (Dossett would later vehemently deny any such arrangment had been made, and would deny going to 23 Mohawk anytime after his medical visit that night.)

Jim said, "If we called the police, either Art's going to be dead, or a police person is going to be dead," Lisa said later.

When they got home, she says, there was another shock waiting.

Jim went into the bathroom and she went into the kitchen, where she saw the answering machine light blinking. She rewound the tape and listened to the messages.

Both of them were from Artie.

"His voice . . . was very scary and threatening. His voice was slurred. You could almost not understand what he was saying.

"He started out by saying, 'You know, Mr. Perfect, this is your brother. You know, this is your brother, Mr. Perfect. You know, it's so bad I had to call Mother about you.

" 'I had to call Mother and tell her what you've been doing.

" 'I had to call Mother.'

"And then he just sort of cut off, and then he started again: 'You told your girlfriend you were going to quit smoking. You told her you were going to quit smoking. Those cigarettes are going to kill you.

" 'But I'm going to kill you first.

" 'I'm going to kill you first, motherfucker.' "

Lisa said that she erased the messages so Jim wouldn't hear them, but he would later say that from the bathroom, only a few feet away, he could hear them just fine.

Trembling, she got a glass and poured herself a shot of cognac and crumpled onto the couch.

She heard Jim walk out of the bathroom and go downstairs to the garage.

Where the gun cabinet was.

She says she got up off the couch, went downstairs and saw him with a rifle in his hands. She begged him, on her knees, crying, on the floor, not to go. She says she still didn't tell him about the messages, but did tell him she was scared that Art would kill him. Again, she says, he told her he had to go, he was meeting Rocky and Skip Dossett at Artie's house.

She said he put the rifle in the car and left about 9:30.

Not too surprisingly, Julie Bajo's account of Artie's phone calls to Jim's house differs from Lisa's.

She says she heard him make the first call, and say something like, "I'm not the only one with the problem. You have a problem too, a problem that will probably take twenty years off your life. Don't you love your kids enough to quit?"

She remembers thinking, God, whoever hears that doesn't have any idea what he's talking about.

Then, she says, he called right back and said "You promised your girlfriend you would quit smoking. What happened to that? Don't you love your kids enough to quit?"

On neither call, she said, did she hear him threaten to kill Jim.

They sat down then to a late supper, and went right to bed. It was about 10 P.M.

It had been a hell of a day for Artie. Now it was almost over.

For a few minutes, he and Julie discussed plans for a trip to Mexico, a trip to scout out places for a longer stay. "I was sort of lying on his chest," she remembers, as they talked about making plane reservations, visiting Storm in San Diego on the way down, finding a house down in Mexico big enough for all the kids to come and stay.

Suddenly she says, with no warning, they heard the front door open, then slam shut. An interior door open and close. Heavy footsteps running through the living room, crashing into furniture. She would say later that it sounded like an army, or a SWAT team.

They both jumped out of bed. Artie yelled hoarsely, "What's going on? Who's out there?" Just at that moment, Julie testified, she heard shots—pop, pop—not loud, but definitely shots. She remembers the pressing sound of the bullets coming through the bedroom door as much as the sound of gunfire.

She recalls hearing more steps then, coming down the hallway toward the bedroom. Oh, God, she thought, how many are there? What are they going to do to us?

She picked up the telephone and stepped into her closet. Artie was standing near the door that led from the bedroom into the hall, the hall where the great scary clumping steps and the hissing little deadly bullets were coming from.

She dialed 911 and hysterically tried to explain to the operator who answered what was going on.

Peeking through the closet door, she lost sight of Artie, and then she heard more shots. She screamed for him not to go out there, because it seemed like he was going into the line of fire.

Then she thought she heard him scream, then she heard more shots.

"I just went into shock," she told the grand jury. "I just started babbling on the phone, just babbling, and my mind started going away."

She thought she heard him fall, but she didn't want to believe it. "I remember sort of hearing a thump, and then silence after that."

Twin Cities Police Sergeant Tom Paraspolo was cruising the streets that misty Wednesday evening, doing what he had spent so much of his twenty-one years with the department doing: looking for traffic offenders, particularly drunken drivers.

About 10:15 P.M., he thought he had found one. The car in front of him on Tamal Vista Boulevard was making some erratic moves. Given the hour, a DUI, or "deuce" in cop jargon—was quite likely.

He radioed Officer Kent Haas to back him up. Haas was a DUI specialist. Catching drunk drivers was, other than his participation on the department's SWAT (Special Weapons and Tactics) Team, his sole responsibility. He was also nearby, and he reached the scene quickly.

By the time Haas arrived, Paraspolo had already determined that they didn't have a deuce this time. The driver of the wobbly car was a pleasant and clearly sober elderly lady. He told her to be careful, wished her a good night, and signaled Haas with four fingers, signifying Code 4—all clear.

Haas, who had not left his vehicle, got away from the traffic stop first. Just after he left, driving southbound on Tamal Vista, and as Paraspolo stepped back into his car, they heard the sound from their radios that quickens any officer's pulse—an "alert tone" signifying a priority message to come. Often it means a suspected crime has just been reported, and may still be in progress. In this case, what they heard next was one of the most worrisome imaginable dispatches in the little upscale suburban enclave they protected:

"Shots fired, 23 Mohawk."

When he got the call, Haas was at the corner of Tamal Vista and Council Crest—less than a tenth of a mile from Artie Mitchell's house.

Paraspolo, about a block and a half behind, immediately hit his lights and siren as they raced down Madera Boulevard, an extension of Tamal Vista, toward Mohawk.

The address rang a bell with Paraspolo, the veteran sergeant. At the briefing at the beginning of his shift, he had been told of the Karen Mitchell–Julie Bajo incident. Guns aren't brandished too often in laid-back Corte Madera, so it seemed logical that there might be a connection. He radioed Haas to tell him that earlier in the day police had, in his words, "removed a weapon from one of the females involved in that residence." He also radioed Bonnie Page and asked her what kind of vehicle Karen Mitchell had. Page, who was half an hour from the end of her swing shift, would work overtime tonight. She was already responding to the call, and she told Paraspolo and Haas about Karen's and Julie's cars.

Paraspolo knew Haas would arrive on the scene first, and he told Haas to be on the lookout for any people or vehicles leaving the area.

Haas did not approach at top speed. He was very close by, and he needed to hear the information he was getting on the radio, to get as much information as possible about what he might be getting into. Once he had heard Paraspolo and Page, he activated his lights and siren and headed toward Mohawk, three blocks away.

Once he got to the street, he shut down the lights, siren and headlights. Again, training told him: entering an unknown shooting situation, don't make yourself any more of a target than necessary. Paraspolo, approaching from the opposite direction on Mohawk, did the same.

As Paraspolo turned onto Mohawk, he started to radio Page and Haas, trying to coordinate their locations so he could make sure all exits to the immediate area were secure. But Haas broke in and said he had a subject in sight.

Paraspolo couldn't understand the whole transmission, but he did hear Haas say something about a gun. He raced his car toward the other end of the street, where Haas was.

Officer Haas had stopped in front of Number 27, a couple of houses down from Artie's place. He didn't want to park right in front of the house, but he wanted to be close. He parked on the wrong side of the street, front wheels over the curb, the nose of his vehicle actually closest to Number 25, right next door to Artie's.

As he started to get out of the car, he saw a man carrying a large umbrella walking hurriedly toward him from the direction of Number 23. He was about ten feet away, and coming toward him, walking quite rapidly.

He wasn't a real big man, about five nine or five ten, wearing wire-rim glasses, a black leather bomber jacket, a little tweed cap, and baggy patterned pants, which Haas would later describe as "camouflage-style," although they were not.

Haas's first thought was, anybody this close must have heard something if there were shots. He wanted to ask the man what he'd seen or heard. But he also was the only person in sight, and not knowing what had happened, Haas stayed behind the door of the car, unsnapped his holster, and kept his hand on his gun.

By now, the man was right next to the car door where Haas was standing. Haas contends that he said to the man, in a loud voice, "Stop."

Haas says that the man ignored him, quickening his pace as he walked away. At this point, Haas says, he realized the man was walking oddly, limping really, holding his right leg straight and grasping the upper right side of his thigh—"as though," Haas would say, "he had a bum leg."

He had gained a little ground, passing Haas and walking maybe fifteen feet past him. Haas drew his gun, got out from behind the car door, which was no longer of any use as cover for him since the man had passed it, and yelled, "Stop! Police!"

Haas would say later that the man increased his speed even more, "to a ridiculous amount of speed for whatever was causing him a problem to walk. . . . He was trying with all his might to run holding his leg."

Haas shouted "Stop! Police!" again, and the man, who had reached the sidewalk in front of 31 Mohawk, suddenly ducked behind a gold Honda that was parked in the driveway.

Haas would testify later:

"At that particular point, the intensity was increased, because the subject's body movements were so descriptive that I knew there was serious trouble. . . . He had, all of a sudden, got behind this Honda car, and I could clearly see the butt of a rifle stock sticking out of his pants. And, still holding the umbrella—he was extremely panicked. He dropped that umbrella down, and he tried like hell to get that gun out.

". . . I told him, 'Stop, or I'll shoot.' I gave him the last directive that I could. He had made two extremely desperate and frantic attempts to get that gun out of his waistband. He was able to pull that rifle all the way out to where I could see the entire wooden forestock . . . the only portion that didn't come out was the front of the barrel.

". . . He took one quick second, and did look up at me. And I had already prepared to do what we hope we don't have to do."

Haas thought, I'm going to have to kill him. Now.

At this critical moment, Paraspolo pulled up, parked in the middle of the street and shone his spotlight on Haas and the man. He leaped out of his car, pulled his service revolver, and yelled, "Freeze. Drop the umbrella or I'll blow your fucking head off."

Haas remembers, "He looked at me, and he—very, very slowly, almost as though he didn't really want to let go, very slowly, still holding on to the umbrella, having ahold of that gun, just slowly looked at me, just started moving his hands. And twice he said, 'Okay. Okay. I'll stop.' And he raised his hands up."

Haas waited for Paraspolo to get in a position to cover him, then moved in cautiously, still shocked at how close he had come to shooting this man, and wrested the rifle out of the man's pants. It was almost completely out, but the front sight had gotten snagged on the fabric.

When he got it loose, he backed up, carried the weapon over and laid it on the grass by the sidewalk, keeping his revolver trained on the man.

Just then the man said, "I've got another gun."

He looked back at the man, who still had his hands in the air, and he could see a shoulder holster. He removed a snubnosed .38 from the holster, then patted him down and found a box of .22 bullets in his coat pocket. Then he cuffed him behind his back, and put him into the back of Bonnie Page's patrol car. She had arrived as he was disarming the man.

Paraspolo told Haas to lock the confiscated weapons in Page's trunk. He saw that another officer, Frank Baldassari, had arrived. He said quickly, "Come with me," and he and Baldassari walked toward 23 Mohawk.

Julie Bajo was still huddled, crying, in the closet, talking to the 911 operator. She knew that something terrible had happened to Artie. She couldn't hear him anymore. But she couldn't make herself go to him.

The operator had talked to Paraspolo, telling him that there was apparently no one else in the house, no weapons that the calling party knew of. Now the operator knew Paraspolo was going in, so she told Julie gently, put something on, the police are there at the front door and they're coming in.

Julie wouldn't put the telephone down until she knew they were there. Once she heard them, she says, she came out of the closet and walked, not looking left or right, down the hall to the living room, where she met Paraspolo and Baldassari.

Julie has given several different accounts of when she turned lights in the hall and bedroom on and off. But Paraspolo remembers that when they met her in the living room, she said, "Where's Artie?"

"I told her I didn't know, and I asked her, where's Artie? And she says, 'I think he's in the back. He may have been hit.' "

He says she spun around and took a couple of steps, then turned on a light in the hall.

Julie Bajo started screaming.

She gazed in horror at the crumpled form of Artie Mitchell, who lay curled in a fetal position, one arm outflung, just inside the doorway to the bathroom off the hall between the living room and the master bedroom they had shared. A circular pool of blood seeped into the bathroom's bright blue carpet.

Quickly, Paraspolo told Officer Frank Baldassari to take her out of there, try to calm her down, get her out of the way, so Baldassari took the hysterical Julie into the south bedroom and closed the door.

Paraspolo then tried to get a pulse from Artie's outstretched left arm, but could detect none. He couldn't see any sign of breathing, or any continuing flow of blood from his wounds. He also could feel no pulse in the carotid artery in the neck.

Haas had already called for medical assistance. Now Paraspolo told Haas to try to get the outside of the house secured. Then the sergeant got on the radio himself and told Sherri Thompkins, the dispatcher, that he didn't want a full rescue unit tramping through the house, messing up the crime scene. Just one medic and one fireman.

Tom Paraspolo knew that a whole army of paramedics could not do any good now. Artie Mitchell had had been shot three times—through the abdomen, right arm, and the right eye—and he was dead.

Paraspolo went back to the bedroom where Baldassari was calming Julie Bajo down. The tall, dignified young policeman was doing well at it. To Baldassari's embarrassment, Julie had brought out her portfolio of exotic dancing and modeling photographs and was showing them to him. She did keep asking him, "How bad is Artie hurt? Is he all right?"

Paraspolo didn't answer. Instead he described the man they had arrested outside, and told her that according to his ID, his name was James Mitchell.

"No!" Julie screamed.

"They're brothers. They love each other. They get along great. There's no way Jim would ever do anything like that to Artie."

PART 5

MITCHELL BROTHER, SINGULAR

Ray DeLeon could not believe it when he took the call from Sherri Thompkins: Artie Mitchell was dead and his brother, Jim, was in custody.

He hurried to the scene, arriving about 10:45 P.M.

His girlfriend, Officer Bonnie Page, was standing by her patrol car as he drove up, and he went over to greet her. He noticed someone in the "cage"—the backseat of her car—and she told him it was the suspect.

DeLeon opened the front door of the car, stuck his head in, and asked the man's name.

"James Mitchell."

"I'm Sergeant DeLeon. We'll need to interview you and process you."

"Oh," Jim Mitchell said. "You're Artie's cop."

"I'm not anybody's cop," DeLeon told him. "I'm just a detective who needs to question you."

DeLeon says Jim told him then, "I know I'm in trouble. I want a lawyer." He paused, then added, "I'll have plenty of time to think about what I've done."

DeLeon had the overpowering feeling that Jim was ready to talk about the shooting. But the moment passed; he said nothing more.

DeLeon took the keys to Jim's new Explorer from his pocket, along with a knife, which he was surprised to find. Someone should have taken it from him before he was put into the patrol car, DeLeon thought.

Then he braced himself to look at his friend's body, talked to Paraspolo, officially took over the crime scene from him, and directed his partner, Detective Jerry Mattos, and Officer Ron Richter in gathering physical evidence.

Jim was taken to the station in Corte Madera, and, after a time, so was Julie. It was there, four and a half hours after the shooting, that DeLeon told her Artie was dead.

A few minutes later, she pulled herself together enough to call Georgia Mae, who remembers it this way:

"Julie called and said, 'It's bad, Mae.' I said, 'What is it?' and she said, 'It's awful bad, Mae.' I asked her again what it was, and she said, 'It's awful bad.' Finally, I told her, 'Julie, I can take it. What are you telling me?' She said, 'Artie's dead, and that isn't all. Jim was found outside with a gun.'

It was 3 A.M., that unholy time of night when the bad news always comes, and the news couldn't be much worse for this 65-year-old widow: one of her two sons shot dead, the other caught at the scene with a recently fired rifle stuck down his pants.

But Georgia Mae Mitchell, for all the love she gave her family, for all her sensitivity, is made of cold-rolled steel, finer than any made in the Antioch mills.

"When she told me the part about Jim, my immediate thought was that to do such a terrible thing, he had to be crazy, and I was concerned for Lisa's safety," she says.

She called Jim and Lisa's number, but got no answer. So she called Art's house, maintaining her composure somehow, drawing every scrap of fortitude from her tremendous personal store, and spoke politely to the police who were standing not ten feet from the body of her youngest son.

She gave the cops Jim's address in San Francisco, and asked that someone be sent over to check on Lisa. They assured her it would be done.

She called her brother in Arkansas, and J.R.'s sister-in-law in tiny Victor, California, told them the grim, bare facts as she knew them, and promised to be back in touch.

Meredith called. The two women were not close friends, and yet they shared something that is irrevocable between mothers and first wives. Divorce, obviously, had twisted it, but even that was a bond of a sort; it had made both of them miserable. Now the ultimate sadness was on them both. Artie had long ceased to be the twenty-four-year-old Meredith had fallen in love with, just as he had ceased to be the five-year-old towheaded scamp who kept Georgia Mae laughing back in 1950. But in a larger way he had still been both of those people, and their common loss was profound.

Meredith offered her house in Lafayette as a headquarters for Georgia and the family as they sorted through the dreadful logistics that would occupy the next few days, and for the time being Georgia Mae accepted.

Moving mechanically, Georgia set a few clothes out on the bed to pack. It was first light now, the first day dawning without Artie Jay Mitchell in her life. She thought back to the day back in 1947 when she lost little Bobby. Only one son now, she thought. Just one left. And goodness knows what will happen to him.

She spoke with Charlie Benton, who had been at the theater all night, calling people, grieving and worrying. I'll be down there, she told him, but not for a few hours. Benton, who had been the first of the inner circle to confront Artie about his drug and alcohol abuse, who had refused to stand by and watch as he destroyed himself, would be at the theater for the next forty-eight hours straight.

Georgia Mae also spoke to Lisa, who had been awakened by the police sometime after 4 A.M., checking to make sure she was all right. She had seen the lights of the patrol car out her window, and had heard somebody banging on the door downstairs. Freaked out, she had called Dennis Roberts, who told her to go down to the garage, staying away from the windows, and find out who was out there.

She had crawled down the hall and down the steps to the garage, then called out, "Who are you? What do you want?"

"We're from the San Francisco Police Department," a voice said, "and your mother-in-law called us because she was concerned about you. What is your name?" When she said "Lisa Adams," they told her, "That's all we need to know." And they left.

Even more distraught by this time, she called Roberts back and got his wife, Sandy, who was a good friend. Sandy told her, Dennis is in his car, and gave her his car phone number. She called it, and told him, "Somebody needs to tell me what's going on!"

He said simply, "Lisa, Art's dead and Jim's in jail. I don't know any more than that. I'm on the way to the Marin County Jail now."

Roberts had discovered what had happened in roundabout fashion. Maureen O'Neill, a respected journalist and Alameda County political heavyweight, had worked in the office of Kennedy and Rhine as a legal secretary in the 1970s, and remains close to both Kennedy and Roberts. At around 2 A.M., she had received a panicked call from close Mitchell confidant Dan O'Neill (no relation), most recently one of the driving forces behind *War News*.

"Jim's shot Art, we need lawyers, help. Call Michael, Call Dennis," he said.

Everyone in the Mitchell group from forever, like Dan, knew that Maureen was a direct contact to both Roberts and Kennedy, so it was logical that the call would come to her. But she just couldn't accept what she was hearing. It was made even more bizarre by the fact that she had spent three hours with Jim Mitchell and Dan O'Neill that day at the *War News* office, and it was the first time she had seen either of them in years.

"Dan, I don't believe you," she said bluntly. "I want to confirm this before I talk to anybody." O'Neill gave her a phone number for Julie Bajo. By this time, Julie had gone to Richard Freeman's for the night. So she called Bajo there, and found out that Dan O'Neill had not been exaggerating. Actually, she was amazed at the detail of the description that Julie gave her.

"She was obviously still in shock, and she was like a machine," Maureen O'Neill recalls. "She gave me a blow-by-blow account, complete with green sweat pants, foaming beer bottle, the works. I asked her, 'Are you all right?' not because she was hysterical, but because she wasn't. She was on autopilot at that point, obviously."

Now Maureen believed. She called Dennis Roberts—only to discover that he had put his answering machine on for the night. She tried several times, with growing frustration. Finally, she looked at her watch. It was almost 7 A.M. New York time, so she called Michael Kennedy.

Kennedy had not been dealing with the brothers over the past few years, and he didn't know just how bad things had been. He knew all was not well; the last time he had been to San Francisco, Jim had told him, "I don't know what to do about Art, Michael. He's really pissing in the soup. He's making the employees unhappy, even the ones who have been with us forever. I've just got to do something." Nevertheless, Kennedy thought the idea of Jim shooting anybody, much less the brother with whom he was so close, was surreal, fantastic. He was absolutely horrified.

Maureen O'Neill told him about Roberts's answering machine. Coincidentally, her son had been babysitting for Roberts and his wife that night, and had returned home, so she knew they were home, and had just put the machine on so the phone wouldn't disturb them. "Go over there and get him up, and tell him to go to Jim," Kennedy told her without hesitation.

She lives only a few blocks from Roberts in the Oakland hills, so it took her less than five minutes to go to his house, wake him up and tell him what was going on. It was shortly after 4 A.M.

Roberts was shocked, of course, but less so than Kennedy. He had done work for the brothers much more recently, and had been more and more put off by Artie in recent years. "It got so I avoided him whenever I went over to talk to Jim," he would say later. "It was a shame. Artie was just as bright as Jim was, but after a while you couldn't have an intelligent conversation with him anymore, the way you could in the old days. If you didn't want to talk about drugs or pussy, there was nothing to talk to Artie Mitchell about. Of course, Jimmy was always fun, very wise, very wry, very witty, very well versed on lots of topics, books, you name it.

"It was no fun going out socially with Artie. You just sat there tense around him. I didn't want him grabbing my old lady's ass, I didn't want him going off on someone. If it was just Jimmy and me, it was great."

It was just Jimmy and Roberts, over at the jail in the Marin Civic Center that night, but it sure wasn't great. It was awful.

There was nothing Roberts could do. "All I could say was, 'I'm here,' " Roberts says. "We couldn't talk. Jim was totally out of it, crying, distraught. He didn't even know where he was.

"It was so sad, so pathetic."

After getting someone to come over and sit by her phone, Georgia Mae went to Meredith's early on the morning of the twenty-eighth. Meredith gave her a ride into the city later, and they arrived at the theater at about noon.

Many things had transpired in that office, around the poker table and in, around, and under the pool table. But the teary-eyed, tight-jawed meeting around the card table now was unprecedented. It was most of the Mitchell inner circle, or what was left of it without the brothers: Georgia Mae, Meredith, Jeff Armstrong, cousins Rocky Davidson and Johnny and Denny Morgan, Ruby Richardson, Charlie Benton. The news that had seemed so surreal in the dead of night had to be faced now in the harshness of the day.

Like a stripper used to sleeping late and using makeup designed for the stage, the O'Farrell was never at its best in daylight. But never had the place looked so forlorn as it did at noon on this gray, final February day.

The cavernous office had the bleakness of a place extinguished by time, like a child's bedroom after the child isn't one anymore. The joyful spirit of that room, where Artie had seduced dancers and shot off guns and won lowball tournaments and shacked up under the pool table with Missy Manners and presided with his brother over the classiest ribaldry San Francisco had ever seen, was gone. And the red-eyed people around the poker table realized it could never be the same again.

A lot of hard, unpleasant work faced them. They split up into groups: one to deal with Art, one to deal with Jim. The Art crew, which included Georgia Mae, Meredith, and the Morgans, had to solve the problems of cremation, which had been Artie's stated wish, and services. The Jim group, of course, had to deal with the reality of his situation, and getting the legal machinery working for him.

Through all of that, the business had to be run, and day-to-day decisions had to be made about that. Of course, the theater would close, but when, and for how long? Dancers were already showing up for work.

Georgia Mae quickly recognized that somebody had to be put in charge, so people didn't go off at cross purposes, and she knew immediately who it should be. "Jeff," she told Armstrong, "you're in charge."

He asked her if she was sure, and she repeated, "You're in charge. You must make the final decisions."

She had picked wisely. Of all the theater insiders, Jeff was the person most qualified to lead in Jim's absence. Everyone would be frazzled over the next dozen days, but Jeff would carry the greatest load, juggling the theater and the press and well-wishers and family and cops and Jim and his own savage grief. He and Artie, Antioch High Class of '63, had been as close as friends get, and as Jeff filled bigger roles with the company he had gotten equally close to Jim. That dreadful morning, he cried for both of them.

San Francisco attorney Tom Steel, a close friend of the brothers who handled many civil matters for them, including the Orange County fight against Keating and the city of Santa Ana, went to the jail to see Jim the morning after the shooting. He was shocked when Jim was led into a little room where Steel could talk with him by phone. "I didn't think it was him," he would testify later. "He was pale and drawn, his eyes were bloodshot. He put his hand up to touch the glass, and I put mine up on the other side. He looked like he was going to fall apart.

"He said, 'My world is shattered.' "

Kennedy had told Tom to tell Jim to call him collect, and Jim called. "Jimmy, don't try to tell me what happened," Kennedy told him. "Just tell me, do you need me out there?"

"I need you," Jim managed.

"I will be there," he said, and within twenty-four hours he was.

Flanked by Kennedy and Roberts, looking as grim as the grave, Jim mumbled "not guilty" at an arraignment on Friday, two days after the shooting.

At the hearing, Kennedy asked Marin Superior Court Judge Vernon P. Smith to allow a psychiatric examination of Jim Mitchell, due to his "profoundly disturbed state." He told reporters afterward, "Jimmy is deeply troubled," and voiced fears that he might try to kill himself.

Those fears were not just window dressing. He had never seen a more remorseful client. "He could hardly speak, and all he would say was, 'I killed my brother. I killed my mother's baby. I killed by nieces' and nephews' father. There's nothing left.' "

Family members were not allowed to see him for several days, and when they were, he was in no better shape. When he first saw Georgia Mae, tears were streaming down his face, and begged her over and over, "Tell those kids I didn't mean to hurt Art."

He had already destroyed part of himself, it was clear, when he shot Artie. The two brothers had been so close, considered by each other and the world as interlocking parts of a single being, that the fratricide was in effect a suicidal act for Jim, and Kennedy would increasingly suspect that Art had used Jim as an instrument of suicide.

Whether or not he was legally sane when he fired them, those eight .22 bullets had fractured Jim Mitchell's psychic identity, sewn as it was like Peter Pan's shadow to that of his younger brother. In the days after the shooting, it was increasingly clear to Georgia and Jeff and the others who were closest that the remaining part of the unit was considerably less than half of the whole.

When he couldn't get Jim into a hospital, Kennedy came to the tactical decision that it was in Jim's interest to stay in jail for a few days, so that it would not appear that he had bought his freedom immediately.

But that didn't mean Kennedy wanted his client to languish in the Marin County Jail forever, and he knew that something would have to be done soon.

At the time of Artie's death, a veteran police officer named Gordon Card was staying at Karen's house.

Karen says, "I had a guy from the Marin County Major Crimes Task Force staying here because they thought Artie was going to kill me. So this guy was sleeping on my couch, protecting me. Art kept calling me, telling me he was going to kill me. I'd hand the phone to the cop, and he'd threaten to kill me to the cop."

The Task Force, however, indicates that no one was ever assigned to protect Karen Mitchell. Faced with this, Karen backtracks, saying, "I'm not sure if it was unofficial, federal, local, or what. Somebody could have hired him to protect me. Jim Mitchell could have done it. He denies it, but he could have. If you find out, let me know."

Card, who worked for the Mill Valley Police Department for years, was assigned for a time to the Major Crimes Task Force. He later resigned and went to work for the civilian security force at Hamilton Air Force Base. But he emphatically denies that he was assigned by the Task Force or by anyone else to protect Karen Mitchell. Rather, he says, he had a personal relationship with her at the time—a relationship that ended, he says, shortly after the shooting.

Karen says matter-of-factly, "I found out he knew DeLeon for quite a while . . . and he was falling in love with me, so I broke it off."

For whatever reason he was at Karen's house, it fell to Gordon Card to tell Aaron, Jasmine, and Caleb on the morning of February 28 that their father was dead.

Then Karen told the kids that it was "all for the best" that their father had been shot to death, because he was so out of it that he was a danger to others, including them.

For a kid who has just lost a father, that's a pretty tough concept to grasp.

The question of a memorial service for Artie was complicated. How many people should be able to attend? Where should it be held? Who should officiate? Jeff and Georgia Mae discussed using the cavernous Great American Music Hall, next door to the theater, but ultimately decided to limit the attendance to family and close friends. Georgia Mae insisted on one thing: anyone who cared enough to call the theater and ask about services should be invited.

Finally, it was decided: the cremation would be done at Marin's Daphne Funeral Home, where Art's body had been taken and autopsied. The memorial service would be Sunday afternoon, at Higgins Funeral Home on A Street in Antioch.

On the afternoon after the shooting, Missy Manners flew into San Francisco to offer her support for the family. Missy was probably closer to Georgia Mae than any of Artie's girlfriends had been, and she was still particularly close to Artie's three older children.

She helped Mae set up a viewing of Artie's body for the family at Daphne on Friday. Martha and Julie and the family all went.

"I went with Mae and the three big kids," Missy says. "Karen said we could pick up the littler kids and take them, but then she backed out of that."

Karen, as usual, tells it differently. She says, "We weren't invited. Everybody else went there except us. I thought that was pretty cold. I was really hurt. Aaron didn't want to go, but the other kids had to. They said, 'Mom, we're going to go. If you don't take us we're going by ourselves.' I said I didn't know if it was a good idea, but they wanted to see him. They wanted to see if he was really dead, so I agreed to take Jasmine and Caleb. We went in, and we all looked at him, and they touched him.

"Jasmine said, 'Mommy, mommy, look at his hair, look at him, he looks so clean. I've never seen him this clean.' It was really sad. I cried.

"Caleb didn't want to touch him, but I think he did, just to make sure he was cold."

The rest of the family had been there earlier in the day, before Karen and the little kids went, and they had brought paper and written notes to Artie, goodbye notes, to be burned with him.

Karen also brought stationery, so that she and the kids could do the same thing. The notes would lead to one of the ugliest incidents of the post-shooting aftermath.

Kristal, too, went to the funeral home to see Artie. "As I walked in, my crystal necklace broke," she said, "so I laid it on him along with a pair of tie-dyed socks for when he got his cold feet. I wanted something to keep me with him forever."

After the viewing, Liberty had gone up to Karen's to try to see the little kids, and Karen was in the midst of doing a live TV interview—wearing a black veil. One of Storm's friends had cut in front of the microphone and said, "You know, everything she says is bullshit." At that moment, Karen was saying, "He just couldn't get over being so in love with me."

Karen Mitchell had been livid about Ray DeLeon ever since he had submitted the declaration to help Artie's side in the custody fight. She kept repeating the accusation that Artie had paid the veteran cop for the statement. "Artie told everybody he paid him off. He was bragging about it," she would say later. "He thought it was really cool. It wasn't cool. It was dumb. And DeLeon's going to prison for it," she threatened. "He'll do two, three, four years. That makes me happy."

DeLeon has always vigorously denied all of Karen's allegations, but her complaining and the friendship he had with Artie would cause the detective more trouble than he could ever have imagined.

The days immediately after the shooting were all marathons for

DeLeon. Jim was the obvious culprit in the shooting, but there was a mountain of evidence to obtain, catalogue, consider.

The case had been assigned to a deputy D.A. named Chuck Cacciatore, a tall, easygoing, personable prosecutor with seven years' experience in Marin County. He had a reputation for courtroom skill and efficiency, although he had only tried one other homicide. He had never handled such a high-profile case before, and he wanted to make sure he got every possible scrap of evidence.

On the night of the shooting, Artie's safe had been locked. Cacciatore had no idea who knew the combination (Julie had told investigators she didn't), and he wanted to get at the safe before any of Artie's friends or family had a chance to get there first. For a house that was supposed to be a sealed crime scene, there had been lots of people trooping in and out.

Twin Cities police were watching the house, going by every hour or so to make sure all was well. On one of their swings past the house on Friday evening, March 1, they noticed that a door that had been previously locked was open. Cacciatore, reached at home, decided he could wait no longer to get a look at the contents of that safe. By the time a locksmith got over to 23 Mohawk late that evening, there was a large law-enforcement team present, including Cacciatore; DeLeon; Twin Cities Detective Jerry Mattos; the husband-and-wife team of D.A.'s investigators, Kathy and Clay Hoffman; and some uniformed patrol officers. Most of them had been there since the afternoon, continuing to examine the shooting scene.

The locksmith drilled the safe dial in short order, and in the wee hours of Saturday morning they inventoried the safe's contents. According to DeLeon's report, they included a cigar box holding $7,800 in cash; loose currency totaling about $148; and several guns, including a .25 caliber Beretta pistol, a .22 Ruger pistol, a Browning Hi-Power 9mm pistol, a .22 caliber Winchester pump rifle, and two air pistols.

(The Mitchell defense would later intimate that one of the guns actually had been out of the safe on the night of Art's death. The forensic evidence would strongly suggest that Artie had fired the Browning at Julie's coffee table that afternoon, and Skip Dossett would testify to seeing a gun in Artie's closet when he visited. But there is no evidence that by the time Artie went to bed that night, the gun had not been returned to the safe, where DeLeon and the others swear it was found.)

Those who knew Artie were surprised that there wasn't a lot of marijuana in the safe, but DeLeon says all the cops found in the safe were seeds. Karen Mitchell, for one, didn't believe there wasn't marijuana in the safe. But she didn't merely accuse DeLeon of swiping a little pot. On Monday, March 4, she told Ruby Richardson that Ray DeLeon had stolen $50,000 from Artie's safe.

By then, DeLeon had already been removed from the case.

Chuck Cacciatore had found one other thing of interest in the safe—a copy of the declaration Ray DeLeon had made for Artie.

"Ray, what the hell is this?" Cacciatore said he asked DeLeon. "What's going on here?"

There was no doubt in his mind DeLeon would have to be taken off the case. Later that Saturday morning, he had a meeting with Twin Cities Chief Phil Green and told him. Green broke the news to his senior sergeant later that day.

In retrospect, it's hard to understand why DeLeon, a veteran officer, wouldn't have seen from the first that his work on the case would present at least an appearance of conflict of interest. Why didn't he duck it that first night? It would have been easy for him to say, "I can't work on this case because I knew the victim."

Was he worried that some embarrassing evidence of his relationship with Artie, or with Martha, would be disclosed during an investigation, and he thought he could best keep a lid on it if he were in charge?

At any rate, DeLeon must have wished before long that he had never been involved, because things just kept getting worse for him.

The *Marin Independent Journal* broke the story of DeLeon's removal on Wednesday, and in that story Chief Green disclosed that he had asked the state Attorney General's office to investigate DeLeon to make sure there were no improprieties involved with the Mitchell case. The AG's office declined to do the investigation, which was shunted to the Marin County Sheriff's office.

Buoyed by the feeling that she had helped get DeLeon into trouble, Karen Mitchell walked into the Twin Cities Police Department on March 18 and swore out a citizen's complaint, alleging that DeLeon had:

- stolen "$30,000 to $50,000" from Artie Mitchell's safe after the shooting;
- looked the other way when visiting 23 Mohawk while Artie had pot plants growing in the backyard;
- taken Martha Rauber up on her offer of sex, made at Artie's behest, after DeLeon's declaration was filed in his custody case.

The Twin Cities department would announce that the sheriff's office had cleared DeLeon of all charges, but it was by far the worst episode of his twenty-eight-year career. During the case he would develop serious heart trouble and be forced to go on medical disability.

Karen would not quit making the allegations to anyone who would listen, but she also had some explaining to do about a visit of her own to 23 Mohawk during the first week in March.

Family members who had gone into the house with police escort to get some things had noticed there were quite a few items missing, including several original paintings and art objects, photographs, a stereo, a Macintosh computer, a camera, two VCRs, a coffee maker, some jewelry, and a brand-new fax machine. Even Artie's stuffed swordfish was missing from above the fireplace.

Then the older kids found out that some of the missing items had been seen at Karen's house, including a very valuable Erté-signed lithograph.

Liberty called the Twin Cities police, who went to see Karen.

She gave back the computer and a few other things, but she kept the painting, claiming she had a receipt for it. The family is still irritated that the District Attorney's office decided not to prosecute.

In an interview, she gave her explanation of how she happened to visit the supposedly sealed crime scene (which seems to have had more people going in and out than a hot-sheet hotel) unescorted and remove several things. Her account takes several leaps of logic that strain credulity:

"I took the kids' clothes, Jasmine's radio, and Aaron's computer. Aaron had a computer class he got a D in because he didn't have his computer. He begged me to get his computer. He was in tears. I said okay. I called the police. They said, Okay, Sergeant DeLeon's off the case but he'll call and arrange for you to go into the house.

"So I thought, well, you [the police] don't have jurisdiction over it anymore. I'll have to call the coroner. So the coroner says we're done with our investigation, we don't have jurisdiction over it anymore. You'll have to talk to the next of kin.

"So I went up to the jail. I knew Georgia Mae would be there, and I said, I've got to get some stuff from the house, the kids' clothes and all, because all their clothes were down there and they didn't have anything to wear. I told her I needed Aaron's computer. So she told me, 'Well, I'll meet you down at the house at two o'clock.'

"So I went down there at two o'clock and she didn't show. [Georgia Mae says she never agreed to meet Karen at the house, instead referring her to the police.]

"The coroner said the family had jurisdiction, so I thought the agreement was I could go into the house, that somebody would be there. And the message from the dispatcher was that Sergeant DeLeon would arrange for me to go in the house. So I thought, well, if he's going to arrange for me to go in the house, maybe he left the door open for me. So I went up to the door. And Liberty, Storm, and Mariah had already been in the house, Melissa [Missy] had been in the house. So I thought, there's not a big problem with me going in the house.

"I got the kids' clothes. It was a very traumatic experience for me. It smelled bad. Blood all over the place, plaster all over. I had a hard time composing myself. You know, it wouldn't be so bad if it wasn't someone you know, but it was Artie's house. The vibes were horrible.

"So I got the kids' clothes and Aaron's computer and then the District Attorneys come over the next day and I said, yeah, I got this stuff out of the house, and they said, you shouldn't have done that. So I told them the story, and I said I didn't know it was a big deal.

"So then DeLeon threw a fit and said, 'She burglarized the house.' And the D.A. said, naah, she didn't. So I said, 'Look, if there's a problem, here, take the computer, take the radio, take Jasmine's answering machine. It's not a big deal. I don't care. The kids care. What you're doing is taking the kids' possessions. You're traumatizing them even more.' But they took it."

Then, asked about the artwork, she said, "Yeah, I took the artwork that Artie had burglarized out of my house. I finally got it back." She laughed. "I had receipts for it. Damn it, it's mine. I knew I wasn't going to get it back from Georgia."

The physical evidence in *People* v. *Mitchell* was beginning to take shape.

For starters, there were the two guns that Jim was carrying when he was arrested—the .38 Special in a shoulder holster, unfired, with a full five-round cylinder, and the .22 rifle that he had stuffed down his pant leg. Officer Richter, whom DeLeon had detailed to gather evidence that night, had found seven spent .22 shell casings on the kitchen floor, near the doorway to the living room that looked down the hall where the shots had been fired. Seven slugs were recovered that night, but one badly mutilated slug, larger than the others, with glass fragments still attached, was almost undoubtedly a 9mm round fired by Artie through Julie's table earlier in the day.

It was assumed that Jim Mitchell had fired seven times, until Detective Mario Watkins examined the .22 at the police station and discovered a spent casing still in the rifle. That made eight shots.

Two slugs were still unaccounted for. One was found the next day in Artie's chest at autopsy, but it wasn't until March 4 that the police realized there was still one slug missing. Mattos went back to the house and found the slug—à la Poe's Purloined Letter—in plain view on top of a dresser in Artie's bedroom.

The .22 also held six unfired rounds. Jim had gone to 23 Mohawk that night with the capability of firing nineteen rounds from his two weapons before he had to reload. If reloading was necessary, though, he was prepared. He had also carried a box of .22 long rifle bullets in his jacket.

The autopsy itself had revealed few surprises. Artie Mitchell died from the head shot, which entered through the right upper eyelid, just below the ridge of the skull above the eye, and exited just behind the left ear. He had two other gunshot wounds. One was a through-and-through abdominal wound, with the entrance almost at the middle of his body, just above the navel, exiting through the left side of the back. This bullet passed through nothing but soft tissue, perforating the intestine but missing the spine and vital organs. Dr. Ervin Jindrich, the Marin County Coroner who performed the autopsy, would later testify that it was a survivable wound.

The third wound was to the right arm and chest. The entry wasn't as small and circular as the other two entry wounds were. It was oval, approximately 1.2 centimeters horizontally by .8 centimeter vertically, compared with the other two circular entry wounds, both approximately .6 centimeter in size. On Artie's right chest, even with the arm wound, was an abrasion and a hard lump under the skin that turned out to be a flattened .22 slug. Because of the size and shape of the wound and the fact that the bullet lodged in Artie's body, the logical conclusion was that this bullet hit something else before it hit Artie, while the other two struck him directly.

The rest of the autopsy revealed that Artie was in amazingly good health, with the exception of some relatively minor fatty degeneration of the liver, certainly to be expected. Jindrich noted in the autopsy protocol that Artie's head was "covered by a fringe of relatively long brown sprinkled with gray hair with a marked fronto-superior balding pattern." That's for sure.

The toxicological screen showed—surprisingly—no discernible levels of marijuana or any drug other than alcohol, but it did show that Artie was smashed. His blood alcohol level was .25 percent—more than three times the legal limit. (*Jim's* blood tested positive for marijuana.)

Jindrich wasn't going too far out on a limb when he signed the official coroner's verdict: homicide.

Artie's girlfriends were all in abject shock. Missy, who had come to town immediately to help the family, just couldn't believe Artie was gone. And she just didn't know what to think about Jim. He had been very kind to her over the years. She had seen him and Artie in conflict, but she would never have dreamed it could come to this. She felt anger, but also sorrow and compassion, because she truly believed that if Jim had killed Artie, he had to have lost his mind.

Kristal too felt the horrible, tearing grief, mixed with anger. But she too felt bad for Jim. "He just snapped," she would say. "He's the type of guy who keeps it all in, and he just snapped, he blew. That's why I can't turn my back on him. I mean, we've all done it, I've snapped at certain times, just lost it."

Even Bana was in deep conflict about her feelings for Jim. She knew how crazy Artie could be, and she could see how it could happen.

Joanne was different. She felt no conflict at all. She felt desolated; Artie was her life, and Jim had taken him away. She thought it was cold-blooded first-degree murder, pure and simple, and she didn't mind saying so.

She thought the way everybody else was sucking up to Jim was disgusting. As for the other women, she thought their attitude proved what she had thought all along: she was the only one who truly loved Art Mitchell.

Sunday, March 3, was rainy and cold in Antioch.

Funeral weather.

More than two hundred Mitchell friends and family members packed the chapel at Higgins Funeral Home to say goodbye to Artie. A few journalists hung around outside, but very few even knew about it. Resourceful *Examiner* reporter Andy Furillo was the only one who managed to get into the service, and he did it the old-fashioned way: he walked in and sat down. Nobody said boo to him. Consequently, the *Ex* had an exclusive the next day. The *Chron* missed it totally; they had run a story the day before saying no services were planned.

The family had requested donations to the San Francisco Fire Department's Surf Rescue Unit in lieu of flowers, but of course there was a profusion of flowers anyway, many of them in elaborate arrangements.

Missy had a huge display made in the shape of a poker hand. Joanne Scott's display was coincidentally almost identical to Georgia Mae's: a big heart with white carnations and red roses, with a red ribbon that said, "Art."

Predictably, it was an affair both raucous and poignant. The crowd was moved to "CAW!" in Artie's style, and also moved to tears as a couple of dozen people eulogized him in an informal open microphone session.

Bill Boyer recalled the summer days he spent riding with Artie in the bed of Frank Grangnelli's watermelon truck, careening down dirt roads with dust and straw flying in the air around them.

"Artie got in the fast lane when we grew up, and it was a lot like riding in the back of that truck with the watermelons," Boyer said. "We were bombarded by things out of our control, and we didn't have sense enough to get into the cab."

Marilyn Chambers, eight months pregnant, was huffing and puffing by the time she got to the mike. "I just know Art would love me to go into labor right here," she said, before remarking on Artie's generosity and unique personality.

The crowd was quiet as the Reverend Bill Mitchell, a Palm Springs minister and one of the brothers' cousins, read a statement from Georgia Mae:

"I know Jim loved Art. He took care of them all their lives. Whatever happened, we don't know. But he never intended to hurt Art."

Mariah, Artie's seventeen-year-old daughter and the youngest of the three children he had with Meredith, said, "I love Uncle Jim. I don't blame him at all. No matter what, he's my uncle, and I love him." Mary Jane brought all of Jim's kids forward and they each spoke briefly, even little Justin, who had to be held up to the microphone to say, "I'm Uncle Art's nephew. The last time I saw him was at the Christmas party, and I just love him very much."

Tears were never far away for Missy that day, but seeing those little kids brought them forth afresh. It was just so touching, these four little kids going up and remembering their Uncle Art, probably wondering when they would see their dad again.

Karen was there with the children, of course. Her twins were crying uncontrollably; she took them out once, but came back and they continued to cry. "The second time I just couldn't stand it," Kristal Rose said later. "I took them and said, 'I'm going outside with them. Go ahead and stay, but they're coming outside with me.' It took twenty minutes to get them to stop crying, and we had no coats, no keys to her car, in the rain.

"And then she didn't even thank me."

Joanne, totally outside the "official" group of relatives, ex-wives, and theater insiders who had always been reluctant to acknowledge her relationship with Artie, sat in the back with her friend Rita Ricardo and Rita's husband, Charles Webb. She had arrived early because she was worried that someone would remove her card from the flowers. She went in before the service and quickly stapled the card to the outside of the envelope on the display.

Even trying to think of what to say on the card had been a strain in the state she had been in over the past few days. She had thought about "Bon soir, mon cheri," but decided on the simple, "I love you very much. Joanne."

After she had finished, she had seen Johnny Morgan and Rocky, at the front of the chapel, making sure all was arranged correctly. Johnny said to her, "Hey, Joanne, how are you doing? Are you keeping under control?" She just nodded grimly at him. Rocky didn't say a word, and she walked away.

She did go up to the front row before the service began and gave her condolences to Georgia Mae, who was sitting with Lisa and best friend Nancy Harrison, another former dancer who was working as a secretary at the theater. All she could do was look at Lisa, and think, you know more about this than you're saying, but she gave Nancy a hug, and they both started crying. Missy, who hated Joanne almost as much as Joanne hated her, was a few feet behind, in the second row, with Meredith and Liberty, Storm, and Mariah.

Joanne quickly went back and sat down with Ricardo and Webb and Mike Weldon, one of the owners of the New Century, and his girlfriend, an Argentine dancer named Isabella. Just a couple of months later, Weldon would die suddenly of a heart attack, and Joanne would be going to his funeral, and empathizing strongly with Isabella as she stood on the outskirts of the "official" mourning party, including Weldon's ex-wife.

Joanne had noticed the woman handing out the in memoriam cards as people walked in, and wondered who she was. She was shocked to find out, when the woman got up to speak, that it was Julie Bajo, whom she had never met.

Julie said, "Artie doesn't like wimps, so we've got to be strong," adding, "he was absolutely the best man I ever met."

To Joanne, the whole open-mike thing was ghastly, and she thought it seemed scripted and weird, particularly Jim's little kids. She couldn't believe there was a minister officiating, even if it was a relative. It seemed so unlike Art.

Liberty, sitting up in the second row, was having some of the same thoughts. The whole thing was an unbelievable ordeal, and it seemed incongruous to her, not like her father at all.

"When they played 'Amazing Grace,' I thought, 'My God, Dad couldn't escape it right to the end. This is so *Okie*.' " She didn't want to offend Georgia Mae, though, so she stuck it out. "I was keeping it together, feeling strong, but I was still really tripping out on the vision I had had that he was going to die—and, of course, really freaking out about Jim.

"Also, I knew that dad would be saying, 'Oh, hell, fuck all this, lighten up.' He hated funerals, and he couldn't stand going to them."

Certainly, there were many moments Artie would have appreciated. Theater employee Phil Brady said, "Art taught me how to roll a marijuana cigarette with one paper instead of two. I think we've saved about 10,000 trees since then." And Artie's friend Tony Pérez, the Dynatones' saxophonist, played "Cry Me a River."

Rebelliously, Liberty wore a bright red jacket and white pants. She knew Artie would have been scornful if she had been creeping around in black. (Dress varied wildly, from Missy's opulent black velvet and pearls to Kristal's jeans and down vest.)

Throughout the service, Liberty's strongest emotion was relief for Artie, that he was finally out of his pain. "I felt good that he wasn't going to have to deal with Karen anymore," she said. "I do blame her completely for his death—at least for the death of his character."

But she and the rest of the family still had to deal with Karen. Liberty saw her right after the service, and asked if the smaller kids could come to Meredith's house afterward for a family get-together. Karen snapped, "No, I don't think so. I read the note Mariah left on your dad's body, and there's some hostility here that needs to be dealt with."

Mariah had written, "I'm sorry your life was destroyed by that witch."

Liberty was amazed. Karen had actually read the notes others had left on Artie's chest, to be burned with him? There must have been fifteen notes there. Had she taken each one off him and read it? (Later, Karen would say that she just "happened to see" the note, and that Jasmine saw it first and pointed it out to her.) Liberty's stomach turned, and she walked outside—into the range of waiting photographers. She wheeled angrily on them and gave them the finger, then went back inside in time to see Mariah and Karen getting into it.

"You read those notes? You fucking bitch!" Mariah yelled.

"Come on, kids," Karen said. "We're leaving." She turned to Mariah and Liberty. "You're never going to see these kids."

"We'll get a fucking court order, you bitch," Liberty snarled.

Artie would have been proud of that.

Artie's wallet, which was apparently in his sweat pants when he died, was recovered by the coroner and turned over to the family. It held $63.

It was a metaphor for his estate: he wasn't destitute, but he wasn't as rich as many people assumed either.

Karen, living in luxury with her Jag and her Harley and her house on the hill, having fed like a great white shark off Artie and the O'Farrell for seven years of ex-wifedom, was quoted in the *San Francisco Chronicle* as saying that Artie "owned nothing" and was "basically broke" at his death.

On Wednesday, March 6, Artie's will was read at the O'Farrell. Georgia Mae, Ruby, Meredith, Mitchell's estate attorney, Hal Forbes, Karen, and Karen's attorney and accountant attended.

The will simply specified that his estate would be divided equally among his six children. In liquid cash, Artie had the money in the safe plus some $23,000 in a bank account, plus some accrued salary from the O'Farrell. The bulk of the estate, held in a living trust set up to exclude it from federal estate tax, was Artie's half interest in Cinema 7, the O'Farrell's parent company. In addition, there was a $1 million life insurance policy with the beneficiary being Cinema 7, designed to be paid into the trust.

The value of his interest in Cinema 7 was unclear, but it was agreed that in the coming months the estate would have an appraisal performed.

It would be a long time before the estate was settled, Georgia Mae knew, and there would be conflict every step of the way.

California may be teeming with young people, liberal people, people of color. But they don't vote. The Golden State's electorate bears little resemblance to its demographics. The people who actually vote are overwhelmingly white, older, and conservative, and their consistent concern is to protect what they already have against the inrushing hordes of new Californians. It is an electorate that produced the notorious Proposition 13, which capped property taxes for longtime residents at the expense of newcomers. It gave Ronald Reagan his political beginnings. And in 1990, these conservative, crime-weary voters passed Proposition 115, a sweeping law-and-order initiative that changed some of the most basic ground rules of the criminal trial. Needless to say, the changes were not exactly in the direction of preserving civil liberties.

The Mitchell case was one of the first two homicide cases that would be tried in Marin County under the full effect of 115. From the very outset of Chuck Cacciatore's case, the new rules would be apparent.

First of all, he made the decision to charge Jim Mitchell by means of a criminal grand jury indictment rather than a preliminary hearing. The criminal grand jury had been all but extinct in California since 1978, when the state Supreme Court had ruled that a preliminary hearing between indictment and trial was a necessary step. Proposition 115 effectively overruled that opinion, giving the criminal grand jury indictment back to prosecutors as a viable weapon for bringing defendants to trial. Before the initiative was passed, defendants charged with serious crimes were given a preliminary hearing, in which a judge would decide, based on evidence presented in court, whether or not there was cause to hold the defendant for the jury trial. The preliminary hearing was open; the defendant and counsel participated, and they could cross-examine prosecution witnesses and present exculpatory evidence of their own.

The grand jury proceedings are held in secret. The defendant is not present or represented. The prosecution leads the jury through its case, and asks for an indictment based on the evidence it presents.

Cacciatore wasted little time. On Thursday, March 7, nine days after the shooting, he convened a grand jury of nineteen Marin County residents who had been called for regular jury duty.

He introduced himself to them, and said, "I am here before you this morning seeking a murder indictment against James Lloyd Mitchell, for the murder of his brother, Arthur [sic] Jay Mitchell.

". . . I'm going to tell you right now, you're not going to hear all of the evidence in this case. It's not required that I present it all to you. But I'm sure that you'll have more than enough evidence to"—he hesitated—"just to look at the case."

Cacciatore kept it short and sweet. The grand jury would hear from just six witnesses.

The first was Julie Bajo, who was destined to be a nightmare witness for the prosecution all the way up to, and including, trial. Understandably, as many people who have witnessed traumatic situations do, she would keep changing her account of what happened that night. In interviews with investigators, in testimony, she would be all over the map in the coming months about the sequence of events that was so critical to the prosecution's case.

But that was only part of the problem. She also came across as a flake.

On this day, Cacciatore was mostly successful in his efforts to keep her focused, but she still managed to wander on occasion. Early in her testimony, he showed her a diagram, and she said, "I am going to get my glasses out." He said, "Sure," and then she said dramatically, "*His* glasses." (The coroner had given her Artie's glasses, which she said were just the same prescription she needed. She had made a big point of wearing them to the memorial service, thereby pissing off just about every other woman in Artie's life who was there.)

Pretty soon, Cacciatore got Julie Bajo to talk about what happened when she and Artie went to bed at about 10 P.M. that night.

"I got into bed with him, and I laid down halfway on top of him, and we were talking about going away to Mexico. He wanted to take a rest, and get away. He said that he had put in twenty-one years, and he deserved at least six months to a year off."

". . . Seven, eight minutes later, ten minutes, maybe, all of a sudden, we hear 'slam.' I mean, hurriedly, the front door opened and slammed closed. . . . And then I heard the second door open and slam closed. Then we heard bumping around. Just bumping around. We knew someone was in the house, and I felt hostility in my stomach."

What next, Cacciatore asked.

"We jumped out of bed. Artie turned on the light switch. I ran to the right closet, which is my closet."

"Let me back up a second," Cacciatore said. "You said that Artie had turned on the light. . . . Were there any other lights on at the time?"

"None except the outside light, which was always left on."

This would be a key prosecution contention—that with the bedroom light behind him and the rest of the house dark, Artie Mitchell would have been like a silhouette on a shooting range that night as he walked down the hallway to meet his death. It was also a point upon which Julie would flip-flop in various versions.

"The front door," Cacciatore said. "Was it locked or unlocked?"

"Never locked," Julie replied. "Artie's slogan was 'My door is always open,' in case somebody needed a place to stay in the middle of the night."

Julie also testified that Artie had asked her for something to wear when they got up, and she had handed him his green sweat pants, which were lying on the floor next to the bed. He asked her for a weapon too, she says, but she had none, and then he was gone. She said she twice heard him ask, "What's going on? Who's out there?" and that the only other thing she heard from him was a scream.

Once she got into the closet, Julie said, she realized that she'd better call 911. She could see the phone on a table in front of her.

"I had heard shots already. So I took one big step, reached for the phone, grabbed it, sort of took that same step back in, to be safe, into the closet." She said she left the closet door open "about an inch and a half," and dialed 911.

Then, for the first of so many times during the prosecution of Jim Mitchell, a jury heard the prosecution's primary piece of evidence— the 911 tape recorded at the Twin Cities Police Department.

It will be argued that the first blood-chilling minute of the tape is the last minute of Artie Mitchell's life:

THOMPKINS: Nine one one emergency.

BAJO: Twenty-three Mohawk.

THOMPKINS: What's the problem?

BAJO: We're in the bedroom and we hear noises, like gun noises outside the door.

THOMPKINS: You hear shots?

BAJO: I—I think so.

THOMPKINS: Okay. Do you know who it is?

BAJO: No, I don't. There's shots outside the door. We're in the bedroom.

THOMPKINS: Okay.

BAJO: The back bedroom.

THOMPKINS: We have a couple of units—

BAJO: We heard a couple of doors slamming. We heard—

THOMPKINS: Hold on, I have a couple of units en route, hold on.

BAJO: (Screams for 1.7 seconds, then:) Somebody's shooting! Oh, my God! Oh, my God! Somebody's shooting! (Sobs for 3.6 seconds, then:) Artie, don't go out there! Artie, don't go out there! (To the phone:) Hello?

THOMPKINS: I'm still here. What's going on?

BAJO: (Crying) I think somebody's shhhh—

THOMPKINS: What's goin' on, Judy?

BAJO: Oh my God.

THOMPKINS: Judy—

BAJO: Artie—Oh my God!

THOMPKINS: Hello?

BAJO: Don't go out there!

THOMPKINS: Hello?

BAJO: There's shots. Artie, don't go out th—

THOMPKINS: 'Kay, tell—what's goin' on?

BAJO: There are shots. I hear people—I hear shots and—

THOMPKINS: 'Kay, can you tell—can you see anything?

BAJO: I'm in the closet.

THOMPKINS: Okay.

BAJO: Artie, get down!

THOMPKINS: Where's Artie at?

BAJO: Artie, get down!

THOMPKINS: What's goin' on?

BAJO: He went to the front door.

THOMPKINS: Oh, Artie went to the front door?

BAJO: Artie went to the front door, and I'm still in the closet.

THOMPKINS: Are you Judy?

BAJO: I'm Julie. I'm in the closet.

THOMPKINS: Julie. Okay.

BAJO: I heard shots, I saw something coming out of the—something coming through the vertical blinds. And—oh my God.

THOMPKINS: Julie—

BAJO: Yes, I'm still in the closet, and I don't want to (crying)— He put a hole through, I think I can see it now.

THOMPKINS: You see—you're outside?

BAJO: No, no. I think I can see a hole through there. Oh my God. No, it's just, I don't have my contacts on, so I can't see that well.

THOMPKINS: Oh, no, okay where's Artie? Where's—

BAJO: I'm still inside the closet—

THOMPKINS: Where's Artie? Where's Artie? Is anybody else with you?

BAJO: No, no, we were in bed.

THOMPKINS: Is anybody else in the house?

BAJO: We were in bed and I heard—we were in bed and I heard doors opening and slamming. Then we started hearing shots, like—

THOMPKINS: How many?

BAJO:—BB shots. Or shots, I don't know what kind of shots. About— I heard like—one, two, three. We got out of the bed, we turn on the lights and I—he said, give me some clothes. I got in—I was putting on my shirt and I heard another shot and I got into the closet. He opened his closet—I think I see a hole right through the vertical blinds, I'm not sure—

THOMPKINS: You mean a—like a—

BAJO: Like a bu—

THOMPKINS:—a bullet hole?

BAJO: I, I think so, if I'm not mistaken, but I don't want to get out of the closet.

THOMPKINS: Okay, no, stay in the closet, but I wish Artie was with you.

BAJO: So do I.

The tape continues until the police arrive, and Julie hangs up.

Cacciatore also called Kent Haas, who described his arrest of Jim Mitchell; Jerry Mattos, who would talk about the physical evidence; Sergeant Michael McDuffie, who would testify to finding Jim's Ford Explorer on Lakeside Drive, one long block and around two corners from 23 Mohawk; Bill Corazza, a criminalist from the state crime lab in Santa Rosa, who would testify that the rifle Jim was carrying fired at least one of the bullets, and could have fired all of them; and finally Dr. Jindrich.

The grand jury got the case shortly after noon, and that afternoon Chuck Cacciatore had his murder indictment.

●   ●   ●

Within the first few days after the shooting, Jeff and Ruby and Mezz saw the need to call a meeting of the Cinema 7 board of directors— the surviving, nonincarcerated members, that is. That was the problem: with Jim, the company's president, in jail and in no shape to make business decisions, the company was paralyzed.

So the board met, and effective immediately, Georgia Mae Mitchell became probably the first and only sixty-five-year-old grandmother to head a major porn corporation, being named president and chief executive officer of Cinema 7. Ruby Richardson was named secretary and Jeff Armstrong treasurer.

In effect, the vote gave Jeff operating control of the company, but the symbolic distinction was clear: the president of the company would always be a Mitchell.

There were also Jim's affairs to be looked after, and they were getting more complicated all the time. Barely two weeks after the killing, Julie Bajo sued Jim for wrongful death, alleging "extreme mental anguish" and "shock and injury to her nervous system." Shortly afterward, her attorney would make an offer to settle "all present and future claims" for $450,000, which was promptly rejected.

Even though her duties as Cinema 7 president were not onerous, Georgia Mae would have little time to grieve. For one thing, she visited Jim faithfully; for another, she was immediately embroiled in matters of Art's estate.

Fortunately, Ruby had recently persuaded both Jim and Art to set up living trusts to administer the lion's share of their assets after death— a move that sheltered their estates from much of their inheritance tax burden. Under the terms of Art's trust, Jim would be the trustee, and if he were not able to serve for some reason, Georgia Mae and Ruby were to serve as co-trustees, and that's what happened. Georgia Mae was also named the executor of his estate.

Beneficiaries of the trust were Art's six children—which inevitably involved Karen, as the legal guardian of the three youngest.

Just because Art was dead didn't mean the fight over his money was over.

All of the children had immediate needs to be met. Mariah was about to graduate from high school, and had already been accepted into Syracuse University. Storm was going to school at San Diego State, and Liberty was in Los Angeles, with the money problems she had outlined to Artie the week of his death. Soon, she would move to Seattle to enroll in acting classes.

Then there were the little kids—and Karen. Ruby and Georgia Mae both felt that the kids should have some therapy to help them deal with what had happened. But Karen and the two trustees had a tough time agreeing on therapists and prices. Jasmine needed braces. And there were always more school clothes to buy, and bicycles, and all the things that kids need.

Meanwhile, the estate had not been valued, and it would be some time before it would be. The trust owned Artie's 50 percent stake in Cinema 7, but Karen and Artie had been fighting for years over what that was worth.

As if it weren't complicated enough, Karen quickly filed a paternity suit against the trust, claiming that the twins were Artie's and the trust was responsible for supporting them—in effect, laying claim to five-eighths of the trust proceeds rather than the one-half that her other three children were entitled to.

Artie had claimed to have had a vasectomy performed long before the twins were conceived, and Georgia Mae hunted desperately for medical records to prove it. She even tried to get some of Artie's blood, which had been drawn at autopsy, tested so that paternity could be conclusively ruled out, because she so strongly believed that the twins were not his.

Then, in April, Karen called the trust's attorney to inform him that she would be filing a wrongful death suit against Jim.

That was too much for Ruby Richardson. When she found out, she wrote Karen a letter that said in part:

> I cannot imagine, Karen, why you insist on keeping everything in a complete turmoil. You will alienate your children from Jim's children and who knows how the rest of the Mitchell clan will react.
> Karen, I have tried to talk to you. I believe I am the only one left in the Mitchell camp who will talk to you. You have done this to yourself and, I must add, quite efficiently. Many people have come to me and talked about the tragedy and I must say most of them feel you are the one most responsible for this whole mess . . . there is a ton of hurt everywhere.
> Try to understand that the fighting has to stop. Art is gone. We are all hurt. You told me yesterday that you loved Jim. Is this how you are going to show your feelings? Is it your intention to run this thing into the ground?
> Karen, I am asking you to please think of what you are doing. Is money so important to you that you will blatantly try to walk or run all over everyone, doing anything you can to get your

hands on *more money*? Do you have no honor or self-respect left?

Art was doing okay. He came to work every day and looked great. But when the fighting started, Art changed drastically. He started letting himself go and drinking heavily and who knows what else. By the time June 1990 rolled in, Art had lost all self-respect.

. . . You should start thinking of what you can do to help your own children emotionally instead of trying to get your hands on *more money*. Please let this obsession with money go!

You will only hurt yourself and your children in the end.

—Ruby

P.S. It has come to my attention that the monthly child support for each child is only $966. The day after Art died I told you we would be trying to keep the regular monthly payments for child support current in order for you to have money to live on. Since we paid you $4,500 per month instead of $2,898 per month you have been overpaid $3,204 to date. Shame on you for not being truthful when the payments were made. There will be no payment in May and the June payment will be $2,592 in order to bring the account into proper balance.

For her part, Karen complained that Georgia Mae and Ruby were trying to make her get by on far less than she needed to keep her household running.

She blamed Meredith. "She's the only enemy I have left," she said in October. "She's always kissed Georgia Mae's ass. She works the trustees and manipulates them. All the furniture has gone to her kids. My kids got nothing, not one thing. Meredith manipulates these people, works them against me."

In July, Karen's attorney sent a letter to the trustees' attorney, claiming that the monthly payments were nowhere near enough to meet her expenses.

In it, Karen pointed out that she was only receiving $3,000 per month instead of the $5,247 she was receiving before Artie's death. She didn't point out that the difference was the amount Artie was paying her in spousal support. It was one of the supreme ironies of the case that Artie's death came just two days before he would have finally been able to stop paying the spousal support. According to the judge's order in the divorce, spousal support, which Artie had been paying since the divorce in 1985, would cease March 1, 1991.

She also claimed that the children were much more expensive to support now because they no longer spent weekends with Artie—which he had suspected all along was one of her prime motivations for trying to increase her custody time. She also argued in the letter that since the children were home on weekends, "a babysitter is needed to ensure proper care and supervision."

The list of expenses itself was formidable, to say the least:

Monthly Support Expenses for Aaron, Jasmine, and Caleb Mitchell

Mortgage	$2,006.10
Property tax	247.50
Home insurance	100
Cable TV	48.98
Auto loan	400.15
Auto insurance	225
Auto maintenance (gas, etc.)	200
Charge cards (Visa, MasterCard, Macy's, etc., for clothing, travel, furnishings)	300
Medical expenses	300
Psychological	400
Copy expense	100
Newspapers, magazines	50
Clipping service	129
Pacific Bell	125
General Telephone	45
Pacific Gas & Electric	200
Garbage	25
Water	60
Distilled water	40
Food and supplies	600
Attorney fees (divorce, probate)	1,000
Accounting fees	100
Home maintenance	300
Beauty (hair, nails for Jasmine)	30
Food, eating out	120
Laundry and cleaning	10
Entertainment	160
Housekeeper	400
Babysitter	300
Piano (Jasmine)	250
Baseball (Aaron and Caleb)	200
Fish tanks (Aaron)	130
School lunches	120
TOTAL MONTHLY EXPENSES	**$8,721.73**

This, from a household in which Karen had been basically unemployed for the last several years. When she got it, Georgia Mae shook her head. She remembered her growing-up years in the Arkansas woods, and she remembered raising her own sons in Antioch. A total of $700 a month for a housekeeper and a babysitter? $360 a year for a ten-year-old's hair and fingernails?

No wonder Artie had such stress, she thought.

Jim was arraigned before Marin Superior Court Judge Gary Thomas on March 14. He pleaded not guilty, and Dennis Roberts urged Judge Thomas to grant conditional bail so his client could enter a psychiatric hospital.

In the motion, Roberts said that Dr. James C. Mickle, a Kentfield psychiatrist, had diagnosed Jim as "clinically depressed with suicidal ideation." A hearing was set for the following Wednesday, March 20.

Michael Kennedy, heavily involved with preparing to go to trial in a little divorce case called *Trump* v. *Trump,* still managed to fly out for the bail hearing.

It was not a pleasant experience.

The motion was heard by Judge Peter Allen Smith, and he wasn't buying what Mickey Kennedy was selling.

Kennedy started by asking for bail to a psychiatric facility, offering electronic surveillance as an added security option. He made reference to the fact that Martin Blinder had also examined Jim, and agreed with Mickle's assessment.

Cacciatore, of course, opposed bail. He had argued in his written brief that Julie Bajo felt great fear of Jim, and that with him free, her life might be in danger. Now he responded to Kennedy's argument.

"From day one the defense got an order signed by this court that Dr. Blinder be allowed access to Mr. Mitchell. I didn't oppose that . . . we see that Dr. Mickle is also seeing Mr. Mitchell, and it appears to me that he has adequate contact with psychiatrists of his choice."

Kennedy retorted, "I don't believe that my colleague is suggesting that he knows better than the psychiatrist . . . and since he did not choose to get an independent evaluation, it seems to me that the record is clear that what ought to happen now is psychiatric treatment in the hospital, and we urge our petition, Your Honor."

Smith replied immediately, "All right. The request for psychiatric treatment in the hospital is denied."

Smith, on the verge of retirement, wasn't interested in subtleties, and he wasn't about to let some hotshot out-of-town lawyer get around him. He clearly did not want to let Jim Mitchell out of jail, and Michael Kennedy's silver tongue wasn't going to cut any ice with him.

Kennedy then asked for a more conventional bailment, with Jim being bailed to his home, electronically monitored if the court wished, and said the defense was ready to meet any reasonable bail amount. Smith denied that, just as abruptly.

But Kennedy had another card to play. After some discussion of trial scheduling, he said to Judge Smith: "I have one other matter. I would like the court to address, if it can, the basis—and I'm not quarreling with the court—but the basis for its ruling.

"If, for example, the court believes that he's a flight risk, I would like to then present additional evidence with reference to that; or if the court thinks he's a danger to the community, I would like to be able to present additional evidence of that, because I feel so strongly that the facts bear in Mr. Mitchell's favor."

Smith walked right into the trap Kennedy had laid so politely.

"It's a matter of broad discretion," he said. ". . . I'm concerned that he is probably a serious menace to society, by view of the serious nature of the offense. Secondly, I'm not persuaded that he would not be a flight risk. Thirdly, because of his mental condition, you yourself have alluded to. . . . and fourth . . . there was a fourth reason in this analysis that I had made that escapes me right now, but those are some of the considerations that I made."

Kennedy had to go back to New York, but he had laid the groundwork. He had expected Dennis Roberts to be able to follow through, but he went on vacation to Mexico.

So Kennedy called Tom Steel, who had his partner, Stuart Buckley, carry the ball. Within days, a petition for writ of habeas corpus was filed with the Court of Appeal, and equally quickly, the higher court set Judge Smith straight.

"Flight risk, while appropriate in determining the amount of bail, is an inappropriate reason for denying pretrial bail for an otherwise bailable offense," the court wrote. "By referring to 'flight risk' and mentioning 'broad discretion,' instead of the requirement of clear and convincing evidence of a substantial likelihood of bodily harm," the court felt that Smith indicated that he had failed to consider the applicable law. "Other statements by the court suggest that it may have improperly shifted the burden of proof to the defendant to show justification for bail," the court added.

"It was then, when the Court of Appeal made its ruling, that the case began to lose its cosmic proportions, to get smaller and more manageable," Kennedy would recall.

The Court of Appeal ordered a rehearing. This time, before Judge Thomas, bail was set at $500,000 on April 26 under the following conditions:

• Jim would remain within the nine-county Bay Area unless the court specifically approved further travel;

• Jim would seek and maintain psychological treatment with Dr. Blinder, and would waive his doctor-client privilege with Blinder to allow the psychiatrist to report to the court with regard to possible flight or any violent behavior.

The defense first proposed to offer real estate as security for the bail. Under the law, real estate with an equity value of twice the face amount was required, which meant $1 million in real estate.

The defense offered the houses owned by Georgia Mae, Jeff Armstrong, Richard Mezzavilla, Dana Fuller, and Charles Benton.

But Marin County took issue with the appraisal of each property, and found many technical reasons to object to the bail security as offered.

"They picked over every word," Steel recalled. They actually got to the point where they were arguing over the placement of commas. "It was clear after a while that they were doing it out of spite."

So the defense gave up on the real estate bond and went to a bail bondsman, James Barrish, who knew Jim. For a fee of 10 percent per annum, he guaranteed the $500,000. And on April 30, after sixty days in jail, Jim Mitchell was released.

The O'Farrell Theatre had been cranking along okay without Jim and Artie. Some even said all the publicity had been good for business. (Later, it would look suspiciously like somebody was trying to exploit the situation: during the trial, the copy on one of the advertisements that the theater ran in the *Examiner* and *Chronicle* every day read: "It's so sizzling, it's almost lethal passion!")

After Jim was released, he spent several days with Lisa and his kids. But soon he was coming down to the O'Farrell, just like the old days. Astonishingly to some, one of the first things on his agenda was giving his brother a proper sendoff.

Of course, Jim had not attended the memorial service. Once he was released, he and Jeff and Rocky began planning a party for Artie. The theater would send out several hundred invitations to what was billed as a "Bereavement Ceremony" on Sunday afternoon, June 23, almost four months after the killing. (Cynics pointed out that the timing of the event, 1 to 4 P.M., meant the theater didn't lose a dime since it doesn't open until 5 P.M. on Sundays.)

By 1:30, guests had already jammed the combined New York Live and Green Door Rooms. An enormous buffet was spread out underneath the baroque erotic murals of the Green Door Room: shrimp, salmon, oysters, carpaccio, finger sandwiches, fruit, desserts, on and on. Lines formed at two open bars.

The crowd was as eclectic as might be expected at a Mitchell Brothers event: everyone from business-suited pols (State Senator Quentin Kopp and County Supervisor Terence Hallinan included) to Hell's Angels and leather-wrapped lesbians chatted and munched and watched the show.

And there was Jim.

He stood by the entrance to the Green Door Room, natty in his trademark Levi's and a peacock blue cashmere golf sweater, stolidly greeting people, making subdued small talk, accepting hugs and handshakes. Nothing untoward happened; it was all very civilized.

It was an ordeal he had determined to put himself through, to face everyone, and although some were horrified, others understood it as the natural progression of things. In reality, it was part wake, part coronation: What was left of Jim was all that was left of the Mitchell Brothers, and this was the first public acknowledgment of the new order.

On stage, Sharon McKnight presided as mistress of ceremonies, making the best of a bizarre situation.

First cut is the deepest: Bana Witt took the stage and reminded the crowd why they were there. She sat on the darkened stage with her legs folded under her, face illuminated by a single ghostly white spot, and ripped out lines with an intensity that Spalding Gray wishes he had. The words, of course, carried their own power:

CROW

I will kill a crow and drink its blood for you
I will wear the hair that you left on the floor
like it was cashmere

I will leave your vodka in the freezer
because part of me has become you
and part of me has died

Was I spared
or was I just uninvited

Let me try one more
of those little white pills

Melting them under the tongue
makes them work faster
though they will never work fast enough
or long enough

I would eviscerate myself
on the spot where you died
but I always hated that house

I will never know
why the sand
does not hold the shape of our bodies
after we leave

I will avoid those who thought they knew you
I will not try to figure out what we had
or why you pulled up stakes just now

I have nothing that smells like you

Thank god we never made it all the way to
mundanity
but I'm hoping for safety there now

I will see things that would suit you
and wear them myself

Picking up the phone will no longer be
emotional roulette

Knowing that art and anarchy
are sisters
who were once joined at the
hip
now they live on different sides
of town

Sisters who wanted to fuck your chaos
thinking you had real estate in paradise
when it was just a plot in the valley

Something big was brewing
and you already knew its taste

Your mouth was the only home I wanted

I watched the young ones fall for you
looking for an epiphany

I watched your chest hair turn to gray
and your head grow naked of its own accord
as wives and girlfriends came and went
time and children sweetened you

I will make turtle soup
and feed it to strangers
I will forgive everyone
who got more of you than I did

Those who bought your underwear
and cooked your food
who nursed you through your fugues

Of all the women who cared for you
I could only write you poems
and visit your arms as a foreigner

When you were at my door
when you came to milk my heart
I wanted to be fast and brilliant for you
and I don't think it mattered

I will feel widowed for years
stuffing pain through the strainer
in the sink
when wisdom tries to visit

I will ignore people with vision
they increase my desperation

I will ferret away
everything you said
in the banks of a river

I will watch the barometer
and learn the tides
hoping for omens and signs

I will learn to forgive
and I will start with you

I am the last of your hostages to come
home
and I don't want to be here.

Many in the crowd were visibly shaken, including some of the ex-wives and girfriends she referred to. Still, Missy, six months pregnant but splendidly coiffed and wearing a lavish white lace dress, Missy who had such a negative experience with Bana while Artie was alive, walked up to Bana and gave her a big hug after her reading. "It took a lot of courage to get up there and do that," she says, and Bana was very touched.

Bana went up to Jim before she left. "His eyes looked just like Artie's," she would say later. "I kissed him goodbye."

McKnight came back onstage. She was the perfect choice for the role this day. A sort of X-rated, punk Bette Midler/Sophie Tucker type, she was funny and tough and acerbic and obviously genuinely moved to be presiding over a wake for her friend Artie Mitchell. She belted out several songs interspersed between other acts, including the other true highlight of the afternoon, the Doors' haunting "Crystal Ship," which is quintessentially Artie (he and Jim Morrison seem to have had quite a bit in common):

Then the strippers began. The first, a tall, elegant brunette in a deep burgundy plush evening dress, did a relatively tasteful strip, sort of cabaret style. The second was another matter altogether.

McKnight introduced her as Summer, and the stage name fit. She was six feet tall, with honey bronze skin ("No tan lines!" McKnight accurately observed), a shaggy white-blonde surfer cut and startling breasts appropriate to her first song, "You're Unbelievable." For her second song, she was completely nude. She lay on her stomach on a scrap of white shag rug—or was it fake fur?—at the front of the stage, stuck her tattooed, shaved nakedness up in the air toward the audience and undulated wildly.

The audience seemed somewhat chastened. It was not your typical New York Live crowd: several women middle-aged or older, including the boys' mother, Georgia Mae Mitchell; several small children; and even a few men who were clearly not used to a real, live Mitchell Brothers show.

Missy Manners sat in the audience and thought about how awful the whole thing was. "Uncle Jim," she thought, "you took our fun away."

The strip shows were punctuated by another open mike, like the one at the memorial service. People were encouraged to come up and offer reminiscenses of Artie. One who did was Nina Hartley.

Nina thanked Artie and Jim for providing a great working environment, then dimpled and added, crinkling her nose in a grin like a wicked six-year-old, "I ate some of my very first pussy *right here on this stage!*" She patted the New York Live stage she was standing next to. "But I've gotten a lot better at it since then," she giggled lewdly, and gave out a fake phone number to laughs.

After a lesbian love act and a few more testimonials, the day was over, and many were moved by the obvious love for Artie that was expressed by the guests. But one man was heard to say as he walked out into the bright June sun, "It was nice, but how could they have a Mitchell Brothers party without Artie? It's just not the same."

Joanne Scott didn't go to the bereavement ceremony. She thought it was a travesty.

One day, after Jim got out, she took a bunch of her phone messages from Art, and strung pieces of them together into a message, and set it up to leave a message on Jim Mitchell's answering machine, using his dead brother's voice: "Hello, partner, it's the O'Farrell, it's today, give me a call."

In the end, she just couldn't do it. She thought Art would have liked it, but she'd been crank-called enough herself, and it wasn't going to bring Art back.

But she sure hoped that somewhere down the line, Jim's karma would catch up with him.

Fortunately for Jim, most people didn't look at it that way. After sixty days in the Marin County Jail, he had emerged intensely nervous about what people would think of him— not only the O'Farrell insiders, but the rest of the city as well. But he began to regain a little self-esteem when people treated him with kindness. Even his neighbors greeted him with warmth, coming over to show their support. And whatever anger over Artie's death that the Mitchell camp felt was tempered by the knowledge of the incredible load that Jim had carried, and most of the public talk was about how out of control Art had been.

Despite his legal problems and his own private horror, Jim must have drawn tremendous strength and succor from the affirmation and tacit forgiveness of this crowd of friends. The reception was as therapeutic for Jim as were his continuing sessions with a psychologist. Slowly, despite the inescapable weight of what he had done, Jim began to regain a little of his personality.

Although almost everyone agreed the trial would never go in August, when it had been set, there was plenty of ongoing legal combat in the case.

It was one of the coolest, foggiest springs Marin County residents could remember, but in the District Attorney's office, Chuck Cacciatore was feeling a lot of heat.

District Attorney Jerry Herman was very skittish about this case, that much was clear. There was lots of media interest, and that meant it was politically significant. Cacciatore got the impression that Herman thought the case wasn't being pushed aggressively enough as he prepared for trial. He felt that there were some philosophical differences too. Cacciatore felt that Michael Kennedy and Dennis Roberts would try to tell the jury a sob story. They would put the victim on trial, that was for sure, and he wanted to develop a strategy to fight that effort tooth and nail. He didn't want to yield the moral high ground to the defense in a case where the accused went into a house firing a rifle.

Nobody would come out and say it, but he got the distinct feeling that Herman thought all that was nonsense. The message was: Develop the physical case. It's overwhelming. You've got the evidence, argue the evidence.

Of course, Cacciatore knew some of the evidence wasn't what it could be. He was discovering what a nightmare witness Julie Bajo was. She had provided an incredible profusion of stories about what happened that night. For Cacciatore, the capper came on May 23, when Julie announced in an interview with Kathy Hoffman that there "must have been someone else there that night with Jim." She said she was certain that she had heard someone running out the back door to the yard, and that the noises she had heard couldn't have been made by just one person. Of course, the defense was entitled under the discovery rules to transcripts of every conflicting account she gave, and it would all come up at trial.

Cacciatore was getting increasingly frustrated. He wasn't getting the support he thought he needed. Just an investigator part-time, and he was even part-time himself. Once, Herman put his name down on the list of attorneys from the office required to attend the weekly plea-bargain meeting, for Christ's sake. And then when he showed up, Herman looked at him coldly and said, "What are you doing here? Why aren't you preparing your case?"

Cacciatore didn't know it, of course, but on the defense side, things were in just as much disarray.

Understandably, Kennedy was in New York almost all the time; he had a lot of heavy-duty cases going on. But it was a pain for Jim, who was paying a ton of money for his defense—the rumor was, high six figures to Kennedy up front—and some things needed to get taken care of on the spot.

Like getting him out of jail, for instance. A perfect example. Kennedy was in New York and Dennis Roberts was *vacationing*. So Tom Steel had to rush around and get Buckley on the case.

It was not just the bicoastal problem. Michael Kennedy was a trial lawyer. His strength, his style, his metier, had nothing to do with writing motions, deploying investigators, working up witnesses. He was a blond-haired, blue-eyed, sweet-tongued, table-pounding, D.A.-baiting, gesticulating, snorting, objecting, hectoring, whispering, weeping, Irish goddamned *trial lawyer*. Don't bother him with details until he needed to know them, and then he'd use each one on the D.A. like a Yaqui uses cactus needles to impale an enemy on the desert floor.

Dennis Roberts was a trial lawyer too. He was brilliant at it too.

But he wasn't exactly Mr. Detail either, and as spring turned toward summer, none of the pretrial motion work was getting done.

All of these problems on both sides of the case would come to a head at a hearing on May 24. Kennedy wanted Jim Mitchell and Roberts to come to New York over the Memorial Day weekend for a major pretrial conference. They were behind and he knew it was time to get serious about the specifics of the defense. And he had an ear infection and wasn't about to subject it to a coast-to-coast plane trip.

But Jim's bail limited him to the Bay Area. So Roberts made a motion to modify the bail conditions to allow the weekend trip to New York.

When it was first presented, they got Judge Smith, who was no doubt none too pleased at being reversed on his original bail denial. He wasn't about to modify another judge's bail order in the defense's favor, and he said so. So the defense managed to get it before Judge Thomas on the twenty-fourth.

As was his habit, Roberts came out punching. "Mr. Cacciatore would have the court believe that the Sixth Amendment right to counsel is spelled w-r-i-t-e. That is not the case. Mr. Mitchell has a right to meet and confer and be in contact with his attorney, not only through telephone, fax, and letter writing."

Thomas let that little bit of smart-mouthing pass, but Roberts pushed his luck, saying that Cacciatore was also trying to deprive Jim of his Fifth Amendment rights in his opposing brief by suggesting a psychiatric evaluation before Jim be allowed to travel.

"It's quite a morning for Mr. Cacciatore where he gets to violate the Constitution in two separate amendments," Roberts said.

"Just a moment," Judge Thomas snapped. "What do you have to say now?"

Roberts cut his oral argument short, but then Thomas, clearly nettled, slammed the door on him. He said that Kennedy's declaration stating the reasons he needed to see his client in New York was inadmissible because it didn't follow the correct form, and then denied the bail motion.

Perhaps because the flawed declaration had come from his office, perhaps because he could tell he was going nowhere fast, Roberts lashed out at the judge. "The last cases I read in which technical rules of pleading were used to thwart constitutional rights of defendants were cases arising out of Mississippi and Alabama in the civil rights movement," he said.

Thomas told him, "Mr. Roberts, you're stretching the futility right now," and cut off argument. "I made my decision. Thank you very much."

Roberts said, "May I ask the court one question?"

"Just a moment," Thomas said again. "There are no other questions. Thank you very much."

"Would the court simply state for the record its reasons for denying the motion?"

"Thank you very much," Thomas said again, and left the bench.

Roberts, steaming, turned to leave the courtroom—and at that moment, D.A.'s investigator Kathy Hoffman handed him a subpoena to testify at trial, presumably about his telephone call to Artie the day before the shooting.

Roberts went absolutely nuts. He was furious. He knew that the subpoena would effectively remove him as counsel from the case. He could not be a lawyer and a witness too. What made it all the more frustrating was that not ten minutes ago Cacciatore had stood by smiling as Thomas had said in denying the travel motion, "The defendant . . . has excellent counsel right here, starting with you." All the time, Cacciatore had known he was about to blow Roberts off the case.

What the prosecutor didn't know was that the subpoena would blow him off the case too.

On May 28, Cacciatore was summoned by two of his superiors, Deputy D.A. Ed Berberian and Assistant D.A. Terry Boren. After he gave them his reasoning for the subpoena, Boren told him to withdraw it.

The next day, Boren called him in and told him that the case was being reassigned to another attorney in the department. Cacciatore was furious. He felt betrayed and abused. Reassigning such a high-profile case during trial preparation was unprecedented, to his knowledge, in the Marin D.A's office, and he thought the subpoena issue was a red herring—just a convenient excuse for Herman and his henchmen.

That day, Cacciatore called Roberts and told him the subpoena was being withdrawn—enraging Roberts all the more. He accused Cacciatore of playing games and trying to sabotage the defense. But what Roberts said to Cacciatore at that moment meant nothing. Both of them were off the case.

Herman reassigned *People* v. *Mitchell* to John Posey, forty-seven, a very senior prosecutor who had handled big cases for him before.

On paper, it looked like a sound decision.

Posey is a Marin County native. He worked his way from junior college to the Hastings College of Law, where he graduated in 1970. He started work in the Contra Costa County D.A.'s office, and moved over to his home county in March 1972.

Other than an abortive two-year stint in private practice, John Posey has been in the Marin District Attorney's office ever since.

He prosecuted his first homicide in 1974, and has handled dozens since. He has been a workhorse, doing literally hundreds of jury trials.

He has earned a reputation as a technocrat, a superb detail man, a little stiff, certainly, but a terrier in court, nipping at the heels of defense witnesses with little questions that rattle them, make them contradict themselves.

By far the biggest case of Posey's career to this point was the "trailside killer" capital murder case against David Carpenter, accused of killing five people in wilderness areas of Marin County and two more in Santa Cruz County to the south.

John Posey spent more than four years pushing Marin County's case against Carpenter, who had already been convicted and sentenced to death for the two Santa Cruz murders when the Marin case went to trial.

Venue was changed to San Diego in the trial because of the massive Marin publicity. For more than a year, John Posey lived in a San Diego apartment while he pursued a conviction against Carpenter. Everyone involved in the case was amazed at his command of the mountain of detail in the case. He put almost 100 witnesses on the stand, and spoke for five hours to the jury in his closing argument.

Finally, in 1988, he got the conviction—and a death sentence. But the following year the case was thrown out and a new trial granted because a juror had been overheard saying that she knew Carpenter was already facing a death sentence in the Santa Cruz cases.

Of course, Posey appealed. The case was still pending before the California Supreme Court at the time of the Mitchell trial.

It was a supremely frustrating experience for Posey. He had put everything he had into the case—even his personal life. The months away from his family proved fatal to his twenty-five-year marriage. Robert Graysmith, who wrote the book *The Sleeping Lady: The Trailside Murders Above the Golden Gate* about the trailside killings, would quote one of the people closest to the case as saying, "That trial took so much out of John Posey. . . . This case *became* John Posey."

To achieve success in the case and then have it taken away was a bitter blow. "Granted, I come with a bias, but that case is a classic example of the judicial system gone berserk," he says bitterly.

Now Posey would have a new challenge. His skill at presenting physical evidence, at marshaling countless details, would serve him well in this case. But some of the attorneys in the D.A.'s office privately wondered if he was right for it. John Posey had a temper, and Kennedy was legendary in his ability to infuriate opposing counsel. Also, the media made Posey intensely uncomfortable. He distrusted reporters and made no secret of it. A big part of that dislike could have been caused by what happened in the Carpenter case, but nonetheless it was there.

Posey's greatest attribute, though, was that Jerry Herman trusted him. And when the District Attorney saw that there were bears in the woods, that this case wasn't the slam-dunk he thought it was, it was completely natural that he would turn it over to his old friend John Posey.

Jim Mitchell went to Tom Steel for advice.

Michael Kennedy was in New York, and it was clear he was going to be there all summer, unless something major happened, and that was all right. He was Michael, he was a Man-God in the courtroom, and he would be ready when the bell rang. He always had been.

But meanwhile, out in California, things were turning sour faster than you could get a parking ticket in a red zone on Broadway. Where were the motions? And who was going to *do the work* so that Michael could come charging in like Eamon de Valera and Kick Ass? It very obviously was not going to be Dennis Roberts. Everyone knew he was a fine attorney, but he had gone on vacation while Jim was in shackles, and screwed up Kennedy's declaration, and hadn't gotten around to writing many briefs, and now he was subpoenaed anyway, which meant that there was a reason to do something, as if there weren't already.

Tom Steel was a pretty natural place for Jim to turn. He had proved he was a winner.

Tom quickly told him, Jim, you know I don't do criminal law. And I've got a full practice going here anyway. But I can get you somebody.

Steel was in the process of taking on a partner, Nanci Clarence. She was young, but not too young. She had experience on big-time cases, and she was damned good. He said, I could ask her, if you want.

I don't know her, Jim said. But if you're going to partner up with her, she's got to be fine. Go ahead. Talk to her.

Tom Steel knew what he was doing. He was about to get a very promising partner.

Nanci Clarence is a Californian; she grew up in Riverside, near L.A. She went to Berkeley, figured out who she really was, and began to explore the possibilities that presented. She did journalism for a while, and then got smart and graduated in English. She worked for the Berkeley Women's Health Collective for a few years, keeping those ideals stoked up, but it wasn't long before she began to sense some futility. Proposition 13 and Reaganomics weren't kind to leftie public assistance agencies. She got smart again and went to law school at Hastings. She realized that she'd get a lot more accomplished if she backed up those humanist ideals with a law degree.

Besides, she had really always wanted to be a lawyer. She was a fighter, a competitor, and she loved not just the cause but the battle as well. She clerked in federal court, then desperately tried to get a job in the federal public defender's office, but there was a hiring freeze. So she went to work in a big firm downtown, Morrison and Foerster, and expected to loathe representing corporate America for big bucks.

But she caught a break and ended up working for Jim Brosnahan, who wasn't exactly your prototypical corporate mouthpiece. He did things like represent the leaders of the Sanctuary movement. He took cases she could identify with and enjoy.

It wasn't always easy, as a woman and as a budding trial lawyer, to play backup for a man like Brosnahan, a fantastic trial lawyer, a serious big-league orator with an ego to match. He relied very much on his staff, which always seemed to consist of smart young women like Nanci Clarence. But it was much better than she expected, she learned a lot, and the money was very good for being right out of school. Also, she was getting experience that would prove invaluable.

A year and a half later, Barry Portman, the federal defender for the Northern California district, called and told her that for the first time in five years, he had an opening he could fill in his office, and would she please come to work. She didn't hesitate, despite taking a 60 percent salary cut, because it was work she wanted, defending mostly poor people, but people with serious issues, people who needed something better than the average court-appointed briefcase.

Again, she caught some great cases and did well. But after four-years-plus of eighteen-hour days for no money, taking abuse from clients and judges and everybody else, she caught herself getting a little sour and told herself, get out now.

Hence the incipient partnership with Steel. She would be the criminal arm of the partnership, but she would also handle some civil stuff. She would make some money. And, she thought, the pace wouldn't be quite so frenetic.

But here was Tom Steel, before the ink was even dry on their new letterhead, saying, how would you like to help defend Jim Mitchell?

Absolutely not, she said, unless we can get somebody on board who knows California murder law. I've been over in the Federal Building for the past five years, and that's not the place to do homicides, and California murder law is complicated and arcane and, of course, critical to this client.

I can do the fact workup, get the discovery moving, no problem, that's the same anywhere, and I can do examination preps, even the examinations if it comes to that. But I can't get these motions written.

Steel understood, and knew she was right. Who should it be?

The list of lawyers with the credentials they needed was not a long one, and one name quickly popped to the top of the list.

Dennis Riordan made sense in every way. He was a distinguished criminal appellate attorney with big-case credentials, earning his spurs as an appellate lawyer in his relentless, ultimately successful fifteen-year fight for the freedom of former Black Panther Johnny Spain, a member of the famous San Quentin Six.

As a law student at NYU, Riordan had been active in the defense of prisoners after the Attica riot, and he had later clerked for U.S. District Court Judge James Doyle, whom Riordan remembers as the strongest civil libertarian in the federal judiciary, in Madison, Wisconsin. He came west, at least partly because the woman he had been seeing got a job in San Francisco. Riordan wanted criminal defense work, and he took his time and found a situation that he wanted.

Which turned out to be second-chairing for Charles Garry, easily the most famous civil rights lawyer on the West Coast, and during the year he did that, Garry defended Johnny Spain on charges stemming from the San Quentin escape attempt on August 21, 1971, in which George Jackson, Black Panther leader, prison activist, and author of *Soledad Brother,* was killed. Johnny Spain was next to Jackson when he died, and in the moments preceding his death three white guards and two white inmates had died.

Spain was charged with conspiring to commit escape, kidnapping, and five counts of murder.

During the trial, which began on March 25, 1975, in the same Marin County court building where Jim Mitchell would be tried, Spain was strip-searched daily, forced to wear a choker around his neck, and chained to the floor of the courtroom.

Finally, in August 1976, after deliberating for a month, Spain was found guilty of conspiracy and two counts of murder. He was given two life sentences in addition to the one he was already serving.

The verdict had to be appealed, but Charlie Garry was no appeal lawyer, and so Riordan decided that for as long as it took to fight Johnny Spain's case, he would specialize in appellate work.

That turned out to be thirteen years. But at the end of the fight, Johnny Spain was free and Riordan's reputation as a legal scholar and a hard-nosed, relentless advocate was firmly established.

Those credentials fit the Mitchell team's needs perfectly. A $5,000 retainer was delivered, and he was on the bus. Which was good, because these motions needed to be done pronto.

Michael Kennedy certainly approved. Chuck Cacciatore's subpoena gave him a chance to do something about the relative redundance of Dennis Roberts. "We didn't need another me," he would say later. "We needed a California legal scholar, and Riordan was a logical choice."

The defense team met for the first time in May, at Steel's offices in the old Victorian at 2424 Pine Street that had been Michael and Eleanore's house. She had decorated it, certainly in part with fees from Jim Mitchell, and it had been one of the hippest salons in the city in those grand old days of radical chic.

Nanci Clarence, the new kid on the block, was going to learn a few things at that meeting.

Gathered around the massive table in Steel's law library were Jim Mitchell, Michael Kennedy, Tom Steel, Nanci Clarence, Dennis Riordan, Dennis Roberts, and defense investigator Eric Mason.

And Eleanore Kennedy.

Clarence had met Michael's wife just moments before, when she had arrived with Jim and Michael. She was quite surprised when Eleanore was seated at the table as the meeting started. Michael wasted no time setting everyone straight about that.

"She will be involved in every major decision," he said. "Unlike the rest of us, who had our intuition stomped out of us in law school, she's very intact. I rely on her and I will do so in this case, and she will be involved all the way."

Gulp. Okay, Clarence thought. Unusual, but I can deal with it.

The conversation turned to the sort of jury they would want, and Eleanore, who always plays a major role in the selection of Kennedy's juries, began talking.

Clarence, eager, excited, agreeing with her, wanting to build on a couple of her ideas, interrupted.

Steel gave her a look, which she didn't quite understand. A few minutes later, she started to do it again and this time got a sharp kick under the table.

Steel took her aside at the next break and said, "Are you crazy? She's important. Don't interrupt her."

Nanci was getting an idea about just how important Eleanore was.

Thankfully, the two women would develop a real friendship. Nanci liked Eleanore. She was smart, and funny, and she had insights into Michael that no one else had.

There was talk of the motions, and it was agreed: Clarence would assist Riordan in preparing them because time was so short.

Other than that, her role was never really defined. It would grow like one of Artie's pot plants as the case continued. Riordan too would play a far more pivotal and comprehensive role than had initially been considered. This was no $5,000 retainer gig.

From that day on, Jim Mitchell's legal bills, already enormous, would grow considerably. But at least he had good people on the case, and it could finally move forward.

In the next few weeks, Dennis Riordan would file a blizzard of paper with the Marin County Superior Court. The Mitchell file doubled in size, and so did John Posey's problems.

Riordan moved to disqualify the entire District Attorney's office because of Cacciatore's subpoena of Roberts, because of statements made to the press and to witnesses, and because of DeLeon's relationship with Artie and with Martha.

He tried again to modify Jim's bail to allow trips to New York, and to Artie's grave in Lodi, which was outside the nine-county area outlined by the judge. He moved for a venue change due to pretrial publicity.

And he moved to dismiss the indictment because of defects in the grand jury process and in its makeup.

Posey agreed to stipulate to Jim being allowed to travel to Lodi, but the New York part of the bail motion was denied again, as was the motion to disqualify the D.A.'s office. The venue change was simply a tactical ploy, and was withdrawn. The object was to make a case for attorney-conducted voir dire, or examination of potential jurors. Proposition 115 had taken voir dire out of the hands of the attorneys and given it to the judges. But the judge had broad latitude, and could either allow attorneys to question potential jurors, or could incorporate some or all of their questions in the questioning by the court. By filing for a change of venue, Riordan was angling to make it clear that the defense viewed the pretrial publicity as an important issue at voir dire, thus increasing the need for the defense attorneys to question jury panel members.

That left the motions to dismiss based on the grand jury's composition, and on alleged defects in the grand jury hearing. In that motion, Riordan had accused Cacciatore of a number of mistakes, including failing to inform the grand jury that it could indict on a lesser charge than murder, and failing to present potentially exculpatory evidence.

The issue was heard August 14, before Judge Beverly Savitt in an unusual double hearing. The other Marin murder indictments under

115 had named Joseph Howard Sherman and Jeffrey David Merrill in a case involving a robbery-killing in San Rafael. On this day, Sherman, Merrill, and their attorneys were in court, along with Riordan and Clarence. Jim had been excused by the court from having to attend.

Judge Savitt is a pleasant-looking but steely-eyed judge with the "tough but fair" reputation to which all judges aspire. On this morning, she wore a stylish gray silk scarf around the shoulders of her robes, which in no way robbed her of her judical bearing.

It was evident from early in the hearing that these murder indictments were in trouble. Judge Savitt said that she viewed the indictments as fatally flawed by the way the grand jury had been selected. (The same jury had issued both indictments.) The nineteen grand jurors had been selected at random from the regular jury pool. Under the law, grand jurors must meet several tests that do not apply to regular petit jurors. They must have lived in the county for at least one year, they must meet a subjective judgment of being "of sound character," and they must not be elected officials.

None of these tests had been applied to the grand jurors.

The D.A.'s office was represented by Judith Brown, its most respected legal scholar, but she couldn't do much about it. Her argument that "only twelve grand jurors have to vote to indict so you'd have to prove there were not twelve qualified grand jurors to have a problem" didn't help. Judge Savitt gently stomped it flat, then said, almost consolingly, that the whole mess had been "a learning process" for the District Attorney's office.

"To go through a trial and have the chance that it would be reversed later would be foolish," she added.

Although the point had become moot, she spoke about the other issues Riordan had raised, indicating that the instructions to the grand jury could also have been grounds for dismissing the indictment, and that the issue of exculpatory evidence would have been a "close question."

From all appearances, the D.A.'s office either expected Savitt's ruling or had been warned. Judith Brown, a heavy, gray-haired, self-possessed woman who looked as if she might be a judge at an English rose show instead of helping to prosecute a pornographer in a homicide case, sat stolidly by herself at the counsel table. Near the end of the hearing, John Posey walked in and stood in the back of the courtroom, his chiseled features set in a pinched expression, looking rather like a parent at a blown piano recital. When the hearing ended, he turned and left, speaking to no one.

Dennis Riordan, by contrast, was quite gregarious. However ephemerally, murder charges had just been dismissed against his client as a direct result of his legal work, in a case he had inherited in terrible shape less than three months ago, and he was going to savor this moment.

Only a couple of reporters even attended the hearing; almost everybody in the press had assumed the motion would be quickly denied. After the bombshell, they quickly huddled around Riordan to find out what had happened. Riordan patiently explained the legal ramifications several times. He told them the prosecution has a choice now: It can go back to another grand jury and try to get another indictment, running the risk that if a second indictment were thrown out, Jim Mitchell would probably never be tried. Or it can rearraign him and take him to a preliminary hearing, but we would get to present our entire case there if we wanted to, and they know that.

Riordan is far more oblique and understated than Roberts or Kennedy, but he did manage to get his digs in at Cacciatore, who had called the killing "cold-blooded fratricide" in an *Esquire* story.

He announced that the defense would do something very unusual: it would hand over the bulk of its case to the D.A.'s office, so that Posey, in order to avoid losing the second indictment on grounds of withholding exculpatory evidence, would have to present it to the grand jury.

It was a bold idea. Defendants and counsel are not allowed in grand juries, but here was a way to put on the defendant's case anyway. There was a certain beauty to the concept of the D.A. being forced to present your case *for* you, and the defense team thought there was a good chance that the next grand jury would indict on a lesser charge.

But of course, like any bold move, there was a significant negative risk. In this case, it was that the prosecution would not only have a clear picture of most of the defense's case, but they would also have a record from the grand jury against which to compare witnesses' testimony—an advantage otherwise reserved for the defense.

Roberts, no longer with any standing in the case, would privately question the decision, but Michael made it and it would be done.

Meanwhile, much of the case preparation itself fell to Nanci Clarence. Michael was in New York; Dennis handled the legal scholarship. But as discovery began to flow in, it was Clarence who learned the case frontward and backward; who organized the discovery; completed files on each potential witness; figured out what the legal issues were likely to be, writing memos on each, for each file; and kept herself at Kennedy's beck and call via phone and fax.

As she saw Posey's case developing, his expert witnesses being lined up, she dug up countering experts for the defense. Kennedy had been gone from the California criminal defense scene for too long to be of any help, so she drew on her own network to find the best people.

Clarence tried to prepare the case as though she were going to argue it herself, although she didn't even know if she would be allowed to assist at trial. Michael doesn't like to ask for help, she was told, although she sure was helping him right now.

John Posey had spent the summer building the state's case. It wasn't easy for him, taking the thing over in mid-investigation. "No one had made any effort, in my opinion, to determine just how the shooting had occurred," Posey would say later. "That was the most important thing. You had all these statements from people, but no real witnesses. So I had to go to work on what actually happened, get the experts on it."

By the end of August, his case bore little resemblance to what had gone before. It wasn't complete in every detail yet, but he had plenty to take to a grand jury. On the foundation of the case—the ballistics and the 911 tape—he had built an elaborate structure of expert testimony, intended to prove exactly how the killing had happened and in the process establishing the basis for first-degree murder.

"I honestly had not made up my mind as to the degree of Jim Mitchell's culpability until the expert work was done," he says. "Then I had no doubt that he was guilty of first-degree murder."

He was confident that this time there would be no mistakes, no technicalities, no defects in the process for the defense to complain about. The grand jury would be formulated correctly, and he would instruct them to the letter of the law. And he would give them the evidence they needed to indict.

As advertised, the defense began to pepper him with information that they said he had an obligation to present to the grand jury.

In a letter to Jerry Herman dated August 23, Kennedy wrote, "The dismissal of the initial indictment against my client, James Mitchell, presents a rare opportunity to ensure that the grand jury functions as historically intended when it again considers his case. The grand jury, to be sure, has long been the means by which the state obtains legal approval of a charge it wishes to lodge against a citizen. At least since 1735, however, when a New York grand jury twice refused to issue the indictment for seditious libel against John Peter Zenger demanded by the Crown, the grand jury has also served as a crucial safeguard against unwarranted prosecution. It is that protection, preserved by Madison for posterity in the grand jury clause of the Fifth Amendment, which Mr. Mitchell now seeks to invoke."

He went on to cite eighty-nine specific references in the discovery material the defense had received from the prosecution's investigation of the case—ranging from Julie's late-developing conviction that more than one person was in the house to Charlie Benton's account of the shooting incident he witnessed at the O'Farrell—which he characterized as tending to show Jim's innocence of murder, and demanded that they be shown to the grand jury.

Then he added a list of nine people that could provide what he considered further exculpatory testimony: Rocky Davidson, Jeff Armstrong, Richard Mezzavilla, Nancy Harrison, Ron Turner of *War News,* Jeanette Etheredge of Tosca, Lisa Adams, estate lawyer Hal Forbes, and Kristal Rose.

"These individuals do not wish to be interviewed by the prosecution, but they are willing to give their sworn testimony to the grand jury and to submit to questioning by its members or by your office in front of its members," Kennedy wrote. "Should there be any doubt that they can provide exculpatory testimony, they will provide sworn declarations establishing the nature of their testimony."

Now Posey had to be very careful. If he chose to withhold any of the cited items or any of the nine people, he would need stout justifications to avoid the charge of withholding exculpatory evidence of which he was aware.

One thing was for sure: with Posey's beefed-up case, and with Kennedy's quirky strategy, this was not going to be another slam-bang, five-hour grand jury.

Posey convened the jury on August 30. The first witness was Sherri Thompkins, TCPD dispatcher, and the 911 tape was played.

Over the next two weeks, the jury would hear nearly two thousand pages of testimony. They would hear several of the witnesses that the defense had offered, including Armstrong, Mezzavilla, Nancy Harrison, Lisa Adams, Charlie Benton, and Hal Forbes. They would get the first look at the prosecution's expert testimony. They would hear from Dr. Harry Hollien, a Florida expert in forensic acoustics, who would maintain that, using computers, spectrographs, and oscillographs, he had isolated five .22 caliber rifle shots on the tape—and, further, after test-firing Jim's .22, he had obtained its acoustic "signature"—and it matched the sounds on the tape.

Last of all, they would hear from Arizona criminalist Lucien Haag. Haag would testify that, based on the trajectories that were able to be traced, and on Artie's wounds, and on Hollien's analysis of the 911 tape, he had been able to arrange the eight shots in sequence—and use that sequence to determine that Artie had been shot in cold blood.

John Posey was staking a major part of his murder case on those two experts, and the defense would launch a thunderous assault on them at trial. For now, though, their conclusions went unchallenged, and Posey's case was clicking along nicely despite the evidence forced upon him by the defense.

Or so it seemed.

All of the witnesses offered by the defense were represented by Dennis Roberts, and all of them prepared declarations outlining what testimony they could offer.

Most were predictable, and Posey did a good job of handling the witnesses before the grand jury.

But not all of them. Rocky Davidson's declaration was the rudest shock John Posey had received yet.

Rocky swore he was with Jim at Art's house that night.

Rocky's statement was tantalizing, and raised all sorts of troublesome issues for the prosecution to deal with, but it sure didn't shed much light on what really happened that night.

The declaration went on at some length about Artie's problems:

"I witnessed the horrifying deterioration of his mind and body due to alcohol and drugs. I witnessed his violent and abusive behavior. I personally observed Art threatening and being violent toward Jim, other family members, fellow employees, and anyone else who tried to help Art or get Art to help himself.

"I saw Art carrying and brandishing a handgun in public and private places before and during the month of February 1991. Art always carried a handgun and frequently threatened to use it."

But when it got to the evening of February 27, all Rocky said in the declaration was:

". . . I met Jim at Art's house on the night of Art's death. I spoke with Jim and others prior to arriving at and while at 23 Mohawk Drive and had occasion to observe Jim's conduct and demeanor on the night of February 27, 1991."

(The wording of the declaration sounds a lot more like Dennis Roberts than Rocky Davidson. Rocky's speech pattern is much more like

Artie's was—colorful and evocative, a bit gruff, very colloquial. Rocky Davidson does not go around saying things like "I personally observed how Jim always took care of Art and seemed to love Art unqualifiedly.")

The fact that Jim had arranged to meet someone at Art's house was pleasing to the defense. It made it a lot harder for Posey to contend that Jim went over there under cover of darkness to slip into Art's house unseen, kill him, and leave.

But what really happened? And what else would come out when Rocky testified before the grand jury?

The night before Rocky was scheduled to appear, Michael Kennedy had something else to do, and he told Nanci Clarence to prepare Rocky for his appearance.

So she and Riordan went to the O'Farrell and talked to Rocky. Jim was there too.

As Clarence tried to prepare Rocky for the questions a hostile prosecutor would ask him in front of the jurors, she became more and more worried. He just wasn't very responsive. The detail that Posey would try to get wasn't forthcoming.

About halfway through, she said abruptly, "That's all for tonight. We'll work on the rest in the morning, before you go on."

She and Riordan wedged themselves into her Fiat convertible in the theater parking lot. She turned to him and said, "Dennis, this is not happening. This will never work. He just won't be convincing."

She really didn't *want* to know what Rocky Davidson had done the night Art was killed. It didn't really matter. What mattered was, his testimony wouldn't help her client one bit.

She and Dennis Riordan sat in the little red car for an hour, trying to figure out what to do about the Rocky situation, but they couldn't come up with much. There really wasn't anything they could do, except get hold of Michael early in the morning and let him know he had a problem.

But in the morning, the problem went away. John Posey tossed the defense into the very briarpatch it was coveting.

After considering Rocky's declaration, Posey told Dennis Roberts that he thought his client should consider his privilege against self-incrimination, and further said that he felt he should admonish Rocky about the possibility of criminal liability.

Roberts said, well, I really hadn't thought about that, let me discuss it with Rocky. Sure enough, he came back with word that he would advise Rocky to take the Fifth.

Posey didn't want that to happen in front of the grand jury. He thought the jurors might get the impression that he was forcing Rocky not to testify, that there was another side to this case they weren't getting to hear.

The issue was hashed out in Judge Savitt's chambers on the morning of Friday, September 6, halfway through the grand jury testimony.

John Posey, Michael Kennedy, Rocky Davidson, and Dennis Roberts stood before Savitt. The first thing Posey did was try to get Kennedy kicked out of the hearing, saying that it was a grand jury matter and concerned only him and Davidson and Roberts, as Davidson's counsel.

Kennedy, smooth as silk this morning, gently argued that since he had elicited the declaration from Rocky, and he had proffered him as a witness to the jury, he did belong there.

While arguing that point, he managed to argue his case at the same time. "Mr. Posey is trying to intimidate Mr. Davidson from presenting the evidence that would be clearly exculpatory of my client," he said. "I have talked to Mr. Davidson at length, prepared the declaration that was submitted. I know of no crime he has committed."

Judge Savitt decided that Kennedy could stay, and also decided that if Rocky was going to invoke the Fifth, it should be done in chambers, to protect the grand jury process.

And, despite Kennedy's high dudgeon, charges of intimidation, and calls for Posey to offer Rocky immunity in exchange for his testimony, that's exactly what happened. Posey was pleased. He thought he had dodged a bullet.

Of course, Kennedy wasn't exactly heartbroken.

Posey was obviously worried that Rocky's testimony would hurt his case, muddy the issues, deflect attention from the physical evidence.

What he couldn't do anything about was that Rocky, just by his enigmatic declaration, his looming presence, would accomplish that much anyway.

And he would do it *without a word of testimony*.

When the grand jury finished its deliberations, though, it looked like Kennedy's bold stroke of presenting evidence through Posey had backfired. The second time around, James Lloyd Mitchell was indicted on five felony counts: murder, burglary, unlawful discharge of a firearm, assault with intent to do great bodily harm (Julie Bajo), and brandishing a weapon at a peace officer.

Presenting all that evidence had not, as the defense had hoped, resulted in an indictment on a lesser charge. Instead, Posey had a tougher indictment that he felt good about, that he thought was bomb-proof from a technical standpoint.

Herman's prosecutorial pinch hit looked good. His old friend had gotten a hit in his first at bat. In fact, Posey was feeling almost cocky.

He told Riordan at a hearing shortly after the indictment: "You guys thought you were pretty smart, getting the indictment thrown out, getting Chuck off the case.

"But now you've got me to deal with."

Riordan just smiled, in his phlegmatic way, from the heart of the briarpatch.

PART 6

"THERE ARE ONLY VICTIMS HERE"

he murder trial of James Lloyd Mitchell was assigned to Judge Richard H. Breiner, one of the most widely respected judges on the Marin Superior Court. Either side could have used a peremptory challenge to get a different judge assigned, and neither did.

Breiner was appointed to the Superior Court by Governor Jerry Brown in 1977. He had spent six of those fourteen years as its presiding judge. He routinely took one of the heaviest caseloads at the courthouse.

Breiner's judicial orientation defies easy categorization. He has liberal credentials, being a Brown appointee and a Democrat, and has taken a passionate interest in civil liberties, particularly in the area of jail conditions and overcrowding. He issued an order in 1983 following a prisoners' suit, demanding that conditions at the Marin County Jail be improved. "The conditions were counterproductive to health and safety," he recalls. "The medical facilities were woefully inadequate, the ventilation was harmful, the exercise yard had no toilet facilities." In the following years, Breiner would often make unannounced visits to the jail, talking to inmates, seeing if his order was being carried out or if there were new problems.

On the other hand, he is known for firmness, particularly in sentencings. "If you knew everything about him except who appointed him, you would not be able to select him as a Brown appointee," San Rafael attorney Albert Bianchi said in a 1987 interview for a legal newspaper's profile of Breiner. "His stances on the bench are strictly legally oriented. They are not politically oriented in any way I am aware of."

One defense attorney accused Breiner of bending over backward to be tough because he is "afraid of being considered a liberal." But the prevailing view is that Dick Breiner is an intellectual, middle-of-the-road judge with a strong concern for civil liberties—and absolutely no patience for shoddy legal work in his courtroom.

Born in Milwaukee, Breiner attended Washington University in St. Louis and took his law degree from the University of Missouri in 1961. He came to San Francisco shortly afterward, working first for the U.S. Department of Labor and then in private practice in San Francisco. He moved across the bridge to Marin in 1965 as a partner in Conn, Breiner, Birkie and Ragghianti, where he quickly became a prominent civil attorney, serving as City Attorney for the affluent suburbs of Tiburon and Belvedere, and at the same time doing some court-appointed criminal defense. His wife, Dorothy, has served for years on the San Rafael City Council. The Breiners are comfortable on the top rungs of Marin County's power elite.

Breiner is of only medium height, which is a surprise after seeing him on the bench. His large head, wavy silver hair, square jaw, and handsome features give the impression of a larger man. He speaks rapidly and has no compunction about cutting an attorney off in mid-sentence if he is belaboring the obvious or heading toward an unsupportable position, and that quick intellect can be intimidating. He is equally quick to crack one-liners, sometimes at utterly unlikely moments.

Veteran Marin trial attorneys say he has mellowed, that he was much more irascible in his early days on the bench, but lawyers who have prepared poorly are still apt to get a raised magisterial eyebrow, followed by a brief but excoriating lecture or a sharp dismissal.

One of his first tasks in the pretrial phase of the Mitchell case was to evaluate Dennis Riordan's assault on the second grand jury indictment.

For all of Posey's care, there were fundamental cracks in a key part of the grand jury—his instructions—and Riordan set to work on those cracks with his hammer and chisel. Six weeks after the indictment was returned, he filed motions seeking dismissal of the murder indictment on grounds of improper instruction to the jurors. He also asked that the burglary, assault, and brandishing charges be tossed out.

The District Attorney's office, with Judith Brown arguing, admitted that errors existed, but characterized them as harmless.

Just before Thanksgiving, Breiner made his ruling. He dismissed both the charges of assaulting Bajo and burglary, but he left intact the other three felony counts, including murder.

It was now nine months since the killing, and finally a trial was imminent. Breiner set December 16 as the date to begin hearing the rest of the pretrial motions and to begin selection of a jury pool. The actual selection of jurors from that pool wouldn't begin until January.

After losing two of the five charges, Posey would have to reorganize his case once more over the holiday season. The Marin District Attorney's office had received its second hard lesson from Dennis Riordan about conducting criminal grand juries.

As you head northward toward Novato on Highway 101, that car-clogged California aorta, past the dreary blur of auto dealerships and motels that the quaint little *American Graffiti* city of San Rafael hides behind, you will see the Marin Civic Center. Or at least some of it. It sprawls across several small hilltops, almost impossibly elegant, looking down on the freeway and its cheap camp-followers, a mall, a motel, an A&W, like a golden eagle contemplating sparrows and starlings.

Frank Lloyd Wright's last great building complements the surrounding green hills, and transcends everything else around it, and yet its own identity will forever be secondary to what it represents. It is edifice as metaphor, for the relentless growth that has turned much of Marin from bucolic to choleric, as implemented by the county supervisors and planning department it houses, and as witnessed by its traffic court, with lines rivaling those forming outside on the freeway, and its coroner's office and its crowded jail.

With its great sand-colored exterior walls and looping arches and sky blue roof and 172-foot spire (that ingeniously hides TV antennae and a smokestack for the building's steam boiler), it is also a metaphor for the beauty that remains in Marin, and for the wealth and pretensions of the place as well.

Perhaps most of all, it represents the endlessness of bureaucracy. It is as confusing to the first-time visitor as the paper chase that will probably ensue once the correct office is found. The two great buildings that comprise it, the Administration Building and the Hall of Justice, are an interconnected mass of interminable hallways, the doors and walls somewhere between the color of brass and the color of mustard, the upper floors festooned overhead with row upon row of bizarre brass/mustard balls. Labyrinthine does not even begin to describe it. The Administration Building is 584 feet long, the Hall of Justice an astounding 880 feet long. Some elevators don't go to the top floor and some staircases don't go to the bottom. One wing looks exactly like another, one entrance looks like another, one parking lot looks like another, and it is *de rigueur* to see people walking the brass/mustard halls with the glaze of hopelessness on their faces.

Not all of them are physically lost. Some of them are being processed by this office or that. Some are the worker bees, looking as if they have been there since before the very first Marin County citizen walked into the County Clerk's office and said, "Is this the Health Department?"

For all its quirks, partly because of them, it is a stunningly beautiful structure, but it almost did not exist. Only after a tremendous political battle did the Marin Board of Supervisors approve Wright's design in April 1958. ("Instead of slicing away the hills with bulldozers, the buildings will bridge the knolls with graceful arches," he said in presenting his plan.) He would die less than a year later, at age ninety-two, but his design would be completed and implemented by a team under the direction of Bay Area architect Aaron Green and Wright's senior assistant, William Wesley Peters.

It is appropriately imposing for a place in which momentous decisions are made, the public trust is held, lives are saved and ruined, fortunes made and lost. Yet it is whimsical enough, with its proliferation of circles and spheres and arcs and crescents, to bring some relief to the stifling mundanity of the desks and countertops where the wheels of government turn so very slowly, lubricated only by cup after cup of horrible coffee.

The cafeteria! It is the adrenal gland of the place, up on the second floor of the Administration Building, pumping out that thin institutional java for bleary-eyed lawyers and such at 8 A.M. and then for a steady stream of secretaries, gossipy courtroom spectators, couples seeking marriage licenses, maintenance men, cops, lost souls trapped on jury duty, expert witnesses, librarians, journalists, and God knows who else the rest of the day. Catering to the Civic Center's 1,200 employees and the hundreds more who visit daily. Serving them doughnuts, salads, hot-lunch specials, and grill items. (The banana nut muffins are delicious, warm from the oven at seventy cents, but the steam table manicotti at $4.25 is risky.) The front eight rows of tables are for nonsmokers, which means that the back of the enormous dining room is forever shrouded in blue haze.

Cognoscenti among the building's bureaucrats have always preferred the jail kitchen. For a time, before Judge Breiner's order and before there was a mini-scandal about the food, the inmates were getting slop while the county employees were getting shrimp omelettes out of the jail kitchen—giving the term "eating at the public trough" a whole new meaning. The prisoners' food has improved somewhat, and there has been some crackdown on eating privileges, but the abuse is said to persist.

It is just one more badly kept secret in a building full of them.

It was raining on the morning of December 16. As they are every day it rains at the Civic Center, the buckets were out.

Wright had envisioned the building's corridors around open-air atriums, but it would never have worked. In winter wind and rain they would have been like the decks of oceangoing ships. So elaborate curved skylights were built, and the light, airy feeling was preserved. It is a wonderful design; every office in the Administration Building has a source of natural light, either from the atrium filled with plants or from the outward-facing windows. But the skylights leak, and no amount of caulking and carpentry seem to be able to keep them from leaking. So, every time it rains, out come the buckets. Marin County's bucket budget must be enormous. Buckets of all colors and sizes line the hallways, from huge rolling trash buckets to little mop buckets. Drip, drip, drip, into the buckets. There was a drought in California, but you would not know it inside the Marin Civic Center.

In the Hall of Justice, below the dripping second floor, confusingly even below the first floor, is the courts floor. There, in the circular wood-paneled confines of Courtroom D, it was time to find out if the high-tech edifice John Posey had built held water any better than the one designed by Frank Lloyd Wright.

Before this first day of the immediate pretrial hearing started, Jim Mitchell sat quietly in the sixth row of spectator seats, staring straight ahead, looking incredibly solemn in a black double-breasted suit. Lisa Adams, sallow and worried-looking, came in with Nanci Clarence and sat next to Jim. There was almost no one in the courtroom—a couple of reporters, Alex Neill of the *Marin Independent Journal* and Diane Curtis of the *Chronicle;* a couple of TV cameramen, and a few other briefcase-toting suits, obviously attorneys.

Clarence went up to join Dennis Riordan and Posey. She too was wearing a tailored black suit, but hers was splashed with a pink yoke across the shoulders, like a layer of raspberry frosting. Slim, leggy, coltish, pushing six feet, with stylish short dark brown hair, she would tower over Posey throughout the trial. Her face dimpled in a smile as she made small talk, but it would be transformed with spark-shooting intensity when she argued in court.

Riordan, looking intellectually rumpled, with a cropped gray beard and a great unruly shock of gray hair coming down across his forehead, greeted her warmly.

Posey allowed himself a smile in Clarence's direction. It is as though he rations them throughout the day.

If ever a man looked like a prosecutor, it is John Posey. He is short—maybe five seven—and wiry. Steel gray hair razor-cut and combed severely straight back with no part, long enough to show a little curl, but controlled with a little dab of Brylcreem, or perhaps just by Posey's own iron discipline. A strong, chiseled face, faintly triangular, with a wide forehead and a small jaw. Deep-set, piercing eyes, used to being narrowed at whatever they look at. A large, hawklike nose, prominent cheekbones, bright white teeth. A little roughness in his complexion, perhaps the remnants of teen acne, somehow helps because it softens his features a little. It is easy to see in him the Cherokee blood that is perhaps the only thing he has in common with Jim Mitchell. He looks tough, intense, feral, predatory.

Hell, he looks like a *vampire*.

The suits he wears are a tad tight—everything about him is tight—and they are cut sharply. It seems like half of them are black, but this day he was the odd man out: he lightened up all the way to gray.

One figure loomed large by his absence: Michael Kennedy is not in court. He would not be, Riordan said, for at least another week.

The desultory chitchat at the counsel table waned as the attorneys popped open briefcase clasps like boxers flicking combinations at imaginary foes before the opening bell. Just before the judge entered, Posey made a point of asking the defense attorneys to bring Jim Mitchell to come up to the counsel table, summoning him to his fate.

First order of business was to hear a petition from Courtroom Television Network, flush from its recent tour de force, the William Kennedy Smith rape trial, seeking to televise the Mitchell case live.

John Keker, a San Francisco attorney who achieved a degree of fame as a Senate counsel during the Iran-contra hearings, presented the case for the fledgling network. He says it wishes to place one silent unlighted camera to record the entire trial, limiting its view so as not to cover the jury.

This will be one of the few things opposing counsel in this case will agree on: they all hated the idea of TV coverage.

At one point, Posey made a crack about the unreasonableness of the request, and Breiner joshed him, "Mr. Posey's concerned that he's not wearing his TV blue suit today."

The defense raised Julie Bajo as a key objection, bitching about her posing half nude on a pool table for *People* magazine a few months back, saying that she will play to the cameras if she's given a chance, possibly skewing her testimony. Also, they fretted about the possibility of the TV coverage contaminating the jury, as did Posey, who said he could offer "nightmare stories from personal experience" about contaminated jurors, no doubt thinking of the trailside case.

Keker argued that the Mitchells fought for the same First Amendment rights he was seeking for CTN, and mentioned the educational value of trial telecasts.

Finally, Breiner took the motion under submission. A few days later he would rule against CTN's request. Then, closer to trial, after an offer by CTN to tape the trial and show it only after the verdict, he reversed himself, reserving the right to prevent coverage of certain witnesses. But the conditions proved too onerous for CTN, which withdrew its request.

Later that first day, the first potential jurors were shown into the courtroom. Jim couldn't resist a quick, apprehensive glance over Riordan's shoulder as they filed in.

It was relatively late in the day, and there were only thirty unassigned potential jurors in the building. They would need many more. The first step would be to winnow out those who have valid hardship excuses that would prevent them from serving on a trial of this length—estimated at four to six weeks.

Breiner explained that court will be in session from nine to noon and from 1:30 to 4:15, with the exception of short morning and afternoon recesses. He went through the anticipated schedule of the trial, then asked how many of the prospective jurors believed they had a hardship that would prevent them from serving. All but twelve raised their hands.

They filed up to Breiner one by one and told him why they thought they could not serve. He listened to each one, sometimes asking a question or two, and one by one they were all excused. Obviously, Breiner wanted to take every precaution to avoid a mistrial or an appellate issue. Posey and Clarence stood close by to hear the excuses, crossing each one off their master list as they were dismissed.

The twelve survivors were told to come back in a couple of days. They would be given a questionnaire made up of questions from both sides. They would fill it out and then return in mid-January, when the actual trial was to start, for individual questioning.

Late that afternoon, the attorneys went over the questionnaire with the judge. The two sides had proposed more than 100 questions. Breiner went through the questions with the lawyers. Some questions were objected to by the opposing side (Breiner settled each dispute with a ruling) and some were simply deleted by the judge because *he* objected to them. Others were added.

So it went for the next few days, with the judge hearing more hardship claims, listening carefully on each one, but ultimately dismissing everyone who complained. The ratio of approximately two hardship claims to one with no claim held steady. Although there were a few Asians and Latinos, not a single black was seen in the jury pool.

Of course, many of the people excused for hardship were relatively young. In these recessionary times not many employers who don't have to are paying for jury duty, so most working people would suffer considerable hardship if they were picked for a trial of this length. It was of obvious concern to the defense that this made the jury pool progressively older and more conservative, but there was nothing to be done about it.

Meanwhile, Breiner also heard arguments on various pretrial motions involving potential testimony and evidence objected to by one side or the other, ranging from Posey's effort to keep out any reference to Artie's 9mm pistol, the 9mm shell casing, and the probable 9mm slug found in the living room (denied) to the defense's effort to limit the number of bloody photographs of Artie Mitchell that will be allowed into evidence (also denied).

It quickly became Jim's habit to step out onto the balcony for a smoke during morning and afternoon recess. Perhaps because of the hypothermia he suffered a couple of years before, perhaps because of stress, Jim shivered noticeably in the chill air on the morning of Tuesday the seventeenth. "Prop 115, it gutted criminal justice," he said, and he said a mouthful. He knew. He was a trial veteran, probably having been a defendant in more trials than Nanci Clarence had argued. "Used to be, we'd take three weeks on the jury selection, a week on the trial. Now they want a jury in half an hour. It's all federal, we're all federalized," he said, flipping his butt away and turning for the door.

"You never think it's going to be you, needing those civil rights."

On December 19, as she headed into court, Nanci Clarence confided, "God, you think Posey whines out here? You should hear him in chambers. Jesus. We cannot sit at the same table for six to eight weeks. It just won't work. I'm gonna bring a chainsaw in here."

The problem was that because of the unusual circular courtroom design, there was only one counsel table, and because it was curved the opposing attorneys ended up sitting quite close together.

Posey could be obnoxious, and it seemed just possible he knew it, and exploited it, getting on his foes' nerves. His voice was nasal and more than a little grating, going up a notch or two during arguments. He also had an annoying habit of starting contentious sentences with, "Frankly, Your Honor . . ." or "In all honesty . . ."

He would carp constantly during this trial about tactics, accusing the defense of springing surprises on him, inconveniencing his schedule, and complaining about the judge not giving him enough time for this or that. Breiner clearly was not disposed to give Posey much sympathy, or more time.

The nineteenth was the last day of hearings before Christmas, and everyone's nerves were a little taut. Riordan argued that based on the grand jury, there was a good chance Dr. Harry Hollien's testimony would not meet the court's standards for expert witnesses, in that it was not based on recognized scientific principles, and he won a chance to question Hollien before the trial, which meant Posey would have to bring him from Florida to Marin an extra time. Breiner was evidently not pleased to order it, being concerned that the hearing would delay the trial, but he felt it was necessary under the law.

A jury pool of 131 prospects had been selected and given the questionnaire, and would be interviewed individually during jury selection, which was set to start January 13. The order in which the juror pool would be questioned, very important for tactical reasons during selection, would be determined by lot.

Tempers had hardly improved over the holidays. At the end of a brief session on Friday, January 3, Posey again complained about the defense changing their argument on the Hollien issue, which meant that he might need to call other expert witnesses for the hearing on admissibility of his testimony.

"I may not be able to do that," he said. "I don't pick up the phone and automatically get witnesses. I haven't been put on notice."

"You have now," snapped Breiner. "See what you can do, Mr. Posey. Let's be positive rather than negative." He turned abruptly and left the bench.

When the court reconvened on the eighth, the arguing continued about the Hollien hearing, set for the following day. Breiner, looking exasperatedly at Riordan and Posey, said, "Why is it so hard to get the two of you on the same wavelength?"

Posey shot back, "I'll tell you what wavelength I'm on. You ordered us to have motions by December 2 and he didn't have his ready. Now here I am, last Friday you tell me to have witnesses ready." He went on to complain that Hollien's approach was hardly new science and shouldn't be challenged.

"They've been using Ouija boards for years too," Breiner said, obviously nettled again. "We'll have the hearing."

But the big show this day was the arrival, at last, of Michael Kennedy.

As he politely introduced himself to John Posey, the sphere of Courtroom D seemed to contract a little. Suddenly, some of the vacant space was very imposingly filled.

Michael Kennedy is tall, about six three. Middle age (and wealth) has polished him like a lapidary's tumbler. He hardly looks like a counterculture advocate these days, probably because he isn't. He looks prosperous, sleek, commanding. His blond hair looks as though it is contemplating skipping the gray phase altogether and going directly to white. Straight as can be, it is combed straight back, barely touching his collar. No one could mistake his face for anything but Irish, and yet it projects imposing, almost Teutonic force. In profile, one can see why: the blond eyebrows that sprout forward aggressively; the classic nose that starts outward and takes a sharp, angular turn south, just as the noses of rich and famous men are supposed to do; and the strong, pugnacious jaw, still well defined but beginning to be softened by time. For men, it is the skin beneath the chin that seems to loosen and lose its form first, and at fifty-four Kennedy has the makings of a true wattle going, but it only seems to add to his distinguished mien as it settles along the edge of his blue pinpoint cotton button-down collar. He wears gold rimless glasses through which his Irish eyes can be as warm as the inside of a saloon when he smiles at a friend and as cold as the North Channel coast in December when he peers mercilessly at a witness during cross-examination. He looks like an older Michael Douglas, maybe somewhere between Michael and Kirk.

Judge Breiner offered him a welcome, to which he replied, "It's a pleasure to be here," courtly, but subdued; one doesn't want one's client to think one is *too* glad to be in court defending him on murder charges.

Of course, it is not just the fat fee that brings him into court; he has had many of those. Jim Mitchell is family, and this case brings Michael back because of that. It is going home again, back to where he began his long upward run, the throttle cranked all the way over as he ascended to the very top rank of his profession.

He argued very sparingly that first day; most of the motions were really Riordan's purview. But partly because of his reputation, partly because he has been absent for so long in this case, the legendary general directing his forces from three thousand miles away, he dominated the scene anyway. Now John Posey could see the first glimmer of what he would be up against.

The next morning, January 9, Dr. Harry Hollien had arrived from Florida.

At this point, the trial had taken on the Hollywood look of a Perry Mason show.

Part of it was the dramatic circular courtroom, which architects say represents the first significant change in courtroom design in more than a century. Both jurors' and spectators' seating—as well as that intimate counsel table—is curved, reminiscent of an intimate theater, with the action occurring in the center. The lighting is appropriately loopy— oddly shaped plastic bubbles like UFOs, all different sizes, scattered around the curved ceiling. They would display an extraterrestrial independence from the proceedings throughout, humming and popping and flickering, and then defying bailiffs' efforts to dim them for slide and video presentations.

But the most striking thing is how much several of the major players look their parts: a commanding, magisterial judge, a feral, barking prosecutor, an elegant, box office defense attorney.

Now Dr. Hollien was the perfect addition. Tall, gray-haired, chubby, pompous, with a neatly trimmed Van Dyke, heavy glasses and a professorial manner, he was almost a caricature of a scientist expert witness.

Only Jim Mitchell looked miscast. He had never looked like a pornographer, and he didn't look like a murder defendant either, with his bald pate fringed with gray, hornrim spectacles, and his stocky little body dressed in what would be a virtual uniform for him during the trial: button-down shirt, conservative foulard tie, dark dress slacks, and a heather green tweed jacket with chocolate suede elbow patches and lapel buttonhole.

The only thing that betrayed his perilous circumstance was his face, set in such a dark, unhappy countenance that there could be no mistake: this forty-eight-year-old man was enmeshed in the crisis of his life, and that was taking in some territory.

Jim, rhymes with grim.

Dr. Hollien settled himself in the witness chair and began to declaim on his personal accomplishments, answering Posey's questions about his curriculum vitae.

Kennedy, peering at his copy, asked Hollien to read some additions that had been made in ink to the typeset vitae, and Posey lost no time snapping at him: "Excuse me, may I proceed with examining my witness?"

Hollien certainly has formidable credentials, and he enjoys talking about them. He is a professor of linguistic speech and criminal justice at the University of Florida, and is the founding director of his own research institute there. He has two master's degrees and a doctorate, with specialties in experimental phonetics and psychoacoustics—the study and identification of sounds, particularly as they are perceived by the human ear.

He has several subspecialties, including underwater acoustics, animal acoustics, and forensic acoustics—the study of sounds as they relate to police and intelligence work, including the authentication of tape recordings, speaker identification or "voiceprint" technology, and the detection of gunshots. He has done research into both the John Kennedy and Robert Kennedy assassinations.

One of the two books he has authored is called *The Acoustics of Crime.* In addition to his expertise in phonetics, Hollien says, he is a gun aficionado. He owns hundreds of weapons, and has fired guns since he was a boy.

With all that established in exhaustive detail, Posey began to run Hollien through his work on the Mitchell case.

Hollien said that Posey sent him a copy of the 911 tape over the summer, saying that there was speech on the tape along with other noises, possibly gunfire, and he wanted Hollien to see what he could find.

"I heard lots of thumps and bangs on the tape, but one of the things I noticed right away was this crack. 'Aha, the first thing I thought of was a .22,' " Hollien said. "It makes a very light, specific crack.

"And then you said, go ahead, see how many there are, so I had to do some processing, pressure pulses, spectography, digitizing sections, some pattern matching," Hollien went on in his didactic fashion. He said that after his experiments, he could state with a high degree of probability that there were five .22 shots on the tape, and that he was able to time them.

Then Posey had Jim's .22 delivered to Harry Hollien in Florida, and the doctor then conducted an experiment that would be one of the most controversial aspects of his testimony. He wanted to record the sound of the .22 as it was recorded the night of the shooting. So he set up an experiment, using his own house. He would testify that his house was "a mirror image" of the 23 Mohawk house, and that "in my estimation, from the type of work I've done in gunfire research, I judged that this was close enough" to the original circumstance. And when he compared the recorded sounds with those from the 911 tape, he said, the sounds had the same "signature pattern."

He displayed the compared spectrographs of the 911 tape and the shots fired in his house. "They are not identical," he said, shaking his pointer didactically at Breiner, "but one must look at the *gestalt*, the whole pattern." He said that the results led him to "conclude with a reasonable level of confidence" that the shots were fired from the same gun.

Posey, satisfied, turned Hollien over to Kennedy. This would be the dress rehearsal for the confrontation these two would have in front of the jury. The defense did not seriously expect to keep Hollien out of the trial, but they did want to set some precise boundaries for what he could and could not say.

Kennedy asked Hollien if a balloon pop or a firecracker exploding would not produce similar sound wave patterns, and if he could be sure to a scientific certainty that the sounds he identified on the tape were shots.

"Science is a process," Hollien lectured. "There is no scientific certainty in the world at all. Even the law of gravity is not a scientific certainty. I think that's a chair over there, but I can't say for certain."

The two kept at each other, Kennedy openly disdainful, Hollien answering with the patronizing air of someone with a store of knowledge that made the questions trivial and boring.

When Kennedy asked whether one could identify gunshots on tape with a reasonable degree of "scientific validity," Hollien said, "Sometimes, yes. You can. In many instances. Sometimes."

Kennedy said, "Was the answer yes, no, maybe, or I can't figure it out?"

"Argumentative," Posey objected.

"It was sarcastic," Breiner said, "but in view of the answer I don't blame him," and instructed Hollien to answer the question.

"I would say yes, ordinarily," Hollien said, still refusing to be pinned down.

At one point he asked Hollien a question, then huddled with Clarence during the answer, and Hollien stopped his answer and watched him.

"How are we going to work this?" Posey said. "He asks the question, the witness answers and they are in conference?"

"Mr. Kennedy can listen with one ear," Breiner said with a smile.

"I know he has difficulty with bangs and pops," Posey said, referring to Kennedy's characterization of the noises on the 911 tape.

"That's very cute," Kennedy responded coldly.

When all the fencing was over, Breiner denied the defense motion to exlude Hollien's opinions, as they were articulated in the hearing. But the defense had still managed to get a clear look at how Hollien would characterize his work on the case, and that would help immensely in a few days when they would replay the argument in front of the jury.

The next day was the final day for arguments on motions, and Riordan started out trying to limit what the prosecution's true star witness, Lucien Haag, could do on the stand.

He objected to Haag's attempt, based partially on Hollien's testimony, to put the shots into sequence. Putting together various testimony into an overall picture, Riordan argued, was the privilege of the prosecutor during his final argument, but he shouldn't be allowed to have an influential expert witness provide his closing argument from the witness stand. "He wants Haag to combine his opinions as a ballistics expert with what he knows nothing about [Hollien's testimony]," Riordan argued. He pointed out passages in the grand jury testimony where, he said, Haag was "parroting" Hollien's conclusions regarding the timing of the shots. "The law in California is quite clear. That's an improper thing to do," Riordan said.

He also objected to any testimony by Haag as to what Artie Mitchell's posture was as he went down the hall—whether he was upright, on all fours, or somewhere in between, in his addled .25 percent blood alcohol state, and what his thoughts were in that final minute.

Breiner conceded that much of what Riordan said "may have merit," but refused to limit Haag's use of Hollien's testimony before the trial started. He did say that Haag could not speculate as to Artie's posture or state of mind as he went down that hall to his death.

With that ruling, Breiner disposed of the last pretrial issue. It was time to pick a jury.

That process began on Monday, January 13, and the tension among the players had increased markedly, as it would every step of the way from here on out.

Breiner reserved the front row for the press, and it was full of writers and courtroom artists. Because the jury pool was seated in the courtroom, there was precious little room for other spectators.

Nanci Clarence was resplendent in a tailored brocade dress, with a peach silk scarf tucked into the neck. She had been taking a good amount of guff from Riordan about her friendly little chats with Posey, but in reality the defense had used her as a liaison with the prosecutor, and it had played to their advantage to have her be on good terms with him; out of courtesy he had outlined the basic order of his case for her, which was of great help in planning. Clarence, who is a lesbian and a feminist, but above all a defense attorney, would say privately later, "Would I flirt with a prosecutor I didn't like, or play the good daughter if I thought it would make points with a judge who wanted that? Absolutely. You use what you have."

Breiner greeted the 131-member jury panel and swore them in. When they all said, "I do," a septuagenarian pool member in the second row muttered, "The last time I said that, I got in trouble."

The questionnaire they all filled out was enormously detailed. The 119 questions included the obvious: education, job history, family status, religion, politics, experiences with law enforcement, feelings about firearms. They also included the arcane: Do you participate in a neighborhood watch program? What movies have you seen in the last year? How do you feel about prosecutors and defense attorneys? In what ways, if any, has domestic violence touched your life? Has anyone in your family or among your close friends had an alcohol or drug problem? What are your feelings about pornography? And on and on.

The jurors were also given a list of ninety-six names of potential witnesses. (There were only ninety-five people; Kristal was listed twice, with her real name and her stage name.) Many would not testify, and some who were not named would testify. Still, the jurors were asked to circle any names they recognized, and list the nature of any relationship they had with any of the witnesses.

Some pool members would be dismissed by stipulation of both sides based on their responses. Breiner would dismiss a few others for cause. The prosecution and defense each had twenty peremptory strikes.

The first fifteen to be considered were ordered up into the jury box. As soon as three were excused, three more would come up to fill the empty chairs.

At 9:07 A.M., Anthony Hill Lucchesi took a seat as the first potential juror. A gangling, handsome youth of maybe twenty-two, he stood out among all the older pool members. He would occupy that first chair for the rest of the day, and as others who came after him were stricken either by the prosecution or the defense, he began to look like a sure bet for the jury.

Posey had retained a jury consultant, a florid, beefy-looking former cop and investigator with a doctorate in psychology named Ray Cameron. "He's a practical guy, not as abstract," Posey would say later, "because he's seen people up close, working as a cop." Cameron sat with him at the counsel table during the selection—one of the few times during the trial that the prosecutor didn't fly solo.

For the defense, Eleanore was the key consultant, but all of the attorneys as well as Jim had some input. They all huddled before Kennedy made each strike.

Eleanore is a thoroughly stylish woman, always poised and alert. She has been described as birdlike, and that's right as far as it goes; she is slim and quick and her delicately drawn features make that superficial impression. But she is considerably more exotic than that. Her features, unremarkable by themselves, combine in a most intriguing way, like the complex bouquet of a fine Bordeaux.

She exudes grace and spirit, and her design expertise showed through splendidly in her courtroom wardrobe. She looked like an ad for Barney's of New York, wearing at least a thousand bucks into court every day, fashionable suits with short skirts and understated gold accessories; not flashy but feminine and sophisticated. Her medium-length brown hair was usually done in a kicky, very young-looking topknot, but sometimes she went for casual elegance with a simple clasp at the back. This woman knows how to maximize her looks, but the presence she displays comes from something much deeper. She is used to being the smartest person in a conversation, and at the same time is endowed with the utterly deadly charm of subtlety.

On this day she eyed each of the would-be jurors like an on-deck hitter studying a pitcher's stuff as Breiner questioned them, jotting notes and occasionally whispering to her husband.

Breiner specifically asked the jurors about pornography, reminding them that the defendant was not on trial for producing pornographic movies.

He drew a laugh when he told the pool that some of them had indicated on their questionnaires that they would believe nothing a police officer said, and others said they would believe everything. He told them that they must judge cops' testimony the same way they would that of any other witnesses.

He gave all of the standard cautions and admonitions, and asked every potential juror about their relationship with their siblings. Bit by bit, various tidbits came out about the pool members.

Joan Dzimian said she knew Martin Blinder socially. She also said she had familiarity with drugs because she was "a child of the 60s," had been to the O'Farrell "with a friend who was reviewing a movie," and also had friends in common with Karen Mitchell. She was Posey's first strike.

Kennedy's was Michael Boyden, a retired navy man.

Phyllis Thompson, a crusty older lady, lives around the corner from 23 Mohawk, and when Breiner asked her if the neighbors have talked much, she snapped, "Nobody's said anything." Sure. She said she liked to go to Reno and gamble on weekends, but she wouldn't miss it too much during the trial. "Want to bet?" Breiner asked to laughter. She was emphatically antipornography: "I know what goes on in those joints," she huffed. Kennedy looked at her without amusement, and a little while later got rid of her.

Regina Kahn Lawrence, a social worker, obviously extremely intelligent and perceptive, was questioned by Breiner about her response to the questions about her feelings toward prosecutors and defense lawyers. She wrote simply, "They're attorneys." Posey's eyebrows shot toward the ceiling. She was a prime candidate for one of his strikes, and sure enough, down she went.

The strikes began to show a pattern: Posey was getting rid of a lot of women, particularly young women, and in general people who seemed to be of a relatively inquiring mind. He didn't want flights of fancy—he wanted attention to the physical evidence.

Kennedy, meanwhile, was striking a lot of the most conservative of the older people, and there seemed to be lots to choose from.

Marin County isn't San Francisco, but it still has a pretty liberal reputation. After the young people had been excused for hardship, though, the group became a lot more conservative, and Posey was doing his best to weed out the rest of the liberals.

The second potential juror, in the seat next to Lucchesi, was Kentner Scott, a gray-haired semiretired real estate man and accountant. He looked a little like an older Gene Hackman, and he was wearing a brightly colored cotton sweater. He too survived the first few rounds of cuts, and it began to look like he would be a juror.

The same with Dorothy Diane Brabo, a middle-aged woman who seemed reasonable and not particularly opinionated, which probably accounted for the fact that she had served on two previous juries.

Gilbert Brook, another ex-navy man, had proclaimed himself "a conservative" on his questionnaire. When Breiner asked him what that meant, he said, "Not liberal." He certainly looked the part, with slicked-back hair, an expensive-looking golf sweater, sports jacket with a silk pocket handkerchief, and round hornrims.

He also said he had trouble with the concept of innocent until proven guilty. Asked to explain this, he said, "I don't think the defendant was picked from the phone book" to be on trial. Breiner bridled a little, and reminded Brook that the grand jury does not determine guilt, and Brook said he understood. On his questionnaire, he also was highly critical of defense attorneys, and said he thought they used tricks and technicalities to evade justice.

Immediate strike? No. Using a quirky bit of strategy, the defense outguessed itself on Gilbert Brook. Eleonore thought that perhaps, being a Stanford man and obviously somewhat of an elitist, Kennedy might appeal to him much more than career county employee Posey. Also, they rationalized, he has a brain, he can be analytical, he could follow our arguments.

So, despite his somewhat incendiary views of the basic tenets of criminal justice, Gilbert Brook survived.

At the end of the day, the prosecution had used nine strikes to the defense's eight, and it looked like there would be a jury sometime the next day.

On Tuesday, Posey returned to his Johnny Cash black suit, which favors his silver gray hair but makes him look all the more dangerous. Is Posey's whole persona something he has constructed for a calculated effect? Or is he just eccentric as hell? After all, he is the veteran of literally hundreds of jury trials, and his reputation is that under most circumstances he is crushingly effective.

Nanci Clarence and Eleanore Kennedy, meanwhile, *both* showed up with royal purple outfits—Nanci a dress, Eleanore another suit. The effect was rather blinding, but certainly attention-getting.

The day started out with a tussle. Something on potential juror Warren Smith's questionnaire moved Kennedy to ask Breiner to strike him for cause. Breiner refused, and Kennedy asked for his refusal to be read into the record for appellate purposes, and Breiner refused, telling him, make your strike, it's your turn. For the first time, Kennedy turned on Breiner in anger. "You want me to go on with my peremptory challenges when I want to make an objection on the record to denying this strike for cause?" he asked hotly. Breiner, resigned, asked the attorneys to come into chambers, and when they came out Kennedy had won. Breiner excused Smith.

After several more strikes, Breiner said to the jurors that he had just been made aware that there was a segment of *Inside Edition* on the Mitchells the night before. He asked if any of the panel had seen it. Carolynne Battaglia, one of the panelists seated the day before, raised her hand, looking very scared, and said she saw it but she gave it no credence. Breiner quite evidently wrestled with the idea of excusing her, but at last decided not to.

A few minutes later, a gray-haired woman named Betty Tutor admitted during her questioning that the show was on at her house, but added, "My husband told me to plug my ears so I plugged my ears and I closed my eyes!" She got a big laugh, and Breiner left her alone too.

After two more strikes, Kennedy finally got around to removing

Lucchesi. The crowd emitted a cry of surprise and disappointment, then laughed at itself for doing so. Lucchesi had obviously thought he was on the jury. He glanced at the ceiling for a moment, perhaps in relief, and then unfolded his lanky frame and left the jury box.

After Posey made a strike, Kennedy said, "After that last outburst, Your Honor, the defense passes." The crowd laughed again. Posey didn't. He and Kennedy traded two more strikes, and then Posey passed.

The defense team consulted once more, and Michael Kennedy said, "This jury is acceptable to Mr. Mitchell, Your Honor. The defense passes."

Posey and Cameron seemed caught off guard, although Posey would deny it later. It appeared likely that Kennedy would have struck at least one more person, and Posey may well have had at least one more strike he wanted to make too.

But it was too late now. The twelve jurors were sworn.

Eight of the jurors interviewed the first day would be on the panel: Scott; Brabo; Brook; Michael Williamsen, a young real estate agent and former recording engineer; Battaglia; Patricia Gorra, a woman in her thirties who also had previous jury experience; James Stein, a portly, balding retiree with a pleasant bearing who had strong feelings against pornography; and Andrew Nance, a big, rangy, ruddy gray-haired ex-marine. On Tuesday, they added young attorney Douglas Roberts; Ralph Harrison, a Korean War veteran and a strong gun-control advocate; Betty Tutor; and Peter David, an intense-looking dark-haired younger man who had voiced skepticism of psychiatric testimony, but said he could keep an open mind.

The twelve were sworn, and the attorneys turned their attention to choosing three alternates. Very quickly, they too were selected: Patrick Ryan, a native Australian in his forties with a wry smile and an air of quiet competence; William Baker Nern, an Episcopal priest who runs a homeless shelter; and Robert Fivis, a thirty-ish man who admitted strong antipornography feelings but said he could be fair.

The alternates were sworn at 1:50 P.M. It had taken a little less than nine hours of court time to pick a jury. After a ten-minute recess, and almost 11 months after Artie's death, *People* v. *Mitchell* would finally be under way.

John Posey stood before the jurors and tried to smile warmly, which was not his forte.

For the next two hours, he would draw them a picture of his case—

in the process, showing its strengths and weaknesses, as well as his own.

He was certainly not an eloquent speechwriter or orator, but he got his point across. He used sentences like:

"Shortly before his death you'll find that approximately a week before his death apparently some sort of problem really started to surface with respect to the relationship between he and his brother, the defendant, and those problems seemed to intensify, of course, apparently the week before he died, or roughly the week before he died, and he died and was shot by his brother on February 27 of 1991 in his home and that week before apparently he had had some difficulties with his brother."

He peppered the statement with matter-of-fact references to Jim killing Artie, as in the "he died and was shot by his brother on . . ." in that tortured sentence, and ". . . on the evening that he shot and killed his brother with the .22 Winchester rifle . . ." and ". . . on the night of the shooting in which he shot and killed his brother." It was a bit heavy-handed, and some of the jurors would comment on it later; at the time, it merely served to infuriate the defense team.

Posey told the jury that his testimony would be from four groups of witnesses: those who would testify about the financial relationship between the brothers; people who knew Artie Mitchell; the police officers involved in the case; and the expert witnesses who analyzed the evidence.

He made a stab at motive, saying he would introduce evidence that showed Jim benefited from the insurance policy Artie carried, but he knew his ground wasn't all that firm, and he didn't dwell on it.

In discussing the second group, those who knew Artie, he spent some time discrediting one of his own witnesses, Julie Bajo.

"You're going to find that some of these witnesses may not be type of witnesses that you might expect to find at church or your parish hall, your synagogue.

"Particularly Julie, who was a nude or erotic dancer who at one time worked at the O'Farrell Theatre, which is a theater run by the two brothers, and you'll find that she did attempt and try to benefit financially after the death of Artie Mitchell." He went on to describe her lawsuit against Jim and the $450,000 offer of settlement; her pose for *People,* her paid appearances on the tabloid TV programs, and her efforts to make a movie deal.

He then went on to describe in exhaustive detail the physical evidence, which he would present—in exhaustive detail—during the trial. "You'll hear a lot of technical evidence . . . and as Judge Breiner has indicated to you, ladies and gentlemen, this isn't *L.A. Law*. It isn't *Perry Mason,* and some of the testimony you may hear from some of these experts is going to be somewhat technical because it all goes to re-create for you and explain for you the evidence and the data that was found at the crime scene and to interpret it for you."

He slogged on through the arrest, the crime scene, the ballistics, and then Hollien and Haag. Describing their conclusions, he referred to the critical issue of the timing of the shots, with which he would try to prove that Jim stalked Artie, waiting for him to show himself so he could administer the coup de grace. Hollien would testify that there was a 28.3-second gap between two of the shots, which Haag would testify were the sixth and seventh of the eight shots. It was the prosecution's theory that the seventh shot was the fatal head shot, and it occurred when Artie, already twice wounded, leaned out of the bathroom to take a look at his assailant.

He ended his opening by playing the 911 tape.

It was shortly after 4 P.M. when he finished, which was good for Kennedy. He did not have to start his statement, then interrupt it and finish the next day. He could wait until the next morning, analyze how Posey had done, make any changes in his preparation he deemed necessary, and get the jury when they were fresh, first thing in the morning.

Some of the inevitable Monday morning quarterbacking in the press row dwelt on that fact, saying that Posey should have cut his statement shorter to force Kennedy on in the afternoon, and it was certainly a point to consider, but that was not Posey's way. He approached this case as a technical exercise, and he wanted the jury to have the expectation of the strong physical case he would present.

Naturally enough, Jim Mitchell was feeling the strain. During the playing of the 911 tape he became furious at a *Marin Independent Journal* photographer who was clicking his shutter. He had a valid argument; the critical issue of what sounds were audible on the tape could be affected. Clarence and Kennedy both objected strenuously, and even Posey agreed with them: "I frankly can identify with that problem. . . . For whatever reason, my experience has been that when there's some sort of outside sound, unless you're the one speaking or if a door opens . . . it pulls you away from what you're doing."

Breiner said, "That's why I can always hear you when you grumble about my rulings."

Jim was still furious as he walked out of court for the day, but he kept a tight lid on his anger. "I'm on trial for murder, and I can't kick the shit out of anybody," he muttered to a friend.

•   •   •

"**E**vidence will show," Michael Kennedy said, "that nobody loved, cared for Artie Mitchell more than Jim Mitchell. So for Jim Mitchell to take Artie Mitchell's life is an event so extraordinary, so complicated, that we may never know everything about it."

Kennedy was beginning a statement that was the antithesis of Posey's. The differences in the approach the two sides employed would be shown in stark relief.

Posey had walked around somewhat informally during his opening. Kennedy gave his statement from a lectern. His words were tightly scripted, chosen for dramatic effect. His statement, as would his case, focused on the humanity of the situation, not the crime scene statistics and the physical evidence.

It is a distinction that would be repeated often, and it would irk Posey. "Their case was emotion, humanity, but they tried to direct the jury away from the evidence," he would say later.

In his opening statement, Michael Kennedy used emotion like Van Gogh used a paintbrush. His voice rising to a crescendo, then falling to a whisper, but a whisper that was completely audible, he painted Jim as the victim of his own love for Artie, his sense of responsibility, and the pressure Artie's behavior and others' demands would bring to bear.

Kennedy told the jurors of the near-drowning incident at Ocean Beach. After describing Jim's attempted surf rescue, he told the jury, "Jim Mitchell, the evidence will show, never intended, meant, planned, desired, wished to kill his brother.

"Jim Mitchell was the only one who cared enough about his brother to risk his own life to save him, because just as surely as Art was drowning in the surf off Ocean Beach in San Francisco in March 1990, Artie was drowning in alcohol on February 27, 1991."

He took a few swipes at Posey's case:

"You are going to hear from experts, and some of them I suggest are real experts, and by that I mean, individuals of legitimate expertise. . . . Ladies and gentlemen, you must keep your eye on the doughnut and not on the hole, because there are going to be two other experts who come in, one from the far reaches of the good state of Florida, and another from Arizona, who will ask you to hear that which is unhearable. Harry Hollien will say to you that he has the most unique hearing of anybody on earth, and he hears things that none of us can.

"And he's going to suggest to you that his hearing is even better than yours, and that what he hears, you should hear, but don't."

". . . A criminalist, Mr. Haag, will come in and attempt to re-create—reconstruct—that which is probably not reconstructable, probably
not re-creatable. Namely, what happened in that extraordinary explosive minute or two when Jim Mitchell enters that dark house on the
twenty-seventh of February of last year. This trial is biblical in its proportions, so don't be—well, be concerned with the science, but don't
lose sight of the humanity as we go through."

Posey had heard enough. "Your Honor, I'm going to object at this
time, that's argument, and I think he ought to summarize his evidence."

Breiner sustained the objection, and Kennedy said, "Thank you,"
knowing he had already made the point he wanted to make.

"Jim Mitchell will answer the biblical question, 'Am I my brother's
keeper?' with a resounding 'Yes.' . . . And if he erred, he erred because
he cared too much. He couldn't let Artie go."

He fired at the insurance motive too: "It is, as we will show, nonsense.
The policy . . . became effective in January 1990, and while it was in
effect, Jim Mitchell, instead of letting his brother die in the surf and
collect the insurance, which he couldn't collect anyway, because the
money didn't go to him, went in to save his brother."

Kennedy also hinted, but did not say firmly, that Jim would testify.
"What is in Jim Mitchell's mind and Jim Mitchell's heart at the moment
he enters the house is the focus of this trial. And he enters, as you will
see, with love, not with criminal intent. He enters with love and not
hostility. Jim enters that house to save Artie from himself. To the extent
anyone knows what occurred in that next few moments, only Jim Mitchell can tell you. The experts can opine, surmise, and guess; only Jim
Mitchell can tell you.

"And you will see that Jim Mitchell did not have an abandoned,
malignant heart. If anything, he cared too much. It is most like, as you
will see, a lifeguard going in to save someone's life, and getting them
in a lifeguard grip, and swimming desperately to shore to save the
person, and in the process cutting off their wind and killing the very
person they're trying to save.

"There's the tragedy. It's an intervention gone awry."

Kennedy was near the finish, and his voice cracked with emotion."The one thing you'll know for sure is that there are only victims
here. There are no predators here. There are no murderers here. This
was a tragedy of domestic violence rooted in frustration and despair,
and not in criminal hostility.

". . . No one condones the killing, and no one regrets it more than
Jim. But we know it's not murder. And by the end of this case, so will
you."

Jim Mitchell wiped away tears during Kennedy's riveting statement, which took just half an hour. When he finished, Kennedy too seemed overcome.

Posey, quite dry-eyed himself, got right to work. Each day, he wheeled into the courtroom a rack loaded with three-inch-thick orange binders, each one crammed with neatly labeled files. It was an impressive array of information, arranged so that he could find any detail in moments, but it irked the hell out of the courtroom artists who were sitting in the first row, because it blocked their view.

Not one of Posey's overwhelming concerns.

Now he turned, took off one of the binders, and opened it to a fat section marked "911." And he called his first witness.

Just as she had been with the grand jury, the first to testify was Sherri Thompkins. She told the jury she had worked the swing shift that day, 3 P.M. to 11 P.M., and had handled radio traffic on both the incident with Julie and Karen around 5 P.M. and the shooting.

Over Kennedy's objections, Posey got two transcripts of the 911 tape into evidence—one with just the conversation with Thompkins and Bajo, and one with all of the radio traffic, including Thompkins's discussions with officers responding to the scene. The jury was given copies, and Posey played the tape twice more.

The jury had now heard the 911 tape three times in twenty-four hours. The first couple of times, it was dramatic and chilling. As the trial progressed, they would get more and more desensitized to the tape as Posey played it over and over. Jurors afterward would say that it had lost all impact by the time the trial was over, and Posey may have made a major miscalculation in not limiting the number of times the jury heard it.

When Kennedy cross-examined, his objection to the transcripts became clear. Under his questioning, Thompkins said she had indeed prepared the transcripts that were offered into evidence by the prosecution, but they had been prepared months after the shooting—and after Harry Hollien had done his analysis and placed the sounds he said were shots. Those sounds, sure enough, showed up on the transcript as "noise." And they were the only unidentified "noises" to be marked on the transcript.

Kennedy then produced yet another transcript, this one prepared on March 3, four days after the shooting, by Thompkins's boss, Sharon Olsen.

It did not make any reference to the "noises."

Kennedy asked Thompkins for the notes she made as she transcribed the tape, and she said she had given them to the District Attorney's office. Kennedy asked that they be produced, and Posey promised to look for them, but they were never found.

Officer Haas then testified, telling his story of Jim's arrest. He shouted "Stop! Police!" very convincingly, and then showed how Jim picked up his pace, trying to walk as fast as he could with the stiff leg from the rifle down his pants.

When Haas told Kennedy on cross-examination that because of the special shift he normally works on his drunken-driver patrol, he was "the only officer that's the odd-ball, that's not briefed," Breiner couldn't resist. He asked, "That wasn't a description of your personality, but of your function?"

"That's what I was trying to depict," said Haas, poker-faced.

"Thank you, Your Honor," said Kennedy. "I wasn't going to touch that."

"That's because you're shy," Breiner said.

The courtroom squabbling reached a new low later in the afternoon, when Kennedy accused Posey of a delaying tactic in connection with the introduction of the 911 transcript the defense offered into evidence.

"That's not true, Your Honor," Posey replied hotly.

"It is true," Kennedy said.

"That's not true," Posey said grimly.

Breiner, half exasperated, half amused, tried to steer around the confrontation, but it flared again after Tom Paraspolo and Bonnie Page had testified and the jury had left for the afternoon.

Kennedy was furious because he thought Posey was trying to keep the original transcript out of the hands of the jury when he knew it was accurate. He protested to the judge, "Mr. Posey is by this obstreperous activity—"

"The adjectives don't help," Breiner admonished.

"The adjectives do help," Kennedy said.

Posey countered, "He's whitewashing this a bit. Had he alerted me that he wanted this part of the transcript to go in, I would have asked her [Thompkins] to . . . verify it."

Posey finally agreed to have someone listen to the tape overnight to verify it. But he added sourly, "To spring something like that in the courtroom and make the allegations that he made, frankly, are very, very unfair."

Breiner said, "The verbs spring and whitewash are as bad as the adjective obstreperous."

"Right. I'm not as guilty as he is," Posey said.

Kennedy rolled his eyes. "Nobody is as guilty as I am."

During Sergeant Paraspolo's cross-examination, Nanci Clarence, displaying a fluent attacking style, had managed to elicit from him that he had never testified to Jim exhibiting a weapon in a threatening manner, nor had he noted that on the police report he wrote about the event of that night.

Also, she took issue with his description of the location of Jim's car being "three blocks" from 23 Mohawk.

Pointing at a map upon which he had marked the car's location in relation to the house, she said, "Would you please stand up for the ladies and gentlemen of the jury and count out how many blocks that is?"

"Okay. Well, by these blocks, it's one, two, and then (you're) there. These are not normal blocks like you would find in a city, though. That's what I meant by three blocks."

"So, in fact, the vehicle is around the corner and then a little bit to the left; isn't that true?"

"It's all the way down this one, up there, and right over, as you see it."

You could look it up.

Jim managed to get past the ubiquitous cameras quickly after court had ended for the day, and he waited in the parking lot with a couple of friends for Kennedy.

"Hey, Jim!" Kennedy was standing on the curb on the other side of the parking lot, next to the street, waving for everyone to come to where he was.

When they got there, Kennedy pointed down triumphantly to the cement around the edge of the curb. "Look at that, gentlemen!"

Someone had written in the cement before it dried: "Not all lawyers are scum."

Jim Mitchell looked at it for a long moment, then looked up at Kennedy. "No," he said at last. "Look at it again." He pointed with his toe.

"That part's fresh. Somebody has just added that 'Not' on the front."

In the morning, Officer Frank Baldassari testified uneventfully, and then Sergeant Ray DeLeon took the stand.

He had heart trouble in the ten months since he was taken off the case, and he looked it; his complexion was florid. Dressed neatly and conservatively in gray slacks, dark blue blazer, and red tie, he looked uncomfortable when he took the stand, and a lot more so during cross-examination.

During Posey's direct examination, DeLeon described meeting Artie in January 1990, befriending him and writing the declaration for him to use in the custody case.

He told Posey that he had been to Artie's house "four [times] that I can recall."

He then outlined his investigation at the crime scene on the night of February 27, as he had with the grand jury—with one important exception.

Ray DeLeon did not mention the conversation he had with Jim in Bonnie Page's patrol car, in which he had earlier claimed that Jim said, "I'll have a long time to think about what I've done."

It was a key piece of evidence. Afterward, Posey would say that he didn't put it on because of fears that it wouldn't stand up under the Miranda rule, meaning that Jim had not been advised of his rights at the time of the conversation.

The way DeLeon had told it before, though, Jim had volunteered the statement. Even the defense didn't feel the Miranda argument was a winner for them.

What it may have amounted to was a delicate game of damage control. Posey knew that if DeLeon testified to anything that damaging, the defense would stop at nothing to impeach him, and the Martha Rauber issue was lurking out there. Posey may have figured that if he could get by without the statement, Kennedy might decide it wasn't worth getting that far down and dirty to discredit the sergeant.

If he figured that way, he figured right. Kennedy had evidence ready to go on the Rauber issue, but he held back. Jim would say later, "DeLeon is a good old cop who helped Artie and liked Artie, and Martha was devoted to Artie too. We didn't want to put them through all that stuff if we could avoid it."

Of course, it was a fine line for the defense too. To attack the credibility of a popular twenty-eight-year police officer in such a basic way might produce a backlash with some jurors.

All of that didn't mean that Kennedy wasn't going to give DeLeon a pretty thorough going-over. It just meant he wouldn't go ballistic on him with the sex and credibility connotations of the Rauber matter.

He certainly gave DeLeon all he wanted and more anyway.

First, though, he and Posey would tangle.

Kennedy asked DeLeon about the two pistols besides the 9mm that he found in Artie's safe. "Do you know where those guns are?" he asked.

"I would hope they're in our evidence locker," DeLeon answered.

"I would like them produced, Your Honor," Kennedy said.

"If he would have asked, I would have brought them today," Posey said.

"I had no idea that he would only present one gun out of the safe," Kennedy said. "I presumed he probably would have presented them all to the jury."

"That's nice to say what he had in my mind," Posey snapped. "If he asks, I'd bring them, rather than the grandstand."

"All right," Breiner said wearily. "Bring them tomorrow, please." This trial was only three days old. It was bound to get nastier, and he didn't like it.

Now Kennedy turned his attention to DeLeon.

"At any time during the three or four days that you commanded the investigation, did you tell anyone that you had had . . . a personal relationship with Artie Mitchell?"

"No, I don't believe so," DeLeon said.

"Don't you think it would have been appropriate for you to have disclosed that information?"

"I didn't have a personal relationship with him," DeLeon said.

"You did not? How would you characterize your relationship with him?"

"I would characterize that as a police officer. . . . People come to police officers and ask them questions about a variety of different subjects. And that—on many occasions, not once, twice, three times, and that was what Artie Mitchell had done. It was not a relationship at all. It was one where he would ask me, the police officer, about what I thought he should do as a citizen in the community, nothing more, nothing less."

"Did you bother to tell anyone at the Twin Cities Police Department that you had been to—that you had had maybe seven or eight contacts with Artie Mitchell over the preceding year?"

"I'll object to that as being irrelevant and argumentative," Posey said.

"It's relevant," Breiner said. "How is it argumentative?"

"He's suggesting a police officer should go to someone who's above him and say, 'I had seven or eight contacts, take me off the case.' It's silly," Posey answered.

"Overruled," Breiner said. "Did you tell any superior that you had any prior contacts?"

"No, I did not, Your Honor."

Kennedy was closing in. He asked if DeLeon had ever called in and told dispatch that he was at 23 Mohawk during this "police officer" relationship. DeLeon said he didn't know, and Kennedy produced the TCPD's log for January 1, 1990, that bore no notation of DeLeon being at Artie Mitchell's house.

Kennedy then turned to DeLeon's internal affairs investigation. Among the documents he had won access to before trial was the transcript of an interview of DeLeon conducted by Lieutenant Spurrell of the Sheriff's Department.

Spurrell had asked him how many times he had been to 23 Mohawk, and he'd answered, "To the best of my knowledge, I'd say seven, could be eight, could be a whole lot more." DeLeon had just come up with the number four on direct examination.

DeLeon, blooded now, had no way to save himself from what was to come. "He never asked you for a favor?" Kennedy asked.

"He never asked me for a favor. There were none to give," DeLeon said.

None? Kennedy then asked about the declaration, and elicited an admission that DeLeon had done it "to help Artie."

DeLeon had had absolutely no contact with Karen Mitchell until he met her the day of the shooting, but, as Kennedy pointed out, he had said in the declaration months before that, "In my employment capacity, I have become familiar with both of the parties in this litigation." Kennedy also established that DeLeon's giving such a declaration in a civil case was against departmental policy.

Kennedy had gotten what he wanted. He made a brief reference to Rauber, but let DeLeon's denial of having had an affair with her stand without challenge. He tried a couple of lines of questioning regarding missing items from Artie's house, including marijuana and his brand-new fax machine.

"Did anyone ever tell you that Artie Mitchell's fax machine was being utilized by TCPD Chief Green?"

Posey squelched that one with a relevancy objection, then tried to repair some of the damage on redirect.

"Sergeant DeLeon, would you lie to this jury to benefit Artie Mitchell?"

"Absolutely not."

"Would you lie to anyone to benefit Artie Mitchell?"

"Absolutely not."

"Would you fabricate evidence or a story to see that this defendant is found guilty of some crime?"

"Absolutely not."

Kennedy just asked one question on recross:

"But you wouldn't hesitate to lie to protect yourself, would you, Sergeant?"

"Absolutely not. I would not lie."

"Thank you."

As hard-fought as it had been, there were positives for both sides in DeLeon's appearance. Posey and DeLeon both knew it could have been worse. And the defense knew they had scored some points by forcing DeLeon to change his testimony on the number of times he had visited Artie's house. Kennedy was also pleased that the most damning part of DeLeon's grand jury testimony had been held back.

Now Posey got into the nitty-gritty of his case. Over the next two days, Detective Jerry Mattos and Officer Ron Richter were called, and the policemen and the prosecutor went through the tedious process of introducing the building blocks of the ballistics evidence: The eight slugs found in the house (seven .22s and the 9mm Artie had shot through Julie's prized glass table earlier in the day), the eighth .22 slug found in Artie's body, the eight shell casings (not counting the one still in the rifle), where they were found, and items from the house that were damaged by the bullets.

This part of the evidence wasn't in dispute, but it was important, because Haag would incorporate it into his controversial reconstruction, in which he sequenced the shots. It took forever to introduce. While Posey was working with Mattos on Thursday afternoon, spectators and reporters in the warm courtroom, bored and full of lunch, began to fall asleep. One after another, heads drooped to chests. Even a couple members of the jury began to nod off. (Kennedy would later kid Michael Dougan, the *Examiner*'s reporter: "You've got to stop snoring in the front row. You were keeping me awake.")

But Posey ground on through it: he had them formally identify each slug, each slug fragment, each piece of splintered wood, and locate them on a large floor plan of 23 Mohawk. The perforated vertical blinds from above the bed, photographs of the sliding glass door frame on the other side where two bullets were found, pieces of Sheetrock and door frame from which bullets were extracted in the hallway—all were brought into court, identified, located, and shown to the jury.

On cross-examination Friday morning, Nanci Clarence managed to establish that Mattos had also found four containers totaling almost a quarter of a pound of marijuana in the house, but those items had not been included in the original evidence log, but had been logged in separately, at a later date.

(In fact, the first the defense knew about the marijuana was when defense investigator Eric Mason saw it on the videotape of the crime scene done by the coroner's office. He had already had a meeting with Kathy Hoffman to examine the physical evidence, and he had been told, this is it, this is everything, and there was no marijuana there. After he saw it on the video and asked about it, an undated supplemental report from Mattos had been filed. It was the first official mention that marijuana had been found.)

When she was finished with Mattos, Posey called Dr. Ervin Jindrich, the Marin County Coroner, who described Artie's injuries and the cause of death.

As gruesome as were the many photographs of Artie's body, crumpled and bloody, that would be introduced throughout the trial, the medical illustration that Jindrich used was somehow equally disturbing—particularly for people who knew Artie.

It was a life-sized, color drawing, representing his wounds, with overlays to show bones and internal organs. The image of Artie's bullet-perforated skull atop a drawing of him, complete with his green sweat pants, was a little tough to take.

Kennedy cross-examined on only one point: as part of their reconstruction, the prosecution would contend that the fatal shot to the head dropped Artie immediately. Kennedy got the doctor to admit, however, that if someone was leaning in a certain direction—and, he pointed out, with a .25 percent blood alcohol level, having already been shot twice, Artie might have been reeling—that the .22 shot to the head wouldn't necessarily have changed the direction in which the person was traveling.

After Richter's testimony, Posey took his shot at establishing a financial motive, calling Sid Cooper, the salesman who had sold Jim and Artie life insurance, and estate attorney Hal Forbes.

Posey treated Cooper somewhat gingerly, establishing for the record only that he had sold the policy insuring Artie's life for $1 million, payable to Cinema 7, and that it had gone into effect January 8, 1990.

Kennedy got some more detail out of him, including that Cooper had been referred to the brothers by Ruby Richardson (who had been after them to buy life insurance to protect the corporation in the event of a death); that Jim told him he didn't like insurance; and that when

Artie took a medical exam that showed he had an alcohol problem, the premium on the policy doubled, and Jim therefore refused both the policy on Artie and the policy on himself, although Cinema 7 eventually went ahead and bought the policies.

Forbes testified that, starting in 1990 and finishing shortly before Artie's death, he had created a living trust for Artie (to avoid probate taxes upon his death) and a will that would "pour over" any other assets into the trust upon his death. Beneficiaries were his six children.

Posey also established that the first-named trustees, or administrators, of the trust were Ruby and Jim, with Georgia Mae as an alternate, and that Jim was the first-named executor of the will, again with Georgia Mae as an alternate. Of course, after the shooting, Georgia Mae assumed both positions in Jim's stead—but Posey's point was that Jim could have been put in the position of being a trustee and executor of Art's estate.

But Kennedy established that, nevertheless, Jim could not benefit financially from the trust or the will because the children were sole beneficiaries. Posey came back on redirect and tried to establish that he could have made business decisions affecting the trust, had he been one of the trustees, but as jurors would say later, that didn't leave much room for a financial motive.

Posey would add later that he had "other suspicions" about financial matters, "but I couldn't very well put on evidence about something I couldn't prove."

Posey didn't prove much with Cooper and Forbes either. Their testimony just didn't add up to a money motive.

Posey next called Detective Mario Watkins, who testified about the weapons found on Jim, and John Clark, a fingerprint expert, who found Artie's prints on the Heineken bottle found in the hallway near his body. Then, after the jury had gone for the weekend, Posey broke the news to the defense that there were no notes from Sherri Thompkins's transcription.

"Why am I not surprised?" Nanci Clarence said sardonically.

"That is stricken," the judge said.

It had been a long week, and Nanci Clarence, with whom he had been relatively friendly up to this point, had wounded John Posey. "Frankly, Judge, this suggestion, that . . . someone is lying, it's just not right or fair," he spluttered indignantly. "I mean, they can make— they can make the arguments that they want to make, but that suggestion really is just not fair. It's not fair. They can make whatever argument they want to make about the transcripts, what was done, but it's frankly not fair to suggest that. It really truly is not fair."

Donald R. Dossett, Artie's best friend, personal physician, and a true wild boy over his years as "Dr. Skip," unofficial resident at the O'Farrell, looked the soul of medical propriety as he assumed the witness stand.

He was wearing a brand-new suit, an olive green double-breasted number, with a stylish robin's-egg blue tie. With his dark hair (just trimmed up by old girlfriend Debbie Do) slicked straight back and his big squarish eyeglasses, he looked a bit like Roy Orbison.

This was an ordeal for him. For one thing, he was genuinely crushed by Artie's death. He had considered Artie his best friend for a dozen years, and he missed him terribly. For another, he hated speaking before crowds because he had a stutter. Third, there was lots of craziness back there in the past, with Artie, that he'd just as soon not talk about.

He needn't have worried. Before he started testifying, he totally endeared himself to the jury by telling them about his stuttering, and asking them to bear with him. When he actually testified, he hardly stuttered at all.

He told the jury that he was very close to both brothers, but Artie was his best friend. He described Artie as an "intermittent alcoholic," because he would be fine for some period of time, then go off on a toot again.

He discussed treating Artie during the last week of his life for a sinus infection, and related the vicious phone call he had gotten from Artie the last day of his life.

"What did he call you?" Posey asked.

"Son of a bitch, motherfucker, nigger, et cetera et cetera . . . and he was screaming and making . . . almost a growling noise to me on the phone," the doctor replied.

Dossett said he got to Art's house around 5:45, and Artie "seemed very weak. In fact, he said he was very weak, and he said he was very glad to see me. He had a runny nose and every indication was that he was run-down, and still suffering from the sinus infection."

He told the jury what Artie told him that night about going into alcohol rehabilitation: "Through a hail of bullets I'll go to a program."

Dossett also testified that the previous Sunday, when he had visited Art, he had seen a pistol in his closet. Posey showed him the 9mm pistol already in evidence, and Dossett said, "It's very similar to this, yes."

Posey quickly got him to repeat that he had seen no weapons in the house on the evening Artie died.

When Kennedy got up to cross-examine, most of his work had been done for him already. He couldn't have been happier with Skip as a witness.

Kennedy got Dossett to reinforce the message of his friendship with Jim. Dossett also talked about the thyroid problem he had diagnosed in both brothers after the Ocean Beach incident. He testified that he prescribed levothyroxine, a thyroid stimulant, for them.

But after a time, he said, Jim told him that he stopped taking the medicine.

"He said he preferred the laid-back feeling," Skip Dossett told the jury.

For the first few days, crowds in the courtroom had been modest. But not today. All 134 seats in the courtroom were taken, and Skip Dossett wasn't the reason.

"The next witness is Julie Bajo," Posey said, and every neck in the room except Jim Mitchell's swiveled to watch her as she came in the door and clacked up the aisle, her four-inch white spike heels punctuating every step.

She wore an odd white very tight linen-ish skirt and vest with black trim, with big black laces on the front. It displayed her O'Farrell Theatre figure to good advantage, and it looked awfully brassy, right out of Frederick's of Hollywood.

On this day, Julie didn't defy any stereotypes. The outfit looked like something a stripper might wear to a murder trial.

Make no mistake: Julie Bajo is a very exotic-looking woman. She has high cheekbones complementing large green eyes set at just the slightest slant, giving her a feline appearance. Her dark hair has a reddish cast, and her skin is a beautiful soft brown that comes not from tanning, but from genes. When she is exhibiting her showgirl smile, as she did a month after Art's death on the cover of *Spectator,* a Bay Area sex weekly ("O'Farrell Theatre Lives On!"), she is dazzling. But on the witness stand, understandably, she looked more scared than sexy.

Under Posey's questioning, she described meeting Artie while she was dancing at the O'Farrell, and then going on the trip to Woody Creek to support Hunter Thompson.

"We got extremely close before we got out of the California state line, and we were absolutely together the entire trip to Colorado and back home to San Francisco. After the trip, I didn't think that we would continue a relationship, but we did, and we got closer and closer, until I finally was spending just about every day with him," she told the jury.

She said that although she "smelled Heineken all over him" when they first met, she didn't realize he had a drinking problem until "deep in the relationship," when "we started having arguments that didn't make any sense. His reaction to me was different than it was at the beginning, and I couldn't figure it out. It didn't make sense. So I started analyzing the situation, and I could see that he was obviously under the influence of something, and that he was changing dramatically."

Her analysis might have been aided by the straight vodka she saw him slam down in between Heinekens.

As Dossett had, she said that it was obvious the brothers were very close. "You could tell they loved each other," she said. Later, she would say that she thought the relationship in December and January was "not as loving," but the answer was stricken after she failed to give any example.

Posey took her through the Saturday night shooting incident at the theater. When he asked her where the gun was before Artie pulled it out, she said, "I was looking down and rolling a joint, so I didn't see where he took it out of."

Just what Posey wanted to hear. He didn't have enough credibility problems with this witness already.

"I had learned one thing with her," he said later. "You never knew what she was going to say at any time."

That's not the feeling you want to have with a pivotal witness. But Posey was really in a spot. He felt constrained to put her on the stand; after all, when the crime was committed, she was *there*. And here he was, building a case around the tape of her conversation with Sherri Thompkins. How could he not call her?

That left him in the position of eliciting testimony from a witness who almost never said the same thing twice—a witness that was on the record with several different versions of events that night. Even worse, she now believed that there was more than one intruder in the house that night—a theory that was anathema to the nice neat case he and Lucien Haag had put together.

So after the lunch break, when Bajo's testimony turned to the day of Artie's death, Posey found himself in the position of having to try to discredit what his own witness said.

And try he did. When Bajo testified that she remembered Artie turning out the light before he went down the hall, he trotted out all the conflicting statements that she had made. The same thing happened when she said she wasn't sure if the bedroom door was open or closed.

And when she said she remembered hearing more than one person in the house, he made a point of the fact that she had first volunteered that information on May 23, almost three months after the shooting, and that it was directly at variance with her earlier statements.

Even further, Posey made her tell the jury about all of the interviews she had been paid for, and about the now infamous picture in *People* magazine.

"How did you pose?" he asked.

"I posed on top of a pool table at the house of a friend in San Diego," she said.

"Were you dressed?"

"I had bottoms on," she said defensively.

A few minutes later, Posey played the 911 tape, and Julie cried as she heard it. It was the fourth time the jury had heard the tape.

After a few more questions, Posey gave up. He had done all he could, but she would not help convince this jury of his version of events, and he knew it.

So did Kennedy, who sat poker-faced as Nanci Clarence said, "Your Honor, we have no questions."

Clarence had worked late into the night on her plan to cross-examine Julie. It would have been her most high-profile assignment in the trial. She concurred wholly with the decision made that day not to cross-examine; Julie had been so bad for the prosecution, there would have been no point. But Clarence still felt a little cheated. "I was ready to rip into her," she said privately the next day. "I felt like a tennis player who had been practicing and practicing for the big match, and it gets rained out."

Her team had won the match by forfeit.

John Posey, having made disastrous forays into the squishy, people-oriented areas of his case—motive and Artie's friends—fell back on the physical evidence.

William Corazza, the criminalist with the state Department of Justice who had testified before the grand jury, gave a concise explanation of tool mark identification in general, and more specifically the methods used to attempt to determine whether slugs and shell casings have been fired from a particular gun.

He gave a rudimentary description of lands and grooves, the high and low places in a barrel after it has been cut. Grooves are cut in a gun barrel in a spiral motion to impart spin to the bullet, which increases accuracy.

He explained to the jury about class characteristics, which will indicate that a bullet was or was not fired from the same type of weapon, and individual characteristics, which are marks made on the slug or cartridge case that are unique to one particular weapon.

(With a slug, he testified, class characteristics include the caliber, or size, of the slug; the direction of the twist applied by the lands and grooves; and the width of the grooves as indicated by marks on the slug. Individual characteristics include the smaller markings that are made on the slug by a gun barrel, and they are unique to each gun. With shell casings, class characteristics include the caliber, and the location and size of marks on the casing made by the firing pin and by the ejector/extractor mechanism. Upon microscopic examination individual markings applied to the casing that are unique to each of those mechanisms would be evident.)

Corazza testified that three of the slugs recovered, including the one from the fatal shot, which had blood and bone chips on it, could be positively identified as having come from the .22 taken from Jim Mitchell. Two more were sufficiently mangled that he could only say they were consistent with having been fired from the .22, but there were not enough individual characteristics left to make a positive identification. Two more were even more distorted, with only class characteristics remaining, meaning they could have been fired from Jim's .22 or any other .22 rifle. And the final slug was so mangled that he could make no determination about what kind of weapon had fired it.

Corazza was able to say positively, however, that all eight .22 casings were fired by Jim's .22.

He also concluded that the slug found in the living room very probably was a 9mm slug, but couldn't identify the gun that fired it. He did confirm, though, that the cartridge case found in the waste basket in the bathroom had been fired from Artie's 9mm pistol.

And he also found that Jim's pocketknife had definitely made the cuts in the tires in Artie's car—one in the tread of one tire, and one each in the sidewalls of two tires.

Posey then called Kathy Hoffman, Mario Watkins, and Ray DeLeon to give their versions of earlier conversations with Bajo, to show that she had changed her story, in order to further demonstrate that his witness, Miss Bajo, was not reliable.

Next came Ken Holmes, assistant coroner, who had made a videotape of the crime scene, and then played the video. It contained few surprises. At one point, as the bed was shown, a dark mass came onto the screen, and Posey asked him what it was. He said, "I believe that's some greenish vegetable matter the police found there." It was the marijuana that Mattos had belatedly logged into evidence.

After the video was shown, Kennedy asked why there was no sound. At first, Holmes thought the sound had been turned down when the video was played, but then it was found that the sound on the original tape had not been included when the tape was copied onto VHS format. Kennedy demanded that the original, with sound, be produced. Posey acquiesced, but said he did not have a camera to play it on. Kennedy, who sniffed something wrong on that sound—maybe some remarks by the cops, something that the prosecution didn't want the defense or the jury to hear—said, "We'll find a camera, Your Honor."

(When the defense finally received a copy with sound a few days later, Kennedy would find out he had been correct. The audio sounded like the police didn't know it was turned on. At one point, as Holmes focused on Artie's body in the bathroom, a voice off-camera asks, "Are you getting some shots of Artie?" Another voice cracks, "Hey, Ray [DeLeon]. I didn't know you were on a first-name basis with the guy.")

Later that afternoon, in a hearing outside the jury's presence, Posey got another rude shock.

Dennis Riordan had shown up with a surprise motion to limit testimony by Hollien, who was scheduled to appear the next morning. Riordan produced a handful of legal cases to back up two premises: One, Hollien had referred to other linguistics experts with whom he had consulted when he was studying one of the sounds on the tape— an indistinct voice in the background that Hollien concluded was Artie saying "What's going on?" Riordan said that Hollien could not quote other experts to support his opinion without the other experts being produced to testify. The other point was that if technicians, not Hollien himself, had produced the oscillographs and spectrographs—diagrams that Hollien would be referring to in his testimony—then they could not be admitted into evidence without the technicians being present to identify them.

Posey was furious, and he played his usual note: "I'm going to object to this, walking on the eve of the testimony of an expert witness when you set hearings, we had full hearings, and he walks in here on the eve of this testimony with a pile of cases. I'm not on any notice. I can't respond to this."

"I wouldn't expect you to," Breiner said, adding that he would listen to Riordan's argument and then make a decision about how to handle it and how much time Posey would need to respond.

After the argument, Posey said, "I can't respond. I have no way of knowing. I haven't read these cases. There's no brief . . . I think it was done deliberately to throw a monkey wrench into this."

Posey demanded a continuance of several days to research the issue, but Breiner denied it. It was noon Wednesday, and there were no more witnesses scheduled. Hollien was due to go on the next day. He told Posey to study the issues during the afternoon and the issue would be discussed further the next day.

The next morning, Posey had some news for the court: Lucien Haag, the criminalist who would cap Posey's case, arranging all of the evidence into the people's theory of what had happened that night, would not be able to testify on Friday, as expected, because he was testifying in a trial in New Jersey that was going longer than expected.

Then, before Hollien started, they briefly returned to the matter of the evening before, and Breiner deferred any ruling until Hollien testified.

Then the good doctor himself took the stand, for the second time in two weeks, this time in front of the jury. After the same lengthy establishment of credentials, with a few added twists for the jury. (In describing what a phonetician is, Hollien used one example from history and another from literature—Alexander Graham Bell and Shaw's Henry Higgins.)

It was evident that Dr. Hollien loved to lecture. When Posey asked him to explain to the jury the procedure used to determine whether or not a tape recording had the sound of gunfire on it, Hollien settled in and began:

"Yes. Well, actually, it all goes back to the sixteenth century, before tape recorders, when Reverend Dereham shot a gun from one church tower and had another reverend in another church tower try to estimate the speed of sound by looking at the flash and hearing the sound." And he went on in that vein for a while.

The jurors were not University of Florida students taking History of Acoustics, or whatever it was Hollien was used to teaching. So Posey gently prodded him back into this century with, "How do you go about studying [a] particular event to find out whether or not it is actually present on the tape recording?"

"Well, actually, of course, you listen to it," Hollien responded.

Eventually he did get around to explaining computer analysis of sound patterns, and visual pattern recognition using spectrograms, which show the range of frequencies that occur at certain times, or oscillograms, which show the amplitude of sound over time. Hollien liked to give the jury explanations, but sometimes they were a bit obtuse: "Oscilloscope is best understood by thinking of your TV set, or science fiction movies, where there's a little round screen and the thing is going, and there's a line across it. What it does is take some signal, and it has a relatively frictionless system, electron beam, and it draws out the pattern of that—of that signal, so it could draw gunfire."

Hollien told of receiving a tape from Posey with a request to see what was on it, specifically if there were gunshots on it. The copy he received was poor, he said, and Posey sent him another, better copy.

He said the first thing he did was listen to the tape, and he recognized the sounds of gunfire, and thought it was probably a .22 caliber weapon.

Then he directed a technician to do some analysis of the sections of the tape where he heard gunfire. The technician turned out to be his son, Kevin, who works for his father's consulting service. "Very good with this thing, very reliable," Hollien said.

Based on Kevin's work, he said, he concluded that there were indeed five .22-caliber gunshots on the tape.

Then, when Posey sent him the weapon Jim had used, he decided to do some test firing with it to try to match the acoustic "signature" of the weapon as he saw it on the 911 tape.

"I was facing some formidable problems," he admitted. The biggest one was trying to match the acoustics of 23 Mohawk, determined by, among other things, the size and shape of the rooms and the amount and type of furniture present.

"I scanned a series of houses that I could use to shoot inside of," Hollien said, and he ended up choosing . . . *his own house.* He called it "almost a mirror image," adding, "it wasn't exact, of course, but it was rather close."

So the Hollien home became a shooting gallery, and Jim's rifle and another .22, this one bolt-action, were fired at a barrel filled with wet newspapers and the sounds were recorded into a phone in the closet.

After this home-brew, keep-it-in-the-family science, Hollien testified, he was able to conclude "at a fairly robust level of confidence that this was the same gun."

Which, of course, Posey already knew from Corazza's ballistics work.

Nevertheless, he drew the garrulous professor out on the subject, showing spectrograms of the various test shots and noises on the 911 tape, trying to buttress in the jury's mind Hollien's capability to determine that those noises were, indeed, gunshots.

Then he had Hollien go through the tape and show the timing of the shots as he heard them: shot number one, 5.5 seconds into the tape;

shot two, 10 seconds; shot three, 25.5 seconds, shot four, 54 seconds, shot five, 55.9 seconds.

That sequence—specifically, the 28.5-second gap between shot three and shot four—was the foundation for Posey's thesis that Jim lay in wait for his wounded brother, then shot him down when he got a bead on him.

It is a sequence that would be under withering attack throughout the rest of the trial.

Finally, Posey would play the 911 tape for the fifth time. But this time, Posey had a new gimmick. The jury—and, of course, the judge and the defense team—would listen to the tape using a special infrared sound system. Soon, everyone was trying on big, bulky Star Wars headphones with little infrared light receptors on them, which gave the whole proceeding a bizarre, comical cast, like something out of Kurt Vonnegut.

"You'll notice at the top there's what appears to be a light-type bulb," Posey said. "This is the part of the headset that picks up the sound waves. So when you put it on, you have to have it toward the system, and you shouldn't have any hair or anything blocking it."

"Mr. Stein, you have an advantage there," said Breiner to the bald juror. Jim Mitchell, bald himself, did not smile. He was getting tired of Breiner's sense of humor.

After a few minutes of fiddling and giggling and nodding and shifting chairs, everybody got rigged up. Hollien told them what the gunshots sounded like, and the jurors listened to the tape.

They were beginning to know it by heart.

Michael Kennedy had been "available" to the media every day after court, making sure the TV types had a sound bite favorable to his client. He was telegenic and experienced in the ways of the press, and he worked the reporters artfully. When Alex Neill of the *Marin Independent Journal* or Michael Dougan of the *Examiner* or Diane Curtis of the *Chronicle* wrote a story the defense liked, there often would be a first-name greeting and a smile the next day from the big guy. He would not be so charitable if they presented the proceedings in a less favorable light.

Posey, by contrast, was always curt with the press, and would only throw a word or two over his shoulder as he wheeled his cart of orange binders in and out of the room, pithy quotes like, "I think we're presenting the evidence." If he was cornered, he looked almost frightened in the glare of the TV lights.

When he was about to begin a key witness examination or argument, Kennedy was not as approachable. He would walk the long halls outside the courtroom during the recess, staring into a world that only he could see. A few times, journalists would think they had a chance for an exclusive word or two as he approached them with that strange fixed gaze, and they would ask a question, only to receive either a cold stare and a "not now" or be totally ignored.

He was in that mode on January 23, during the lunch break. When court reconvened, he would have his shot at Harry Hollien.

He started relatively gently, inquiring after a few preliminary questions how much Hollien's testimony was costing Marin County. "That is, for your time and your research, and of course, include your son Kevin and Mrs. Hollien [who did his accounts and assisted him with records, Hollien had testified], and whoever else participated."

Eventually, Kennedy established that the tab would be somewhere around $12,500, and then he moved on to more substantive matters.

"I'd like to read you a quote and see if you recognize it, sir, I'll even hold up your book. Quoting from page 310: 'In short, it may be possible to determine if a particular gun was fired, but if you are to do so, all aspects of the environment must be exactly replicated during the test.' End quote. You wrote that, did you not?"

"I'm sure that you read it correctly, sir, yes."

"All right. And this is your book? You are Harry Hollien, the author of *The Acoustics of Crime: The New Science of Forensic Phonetics,* correct?"

"Yes, I am, sir."

"All right. I think it would be fair for us to note that you didn't exactly replicate the conditions in your home of 23 Mohawk, did you?"

"That is correct."

"Well, do you want to change your book now?"

Hollien admitted that "When I do the second edition . . . I would change that a little bit." He went on to say that he had done more research since the book was written in 1988.

"Well, this book says here, it was published in 1990?" Kennedy asked.

"I didn't write it on Monday and have it published on Friday," Hollien snapped.

"Well, we'll look forward to the revisions," Kennedy said in a tone of utter disdain.

"They're being written right now," Breiner said.

"We're part of the research project," Posey threw in.

Kennedy did not acknowledge the banter. He bore down on Hollien. He pointed to an oscillogram of Hollien's shot number four. "Would you stake your reputation on your belief that this is a gunshot you have circled, as opposed to a ricochet?"

Posey objected to the question as argumentative, and Breiner sustained it. Kennedy asked him again if he was completely certain that he had identified the gunshot correctly.

"Please don't think that I'm being flip, but you shouldn't be so naive," Hollien said haughtily. "This is not the only evidence."

When Kennedy continued to press, he said that in "all probability," it was a shot, but he could not be certain from that illustration alone, and he had other evidence to back up the assertion.

"So you're telling us that what you have circled may or may not be—"

"No, I'm not."

"What are you telling us?"

"I'm telling you that pushing the brake doesn't allow you to drive the car. You have to—"

"That's very helpful. Would you mind answering the question?"

The two kept fencing over each point. Kennedy questioned the identity of shots two and four as Hollien represented them, and then moved back to the test Hollien did, pointing out all of the differences: the imprecise distance from gun to microphone; the fact that the recording system was different from the one used by the police department, and that the police recorder had an automatic gain control, which would tend to compress the higher-amplitude sound waves, which had not been taken into consideration; and most of all the many physical differences between Hollien's house and 23 Mohawk.

Close enough, Hollien insisted.

Kennedy then asked him if Julie's screams could not have masked other shots on the tape, particularly since the recording was made with an automatic gain control.

After some quibbling, Hollien agreed it was possible.

Hollien was done, finally, but his testimony would continue to be debated throughout the trial.

Now, it was Posey's turn to spring a surprise, and it was a beaut.

On the afternoon of Friday, January 24, he gave the defense a copy of a computer-generated video animation of the shooting. In it, Artie was represented as an androidlike figure who went to the door of the bedroom, opened it as the shots began to come, walked down the hall, arms at his sides, and was shot twice, then showed him going into the bathroom, then sticking his head out into the hallway and getting shot the final time in the head, crumpling to the floor. The shots were represented by red laser beam–type lines against a blue background.

Not only did the animation use the physical evidence to locate the shots that struck something in the house—but it purported to show *the order in which the shots came*. The tape was a visual representation of the crime reconstruction Haag would testify to, and it incensed the defense.

On Monday morning, Haag was still stuck in New Jersey, so the attorneys and Breiner met without the jury.

Kennedy told the judge he objected to the proposed use of the "Nintendo-like" video, saying, "It assumes facts not in evidence. It assumes facts that could not possibly exist because it is done in a computerized programmed video way. It is argumentative throughout . . . the trouble with something like this is the undue emphasis these jurors and people in general tend to place on computers and . . . television.

"When we see it, it is almost a form of computerized hypnosis becasue we look at it and say, 'Oh, my God, that must be real because it's on TV.' It overwhelms us. It overcomes our own judgment. . . . It attempts to usurp both directly and subliminally the very function this jury is supposed to play, which is to decide, ultimately, what happened.

"It purports to be . . . a computerized mechanized eyewitness to events that there were no human eyewitnesses to. It is as pernicious a piece of evidence as I could imagine."

Posey, obviously pleased with himself, told the court that it was the defense's insistence during pretrial that Haag had incorrectly relied on Hollien's testimony that had spurred him to have the animation done.

"All it is is a diagram, Your Honor. It's based on the diagrams [Haag] prepared in his report."

When Riordan presented some cases to argue the defense position, Posey said, "I anticipated something hot off the press, so I had a document prepared on this issue.

"It's what's known as anticipation," he added rather vaingloriously. For once, he had the upper hand, and he was going to make the most of it.

Posey told Breiner forcefully that the defense's argument ignored the crime-scene facts and the work that Haag did. He maintained that the sequence of shots could indeed be established by the physical evidence, as Haag would demonstrate when he testified.

"This is a very difficult case to explain verbally. I mean, I can talk forever. I have in my mind the way it's been explained to me by these people. It's extremely difficult to explain essentially what happened, the way a bullet turns, the way a bullet looks, this height, that height, and tie it together. That video is nothing more than a diagram that shows the trajectories of the bullets, based on the reconstruction. . . . As you'll see, it's not gruesome, not gross. It simply has a person walking down the hallway, giving the perspective where he was and where those shots occurred through this sequence."

The issue was hotly argued back and forth before Breiner issued a ruling later that afternoon.

He started by saying that the visual nature of the exhibit didn't bother him at all—that the fact it was a high-tech presentation didn't affect its legality.

But Breiner did have problems with the fact that the re-creation showed Artie in a completely defensive posture, arms at his sides, as he went down the hall. "Whether the victim had anything in his hands, whether it would be a weapon or anything else, and how and when he held and failed—stopped holding the beer bottle, is for the jury's determination based on all of the evidence.

". . . I have no trouble with allowing the rest of the video, even that portion showing the victim in the bedroom before he purportedly opens the door. Now to the extent that is based on conjecture, I think that is harmless.

". . . But it's once he opens the door and leaves the bedroom that the prejudicial effect outweighs the probative value. That's what I have a problem with.

"I have no trouble at all, also, with the video showing the location of the shots or the sequence of the shots, provided that's based on evidence or on a hypothetical question [posed to Haag].

". . . But again, commencing with the portion where the model shows the victim opening the bedroom door, through the fatal shot through the eye, I would hold that the model can't be introduced for those reasons."

Breiner suggested that the model be modified to eliminate the objectionable part, and Posey seized on that possibility.

Posey asked if it would be acceptable if a box, a rectangular shape, were substituted for the human shape representing Artie, and Judge Breiner said it would. Posey argued a little more about the final shot, saying that the evidence indicated Artie had to have been peeking out of the bathroom, but Breiner disagreed, saying it was prejudicial to show him doing so. If you substitute a block for a body, he said, that would take away the problem. But there just isn't evidence to show he was definitely in the bathroom when he took that shot.

Now Posey became concerned that he couldn't even argue the peek-ing-out-of-the-bathroom theory.

"There might be a hypothesis," Breiner said. "Certainly you can argue that. And perhaps the witness can hypothesize. But he can't render an opinion to the jury that is where the defendant was standing, the victim was standing, that is what the victim is doing at the time."

"Why?"

"Having an expert tell the jury that that is what he thinks was hap-pening based on his conjecture is not admissible."

"But . . . that's the whole point. That's what crime scene reconstruc-tion is all about."

"So, see you tomorrow, nine o'clock." Breiner ended the hearing.

The defense was mad enough about the computer animation. The morning paper didn't make them feel much better.

"Mitchell Judge OKs Simulation of Crime" read the banner headline across the top of page one in the *San Francisco Chronicle*.

They just couldn't believe it. The judge had ruled their way, and the headline said just the opposite.

The judge's exact words had been: "So the motion is granted. The animated diagram is precluded, will not be admissible, will not be shown to the jury, unless that portion showing the victim from the time of opening the bedroom door through the fatal shot is deleted or somehow modified."

Chronicle reporter Diane Curtis didn't write the headline, but she did write the story, which began, "Jurors in the Jim Mitchell murder trial may be among the first in the nation to view a computerized video re-creation of a slaying." And the *Chron*'s editors took it from there.

Turns out, they were prophetic, and the defense was in for another nasty surprise.

John Posey had suggested "a box," or "block," instead of a person, the day before when he was fighting desperately to get the video in front of the jury. But when the modified video was shown to the court the next day, there was no block. There was the same humanoid, but shown from an angle so that his arms could not be seen.

The defense angrily argued that the figure had arms later, when he fell to the ground, and that just because the jury couldn't see arms as he went down the hall simply meant that they would assume the arms were at his side in a defensive posture, because if they weren't they would be able to see them.

"We have our theory and they have their theory," Posey maintained. "If they want to do a video they can do a video."

He said, "Certainly through cross-examination it can be brought out through Mr. Haag that he can't say exactly where his arm was, whether it was here, there, up, down, whatever. But what he can say is based on the video, the trajectory of the bullet and where it struck the victim . . . that, I submit, would aid the jury in assessing the testimony."

Riordan responded, "The video portrays them [arms] at his side. You have said that is unacceptable; give me a block that doesn't portray that and I'll find it acceptable. Mr. Posey has adamantly refused."

"Just one comment on the block [idea] that I threw out yesterday," Posey said. "In trying to reestablish and re-create this in a way that made any kind of sense, it doesn't work out that way.

". . . All the physical evidence shows that he got cornered in that bathroom and got shot in the arm and in the head after he was cornered in the bathroom and was creeping around that corner. That's what the blood evidence indicates. All that is removed from this video. What's left is simply this man, who's depicted with what Mr. Riordan feels, I guess, is something damaging and jeopardizing to their case, because his arms are at his side."

After Riordan argued again that not showing the arms from the top view but showing them later was tantamount to showing arms at sides in a defensive posture, and again raised the issue of a block, or a body with arms sheared off, Posey snapped, "Well, what are we going to do? Pretend it wasn't a human being that was shot, that he didn't have a body?"

Riordan was tired of the endless argument, and he knew he was in a tough spot. Posey had been very skillful. He had not done what he asked, precisely, but he had done enough that it was a close issue.

"I've had enough argument. The motion to exclude the video is denied. I will advise the jury that the video does not show arms. It's not intended to show arms."

"That makes it all the worse," Kennedy said, "with all due respect, because what you are doing is giving imprimatur to this . . . and saying that but for the arms, all of the rest is correct." He asked the judge not to make such a statement, and the judge agreed.

Had Posey decided to use a block in the video, Lucien Haag could have modeled for it.

Short, stocky, muscled, Haag looked like what he was: a tough, smart former cop. The combination of his chestnut hair cropped close in a military-style haircut, his thick neck exactly the width of his head, and his occupation quickly gave rise to the nickname "bullet-head" among the less reverent types in press row.

He was an extremely impressive witness. No one could fault his intelligence, his credentials, his command of the case, or his skill as a witness.

As he testified, each little scrap of information Posey requested came out crisply, easily, straightforwardly, like a carrot tugged from soft earth. Unlike Hollien, Haag lectured only when asked to explain something, not just for the joy of hearing himself talk. There were no flights of verbiage, no voyages to the sixteenth century.

At some time in his long career as a witness, Haag had learned to answer questions to the jury, but he was nowhere near as patronizing as his predecessor on the stand.

Posey spent a long time on Haag's credentials, and the criminalist made it all sound matter-of-fact and admirable, without sounding boastful.

Haag runs his criminalist consultant work from a crime lab in Phoenix. During his entire police career, Haag worked in the Phoenix Police Department crime lab, starting in 1965 and advancing until he was the department's top criminalist, the position he held in 1982 when he formed his own company to take advantage of the lucrative market for criminalists of his skills.

Like Hollien, he told the jury he had a strong personal interest in firearms, having done a lot of competitive rifle shooting.

Posey questioned him at length about the papers and presentations he had done, and his professional association memberships and honors, and the many cases in which he had done reconstructions. He did not neglect to mention Haag's after-the-fact investigations of both the Lindbergh kidnapping and the shooting of Huey Long. Finally, he got down to business.

Lucien Haag also had test-fired the well-traveled .22, in order to see if it worked correctly (it did), if it was accurate (it was), where the shell casings would go upon ejection (in a fan-shaped pattern, six to eight feet away). Jim looked especially grim as Haag demonstrated how the rifle's lever-action worked.

He talked of studying Jindrich's autopsy report. As if he were letting the jurors in on a professional secret, he explained how important to a reconstruction it was to know how the wounds tracked through the body, pointing out that if there were an exit wound, there had to be a slug somewhere to correspond with it, and "there stands to be some other object beyond the individual" that was also struck by the bullet.

He discussed the evidence the police gathered, and Corazza's ballistics work, and then described the many tests he performed on the evidence.

He identified the fatal bullet, which he had photographed. "It has one particularly very large bone particle embedded in it," he reported clinically, and later his slide of the bullet would be shown to the jury.

He told jurors about going to 23 Mohawk on the twenty-seventh of July, and working to determine the trajectories of the bullets. Posey seemed particularly fascinated with his use of a small laser light in working out trajectories, and he got Haag to tell the jury about it.

"Well, in all candor," Haag said with just the right amount of self-deprecation, "it's a fancy string. For years, criminalists . . . have used probes, dowel rods of various sorts, sometimes tautly drawn line or cord, all of which are useful.

"A laser . . . has some advantages in that, for example, a string line you can't step into and position yourself. A laser very handily allows us to set up for a bullet hole or bullet impact mark, or both, appropriate trajectory, and then position a person of comparable stature . . . most importantly if we know where an injury wound is. Could it work this way, or is that possible or not possible."

Haag did just that with the fatal shot, and over Kennedy's objection, testified, "Such a shot could easily be made in the kitchen area, and a subject could basically stand in the doorway and expose his head, turn and look . . . and sustain such an injury."

Then Haag talked about the bullet that struck Artie in the arm and lodged in his chest, which had to have struck something else first because of the size of the wound.

"There's only a couple of places in the house where bullets had gone through something. One of them was by that bathroom doorway, again where wood and drywall material were present.

". . . There was no bullet damage opposite this area, no damage down the hallway that represented a destabilized bullet. There are a couple of bullet holes, but pristine bullet holes, through a door. That raised the clear possibility that this bullet may indeed have gone into the decedent. The wound would also suggest that."

But more conclusively, Haag testified, he examined the bullet recovered from Artie's chest under a scanning electron microscope and found embedded calcium sulfate, or Sheetrock material from the wall.

Looking at the crime scene photos, he also noticed several white specks on Artie's beard, arm, and armpit that he theorized were also Sheetrock.

Noting in the photos that Artie had been wearing sweat pants, he asked for them to see if he could find any more particulate matter on them that might have come from the wall. Almost six months after the shooting, he found a little wood chip hanging on to the bloody, putrefied pants that he tested for traces of lead from a bullet with a reagent, sodium rhodizonate, and sure enough, it tested positive.

"That fit with all the other inferences I had that this injury was that bullet that came through that archway next to the bathroom in the entryway to the hallway."

He would use one particularly dramatic piece of evidence to estimate the length of time between that shot and the fatal one: the blood that had oozed down Artie's arm. Haag said it showed conclusively that Artie was basically upright—and alive—for a certain length of time after the arm injury before collapsing from the head shot. The blood came from the wound straight down Artie's arm for that time, then, after he had collapsed and his arm had splayed out to its final position, the blood already on his arm ran downward.

He called it a "liquid hourglass."

He then described the trajectories of the other bullets, including the shot that struck Artie in the abdomen. As Dr. Jindrich had observed, that shot passed through Art's body without hitting anything solid, and it still had considerable force when it exited, Haag said—enough to hit the edge of the bedroom door frame and ricochet diagonally across the bedroom, striking a window frame, and landing on top of the dresser, where it was found a few days later by Mattos and Richter when they realized they were one bullet shy.

Haag contended the bedroom door had to be open at least forty-five degrees for the ricocheting bullet to have gone through without striking the door. He said the two bullet holes in the door correlated with bullets that struck the sliding glass door above the head of the bed—one at the center post and one at the end.

The bedroom door itself, People's Exhibit 94, with two bullet holes in it, was wheeled into court, mounted on a crude frame of two-by-fours, constructed so that the door could be opened, closed, and easily moved. For the rest of the trial, it loomed ominously in the aisle next to the defense table, reminiscent of a gallows, with the two malevolent little holes, marked "A" and "B," forty-six and forty-five inches, respectively, from the bottom.

Haag testified that in tracing the trajectories of the bullets, through the door and beyond, he discovered that the door must have been closed for shot A, and open "thirteen or fourteen inches" when shot B passed through it.

Another bullet was found above the hallway door, some seven feet, two and three-quarters inches above the floor. Another penetrated the Sheetrock and lodged an an interior wallboard to the right of the bedroom door, about forty-four inches high. And yet another lodged nearby in the door frame, forty-seven inches high.

With respect to the two bullets that passed through the door, Haag testified that because one of the bullets traveled nearly horizontally through the door, and another passed through on a descending angle, of four and a half to five degrees, the shooter probably changed positions in between those two shots.

Haag went so far as to buy another similar door and shoot some test rounds through it to see what effect the deflection from the door would have on the vertical angle of the bullets, and he found that effect to be only two or three degrees.

He demonstrated—after Kennedy's objection was overruled—that he felt shot A through the door was probably fired from a standing position, while shot B was probably from a kneeling position.

Now Posey went for the whole enchilada.

"Can you indicate to the jury if you have the capability, through your investigation or analysis of crime scene evidence, to determine the order the shots were fired in?"

"Yes," Haag said, "presented with certain factual information. Some of that I already have."

This was where Posey's theory—and Haag's theory—was on the shakiest ground. Because now they had to rely on the 911 tape, and on Hollien's analysis, to complete their shot sequence.

"I'm going to ask you to assume certain facts, and then ask you some questions based on those facts," Posey said. "I'd like you to assume that we have a man and a woman who are located in the easternmost bedroom . . . that they hear noises like doors slamming, and that shots are fired.

". . . I want you to assume that they get out of bed and that the woman eventually picks up a telephone and calls the 911 operator. . . . The woman is asked a question about how many shots were fired. . . . The lady making the phone call says . . . 'I heard like one, two, three. We got out of bed, we turned on the lights, and then I— he said give me some clothes. I got in—I was putting on my shirt and I heard another shot and I got into the closet.'

"I want you to assume further that at another point . . . the person says . . . 'I heard shots, shots, shots' . . . so on two occasions the person making the phone call used multiples of three."

In an injured tone, Kennedy said, "Excuse me, Your Honor, 'Shots,

shots, shots' means using the word three times. That doesn't mean a multiple of three shots."

"Sustained. That's correct."

But Haag said, as if ignoring the objection, "I followed. You used that word three times."

"I want you to assume further," Posey said, "that the 911 tape was analyzed by an expert in the analysis of tape recordings, and that this person concluded that the tape recording . . . revealed the sound of five gunshots during the course of the telephone call.

"Now, with those facts that I've asked you to assume, and in light of the evidence that you've gathered and with respect to the work that you've done on the case, can you say whether or not you can put all that evidence together to give a sequence within which shows the shots might have occurred?"

Posey had reverted once more to the George Bush school of syntax, but Haag knew what he meant.

"Yes," he said.

"I have to object. Excuse me. I move to strike that until I can complete my objection," Kennedy said, glaring at Haag.

"Sorry," said Haag unrepentantly.

"I move to object to that particular question on the grounds that it does not include a variety of salient facts, such as, the credibility of Julie Bajo was impeached by this gentleman"—he waved at Posey—"for several witnesses, for some time.

"She has said subsequently that she thinks there were maybe two shots. She has said subsequently she's not sure how many shots whatsoever because she was under such extreme stress.

"Professor Hollien said, in fact, that there could have been other shots on that tape not discernible by him because they could have been masked by the screaming."

"Well, Your Honor, my hypothetical is based on the assumption of what she said during the 911 call. If he wants to pose a different hypothetical to the witness based on what he contends the correct evidence is, he's free to do that."

"He doesn't have to," Breiner said. "The objection is sustained. It's not a complete hypothetical."

"Well, let's add in what Mr. Kennedy just indicated he felt should be in the question," Posey said. Turning to Haag, he said, "Did you follow what his objection was?"

"No, I'm sorry, I did not," Haag said virtuously.

"Well, his objection is that the woman, after the 911 call, has given various statements with respect to the number of shots that she heard before she called 911.

"One of these statements was that she only heard two. . . . As a matter of fact, that was a statement she gave several months ago, and she wasn't clear as to how many shots she had actually heard before she made the—"

"I'll put you out of your misery, Mr. Posey," Breiner interrupted. "This is not a proper hypothetical. You're asking this witness to do what the jury will have to do."

"But why—what, you're precluding me from askng the hypothetical question based on the 911 call?" Posey asked, seemingly horrified.

"I'm precluding you from asking this hypothetical question," Breiner said irritably. "The objection is sustained."

Posey tried all kinds of ways, but Breiner didn't let Haag tell the jury his theory of the sequence of shots.

But he did allow the edited version of the video animation—which *showed* the sequence—to be played. It showed the fatal shot as the next to last, with the shot high into the wall above the door as the final shot.

After it was played, Posey asked Haag, "The display we just saw— that is based on your reconstructive work, is it not?"

"That's right."

"That's all I have."

Now Michael Kennedy would face the toughest challenge of the trial—one of the most experienced, effective criminalist professional witnesses in the business. A witness with a rep almost as good as his own.

The courtroom tightened palpably in anticipation.

There was an overwhelming urge to cast this confrontation in the metaphor of competitive sport. It was like Ali, after fighting Zora Folley and Cleveland Williams and Ernie Terrell and an old Floyd Patterson, running up against Joe Frazier. Like Whitey Ford glaring in at Yaz. Jim Brown running into Night Train Lane. J.R. Mitchell vs. Amarillo Slim.

But this wasn't a sport, and the stakes were higher than any you could lay down on green felt. This was life.

Maybe, for Kennedy's friend and client, life in prison.

After eliciting from Haag that his fee would be $175 an hour for "fifty to 100 hours" plus expenses, Kennedy started in on Haag.

The answers that had come so smoothly for Posey were now having to be extracted like impacted wisdom teeth.

Haag went to extraordinary lengths to avoid saying the word "yes" in reply to any of Kennedy's questions. He was brittle, argumentative, at times openly hostile. He would not give anything up that he didn't have to.

If he had a weakness, that was it. Kennedy sensed that the jury didn't care for Haag's quibbling responses, and so he tried to push him into more and more of them. Haag had just flown across country, he had been on the stand all day, and he had to be jet-lagged and exhausted.

There were also some cracks in his presentation—mainly that in order to defend the sequence of shots he put forward, he had to rely on Bajo and Hollien.

Kennedy asked him about the shot high above the door that he had identified on the video as being the last shot.

"As a matter of fact, it could have been the first shot, could it not?"

He got Haag to admit that it could have been any of the first three shots.

"But it also could have been the next-to-last shot, could it not?"

"Well, at that point, I have two ways to go. If you totally disregard the assistance of Dr. Hollien, then I'd agree with you. If I utilize the data provided by him, there's an argument against that." He brought up the groan Hollien said occurred between the last two shots.

"But isn't that just speculation on your part?" Kennedy asked.

"There are speculative elements of all scientific testimony," Haag replied.

Kennedy then spent several minutes pinning him down to repeat what he had said easily on direct examinaton—that the trajectory of the shot more than seven feet above the door was basically horizontal, which, if accurate, would mean that the shooter would have had to hold the gun over his head to fire that shot, or have used a ladder, neither of which seemed likely. Kennedy used this to try to cast doubt on Haag's hypothesis based on trajectory angles that the shooter had changed position. Posey and Haag had cited that as evidence that the shooter had consciously tried to get a better angle for a killing shot.

Next, he wormed out of him that if Julie Bajo's original estimate of the number of shots before the 911 tape—three—were not factored in, there would be no way to sequence any of the three shots that missed Artie and hit only one place in the house.

And that the shot that struck Artie in the abdomen could have been the fourth, fifth, or sixth shot.

Posey watched Haag intently during cross-examination, occasionally making abrupt, chopping, emphatic motions with his hands, as if he were answering Kennedy himself.

Finally this day was over, but the cross-examination wasn't. The next morning, Haag and Kennedy were at it again, arguing about everything from Haag's ability or lack of same to sequence the shots (again) to his "liquid hourglass" theory of the blood from the arm wound. Kennedy made the point that the rate of flow would have depended on blood pressure, how many capillaries or arteries were damaged, etc.

Haag described an experiment he did, running blood from a tube down his arm in the same manner the blood flowed from Artie's wound. He did it twice, he testified, and once it took twenty seconds to make a similar path and once it took thirty—fitting nicely with Hollien's 28.5-second gap between the third and fourth shots on the tape.

But Kennedy pointed out that he was able to control the rate at which the blood flowed during the experiment, and it might or might not have corresponded with the flow from Artie's arm wound.

And he also got Haag to agree that with eight shots, there are more than forty thousand possible sequences to consider.

And he pounded away at Haag's contention that the shooter probably changed his position at some time during the shooting, the two men knowing each other's styles now, wrangling at each other like an old married couple. Occasionally, Haag looked over fiercely at Jim Mitchell, sitting not six feet from him, staring straight ahead.

Finally, well into the afternoon of January 30, Haag's second day on the stand, the inquisition was over, and with it Posey's case. The prosecution rested.

Warren Hinckle, the eye-patched, vodka-swilling San Francisco leftie media darling, former editor of various magazines, former *Chronicle* columnist, former *Examiner* columnist, had been a close friend of the Mitchells ever since his columns critical of the Marilyn Chambers bust got *him* busted by vindictive cops for a dog leash law violation and got the brothers' business barrels of great free ink.

Now he and his wife, Susan Cheever, were ostensibly writing a Mitchells book, and covering the trial, but Hinckle was busier writing the Mitchell company line in his colorful way. Not for the *Examiner* or the *Chronicle,* who had cooled considerably to his screeds, but for the *Anderson Valley Advertiser,* a tiny firebrand weekly from the hills of Mendocino County, fifty miles to the north. Run by irascible, irreverent publisher Bruce Anderson, replete with well-written polemics decrying this and that in local politics, the paper had a cult following around Northern California that amounted to only a few copies outside its primary circulation area, the tiny hamlet of Boonville and surrounds.

Now, Hinckle had both a cause—Free Jim Mitchell—and a target, the easily lampooned Posey. He and a posse of the raffish, talented counterculture artists that the Mitchells had always supported (led by Dan O'Neill, who was still trying to open a nightclub in the old *War News* space) basically took over the paper for the duration of the trial. Jim bought hundreds of copies at twenty-five cents apiece (the price in Boonville is seventy-five cents). He had Rocky, still a potential trial witness, and Johnny Morgan and others distribute them around Marin and San Francisco. Suddenly, *Anderson Valley Advertiser* giveaway newsracks sprouted all around the many Civic Center entrances, with rack cards that trumpeted "The Truth About the Mitchell Trial." A stack of *Advertisers* even showed up in the Civic Center cafeteria. The unspoken possibility was that a juror or two might snag one despite the admonition, which Breiner gave them daily, not to read about the case.

Bruce Anderson was to learn what so many editors and publishers had learned before—editing Hinckle was no picnic. Hinckle routinely flouted deadlines, and as a result his stories were jammed in without proofreading, so they were rife with errors typographical and factual, from the spelling of the judge's name to Artie Mitchell's address. One week, a huge segment of his story was repeated.

The whole thing was a zany move that was typically Mitchellesque. It was not without risk, of course, and the attorneys were privately nervous about it, but it did boost Jim's flagging morale.

"High school journalism. *Bad* high school journalism," one insider sniffed, reading the *Advertiser* outside the courtroom. Of course, Hinckle is more colorful than clinical, and in covering the trial he tended to come late and sleep often. But that wasn't the point. It was outlaw, insurgent, tail-twisting fun, and it was a reprise of some of the Mitchell antiestablishment stunts of yesteryear.

Posey swore up after the trial that he didn't read any of it, but there were certainly copies making the rounds of other desks in the District Attorney's office.

Michael Kennedy couldn't start right off with the warm, fuzzy, human case he wanted to present. First, he had to put on experts to bash Posey's experts, a forensic version of Star Wars, or maybe Spy vs. Spy.

For all their credentials, technical expertise, and attitude, both Hollien and Haag were bashable. Particularly Hollien.

But Kennedy wouldn't call any bulletheads. He chose an improbable-looking leadoff hitter instead—Dr. Vincent Salmon, a seventy-six-year-old Stanford professor and MIT-educated acoustics expert who spent thirty years of his career at the prestigious Stanford Research Institute.

Vincent Salmon looked like a sweetly disheveled little old man, because he was. A few gray hairs sprouted here and there on his bald pate. His glasses were a little cockeyed and his jacket tweedy and seedy. This was the warm and fuzzy version of the expert witness. Lucien Haag had worn a bullet cartridge as a tie tack; Vince Salmon held his tie to his shirt with a paper clip.

Yet there was nothing disheveled about Salmon's brain or his manner.

Kennedy wanted him primarily to discuss room acoustics, specifically Harry Hollien's representation that his house was "close enough" to 23 Mohawk to conduct a valid scientific experiment.

Salmon said that upon examination of the data from Hollien's testing, he concluded that it "was not a sufficient simulation of the actual case to permit evidence gathered in Professor Hollien's residence to be directly comparable to what happened, presumably, at the Mohawk residence."

He said he had read Hollien's book, recalling that the Florida professor "was very emphatic in that the acoustical environment was so important [that] it dictated what was heard."

"Well, he became less emphatic in court here, sir," Kennedy said wryly. "But do you agree with that statement of his in the book?"

"I completely agree with his statement in the book," Salmon said.

On Monday morning, February 3, before the trial started for the day, Breiner told the attorneys that juror Peter David was in bed with the flu and a 104-degree fever, and could not come to court. So an alternate was chosen by lot to take his place, and it turned out to be Rev. William Baker Nern.

Now Posey confronted the question of how to go about cross-examining Vincent Salmon. He didn't want to come down too hard on him, because he sensed that Salmon was an enormously sympathetic figure with the jury. But he had, in his gentlemanly way, ripped up the validity of Hollien's test, which wasn't so big by itself, but it did tend to impeach Hollien's overall credibility. So Posey had to try, in turn, to impeach Salmon.

"With respect to guns, do you use them?" he asked Salmon.

"I fired a pistol once."

"When was that?"

"About fifty years ago," Salmon said cheerfully, provoking a belly laugh.

"Was it a flintlock?" Breiner inquired.

Posey elicited from Salmon that he had testified in only six or seven cases before, and only two of them had had anything to do with gunfire.

He asked him if no tests or re-creations could ever be valid unless the conditions were exactly duplicated. Salmon replied that he would not be completely comfortable with the results if the conditions were less than exact, but "as you approach exactness, the final result will be closer and closer to a complete re-creation."

Posey kept at him for a while, getting him to misread the scale on a chart at one point, but he deliberately didn't press him as hard as he could have.

There was another, more important acoustic witness coming up. He was Fausto "Tito" Poza, and he was the defense's main weapon against Hollien's testimony.

Poza had also spent twenty-five years at Stanford Research Institute before becoming a forensic consultant, primarily in the field of speech research.

Among his qualifications, he testified that he had been hired by the federal government in 1983 as part of a peer review board to check out a project that the Department of Justice was funding. The object of the scrutiny was research by Dr. Harry Hollien.

Which of course was what he had been hired to do in this case.

Certainly, this time around, he didn't think much of the Florida doctor's work. First, he also agreed with Hollien's published view—as opposed to what he actually did in this case—that for gun signature tests to have any validity, conditions must be exactly replicated in the tests.

Next, he pointed out that the software Hollien used in his analysis was twenty years old and, in his view, obsolete.

Then, Poza took the two wave forms—one produced from the 911 tape and one from one of Hollien's test shots—that Hollien cited as evidence of a matching "signature." He overlaid them and pointed out the dissimilarities as well as the matching areas. ". . . The match is very bad, but of course I would find no reason to expect it to be very good," Poza said. "You do not expect to find matching time wave forms in the situation that we've got here."

Instead of bringing diagrams of wave forms into court, like Hollien did, Poza brought his computer, with three monitors, into court so he could isolate various segments of the tape and show what they looked like in graphic form and what they sounded like. In order to do that, he took a digital feed of the 911 master directly into a Macintosh II, FX, a super-high-speed Mac. Using Mac Speech Lab II software, he was able to do the analyses that Hollien did—with more precision, he maintained—and also analyze the work that Hollien himself had done.

As Kennedy questioned him, Poza displayed powerfully for the jury on the Macintosh screens, and through the computer's sound output, that there seemed to be big-time problems with at least two of the shots identified by Hollien.

The second shot, which Hollien said came ten seconds into the tape, just as Sherri Thompkins is saying, "You hear *shots,*" wasn't a shot at all, Poza maintained. "It's not even close." The sound was actually merely Sherri Thompkins pronouncing the "ts" of "shots"—specifically, releasing the "t" sound, Poza contended.

Furthermore, Poza claimed that the wave form that Hollien marked as "shot four" was also probably not a shot—that a wave form just before the area he marked was probably the actual shot instead.

Poza also identified several places on the tape where Julie Bajo's screams could have, in his opinion, masked wave forms caused by gunshots—in an effort to negate the timing established by Hollien's analysis.

Tito Poza wishes his testimony had stopped there.

But it didn't. He took another random short sound from much later in the tape, printed out a graph of it and overlaid it on the 911 tape shot that Hollien had used for his comparison—and told the jury that the overlay was a better match than was the demonstration shot that Hollien claimed as a "robust match."

It was a dramatic, visual example.

The next morning, it turned to dust before the eyes of the defense. Posey had enlisted the help of one of Hollien's former students, Dr. Ruth Huntley, an acoustician from North Carolina, and overnight she had examined the overlay Poza had made.

And she discovered that, somehow, the amplitude of the sound Poza had picked for the comparison had been reduced by 50 percent before the comparison was made.

Up to that point, Poza had been an incredibly persuasive witness, careful not to overstate, straightforward, good at explaining the computer stuff and making the Mac operate so the lay jury could understand it. He had made Hollien look incompetent and unprofessional.

But this mistake cost him, and the defense, dearly. It looked as though he had manipulated the evidence to strengthen his argument.

The defense will tell you that is ludicrous, that it was a freak error, that Poza is such a stickler for accuracy that he was forever understating the evidence, not exaggerating it.

Posey, desperately fighting the damage done to Hollien over his elusive "shot number two," tried to suggest to the jury that a small wave just after the "t" sound that Poza had isolated was actually the shot Hollien had identified.

Poza retorted, "For his sake, I hope not," adding that it was far too short and lacked the classic wave pattern of a gunshot. On redirect, Kennedy dubbed it "Posey's blip" and elicited Poza's opinion that it was nothing more than the "s" in "shots."

All of which was convincing. Nevertheless, the error on the overlay loomed large, and Posey made it clear he felt he had caught Poza cheating. "He altered evidence," he said flatly after the trial.

In some jurors' minds, it was the last straw, the final disillusionment in a tangled maze of "expert testimony." One juror would say later, "I think a lot of us just threw out all the experts."

Kennedy would call one more expert witness, but first he began his promised "human side" of the case. Most of it would be a milk run for him, questioning devoted friends and family. But not all of it. He started with Liberty Bradford, which was a ticklish business indeed.

Liberty loved her uncle, but she still felt a lot of anger about what had happened. She didn't want to testify. She wanted to get on with her life. She was caught between her mother, who also remained very angry with Jim, and her grandmother and uncle and the rest of the Mitchell family, from whom she felt a great deal of pressure.

Liberty was really important to Kennedy. She was personally involved in several events that he wanted to use to show Jim's love and concern for Artie. But he knew that she could very easily blow up in his face and say something hostile on the stand.

Finally, after a lot of soul searching—and a subpoena—Liberty came through for her uncle Jim.

Her drama training paid off, helped her get through this latest ordeal. With her blonde hair upswept, conservative black skirt, green plaid blouse and dignified air, she looked almost Grace Kelly–ish. She spoke in a strong, level tone.

Kennedy was very careful with his questions, and she answered him without adornment. She told the jury about the Ocean Beach incident. She told them about the meeting she had with Jim and Art at the theater in January, about the argument she had with her father the last time she saw him, and about her discussion with Jim the Monday before the shooting.

"He said, 'Well, we could possibly do an intervention, but we've got to take legal steps to do that,' and we both knew it just seemed like a horrible prospect of trying to put my father forcibly anywhere he didn't want to go," she testified.

Posey, who had talked to Meredith, knew that Liberty was ambivalent about testifying, and he tried to get at that fact on cross-examination.

"Were you subpoenaed to testify here today?" he asked.

"Yes."

"Do you want to be here?"

Liberty set her jaw grimly. "I'm here. I'm not particularly excited about this," was all she said.

Posey had another avenue of attack. "Now, since the death of your father, have you become a stockholder in the business?"

Kennedy saw trouble, and was on his feet immediately. "Objection, Your Honor!"

After a discussion at the bench, Breiner dismissed the jury so the issue could be argued out.

Once the jurors were gone, Posey said: "Ms. Bradford, I want to ask you a series of questions dealing with your stock interest in the business. You own stock through a living trust created by your father; is that correct?"

"Yes."

". . . Can you tell us whether or not someone approached you suggesting you should sell your stock back to the defendant?"

"Ruby—I talked to her on the phone, and she suggested that we sell the stocks and diversify our interest."

"And who did she say you should sell them to?"

"It would be selling them back to Jim or the company would buy us out."

"Well, the company or the defendant?"

"I guess Cinema 7."

"Please don't guess," Kennedy said irritably, in a tone he would never have used with her in front of the jury.

"We don't want you to guess," Breiner said. "What did Ruby Richardson tell you?"

"She told me that we should sell the stocks and rediversify them."

"And to whom did she say you should sell the stocks?"

"To Jim," Liberty said finally.

"That's the area I want to elicit from this witness," Posey said.

Kennedy argued that, first, it was irrelevant to the case, and, second, it called for hearsay, and that Ruby herself would be a witness. "We have a very complicated trust circumstance in which Jim Mitchell has absolutely no interest. It is not possible for him to buy or sell or hypothecate these shares in any way."

Breiner ruled with Kennedy, saying that the line of questioning was not relevant and more misleading than useful, and the rest of Posey's cross-examination passed without incident. Kennedy had gambled and won. "Now we're getting to the heart of the case," he told reporters ebulliently after Liberty's testimony.

"I felt used," Liberty said afterward. "But there was nothing else I could do." A few weeks later, she filed a wrongful death suit against Jim, right before the deadline of one year after the shooting, "just to keep my options open." She said her mother was her "legal adviser," and she also had hired another attorney. One person close to the family would say it was Meredith's hatred for Jim that fueled the three older children's suits.

As they had been almost all their lives, Art's kids were caught in the middle.

The Associated Press photo desk in San Francisco had arranged with a Marin stringer, Richard Johnson, to cover the trial. He had been assiduous, always courteous, always right there. Several of his photos had moved on the AP network. But for some reason, this day they decided to send a staffer, who came in and haughtily told Johnson, in front of the other journalists, that he could leave. He had been "relieved." Johnson, quietly angry, went nowhere.

At the morning recess the AP staffer, Alan Greth, got about two feet from Jim's nose and started banging away, the strobe popping repeatedly in Jim's eyes. Jim gritted his teeth and walked faster, but Greth matched him stride for stride.

Michael Kennedy saw what was going on and stepped in front of Jim. "What the hell do you think you're doing?" he snapped at Greth, who responded, "Just doing my job."

Kennedy, red-faced, poking a finger in Greth's face, said, "You're not doing your job. You're an asshole."

Greth shrugged and waited for Jim to reappear in the corridor, but when he did, several of his friends, plus a few trial spectators and even a journalist or two, stepped up and neatly blocked Greth's view.

He did not come back. Johnson shot the rest of the trial, very capably.

The Ocean Beach incident did not merely present the defense with a stirring example of Jim's love for Artie, and a refutation of the insurance motive. It also gave them an opportunity for a little courtroom pageantry.

Kennedy very much wanted to get the firemen involved in the rescue onto the stand. Jim had gotten to know them pretty well after the incident, and he knew they'd be happy to do it, and they'd make a great impression.

But there was almost a disastrous miscue. Nanci Clarence had thought that Jim, through his friendship with Lieutenant Tilden Hansan, an officer who had supervised the rescue from the shore, had lined them up to testify. But it wasn't that simple, and just a couple of days before they were needed, she discovered that it wasn't a done deal.

She called the Fire Department legal office and was told, get the subpoenas to us two weeks ahead of time. Thanks a lot.

So she called the chief's office, and dealt with some assistant chiefs who were all business, and she wasn't getting much of anywhere with them. Finally, she asked them just to give the chief a message. He called, and she got him on the phone with Kennedy.

Of course, the Mitchells had incredible juice in City Hall, particularly after supporting former Police Chief Frank Jordan, who had just been elected mayor. And the Fire Department had received thousands of dollars in donations for their surf rescue unit, both from the grateful Mitchells themselves and from memorial donations in Artie's name.

Fire Chief Fred Postel intervened just in time. The day before the defense needed the firefighters to testify, they got the okay, leaving one final issue for Kennedy and Clarence to wrestle with. It was against Fire Department policy for the officers to testify in uniform except on city business, and the defense really wanted them to look sharper than Posey's police witnesses, who had testified in their civvies, most of them sort of clumpy and polyesterish.

On the eve of their testimony, the chief took care of that too, waiving the rule for this occasion.

Now all they had to worry about was getting Breiner to let all of them testify. Posey objected to all of them on grounds of relevancy, but the judge denied that objection; Kennedy had mentioned the rescue in his opening statement, and the rescue itself touched on several issues, including the health of victim and defendant and also their relationship. And nobody raised any fuss about the closer issue of how many firefighters it takes to tell the story of one beach rescue.

So on the afternoon of February fourth, you could almost hear strains of John Philip Sousa in the background as Kennedy paraded not one or two, but *four* rugged, heroic firefighters to the stand, one after the other. All were wearing their best sharp-creased dress blues, shoes spitshined, and brass buttons gleaming.

First was Captain Steven Freeman, who told of his own serious injuries that day, and related how Jim had asked after Artie when the three of them were in the ambulance after the rescue.

Then came Fireman Ralph James Blanchard, who rescued Jim and Storm. He was followed by the handsome Mark Allen Evanoff, who singlehandedly pulled Artie to shore after Freeman was injured.

"You received from the California State Firefighters Association, the San Francisco Fire Department, and other agencies, citations for valor and heroism?"

"Yes."

"For risking your own life on this occasion?"

"Yes."

"Was your life in jeopardy?"

"Yes."

Finally, Lieutenant Tilden Hansan testified that he had just returned from work the day before, having had a recent surgery. Arriving after the others, he supervised the operation from the beach.

"Lieutnant Hansan, as the officer in charge . . . had you gotten there before the firefighters entered the water, would you have permitted them to enter?"

". . . I would have asked that they didn't go in . . . conditions were so dangerous that you would not order your firefighters into the surf. I would try and order them not to, but the firefighters as a practice are not ordered to go into the water. It's always voluntary."

Posey was smart enough not to try to cross-examine.

Georgia Mae Mitchell was next, and Posey knew how dangerous she was as a defense witness. He tried a bit of last-minute containment, arguing before the jury was brought in that her account of the phone conversation she had with Artie the night of his death should not be admitted, because there was no evidence that Jim had known of the threatening remark he had made.

But Breiner had already ruled the statement admissible in the pretrial motions, and he wasn't changing his mind now.

He did throw Posey a bone, agreeing with him that a family portrait

Kennedy wanted Georgia Mae to identify, and thus enter into evidence, was irrelevant.

Georgia Mae Mitchell looked grandmotherly but somber, wearing a smart charcoal suit that nicely complemented her gray hair.

Kennedy started by trying to establish that the only reason she hadn't been in court before was that she was not allowed to attend before she testified. Posey objected successfully, but Kennedy got the point across. He asked her if she had testified voluntarily before the grand jury, and she said, "Yes, I did. I wanted the grand jury to know about my sons, so I was happy to do it . . . and I want these people to know also."

"Tell us where and when you were born and what schooling you had, please?"

"I'll object to that as being irrelevant," Posey said. He was going to make this as tough as possible.

"Your Honor, I'm trying to paint a family portrait of a family tragedy. The prosecutor would like to focus on high technology," Kennedy said with a withering glare at Posey, "and I would like to focus on the humanity."

"Her history is not relevant," Posey said shortly.

"Well, her age would be, if she wants to tell her age," Breiner said with a smile, "so the jury knows something about where she's coming from, but her history and schooling wouldn't seem to be."

"Well, does there come a time, Your Honor, when your mother becomes relevant?" Kennedy asked aggrievedly. "I don't know where to begin."

"I don't want to do the questioning for you, Mr. Kennedy."

Kennedy figured it out pretty quickly. He managed to pick up Georgia's biography with her marriage, J.R.'s occupation ("He played lowball, and he was good at it"), and the birth of Jim and Art.

He took her through the early years in Antioch, and how she and J.R. reared their boys.

"And did you and Mr. Mitchell attempt to impart to Jim Mitchell a sense of responsibility about Artie?"

"Yes. That was their training. Jim grew up to take care of Artie, and he took that responsibility seriously."

Talking about the boys in junior high and high school, she said, "Art was always the funny one, oh, the clown of the family . . . and even at those early ages, Jim took responsibility more seriously than Art did. They seemed to grow up with those traits."

She told the jury how J.R. taught them about guns, and how they were both "crack shots."

"What did you think, as a schoolteacher, of your sons going into the pornography business?"

"You know, to me, it was great. . . . Many people don't understand how much they've given for the rights of other people, to have the right to choose. If you don't choose pornography, it's fine. It's just wonderful, if that's not what you want. But if you want to see it, it should be your right.

"And Jim and Art, my sons—I'm proud of them that they would stand up and they fought in court for years so people could have that right."

She testified about the boys' marriages, and children, and divorces, and about Art's deterioration during the endless fight with Karen.

"Karen Mitchell was forever wanting more money," Georgia Mae said, adding that Artie told her, "I might as well just give it to her. When we go to court, she's going to get it anyway."

And she talked about the phone call that night, struggling then to keep her composure, finally succeeding.

A few minutes later, Kennedy handed her over to Posey, who would have been better off not to question her at all, like the firemen.

She knew what the professional witnesses like Hollien and Haag had seemed to forget about cross-examination—stay unruffled, be helpful and polite, make the other guy look like a hothead and a bully.

Which of course is relatively easy to do when you're a petite gray-haired grandmother made of steel.

Posey tried to nibble at her. He asked a zillion innocuous little questions, and everyone waited for him to tie it all together, ask the zinger. But the zinger never came. Just a lot of the innocuous little questions, adding up to nothing, that just helped her win sympathy: "How old was your husband when he died? How old were your boys when your husband died? When he did his gambling, would that be in the daytime or evening hours?"

Some of his questions even enabled Georgia Mae to emphasize points the defense had made on direct. "How young would you say your son Jim Mitchell was when this responsibility [to take care of Artie] was passed to him?"

"It was even before they started to school. It was a way of life from the beginning, maybe two and four years old: 'Look after your little brother, Jim.' They just grew up that way, Mr. Posey, and Jim took the responsibility and accepted it."

For an unaccountable reason, he even asked her, "Were these the only two children that you had, Jim and Artie?"

Now there aren't many answers to that question that could be considered helpful to the prosecution.

Whatever he was after, of course, what he got was more points for Georgia Mae when she answered, "We had three sons. Our baby died when he was four months old. He was approximately two years younger than Artie." Kennedy said later that he had considered asking that question, but rejected it as too blatant a sympathy ploy.

She even managed to repeat three times that Jim's attitude toward Artie reminded her of the Boys Town motto, "He ain't heavy, Father, he's my brother."

She called the prosecutor "Mr. Posey" throughout, treating him like she would a misguided former student, nice enough, but never really was too bright. "I must have confused you, Mr. Posey," she said once, sweetly.

It was a magnificent performance, and nobody on the defense team could believe Posey let it go on so long. After the trial, Posey admitted he had a tough time with her, which was an understatement.

"The mother problem," he called it ruefully.

Georgia Mae was the quintessential tough act to follow, and Lisa Adams would not play so well to the jury.

Of course, she was a much less sympathetic figure: a former stripper living with a man accused of murder versus a widowed retired schoolteacher with one son dead and another in the dock.

Also, testifying was much more of an ordeal for Lisa. The whole trial had been, of course, not to mention the preceding nightmarish year. She had been prevented from watching the actual trial until she testified, so she would wait for Jim in the corridor, the picture of domesticity in her long dresses, doing needlepoint, talking quietly with her brother, Matt, while her man grappled with his fate in the courtroom.

But now she was on center stage, and in a decade of dancing nude at the O'Farrell, she never had a tougher gig. In a fawn sweater and a long floral print dress, high at the neck, looking pinched and nervous, older than her thirty-two years, Lisa nevertheless held her head high and joined the battle with her chin thrust forward.

Questioned by Nanci Clarence, Lisa told the jury she had grown up in the San Francisco suburb of Redwood City, the daughter of a kindergarten teacher and a Sears store manager.

"What do you do now?" Clarence asked gently.

"I consider myself to be a homemaker," Lisa said. "I live with Jim Mitchell and his four children. I take care of our home and our children. I prepare our meals and take care of our garden and our pets and just try to make a pleasant home for all of us."

Lisa Adams was eighteen when she started dancing at the O'Farrell, and that's when she met Jim, the jury learned.

And it was just one big happy strip joint: "They'd often have parties on holidays, or they'd have movie openings, and they'd invite all the people from the theater. I remember going to some Easter parties where they invited all the people who worked at the theater. It seemed to me that they considered all the people that worked with them and for them to be part of their family. It was a wonderful atmosphere."

She talked about working both as a dancer and a secretary, and about the brothers' brainstorming sessions in their cantina-style office, which she accurately described as "a real revolving door. People were always coming and going. They had a lot of friends that they golfed and fished with, and those people would always drop by to say hello."

Lisa described Artie evolving into Mr. Hyde the same way that everybody else had: "When I was working in the office in the later 1980s, it seemed like the sweet guy that I knew was there less and less often, and in his place there was a lunatic who was very frightening, and you never knew what his next move would be."

She talked about how abusive he was to the performers, and as a prime example the defense tried to enter into evidence the phone messages Artie had left for the stripper Lady T after their argument at the theater back in 1988.

During a hearing outside the jury's presence, the tape was played, and it was an uncanny moment. Suddenly, Artie was in the courtroom, the bad Artie, not the cute, funny Artie. The Mr. Hyde Artie everyone had been describing. All the descriptions, all the witnesses' recollections, all the horror stories were at once confirmed and relegated to the category of pale imitation.

Here, then, in an ultimately inadmissible piece of evidence, was the essence of the trial, for here was the Artie, slurred, malevolent, menacing, who had driven Jim to kill:

> Lady T: This is Artie, I have a message for you. You scraped the shit out of my back, for no reason, OK? You ripped two or three holes in my back. I've gone to a doctor, his name's Dr. Dossett, he's already, uh, uh, immediately treated me, and he says yes, you've lacerated me. He saw it, he's an eyewitness. He's a doctor of medical practice. You're a swine. I'm mad at

you, OK? You're out of a job. You'll never ever—if you work
here again, Mrs. T, let me give you a guarantee: Artie won't
work here. It's me or you, OK? Now you take your fucking
choice. You want to go to a lawyer, go. You know why? Because
I'm going to sue you for all you're worth. Which is what? It's
like five peanuts and two pretzels. I'm gonna take you for all
you've got. You fucked up, you're out of line. You made a big
mistake. You know you had a nice deal going. You had a real
nice deal. I've never, ever been mean to you. I've always respected you. I've been nice to you. And you're out of line. OK?
I have a real credible witness, Dr. Dossett. Show you—for no
reason, rip holes in my back. What are you, mad at me? What
did I do to you? I'm a man, you're a woman. Well I got a real
hint for you. You can take it to the Labor Relations Board, you
can take it to God. 'Cause I got a lot of witnesses. You're fired.
You understand? You're fired. I'm gonna tell Vince tomorrow.
You're never in your life ever, Miss T, ever working O'Farrell
Theatre again. If you do, you do, fine—Artie Mitchell won't
be working there. You know, because you ripped holes in my
back, with witnesses, you're a swine, and I'll tell you something.
You're vicious, you're deceitful, you're hateful, you're a traumatic dyke, and you know what? I have no more respect for
you anymore, none. Now you can take it and do what you want
with it. If you don't like it, come and talk to me face to face,
OK? And I'll tell you what: You're fucking fired. You're finished.
    (Hangs up)
    (Calls back)
    Hey, slut, I'm glad you're taking messages (tape
slips). . . . You know why? If I get your fucking face, I'm gonna
stomp your face. You know what, Lady T? Get your biggest
boyfriend and bring him to Artie. Artie and all the Mitchell
brothers want him. You'll never work here again. I'm gonna
kick your face. You slut. I hate your guts. You know? You're
fucked. You, you are out of line. You scratched me, unless you
wanna scratch my back up, you know what you get? You got
hate, from all the Mitchell brothers, who give you nothing but
love (tape slips) . . . you slut.
    (Hangs up)

    The defense wanted it as a substitute for the threatening phone
messages of the night of the shooting, which Lisa would testify she
erased immediately. It was a graphic example of his frightening tone
and manner.
    But Judge Breiner was rightly concerned about the provenance of
the tape. The defense couldn't prove where it came from, other than
to say that Linda Bright, a dancer with the stage name Lioness, and a

close friend of both Lady T and Lisa, gave Lisa the tape a couple of months before the trial.

"You don't plan to call Lady T as a witness?" Breiner asked.

"Unfortunately, Your Honor, Lady T killed herself shortly after this telephone message," Nanci Clarence said.

Breiner said the rules of evidence clearly precluded him from allowing it in, so the jury never heard it, but courtroom spectators did.

For the people who had known Artie, it was extremely disconcerting.

Lisa Adams told another Artie story or two, talked about his decline during the last year of his life, told of Julie calling a couple of weeks before he died, saying Artie had agreed to go into rehab, which of course he hadn't, and the elation followed by disappointment that false report caused in Jim, and then gave her account of the day and night of the twenty-seventh of February.

She talked about being in the O'Farrell when her friend Nancy Harrison had taken the call from Artie threatening Lisa's life, and then, distraught, sitting with Nancy as she called Jim at the *War News* to tell him.

Lisa said she got on the phone and told Jim, "I'm not asking you to do anything, but I have to call the police and swear out a complaint against Artie, because I'm not only afraid for myself, I'm afraid for anybody that gets in his path. If it's not me that gets killed, it's going to be somebody that doesn't deserve to die, someone that happens to be in his way, and I couldn't live with that."

She testified that Jim begged her not to call the police. "He said, 'Don't you understand that if you call the police, there's a chance that Art will get killed, but there's a better chance that . . . he'd kill a policeman or somebody that came to the house?' And as much as I wanted to call the police, I knew that what he was saying was true."

She said Jim asked her to wait, that he was calling lawyers, and was going to ask them what steps could be taken. He asked her to call him back around 4 P.M.

She said she went out with Nancy for a dreadful lunch, and the two talked about what had happened. Then she dropped Nancy back at the theater and drove home. At about four, she said, she called Jim back, and he pleaded for more time. He hadn't got any calls back from Dennis Roberts or Tom Steel yet. Then she told the jury about going to get Jim at the *War News*.

When she got to the phone messages from Artie that she found when they got back to the house, Lisa's self-control finally cracked.

"I remember just taking my hand and slamming it down as hard as

I could on the buttons, just get rid of them. I never wanted to hear that voice again."

"What were you feeling when you heard that message?

"That Art was going to kill his brother. I was so scared for both of us. I thought maybe he would kill us both," she said, and began to cry.

After a ten-minute recess, she finished her account of that evening, including Jim's loading the guns and leaving, getting a call from Rocky around 10 P.M., and then finding out from Dennis Roberts early the next morning what had happened.

Posey the Nibbler went to work again. He didn't have to be quite as polite to Lisa, and he wasn't. He did manage to establish that in the first interview she had with defense investigator Jack Palladino, she made no mention of the phone call with Rocky. And that Palladino wrote in his report that she watched as Jim listened to the phone messages. Lisa said, "Mr. Palladino . . . seems to have misconstrued what I was saying to him."

Posey's favorite strategy seemed to be the Swarm of Gnats attack, asking those little questions, and also skipping around quickly from subject to subject, apparently trying to confuse the witness into making a blunder. But he ran the risk of befuddling the jury at the same time.

With Lisa, he asked about her career at the O'Farrell until he was stopped by an objection, then hopped from the night of the shooting, to her relationship with Jim, to the brother's relationship, back to the night of the murder. These broad subject areas were interspersed with questions like "Do you know what kind of glasses Jim was wearing?" ("Similar to what he has on right now.") and "Were there any other cars at your house that evening?" (Yes, a Mustang, in the garage.)

So what?

He asked Lisa, "Have you gone from where you were living in San Francisco to the house that Artie Mitchell was living at on the day he was shot, which was 23 Mohawk in Corte Madera?"

"Yes, I have."

"How many times?"

"Maybe three or four times total."

"How long of a ride is that?"

"I don't know, twenty minutes, maybe. I'm not sure."

Fifteen minutes later, after a couple of other lines of questioning, he asked her, "Now, your house is how far from Artie's house?"

"I just said, Mr. Posey—"

"Twenty minutes," interjected Breiner.

"I mean distance, if you know?"

"I have no idea," Lisa said wearily.

The cross-examination finally trailed off. No revelations, no forced admissions, no dramatic "gotchas." Just a mountain of minutiae that had little to do, ultimately, with what the jury would make of Lisa Adams.

Political consultant Jack Davis, one of Artie Mitchell's closest friends, took the stand with the panache of a celebrity, which, in Northern California political circles, he was.

He is tall and rotund, probably close to three hundred pounds, one way or the other. Dressed in an expensive, expansive glen plaid suit, a gold Rolex glittering on his wrist, his fleshy face animated and intelligent, Jack Davis dominated the courtroom from the witness stand.

Breiner was obviously impressed with him, and his reputation. Breiner asked him, "How are you, Mr. Davis?" after he was sworn, and the two men would joke with each other throughout Davis's appearance. Kennedy obviously loved it, and even Posey, seeing the judge's reaction, was low-key and respectful.

Kennedy started pitching batting pracice to Davis:

"Have you managed any campaigns lately?"

"Yes. Fortunately, I have been employed on a regular basis, Mr. Kennedy. I just completed Frank Jordan's successful mayoral campaign in San Francisco."

"Frank who?" Breiner deadpanned.

"I know it's provincial in Marin a little bit, sir, but he was the police chief who was elected on December 10, fortieth mayor of San Francisco."

Davis testified that he had known both brothers for about seven years, meeting them at an AIDS fund-raiser. "I was impressed by the fact that here were two notoriously heterosexual individuals who were involved in raising money to help with the battle against AIDS at a time . . . before there was the general kind of support that exists today."

He described various other fund-raisers the Mitchells had been involved in, including a fortieth birthday party for Davis that just happened to have raised funds for a well-known Marin charity.

He described Artie as "smart, caring . . . incredibly entertaining and gentle and nice, at times, irreverent, impish, mischievous. . . . But he also had a dark side."

In describing that, he said, "He had a well-renowned call . . . he would go CAW, CAW"—Davis demonstrated at the top of his lungs to the startled courtroom—"and when he gave that call, you could see that he was just about at that point where people who knew Artie well knew that it was either time to cut on out or batten down the hatches."

That led nicely into the pool cue–throwing incident, which Posey tried unsuccessfully to keep out, and then to the gunplay at Maye's Oyster House, followed by the assault at the O'Farrell.

"He said to me, 'I know you have that effing gun. I don't think this is effing funny. I want that effing gun, and you're going to give it to me,' and he still had me in a choke hold. I . . . nodded that he could have the gun, and he stopped."

Davis said that when he handed the gun back, he said, " 'Artie, you're the last person in the world who should be walking around with a loaded gun in the condition that you're in,' and he said, 'Eff off,' and that was the last time I saw Artie Mitchell."

Davis testified that Artie called him later, and was abusive over the phone to him, and that he then did what everyone always did. He called Jim and told him about it, on the night of Tuesday, February 26, a day before the shooting.

On cross-examination, Davis said what nobody else had said yet: that Julie Bajo was part of the problem. "Personally, I watched Artie go through three different girlfriends and felt that Julie Bajo cared little about Artie and was part of the downward spiral that existed in the final year of his life."

"So she was the cause of his death?" Posey asked sarcastically.

Later, Posey quizzed Jack Davis about the attractions of partying at the theater, and Davis delivered one of the trial's better ripostes: "I'm gay, Mr. Posey, so the O'Farrell Street Theatre offers very little for me."

As the defense case continued, the time of reckoning for Jim Mitchell drew nearer. There was a lot of sympathetic testimony about what a great guy he was, and how bad a problem Artie was, but the jury had heard nothing from the defense about what had actually happened that night. That would be up to Jim to explain, the best he could, and he felt the pressure.

"One thing I've learned from this," he said during a smoke break one day. "You can get it anytime. At a street corner, on the way home. Anytime.

"The world fell in on Art that night, but it fell in on me too," he said, in a rare burst of candor. "I would never have dreamed all of this could happen."

•   •   •

Rocky Davidson wasn't destined to help elucidate matters much for the jury. But Kennedy played the Rocky card to maximum effect.

He called Rocky and had him take the stand, so the jury could see that the defense was eager for him to testify.

Then Posey asked the judge for a conference, and a few moments later Breiner dismissed the jury.

Rocky, represented by Santa Rosa lawyer L. Stephen Turer, sat impassively in the witness box as the fight raged.

Posey started by saying that the court had been advised in an earlier conference that Rocky might take the Fifth. "It's my feeling that in light of that conference, that we should have had a hearing before the witness was called to the stand in front of the jury. And when I raised that objection, Mr. Kennedy indicated I was a fraud for raising that objection. I'd like the record to indicate that."

"Good, I'd like the record to reflect I think he is a fraud, Your Honor. He's demonstrated it in a variety of ways to which I could speak endlessly."

"Well, not on my time," Breiner said.

Kennedy then gave Breiner his version of what had happened in the hearing during the grand jury. He told Breiner that he would offer a summary of what he expected Rocky's testimony to be.

He said Rocky had been checking on Artie almost daily because of his worsening condition, and that on the morning of the twenty-seventh, he had gone to Jim at the *War News* and told him, "Art is really in bad shape. He even scared me." Kennedy said Rocky told Jim he had spoken with Skip Dossett, and that he and Dossett were going to go over there tonight. He said Rocky offered to go and tie Artie down, subdue him in some way, if that's what Jim wanted, but Jim rejected that idea. Later in the day, he tells Rocky that he will meet him at 23 Mohawk around 9 P.M.

"Rocky gets there first," Kennedy says. "He waits for what he says is a half hour or forty-five minutes . . . Jim arrives . . . and parks the Ford Explorer on Lakeside.

". . . Rocky comes over, meets Jim, they talk—they walk down. Jim is carrying the umbrella, he's carrying the .22 rifle. They walk down Mohawk and they cross—they are on the opposite side of the street from where 23 Mohawk is, and the house is completely dark. They come up to—"

Breiner interrupts, "And you contend the evidence will show that Davidson knew the defendant was armed as he was?"

"Yes, he was," Kennedy says. "He not only knew it, but he saw the rifle, Your Honor. And there was some discussion about it. . . . Concern about the neighborhood watch, which I think is an organization keeping an eye out for criminals and crime or what have you. . . .

"They walk down the street on the opposite side of 23 Mohawk. Come back up the front of 23 Mohawk. The house is completely dark. . . . Jim Mitchell knocks at the door. There's no answer. Rocky Davidson is very familiar with the house. . . . Jim asks Rocky to go back around to the back of the house. He goes through an unlocked gate—by the way, they've tried the front door, and the front door is locked, according to Mr. Davidson. He goes around to the back and he comes back and reports to Jim Mitchell that there are no lights on. It doesn't look like anybody's at home. Jim Mitchell then . . . asks Rocky to go make some phone calls, to call the O'Farrell Theatre, to see if Artie is there . . . and to call Lisa Adams.

"Mr. Davidson does, and he goes and he finds a telephone in a neighboring mall. At that mall, he makes two telephone calls. . . . He calls the theater, and he speaks to Charlie Benton, asks Charlie if he had seen Artie. . . . He also calls Lisa Adams . . . telling her . . . Jim says not to anwer the door if Artie comes.

". . . Rocky comes back. His estimate is it could be fifteen to twenty minutes later. He comes back and he comes down by Mohawk, he sees a patrol car at one end of Mohawk with its lights on parked somewhat blocking that entrance to Mohawk. He drives his vehicle down to the other entrance of Mohawk, because as you know from the photograph and the evidence, Mohawk is a kind of a large ellipse of a street. He comes down to the other end, there's another patrol car there, and he leaves at that point. He doesn't want anything to do with the police at that point, and he leaves and goes back home. That is his testimony."

Kennedy suggested to Breiner that, "We work out some way in which to present his testimony, so that Mr. Mitchell can have the benefit of his testimony, which is extremely important from Mr. Mitchell's standpoint, and that Mr. Davidson's rights can also be protected."

The "only solution" he had been able to come up with, he told the judge, was for Posey to immunize Rocky. He said that in order to allay Posey's fears that Rocky, once he got immunity, would confess to shooting Artie himself, his testimony could be taken in advance, outside the presence of the jury, and then if he deviated from it he could be charged with perjury.

Posey wasn't having any. "I am not going to grant any immunity to this witness at this time in this matter, particularly in light of the way that it's been presented to me."

Then Kennedy asked the court if Rocky could testify to his knowledge of Jim and Artie over the years, not mentioning what happened on the day of the shooting, without losing his right to refuse to answer questions about that day, since Posey was refusing to immunize him.

After some discussion, Breiner said he thought that if Davidson avoided any mention of what happened that day, he could testify and avoid waiving his rights against self-incrimination.

Then Kennedy told him that since Jim would testify that he had met Rocky that night, the jury might wonder why the defense had not asked Rocky any corroborating questions when he was on the stand. He asked Breiner to instruct the jury something to the effect that "Mr. Davidson was not asked about events of the twenty-seventh for reasons that don't concern you, and you cannot infer, speculate, whatever about them."

"That's one alternative that you and Mr. Posey might talk about during the noon hour," Breiner said. "Another alternative is not to call him at all, and you don't have that problem. Because I will instruct the jury that neither side is obligated to call any witness that has knowledge of the events."

"The only observation I would make here," said Posey, "is that I don't believe the defense has truly thought out all of the legal ramifications that can come from the testimony of these two people. And maybe they should discuss it a bit further, because I don't think they really realize, frankly, the potential."

"I wonder, was that a threat of some sort?" Kennedy said.

"No, it's not a threat," Posey said. "They can do whatever they want. It's their decision. But I'm not going to grant him immunity."

"Could I ask all of you to meet pleasantly during the noon hour?" Breiner asked.

"As long as I don't have to follow the 'pleasantly,' I don't mind meeting. Because meeting with Mr. Posey I couldn't describe as pleasant," Kennedy said churlishly. Later he would blast Posey in the media, calling his decision not to offer immunity "an outrage."

Beneath the bluster, the defense had to be delighted. Rocky never testified, but the jury did see Kennedy call him to the stand. He had created a silent corroborating witness for the story Jim would tell.

Without letting Posey get his hooks into Rocky on cross-examination.

•   •   •

It was easy to see why the brothers trusted Ruby Richardson with their money. As she settled herself into the witness stand and began to give Michael Kennedy her personal history, both her acumen and her fierce Mitchell loyalty quickly became evident.

She told the court how the brothers "always got the same amount of pay, the same benefits, the same cars. Everything was 50-50."

They set their own salaries at around $100,000 in the early 1980s, raising it to $207,000 by 1989.

But in 1990, she said, they took a little less, only about $160,000, anticipating a downturn in revenues after the closing of the Santa Ana theater. But that downturn never occurred, and at the end of the year, both brothers planned to take bonuses.

But Jim planned to give his bonus to Art, Ruby said, because what with the Karen problem and everything else, Art needed the money more.

"I went to the theater and Richard [Mezzavilla] told me that that's what Jim was going to do. I went in and talked to Jim, and I said, 'You know, this is going to put you in a big tax liability if you don't take a bonus this year and you take a big jump next year. It's going to put you in a higher tax bracket and everything.'

"He said, 'No, I really think that Art needs the money more than I do, and . . . this is what I want to do.' "

On cross-examination, Posey asked Ruby, "Approximately, what was the gross per year of the corporation?"

"Well, I was hoping you were going to ask me that, Mr. Posey, because I brought some figures with me today," Ruby said.

Her figures showed that in 1986, Cinema 7 had grossed $3.5 million, and each of the next four years the number was almost exactly the same, right around $3.3 million.

Posey asked Ruby if she hadn't told Detective Mario Watkins about Jim's three-part goal for Artie: get him to seek and accept treatment for alcoholism; keep him out of the theater, as long as he was disruptive; and set him up with a comfortable income, outside of the corporation.

Ruby said she didn't remember saying those things.

Nanci Clarence questioned two of her law firm colleagues, secretary Farshid Arjam and her partner, Tom Steel, to establish that Jim had called Steel twice on the afternoon of the twenty-seventh to ask him what to do about his brother, and that Steel never got either message until the next morning, after the shooting. Arjam testified that the second time he called, Jim told her, "My brother is threatening to kill someone."

On cross-examination, Posey asked Arjam to identify some notes, which turned out to be Nanci Clarence's notes about the issue of the phone messages, which she had turned over to him in discovery. Posey, angry about being surprised with Arjam's testimony about Jim's corroborative statement, was trying to make the point that he had never been told about it in advance, and that Clarence had deliberately left it out of her notes.

The judge denied Posey's request and, seeing that both Posey and Clarence were steaming, called a recess and dismissed the jury for a fifteen-minute break.

"Mr. Posey's rigamarole with my notes with this witness on the stand is entirely improper," Clarence raged. "Those are hearsay, he knew they were my notes, I turned them over to him. . . . And for him to take those notes and try to create some sort of a stir in front of the jury is entirely improper, and I ask that he be admonished."

"I think the defense—she deliberately left them out of her notes," Posey said.

"I'm sorry, left what out of her notes?" Breiner said.

"The statements of what the defendant said on the telephone call. It's not in those notes and it's not in discovery."

"For Mr. Posey to accuse me of deliberately leaving something out . . . is entirely unfounded and inappropriate, and I ask the court to admonish him. I resent the suggestion that I would do such a thing," Clarence said angrily.

There was nothing Breiner could do with this one, and he knew it. "We'll take a recess for the rest of the fifteen minutes," he said.

All pretense of collegiality with Posey shattered now, Nanci Clarence strode over to his end of the counsel table, pointed down at him and spat, "You owe me an apology, punk!" Then she turned and stalked out of the courtroom.

Putting the victim on trial is, of course, a time-honored defense tactic, but rarely does a defense attorney have such an open-and-shut case against the victim as Michael Kennedy had here.

Artie Mitchell was not only put on trial, he was convicted. By this stage of the trial, there weren't too many jurors who didn't realize that Artie might have had a few behavioral problems when he was drinking, which during the last year or so was pretty much whenever he was conscious.

After trying and failing to establish a money motive in the jury's minds, Posey would try to turn this in his favor, and he postulated that Jim had simply killed Artie because he was fed up with him.

That theory seems much closer to the truth, but for purposes of the trial, there was a problem with it: by now, the jury was fed up with Artie too.

Kennedy knew it. And he just kept feeding them more Artie stories.

Charlie Benton knew a lot of them. As the theater manager most often around in the evening hours, he had lots of chances to see Artie at his most swinish. Before he got to the heavy-duty story of Artie putting a gun to his head, Kennedy had him relate an abusive incident that had a sort of Three Stooges slapstick quality. And in the telling of it, Benton and Kennedy and Posey got into a Moe, Larry, and Curly themselves:

Charlie Benton related, "One evening after closing—it wasn't uncommon for there to be some people up in the office, having a few drinks, just partying, talking, playing pool—I saw everybody was pretty well toasted. They were under the influence.

"Drunk.

"I saw Julie was complaining about her leg. Artie said something . . . and she came back, 'Well, if I walked by, you would probably kick me.' "

Posey hopped up. "I'm going to object to that as hearsay, ask it to be stricken. I'm going to object to this line of questioning as being irrelevant. I don't believe Julie Bajo was asked any questions in this area."

"I'm not trying to impeach Julie Bajo, Your Honor," Kennedy said. "What I'm trying to do is demonstrate the propensity for mindless violence."

"When did this happen?" Breiner asked.

"This was a very short time before the incident happened," Benton said euphemistically.

"The shooting?" Breiner asked.

"Yes."

"Overruled."

Kennedy said, "But you cannot tell us, Mr. Benton, what Ms. Bajo said. Just go on and describe."

"If I walked in front of you, you would probably kick me," Charlie said again.

"Same objection," Posey said.

"The witness didn't understand," Breiner said.

"That's all right, Mr. Benton," Kennedy said happily. "Your Honor, that will be stricken?"

"Yes, that's stricken. The jury will disregard that last answer."

"What happened next?" Kennedy asked.

"She walked in front of him, and he kicked her. And she fell to the ground crying and screaming. She was in a lot of pain, and she was crying.

"And when she did get up, she said, 'If I walked by you again, you'd probably do it again.' "

"Judge!" Posey groaned. "Same objection!"

"Sustained."

"I think by now he should have caught on," Posey grumbled.

"Did he kick her again?" Kennedy asked.

"He kicked her again. She fell down again," Benton said.

"He kicked her twice in her bad knee?" Kennedy asked in a shocked tone.

"He kicked her twice in her bad knee," Benton said. "Then I finally said, 'This is it. Let's go.' They finally got out of there."

Benton went on to describe the gun incident, Artie's general bad behavior, and the call from Rocky the night of the shooting.

Then Kennedy asked him, "Over the years of knowing Jim Mitchell as closely as you have, can you tell us what kind of a man he is?"

"He's very calm, cool, collected. He's got energy. He's a no-excuses guy. Get the job done. Hardworking, very family-oriented. Somebody you can depend on and trust. Someone that has a real good understanding and makes everybody feel comfortable with him."

"Did you ever know him to lie to you?"

"No," Charlie Benton said, and then he thought for a moment.

"Maybe in a card game."

Kennedy was ready to present his antidote to Lucien Haag: criminalist Charles Morton.

Morton, who owns a criminalistics laboratory in Oakland, went through his credentials, which included several years of work with criminalistics pioneer Professor Paul Kirk before he established his own lab.

Morton studied the physical evidence, went to the crime scene, and read all the reports, including Hollien's and Haag's. He had sat by Kennedy's side as Haag testified.

His message to the jury was simple: what Haag tried to do not only shouldn't be done by criminalists, but couldn't be done with any degree of reliability in this case.

He said that he and Lucien Haag were apparently on opposite sides of an issue currently being discussed among criminalists: how far a criminalist can or should go into the reconstruction of an entire event.

"A reconstructionist really goes beyond the examination and interpretation of specific elements of evidence, and attempts to put together the entire package.

". . . And I think the problem that you have there is that when you start putting together an event, you have to start interpreting the individual elements in light of other elements. And then you tend to weigh those various components differently because of the fact that you're sort of being pushed into a reconstruction."

Kennedy asked him, "Why is the reconstruction of an element of a crime scene different from the reconstruction of the entire event?"

"Because the reconstruction of the element depends on very specific issues of physical evidence: Is there evidence of a bullet entry and exit hole on a victim? Are there impact points at a crime scene that would support the conclusion that a bullet traveled through a particular trajectory or series of paths? . . . Although there are inferences drawn from those, they are supportable by certain physical facts.

"Once you start getting beyond those physical facts and start interrelating everything, then you're having to rely more on less-scientific and less-reliable kinds of observations."

Morton said he thought Haag's version of events was certainly possible, but it was only one of a wide range of possibilities. He specifically mentioned the single-impact shots, or shots that only hit the walls in the house and nothing else, as being impossible to sequence with any degree of scientific certainty.

"I think in Mr. Haag's testimony he indicated that the shot over the hallway entry was in his opinion the final shot because the shooter would be in a hurry, hasty or excited." He said there was no scientific basis for such an assumption.

Morton also reemphasized the point Kennedy had made during his cross-examination of Haag about the trajectory of that shot. "He [Haag] was willing to accept the five-degree horizontal angle as correct, even though he felt the vertical angle was not reliable.

"And that suggests a willingness to ignore what doesn't fit and accept what does fit to the reconstruction."

And so it went, with Morton questioning everything Haag said that wasn't based on concrete physical evidence—the blood flow of the arm wound, the position of bullets found after people had walked in the area, possibly kicking them; and most of all, the sequence of shots that depended on Hollien's work and Bajo's statements.

Posey picked at him for a couple of hours of cross-examination, but Morton was obdurate. He and Haag, both respected experts in their field, had agreed to disagree, and that was it. Haag was a very aggressive, skilled criminalist who believed he could take the physical evidence in combination with witnesses' statements and other experts' work and put it all together for the jury, draw them a completed picture of an event.

Morton, much more conservative, felt the criminalist's role was simply to analyze the physical evidence and go only as far in reconstruction as that took you. The rest was up to the jury.

That debate would be carried on in hundreds of courtrooms, in the journals of various professional associations, and over cocktails at various conventions and symposia for criminalists.

But this jury couldn't wait for somebody else to settle it. There was a verdict and a life in the balance. They had to decide which theory to embrace, which expert to believe.

But by Monday morning, February 10, they had something else to think about—something to push the experts onto the back burner.

Finally, 358 days after the shooting, four weeks after the trial began, James Lloyd Mitchell was ready to talk about what happened. At least, he'd better be, because he was taking the witness stand in his own defense.

T his trial had not been easy for Nanci Clarence. As a rookie, not in her own career but in the legal annals of the Mitchell Brothers, and as a woman, she had been made to feel like an outsider all the way through.

In a lot of ways, second-chairing for Michael Kennedy was really rewarding. When you did it for lesser attorneys, you busted your guts preparing the case, handed them a magnificent package to argue at trial, and they dropped half of it on the floor. Not so with Michael. She had been apprehensive about his absence during preparation, but she was amazed at his command of the evidence: the discovery, the witnesses, the detail, the nuance. He had every scrap of the case in his brain, and if he didn't use something, it was for a damn good reason, not because he didn't remember it or didn't apprehend its significance. Posey was supposed to be the detail man, but Kennedy was able to jet in at the last minute and match him point for point.

But he never made her feel like a full partner in the effort, and neither did Jim. Michael Kennedy and Jim Mitchell were bonded by more than twenty years of war stories and secrets and shared victories, and she was a part of none of that. It didn't help that they were both close-to-the-vest people, both strongly independent, both frequently distracted and aloof.

Jim had been through so many trials that he thought he knew it all, and he had criticized her sharply in the early going for not being more confrontational with the judge. Jim had been through years and years of hostile judges, and he thought the only way was to go in and rip their nuts off.

It was her opinion that Breiner was a favorable factor for them, and they stood to gain nothing from pissing him off. She respected Jim's prior experiences, but she knew it just wouldn't work this time. She thought that Posey would alienate the judge as the trial progressed, helping them even more, if they didn't jump down his throat early. So she did it her way and took her lumps, and it was not the first time Jim had been difficult.

It was a weird position for her, as an attorney, as a woman. It was such a *boy* deal, top to bottom. The coterie of old friends, the theater itself, the attitudes. As an attorney, all of that had to be ignored. She had to stay focused on the case and the legal issues, and she had, completely.

But that didn't mean she had to enjoy taking shit from her client, and never knowing if she would get backup from her partner.

Given all of that, she had tremendous sympathy for Jim Mitchell right now. He was impaired by what had happened, really suffering, and the trial was an absolute nightmare for him. She could not work for months as a relentless advocate for a man and not feel concern and compassion for him as he faced his ultimate test.

So her heart went out to him on the weekend of February 8 and 9 as he spent grueling hours preparing for his testimony at the Kennedys' house in San Anselmo.

During the trial she had gotten used to Kennedy's harrowing style of last-minute preparation. The house, borrowed from friends for the duration of the trial, was the scene of many late-night sessions preparing witnesses and arguments for the next day.

All of that was prologue to this moment, at 10:40 A.M., Monday, February 10, as Kennedy ushered Jim up to the stand and he was sworn.

Now all Clarence felt was worry and affection for this mild-looking little guy with the bald dome and teddy bear physique, wearing the tweed sports jacket with suede trim that had been almost like a uniform throughout the trial, eyes black and flat behind round brown-framed glasses.

He had been in really tough shape over the weekend, and he looked so forlorn and vulnerable now, hunched into the witness chair, squinting out at the mass of faces fixed on his, steeling himself for what was to come.

Was this the guy who knocked the porno industry on its bare ass? Who built a dream from nothing, made millions before he was thirty, backed off the mob, the cops, the courts, and Charlie Keating? Who turned his family from Okie to elite?

Well, yes, it was. One of them. There were two of those guys. The other one was dead, you know, and that was the *problem*. That's why Jim's mouth was quivering and contorted as he sat, perched in that chair like a treed coon in front of his mother and his friends and the clicking cameras and a neck-craning mass of strangers and a prosecutor in a black undertaker's suit. Getting ready to talk, finally, about why he had fired eight ugly little bullets into his crazy brother's dark ugly little house, shredding his dark diseased brain and ending his dark and ugly life.

The jammed courtroom was hushed as Kennedy began: "Jim, next to your mother and your four children, who was the most important person in your life?"

"My brother, Art," Jim replied in a soft, hoarse monotone.

"And that was one of the reasons you decided to go into the surf on March 18, 1990?"

"I'm going to object to his leading the witness, Your Honor," Posey said.

"Sustained," Breiner said.

"Why did you go into the surf on March 18, 1990?" Kennedy asked.

"I couldn't not go in. Storm—Art had gone in after Storm. I went in after both of them."

As his testimony continued, a cadence developed. Each answer was preceded by a few seconds' silence, as though Jim was fighting for control every time he opened his mouth. His face did nothing to belie that impression. His mouth worked torturously and his brow was furrowed in a rictus of pain. It was as though each monosyllabic answer was being ripped from his cortex like flesh from an open wound.

"On the day Art Mitchell died, did you love him?" Kennedy asked.

Pause. "Yes. I did." It's an excruciating android monotone, every word ending out in the blackness of space like a dead dream, hopeless.

"I mean no offense, Jim, but we've heard evidence in the last few weeks of his life that Art was diseased with alcohol, violent, threatening, abusive, out of control, not himself. Are you telling us you still loved him?"

Pause. "Yes. Yes. I loved Art." The monotone. God. Harry Hollien should do a spectrogram: the sound of agony.

"Did you ever give up on him?"

Pause. "No."

"I want to direct your attention, Jim, to twelve hours on the twenty-seventh of February, 1991. You know that's the day Art died?"

"Yes."

"That's the day you killed him?"

"That's correct." So many people who love them both were watching him now, thinking, Oh, God, Bobby, no, Big Bob, no, it's *not* correct, why are you all ripped up inside and why is Little Bob turned to ash and gone?

Kennedy took him through the morning at the *War News*. Jim said he and Rocky and Dan O'Neill went downstairs at one point for a "smoke break."

"What kind of a smoke break were you taking?"

"Smoke a joint."

"Marijuana?"

"Yes."

Jim said Rocky reported to him about his visit to Art's house the day before. "Art came out . . . and got in his face up close, started beating on his chest and screaming in his face, 'Do I look like I'm washed up?' And Rocky said he told me that it scared him."

"Scared Rocky?"

"Yes."

"Have you ever known Rocky to be scared in his life before?"

"Not that I ever knew of."

About noon that day, Jim said, he got a call from Art. "He basically opened up the conversation with something like, 'You're a chickenshit bastard.' . . . He was agitated, he was upset. . . . He said something along the line, 'If you want to talk to me, you talk to me. If you want to see me, you come and see me.' . . . The way I knew him, he was kind of calling me out. . . . trying to act tough." *Johnny Concho. Calling his brother Red Concho, the gunfighter, out into the street.*

Jim testified that he thought Art was referring to the call Dennis Roberts had made to him the day before.

"His behavior had been very erratic and very violent and intimidating, actually hurting people and going after people in the past couple of weeks, a lot more than generally.

"And it just kind of got to the point that I had talked to Art myself several times. . . . I called Dennis to try to put a little more heat on Art, to tell him that, you know, it's not just me talking to him. . . . I asked Dennis as a favor to do it, give him a call, and tell him, you know, he had to shape up or . . ."

"Or what?" Kennedy asked.

"Well, we were going to have to do something about it. He was going to have to go one way, and I was going to have to go the other way."

A few minutes later, he said, the call from Nancy Harrison and Lisa came. She didn't want to put it on him, didn't want him to do anything, but she wanted to call the police.

The police? No. The police are the fucking enemy. Always had been. J.R. didn't turn Artie in to the cops for drinking underage. He solved it himself. You didn't call the police to solve your problems. You didn't let your woman call the police to solve your problems. You solved them yourself.

He said he asked Lisa not to call the police, and to hold off and let him see what he could do. *Do something.* He promised to call her back by 4 P.M.

Kennedy asked, "Were you beginning to feel some pressure, Jim?"

"Yes." *Fuck, yes, he was feeling pressure, like a horrible fat brother beast squatting over his shoulders, crushing, suffocating, hairy spider arms wrapping around him, mouth looking for a place to suck out his blood. Pressure, Jesus, all his life he had felt pressure, but not like this.*

Jim said he called Dennis Roberts back, and left a message, and then left the first message at Tom Steel's office.

Jim said he next talked with his friend Dana Fuller, who gave him a crisis hotline number, and he called that. He said he was told, bring everybody in for counseling.

Bring everybody in for counseling. Sure, why don't we all go out for brunch first, and then come on by for a little counseling? Thanks a lot. Counsel this, motherfucker.

He said Lisa called him back, and wanted to know what was going on, and said again that he didn't have to do anything, but she wanted to call the police. He said he asked her for a little more time, and she relented again.

Don't do anything, but do something. Do something.

Jim said he saw Rocky then, and took him aside, and asked him to meet him "around the corner" from Artie's house at 9:30, and Rocky agreed.

"Did you talk about what you were going to try to do, you and Rocky, when you meet and go see Art?"

"Generally, just—just trying to settle Art down. And I said I think it would be a good idea if we could get Art's guns out of the house."

"When you said to Rocky, 'Let's meet around the corner,' why did you say that? Why didn't you just say I'll go to Art's, and I'll meet you at Art's?" Kennedy asked.

"Because we were both fairly apprehensive about Art's state of mind, what he might do. I didn't want to just drive up out front and have him start shooting through the window at us."

He made the second call to Steel's office. Then, he said, about 7 P.M. he went to Tosca and drank two margaritas. When he came back, Lisa was there, upset because he hadn't called her back and hadn't left word where he was. She had been waiting for forty-five minutes or so.

He told the jury about the drive home, and said he parked the car out front because he knew he'd be going back out again.

Kennedy asked, "At that point had you given any thought in your own mind to taking guns over to Art's house?"

"No."

He said that they walked in the door, and he went to the bathroom, and Lisa went into the kitchen and hit the message playback button on the answering machine. In the bathroom, with the door closed, he heard the messages from Art clearly, he said, because the kitchen phone was just across the hall.

"I could tell it was Art. Seemed like there were a couple messages, kept going, made a couple beeps, and came on again. It was—I had never heard Art that garbled . . . his voice was a voice not of Art. It was very husky and growling almost, and it was so unintelligible almost that I wasn't even really trying to listen to what he was saying. I was just—listening to more about—what bad shape he was in.

". . . At the end there was . . . I could make out, seemed like it was toward the end that he said, 'You're going to die.' And he goes, 'I'm going to kill you first.' "

"What did you do after you heard that?"

"Just immediately, I left the bathroom and walked down the hall, down the steps into the basement garage and went to the locker, a paint locker actually, it was a wooden locker with a padlock on it. I took the key out from above, and opened the door, and took out—I had a .38 caliber revolver inside a little bag. I had five bullets with it in there that I kept at home.

"And I loaded that. I had a shoulder holster, and it was in the shoulder holster already. I put that on—took my jacket off and put it on. And there was a .22 rifle in there, and I took that out, and there was a box of shells, and I loaded it."

"Were you planning to go over to his house and kill him?" Kennedy asked.

"No."

"What were the guns for?"

"I kind of—I thought to myself . . . that I was going to have to have some bluffing power or something to show him, that he was in a state of mind that it was going to be—you weren't just going to come in and talk him down.

"You were going to have to, you know, I don't want to say bluff him, but . . . you were going to have to have something, because he was—"

Jim was really struggling now. How could he explain this to someone who didn't know? "You know, I was—I was wondering—I was—it was—wasn't very —wasn't real clear to me, but I knew it was—it was—I'd never been in a situation like that with Art," he finally finished chokingly.

He said Lisa came down and saw the rifle, and started crying hysterically, sobbing, begging him not to go. "I told her not to worry, everything was going to be all right, just to take it easy. And that I was going to go over there, going to meet the guys over there, try to get Art's guns out."

He left, stopped to get gas, then drove to Art's house. He said he cruised by the house, saw it was dark, then went around the corner, saw Rocky's pickup and parked on Lakeside.

"I opened the back door of the car. I had thrown the rifle in the backseat on the drive over, and I took it out.

". . . I never carry a loaded gun in a car. . . . In my life I've never carried a loaded gun in a car before that night." *J.R. told him, never carry a loaded gun in the car.*

I'm sorry, Dad. Oh, God, Dad, this is such a mess.

"As you're driving over there to Art's house, are you thinking at all that you might hurt Art?"

"I'll object to that as leading," Posey said.

"Excuse me, strike that," said Kennedy.

"Overruled," said the judge.

"Thank you, Your Honor. I'll leave it as it is."

"No, I wasn't," said Jim. . . . All during the day I'd been thinking I wanted to get him to apologize to Lisa, see if we couldn't get her backed off a little bit. And I had . . . talked to Rocky about the idea we had to pick up all of his guns. He had I didn't know how many, but he had several."

Rocky told Jim that they "probably wouldn't even get to Art's house, carrying that rifle down the street, that the neighborhood watch would call the cops," Jim said. So he took out his umbrella, which was on the floor of his backseat, and put the rifle next to it and carried them together.

They walked on the other side of the street up to the house, still saw no activity, then crossed the street. Artie's car was there.

The car was actually registered to Jim. Kennedy established that Jim had bought the car for Art.

Jim said he knocked on the door and got no answer, tried the door and it was locked. Rocky went around back, then came back and reported there were no lights on and he couldn't see anybody.

"I asked Rock to go . . . find a phone and call the theater and ask if Art had been there. And while he did that I asked if he would call Lisa and tell her to just stay away from the door."

Jim testified that after Rocky left, he got uncomfortable outside the house. "I thought that I looked like a prowler or something along that line, standing out in front of somebody's house, you know, ten o'clock at night."

"Why didn't you just leave?" Kennedy asked.

"I just couldn't . . . I wanted to leave, but I had to make . . . I had to try again to get Art up, to wake him up if I could. I couldn't just say that was the effort I had made to reach Art that night."

Do something. Do something. Do something.

". . . I lit a cigarette, was looking at his car, and I was . . . thinking about how unappreciative he was about the car, the fact that I had got him the car on a short notice, and that he had to have an automatic transmission.

"And after I got it for him and put it in my name, got the insurance in my name for him, he told me it was really no good because it didn't have automatic door locks."

Asshole. I give you $50,000 of my money. I give you a car. I put you on my insurance, because you keep fucking up. And as always, it's still not enough to keep you from ruining my life.

"And I took my pocketknife out, stuck it in the tire. And I guess I stuck it in the tread first. Nothing happened. Then I went around and stuck it in the sidewall, and it went right in, popped the tire, then I went around and popped the back tire."

"Why did you stab the tires?"

"It was a combination of reasons. It was like a frustration. It was the way Art sounded. There was no way he should be driving, period. And we always had a big joke in the family that Art couldn't change a spare tire.

"When he was a kid, he had a flat tire a block from the house. He came home and asked his father to do that, the old man. Art couldn't change a tire.

"So, I knew if I knocked both of them out, he wasn't going to drive that car anywhere soon."

Jim said he figured that Art had to be out partying somewhere. The way he had sounded on the phone, he didn't think it was possible that he was asleep already.

"I was going to move out myself."

"You mean leave?"

"Leave. And I went over . . . I went back up to the front door, and I kicked it."

"Why did you kick the front door?"

"It was like I wanted to make some noise. I wanted to wake him up if he was home. I wanted him to get out there."

He said he kicked the door two or three times, and he was surprised that the last time he kicked it, it popped open. He went inside.

His words were coming a little more quickly now, but the pain in his face was horrible to see and the vocal cords were still pinioned in that deathly monotone.

"I was pretty scared . . . I started screaming at him. . . . If he was home, I wanted him to be really aware that it was just me, and it was not a burglar or somebody had broken into his house. It was me, and he would recognize my voice.

"And so, I was screaming. . . . I was upset with him. I was screaming, 'Hey, killer,' I mean in a really loud voice, 'get your skinny ass out or get down here. If you're home, you know I'm here,' along that line."

"And you're screaming this?" Kennedy asked.

"I'm screaming it for all I've got.

". . . I went into the kitchen. I don't know if that door . . . I think that door might have been closed. I think I opened the door pretty loud, slammed it, and went into the kitchen area, and was just standing there. And I was continuing to scream at him."

"What happened next? Were there any lights on?"

"No . . . the house was dark. And when you got inside the room, the kitchen there, the ambient light was coming through. There's a big plate glass window in the kitchen on the street side. I could see.

"You could see?"

"Yeah."

"You kept screaming?"

"I continued to scream."

"What happened next?"

"Art came down the hallway." *Just like his warrior ancestors, charging the cavalry: today is a good day to die.*

"You saw Art?"

"I saw him."

"How did he look? How did he appear? What was he doing?"

"He was coming down the hallway fast, aggressive. He was crouched, had his gun out. Had his hand out, right hand pointing at me. And he was pointing that gun. He was aiming at me, and he yelled at me."

"What did he yell at you?"

"He yelled at me, 'Okay motherfucker, I'm going to blow your fucking brains out.' "

"What did you do?"

"I shot—I shot the rifle off. I shot it up. I think it was in the ceiling. And I thought—I mean, I shot it, and I don't know. I thought I heard another shot that he'd shot at me about the same time."

"What happened next?"

"Next thing was it was a bright light in my face, and I heard somebody say, 'I'm going to blow your fucking brains out.' And I turned. And there was a couple policemen maybe four, five feet away, had their guns drawn down on me, pointed at me.

"And I think the guy said, 'Drop the umbrella. I'm going to blow you away.' "

"What happened, Jim, between the time you see Art with the gun screaming, 'I'm going to blow your fucking head off,' and you shoot, and he shoots, what happens between then and you get out in the street with the police?"

Jim, fighting tears, croaked, "I don't know, I don't know. I don't know how I got out there."

"So you don't remember shooting your brother?"

"No."

"You know you did it?"

"Yes."

"Do you remember being in the back of the police car?"

"Yes."

"What do you hear when you're in the back of the police car?"

"I could hear the police radio," Jim said.

"What does it say, Jim?" Kennedy asked softly. "What do you hear when you're in the back of the police car, and you hear the police radio?"

"I could hear a lot—a lot of radio traffic. And I—I heard them call for a fire department, and the fire department was responding. And then I heard someone come on the radio and say, 'Cancel, cancel the paramedics' . . . because there was a DOA."

"What does DOA mean to you?"

"Dead on arrival."

"Did you know then that you'd killed your brother?"

"Yes." Tears ran down his face, and he bowed his head. *Sorry, Dad, sorry, Mom, sorry, Artie, my brother, half of myself, I love you, you rotten little prick.*

He asked Jim if any of Art's kids had asked him what had happened, and Jim said that Storm came to the theater one day in the summer, and that he told him, "I went in the house, and there was a lot of shooting, and I never saw his dad, and that it was an accident, and I was very sorry."

"You told us you did see his dad?"

"Yes."

"And you lied to Storm?"

"Yes."

"Why did you lie to Storm?"

"I didn't want to tell Storm that his dad had tried to kill me."

"Jim, having sat through this trial, do you know now what you did in that house?"

"I think so now."

"What did you do?"

"Killed Art."

"Do you remember killing your brother?"

"No, I don't."

"Did you have any hostility toward your brother?"

"No."

"Did you intend to kill your brother Art?"

"No."

"How do you feel about having killed your brother, Jim?"

"I don't feel good about it." The answer was a raw hoarse cry.

"Nothing further, Your Honor."

"**O**kay, Mr. Posey," Richard Breiner said soberly. "You may cross-examine."

It was five minutes until noon. John Posey had been sitting with his legs crossed, right ankle on left thigh, staring intently at Jim, making that nervous emphatic gesture with his hands during the direct.

He stood and walked to the other side of the table, closer to Jim.

His harsh nasal voice was a marked change from Kennedy's sibilant, soft-voiced questioning. "Mr. Mitchell, did you go to 23 Mohawk on February 27 of 1991 to murder your brother?"

"No. I didn't." Jim's voice was the same.

"Were you mad at him?"

"I was upset with him."

Posey asked Jim if he had been concerned about Lisa's safety, and Jim's answer was revealing: "I was a lot more concerned about Art. Lisa Adams was home, at my home, safe. And Art was in the middle of a mental breakdown."

Posey asked, "Did the thought ever occur to you that maybe you should call the police and have them go by your house in case this raging maniac with guns went by?"

"No."

"You wanted to control the situation yourself, didn't you?"

"We were hoping to."

"You wanted to be in charge, didn't you?"

"I don't think I wanted to be in charge. I don't think I had much of a choice."

Mercifully for Jim, the court broke for lunch at noon, but at 1:30, Posey was waiting for him as he took the stand once more.

"You purchased that rifle, did you not?"

"Yes, I did." The gun dealer had already testified that Jim bought the rifle in 1980.

"Was that supposed to be a gift to Artie's son Storm someday?"

"It was a gift for Storm's twelfth birthday."

Jim said Meredith didn't want Storm to have it then, so he kept it, intending to give it to him someday.

"Let me show you the rifle we're talking about, Mr. Mitchell, people's exhibit number 10." He walked over and picked up the rifle, then took it and tried to hand it to Jim, who wouldn't take it, and then put it down in front of him on the witness stand. "Take a look at that. Is that the rifle you took to your brother's house February 27 of 1991?"

"Yes."

"Was that rifle unloaded when you took it out of the locker?"

"Yes."

"Did you load it?"

"Yes, I did."

"Could you show us how you loaded it?"

"I don't want to touch it."

"Well, you put bullets in it, didn't you?" Posey pressed.

"That's argumentative," Breiner interceded.

Posey then showed Jim the box of bullets and went through the grisly math with him: fifty bullets in the box originally, eight fired, six found in the gun, thirty-five found in the box made forty-nine, one bullet missing.

"Did you test fire that rifle before you walked to your brother's house?" Posey, obsessed with the missing bullet, would ask this several times.

"No."

Then Posey turned to the .38, and asked Jim to show the jury how he put it on.

"I don't want to."

"You don't want to show the jury how you strapped it on? Can you hold it up and show us how it straps on?"

"I don't want to touch it."

"You don't want to touch it. You didn't have any trouble touching it that night, though, did you?"

"Argumentative," said Kennedy irritably.

"Sustained."

". . . If my arithmetic is correct . . . when you entered your brother's house you had the capability of firing nineteen rounds without ever having to reload, isn't that right?"

"Yes."

(Later, several members of the jury would say they had been offended by Posey trying to get Jim to handle the guns. Juror Michael Williamsen would say, "Right then I was so mad at Posey I thought, 'If you want him to demonstrate, why don't you go over and stand behind that door, and we'll have a real demonstration.' ")

When Jim talked about calling the crisis hotline, Posey said, "Now they didn't suggest to you that you should go to your brother's house with two weapons that had fifteen live rounds, did they?"

"No, they didn't."

"I'm sorry, I misspoke. Nineteen?"

"No, they did not."

A few minutes later, Posey said, "Would you scream just like you did that night, exactly what you said you did when you entered that house?"

"I don't think I probably could."

"Well, give it your best try. . . . Well, you're looking to Mr. Kennedy."

"I'm saying he doesn't have to," Kennedy said, white with anger, red spots high on his cheeks.

"Give it your best try," Posey pressed. "Let the ladies and gentlemen of the jury know how loud you screamed when you entered the house to alert your brother you were coming in."

"You don't have to do that, Mr. Mitchell," Kennedy said.

"Well, Your Honor," Posey said, "I'm asking the court to direct him to illustrate for us what he did."

"If he's unable to do that now, I won't force him to," Breiner said. "Can you do that for us, Mr. Mitchell?"

"No."

A little later, Posey asked him, "You were just bluffing when you put those live rounds in the rifle?"

". . . When I went down and got the rifle, I just loaded it up."

"Now that was part of the bluff, live ammunition in the rifle?"

"I didn't think about it."

"Were the five live rounds in the .38 revolver part of your bluff?"

"It was the same kind of situation."

"You didn't think about it?"

"I thought about it from the standpoint that I was scared, that I didn't know exactly what I was going to be getting into."

"You were going to bluff him with live ammunition?"

"Well, I—the gun was more of a bluff."

"Mr. Mitchell, my question was: were you going to bluff him with live ammunition?"

"I don't think that there's any way he could have known if the gun was loaded or not."

"And you could have bluffed him without having ammunition, couldn't you?"

"I could have."

"And you felt that you might need extra bullets, didn't you, that's why you took the box that contained fifty .22 long rifle shells?"

"I—I didn't remember even putting those in my pocket."

Posey hammered on for several more minutes about the bullets. It was an extremely strong point for him, and he knew it.

He forced Jim through the rest of the chronology, driving to the house, meeting Rocky.

When he asked Jim what he was wearing, he told him, his new dark leather jacket, baggy batik-print pants (the prosecution had called them "camouflage-type"), trademark English-style wool cap.

And "my white bucks, that were pretty old and kind of scuffed up."

White bucks, like the ones he borrowed from Art the night of the dance, old, scuffed up, like the battered dreams of his adolescence, the end of innocence. That night, those Jim and Artie dreams, so soiled and scuffed over time, had finally died, and white turned to black forever.

Art would never wear his white bucks again, and neither would Jim.

Jim had asked Art to stay away from the *War News* because of his behavior, and Posey asked, "He was an embarrassment to you, wasn't he?"

"Well, he was my brother, and he was having a hard time."

"Well, was he an embarrassment to you when he did that."

Jim stared back at the prosecutor. "I think I was beyond the point of being embarrassed by Art," he said quietly, and Posey changed the subject.

When Posey asked him if his brother got more attention than he did by being a social rebel, Jim said, ". . . He had a lot of moves, as we say . . . you know, he had style, and we all considered ourselves to be rebels."

Posey, pressing the issue, wanting to make Jim out to be jealous of all the attention Artie got, asked if Artie was the "PR man" at the theater.

"We could both be whatever we wanted to be there," Jim said. "I think as the years wore on . . . Art sort of became the victim of the business. . . . I think that the drinking and the partying just over the years had gotten to him."

"So what you're saying is the pornography business that you had started finally got to your brother?"

"I don't think it was. It's more than a business, per se. He was just basically unable to handle the prodigious amounts of alcohol."

Posey tried to push the life insurance idea around a little bit, but he didn't make much headway. Finally, in an answer to who would make decisions for Cinema 7, Jim said, "I haven't—I haven't been active in the company since this"—he hesitated—"since I killed my brother."

After a few more questions about the will and the estate, Posey shifted direction suddenly and began hammering at the night of the killing again. For an hour, he asked his patented little detail questions, his tone dubious, bordering on surly. He asked a series of questions about Jim and Rocky's approach to the house, and after each answer asked, "And you remember that?"

Finally, he got back to the point of Jim approaching the door.

"Did you think Artie would say, 'Jim, I'm going to give you my guns. Come on in and get them,' never mind the fact that you happened to have a rifle for show?"

"Excuse me, Your Honor, that's hardly a question," Kennedy said.

"Sustained. It's argumentative."

"Did you think Artie would say, 'Come on in, take whatever you want, take the guns?' "

"I was hoping that we could talk him out of it, settle him down a little bit, maybe smoke a joint with him, and just try to be there with him. We knew he was having a really bad time . . . we were there basically not to ignore him and to be there and let him know that he was getting to the point where people . . . were going to call the cops on him."

A little later Posey asked, "Which foot did you kick the door with?"

"I think my right foot."

"Can you show us how you did that or is that too difficult or embarrassing?"

"That's argumentative and uncalled for," Kennedy said.

"Sustained. The jury will disregard that last question."

"Would you show us how you did that, Mr. Mitchell?"

"Just lift your leg up and push it out," Jim said.

"Well, how hard did you try to kick the door?"

"Your Honor, this is sadistic!" Kennedy glared at Posey. "He doesn't have to ask these questions."

"Overruled," Breiner said.

Jim finally satisfied Posey that he kicked the door firmly, up near the knob, and he went on to the shooting itself.

"Did you see your brother go into the bathroom after you shot him in the abdomen?"

"No."

"Did you wait approximately thirty seconds, twenty-eight or thirty seconds, for your brother to peer out of the bathroom, then shoot him again?"

"I don't remember anything like that."

"You don't remember that."

"No."

"Did you see your brother come out of the bathroom again and then shoot him in the head?"

"I don't remember any of that."

"Do you remember firing two rapid shots in succession, one of those shots hitting your brother in the head?"

"No."

Finally, with Posey still peppering Jim Mitchell with questions about the confrontation with Haas and Paraspolo, Breiner called it quits for the day at 4:20 P.M. Then, the defense's fury with the prosecutor boiled over.

As Posey tried to discuss the scheduling for the remainder of the trial, Kennedy said, "I don't want to go up there [to the bench] with that bastard," and walked out of the courtroom.

"I want that reflected on the record," snapped Posey. "Mr. Kennedy—maybe he should come back, Judge. He's part of the—"

"You said you want something on the record?" Breiner said.

"I said we could talk about scheduling. He just said on the record that he doesn't want to come up here and talk with that bastard."

"I didn't hear that," Breiner said. "We'll do that first thing in the morning, without the jury."

As Posey walked out into the crowded corridor, wheeling his omnipresent rack of orange notebooks, he shot a look over to Kennedy, who was standing with a group of reporters.

"Don't glare at me, you little shit!" Kennedy shouted at him as Posey, white-faced with anger, got onto the elevator.

On Tuesday morning, the cross-examination resumed, and Posey played the 911 tape for the sixth time.

"Mr. Mitchell, did you hear Ms. Bajo screaming when you were in the house?"

"I don't remember hearing her at all."

"What we just heard on that 911 tape, Mr. Mitchell, you don't remember any of that? Is that correct?"

"No, I don't."

"That's all I have."

An audible sigh of relief traveled through the courtroom.

Kennedy had a few questions on redirect. He asked why Art's car registration and insurance were in Jim's name.

"Because Art had a drunken driving record and his insurance was up over, I guess, $18,000 a year."

"And you said on cross-examination that seeing Art's car in the driveway didn't mean to you that Art was in the house. Why?"

"Because he had gotten to the point that he was rarely driving."

Kennedy asked, "Why did you enter the house, Jim?"

"Because I had to go in and help Art."

"Did you think that Art could have sobered up, that Art could have conquered his alcoholism?"

"For sure, we never gave up on him. I knew he could do it."

"Did you feel any hostility toward your brother?"

"No."

"Well, what did you feel toward your brother?"

"Primarily toward the end I was feeling more inadequate, because he was falling apart, there was nothing I could do, almost."

"Did you intend to hurt or kill your brother, Jim?"

"I wish it could have been me!" Jim Mitchell cried out in anguish, and dropped his head into his hands.

"Nothing further."

PSYCHOGENIC AMNESIA.

Michael Kennedy scrawled the two words in six-inch-high capital letters on the blackboard behind the witness stand as the jury watched.

He was examining his next defense witness, Dr. David Kessler, and the psychiatrist had just defined those words: "Psychogenic. 'Psycho,' that's the mind, 'genic' means caused by. . . . 'Amnesia' is forgetting. . . . So it's an amnesia that has a psychological causation."

He told the jury that there was no foolproof way to determine whether or not a claim of amnesia is legitimate or phony, but that there are factors that can be taken into consideration in order to make an evaluation.

"You look at such factors as what's the context in which this claim of amnesia is being made? For example, is it . . . a criminal defendant who's asserting this claim? Skepticism arises if it's in that context."

"And that's certainly the context in which it's being raised here, do you understand that?"

"Yes."

"So that causes skepticism initially?"

"Certainly in my mind, yes. I don't mean to discount the claim. . . . You have to wonder—look for evidence.

"Another factor is the . . . individual involved, his past history. . . . Is this . . . an individual who would fit under the heading that we call antisocial personality, somebody who characteristically misleads people, lies, gives self-serving statements, is a con artist? . . . Does the claim hang together? Is it consistent from one time to the next?"

After he had elaborated on such potential signs of faking, Kennedy gave him a lengthy hypothetical that conformed to the facts of the case as they were in evidence.

And Kessler said the facts as presented were more consistent with genuine amnesia than with malingering.

Posey asked for a continuance before cross-examining because he had such short notice of Kessler's appearance. Breiner gave him until after lunch.

The cross-examination was brief; Posey did manage to establish that Kessler was not giving a diagnosis but an opinion based on a hypothetical question, without doing a personal examination. But Kessler, a veteran of hundreds of trials, didn't give him much elbow room.

Later that afternoon, Martha Rauber, Artie's worshipful housekeeper, finally got her wish: she got to testify. She had thought she might be called to testify regarding the DeLeon matter, and she was very nervous about that (as was DeLeon). But when it had become unnecessary to call her on that issue because DeLeon's testimony wasn't nearly as damaging as expected, she was terribly disappointed not to get to be part of the show.

But the defense needed her briefly to describe the phone call she made to Georgia Mae the night of the killing, so Martha, svelte in a heather green sweater, finally got her moment of glory.

A moment was all it was—just long enough to describe the call and identify a telephone record. Posey had no cross-examination, and Martha was free and happy.

A few minutes later, the defense rested its case.

John Posey would call several witnesses in rebuttal—first of all Kent Haas, to determine that he did not notice Jim Mitchell to be intoxicated. Next came Mario Watkins, whom Posey wished to ask about the statements Ruby Richardson allegedly made to him, but Kennedy was successful in arguing that such testimony would not be proper rebuttal.

Ray DeLeon was called to emphasize that he had never played golf with Artie, despite the fact that Nancy Harrison had testified earlier that he had left a message about golf for Artie at the theater. He denied ever making such a call.

Richard Freeman testified that the last time he saw Artie, the day before his death, he "appeared fine, in good spirits."

But the rebuttal witness who caused a ruckus was, naturally, Julie Bajo.

When Posey asked her what her recollection was of the date she had heard Artie making the call to Nancy at the O'Farrell, she said, "I believe it was one or possibly two days before the murder, but most probably Tuesday before the murder."

Breiner immediately admonished the jury to disregard her use of the word "murder." She was the last witness of the day, and the jury was dismissed a couple of minutes later.

Then, Kennedy vented his rage. Posey had been directed before the trial to admonish Bajo about the use of that word.

"Your Honor, I am obligated to move for a mistrial at this late date. Because I believe Mr. Posey deliberately elicited the word 'murder' from Ms. Bajo. The reason I say that is because the word 'murder' is in his notes. His notes of his conversation with her are here, and it says, quote, 'one to two days prior to the murder.'

"Any experienced lawyer, any lawyer who is interested in any kind of fair trial, would have instructed a witness that that word is totally inappropriate, doesn't belong in the trial, and do not say that. . . . I suggest . . . first of all that there ought to be a mistrial declared with particular reference in this case. And secondly, he ought to be chastised as severely as you possibly can because it's outrageous conduct by this person."

Posey replied, "Your Honor, first of all, those aren't my notes. That is the handwriting of Kathy Hoffman, who took those notes the other day when we talked with Julie Bajo.

"Secondly, I did not deliberately elicit that statement from her. I have told her not to use that . . . and she was directed not to say that, and she obviously chose otherwise. But I did not deliberately elicit that. . . . Mr. Kennedy is 100 percent wrong when he suggests that I would do that at this stage of trial."

Breiner, irritated with absolutely everyone now, denied the motion for mistrial.

The trial's last witness was Sherryl Skidmore, a Southern California psychologist that Posey hustled up at the last minute in an effort to impeach David Kessler.

Although Dr. Skidmore was not a psychiatrist, like Kessler, she did have a doctorate in psychology and specialized in forensic psychology.

She came out swinging, accusing Kessler of a breach of ethics for offering his opinion based on a hypothetical, without examining Jim Mitchell.

She also testified that psychogenic amnesia usually lasts from six to twenty-four hours.

On cross-examination, Kennedy got her to admit that such episodes of memory loss could conceivably be shorter or longer, and then he asked her, "Are you telling us that it is unethical for a medical doctor with a specialty in psychiatry, in response to a hypothetical question, to say whether or not certain facts are consistent or inconsistent with a disassociative disorder?"

"Yes, I am."

It was the end of a long trial, and the cross-examination was probably

Kennedy's least effective. He ended up eliciting information from her that Posey didn't but should have, including a psychiatric text's admonition regarding psychogenic amnesia and malingering: "Involving simulated amnesia patients, a particularly difficult diagnostic dilemma, attention to the possibility that amnesia is feigned is crucial. Careful questioning under hypnosis or during an amobarbital [truth serum] interview may provide useful information, although . . . some people continue to malinger."

Finally, the testimony was over, and it was time for the attorneys to make their final arguments to the weary jury, who had already heard plenty of arguing, thank you.

John Posey knew when to hit his peak. His closing argument was by far his best performance of the trial. Kennedy had kept him on the defensive through most of the evidentiary phase, but now he could put all the complex pieces of his case together for the jury.

He had some work to do too. He had to explain to the jury the various levels of culpability they had to choose from. In this case, where the actual fact of the shooting was not in dispute, those distinctions were paramount. And, for Jim Mitchell, the stakes were high: first-degree murder would mean twenty-five years to life; involuntary manslaughter would mean two to four years.

Posey succinctly described the two types of malice aforethought: express malice, in which there is a manifest intent to kill; and implied malice, in which an intentional act is committed that has as a natural consequence danger to human life, performed with conscious disregard for that life.

As regards implied malice, Posey said, "I submit to you that firing a weapon in that house meets those criteria."

Posey had prepared a chart outlining the events leading up to the crime that wrapped clear around one curved side of the courtroom, and he went through them step by step with the jury.

When he got to Julie Bajo calling 911, he said, "Ladies and gentlemen of the jury, the fact that Julie Bajo had enough composure at that moment to do that, to dial 911, was this defendant's undoing. Had she never done that, he would have gotten away, and he would have been the bereaved brother, and we wouldn't be here with this trial."

Every time he could within the context of his argument, Posey mentioned the fact that "the defendant shot his brother three times." He used the words like a bludgeon, and soon each time he said them, Kennedy's eyes would roll and he would shake his head in indignation.

Posey outlined the three theories of first-degree murder that he had presented: first, that it was a willful, deliberate, premeditated killing with express malice.

"You can infer the way he entered, the way the gun was fired, the timing between the shots, that he arrived at or determined this as a result of careful thought in weighing the considerations.

"He drove from San Francisco.

"He was getting ready to go to war.

"He had a rifle, a handgun, a dark coat, a hat, the knife, and thirty-five rounds. He entered that house with the capability of discharging nineteen rounds before having to reload. And yet, he tells you from the witness stand that he went there just to bluff.

"Once again, it's all that evidence, the evidence of the crime scene . . . that shows it's premeditated."

Posey stalked back and forth in front of the jury like a caged animal, returning every so often to his notes on the counsel table.

"Now, there's another way that one can arrive at a first-degree murder under an express malice, and that is murder by means of lying in wait. . . . Waiting and watching for an opportune time to act."

Posey went through a detailed description of the pattern of bullets once again, and the sequence Haag propounded, and the timing offered by Hollien's testimony.

"After Artie took refuge and sought safety in his bathroom, his brother waited for him and fired the last shots. . . . And based upon the analysis of the 911 tape, there is a time lapse. You can hear it before you hear those pops, about twenty-eight seconds. And that's when he came out, and he got shot."

Posey decided to present the case for second-degree murder and manslaughter before giving the jury his theory of felony murder, which was the third way they could get to first-degree murder.

For second-degree, he argued, all the jury needed to find was that firing those shots constituted implied malice.

At that point, in the middle of Posey's argument, the court recessed until the next day, Friday, February 14, Valentine's Day, and almost certainly the day the jury would finally be given the job of deciding Jim Mitchell's fate.

The next morning, Posey's intensity was unabated. If anything, it was greater.

He started by telling the jury the basic definition of manslaughter: intentional killing without malice aforethought. There were two ways they could get to voluntary manslaughter: one, if they thought Jim had shot Artie in the heat of passion, or in a sudden quarrel; and two, if he had an honest but unreasonable belief he had to defend himself against imminent peril.

And he argued against both scenarios. "He drove all the way from the city, twenty-, twenty-five-minute ride, and then violently went into his brother's house. That is not an honest but unreasonable belief that he had to defend himself.

". . . We spent a large amount of time in this trial . . . focusing on the conduct of Artie Mitchell. . . . but look at the conduct of this defendant. It's time now to look . . . at what he did, and ask, what rights did Artie Mitchell have?"

He hit motive once, but not too hard, because it was the weak spot in his case: "One of the things that the defense . . . has attempted to do is suggest to you that there's no motive for this killing. . . . But I suggest to you, ladies and gentlemen of the jury, that the evidence suggests motive.

"He was tired of Artie Mitchell."

The prosecutor repeated his contention that had Jim gotten away, he would never have been a suspect, and that Karen Mitchell very well could have been charged with murder.

"He would have walked away free, and they would have never suspected him. He would have controlled that corporation, he would have controlled that living trust, and he would have been the bereaved brother."

He spent only a moment discussing involuntary manslaughter, the least serious result possible short of acquittal. It required that the jury find no intent at all to kill, but to find an unlawful shooting that resulted in death.

Then he went back to the third theory of first-degree murder: felony murder. Under Proposition 115, a killing committed during the commission of another felony was first-degree murder. Posey's "underlying felony" for this theory was burglary by false imprisonment, in this case breaking into Artie's house to hold him against his will.

He based this in part on the fact that Jim had flattened the two tires on Artie's car. "He was going to confine, detain, deny Artie Mitchell his freedom of movement, if you will, his liberty. And he had no right to do that."

He played for the jury the computer animation of his version of the crime again—that "most pernicious piece of evidence" that Kennedy had already vowed to base an appeal on if there was any conviction in the case.

Then John Posey did perhaps the most dramatic and unconventional thing he had done in the case so far. Talking about the gaps between shots as Hollien analyzed the 911 tape, he counted out loud, first to fifteen for the fifteen seonds between the second and third shots on the tape, what Haag theorized were the fifth and sixth shots fired. He contended that Artie was hiding in the bathroom, then stepped out and was shot in the arm through the door molding after those fifteen seconds. "He retreats back into the bathroom." And then to twenty-eight, for the gap between the sixth and seventh shots, as Haag contended, the arm shot and the fatal head shot.

"See what kind of time we're talking about: One. Two. Three. Four," he barked. "Five. Six. Seven. Eight. Nine. Ten." Standing right in front of the jury box, gesturing with each number. "Eleven. Twelve. Thirteen. Fourteen. Fifteen. Sixteen. Seventeen." Angry, staccato counting. "Eighteen. Nineteen. Twenty. Twenty-one. Twenty-two." Staring intensely into each juror's face, one by one. "Twenty-three. Twenty-four. Twenty-five. Twenty-six. Twenty-seven. Twenty-eight."

He paused for a moment, and then continued. "His brother cornered him in the bathroom *and shot him in the head.*"

A few minutes later he played, for the seventh and final time, the first minute of the 911 tape.

"Ladies and gentlemen of the jury, you just heard what was the last fifty, sixty seconds of Artie Mitchell's life. You just heard how his brother went into that house by force and by violence and gunned his brother down.

"That, along with the other evidence in this case, leads to only one conclusion when all the evidence is considered and heard by you. That is, that the defendant, seated in this courtroom, James Mitchell, murdered his brother and that under any of those theories that you'll be instructed on, it's a first-degree murder. And that's what your verdict in this case should be.

"Thank you."

Michael Kennedy's task was made all the harder by the expectations.

Everyone in the courtroom *expected* to be electrified by his summation. Nothing less would do. He had wowed them with his opening statement. He had fought through a morass of damning physical evidence during the trial. Now he was *expected* to perform another miracle, to convince the jury by the power of his words and his logic and his histrionics that despite all of it, his client should go free.

It wasn't that easy. However strong was the defense's animus toward John Posey, however amateurish Kennedy had made him look from time to time during the evidentiary phase, the silver-haired prosecutor had just presented a thoroughly compelling argument for a murder conviction.

At 10:40 A.M., Friday, Kennedy took off his watch, put it on the lectern beside his notes, hitched up his pants and began. After he had echoed Posey's thanks to the jury for their lengthy tour of duty, his words began to flow, just as eloquently as anyone could have demanded:

"What a wonderful world this would be if it were the way I think my colleague, Mr. Posey, and even Mr. Haag, see it. That is, a world where there is no doubt, a world where everything is known, everything is mathematically measurable. Everything is computerized, computable. Everything can be known with certainty, with certitude.

"That's not the real world. That's not the world we live in. It's not the world Jim and Art Mitchell lived in. It's not the world Art Mitchell died in. It's not the world Jim Mitchell killed him in.

"No, it's a much more complicated world than that: it's a world with us human beings, with all our foibles, our frailties, and our errors, and our aspirations, and our falling short of the mark, our negligences, our derelictions, even our courages, our braveries, those moments when we shine."

". . . We've had some high-tech and low-tech and no-tech, I suggest, with reference to a couple of witnesses. We have had a family tragedy of biblical proportions, and we have had sex and drugs and murder.

"What we have had the least of, and what we want the most as human beings, are answers. It's our natural tendency to want to know, what happened? What happened to an individual about whom the record is without contradiction, in forty-eight years of his life, that he is a fine, decent human being? What happens when we try to show you forty-eight years of a life, but we can't show you two minutes of that life, because Jim can't remember? It's for you to decide whether you believe him or not."

He spoke of stress and pressure and the mind giving way. "Now, I don't know what happened. I can say to you Jim snapped. It could be. But if you want, as the prosecution is committed to do, to ascribe every sinister, murderous interpretation conceivable to Jim Mitchell, you can find first-degree murder."

Predictably, just as Posey gave motive once over lightly, Kennedy dwelled on what he characterized as the total absence of motive, reminding the jury that absence of motive must be considered as possibly tending to establish innocence.

He told them again that the insurance policy was in force the day Jim tried to save Artie's life in the surf.

"There's no money motive here. There's no money motive. So he's backed and filled now, has my colleague, to a point where he's saying [Jim] wanted to get rid of Artie because he was tired of him. Well, I think the record is clear that Artie was a pain in the you know where, and had been for a long time. Is that a reason to kill him? If you want to kill Art Mitchell, you abandon him. You leave him to his own disease of alcoholism and let the poor wretch die of alcoholism. That's what you do if you're tired of him.

"But that's not Jim Mitchell. Because you know what Jim Mitchell did not have? He didn't have malice toward his brother."

He talked about Georgia Mitchell's testimony about the brothers' childhood, showing that they were, as he put it, "inexorably joined."

But for much of his closing, he talked of the prosecution's witnesses. He treated Skip Dossett like his own witness, which in point of fact he turned out to be.

He lampooned Harry Hollien and his "close enough": "It reminds me of the old 'close enough for government work,' " he said scornfully. But Kennedy saved most of his scorn for Julie Bajo, pointing out one after the other the contradictions in her testimony. She "wasn't even a witness," he said. "I mean her no disrespect. But Julie Bajo was an exhibit. She was brought in by the prosecution to sit up there and tell a story, and then they spent a day and a half impeaching her, impeaching her beyond what anyone could imagine."

He whacked away at Haag's shot sequence and Hollien's timing. "Like you, I had to sit and wait and listen while the prosecutor counted from one to fifteen, and then counted from one to twenty-eight. It's a long period of time. But what is important is that both Hollien and Poza said that during that long stretch of time, that time when the prosecution would have you believe there's a cold-blooded killer lying in wait, there are several masking moments, those moments when Julie Bajo with the receiver right next to her mouth, in the bedroom closet with the door closed all but one inch, screaming into the phone. Is it not surprising that some of those shots would be masked?"

He went through the legal definitions as Posey had, citing all of his reasons why the definitions did not apply to what Jim Mitchell undeniably did do that night. He not only argued against the murder theories, he also argued against the manslaughter theories, including heat of passion. "This is a case where Jim goes in, not out of blind passion, but out of blind love, if anything."

And finally, Michael Kennedy told the jury: "Jim Mitchell's life is in your hands.

"That's a good place for it to be. We'll await your verdict. Thank you very much."

• • •

Posey argued as forcefully as before in a twenty-minute reply to Kennedy's summation, and then Richard Breiner painstakngly read to the jury 112 pages of incredibly complex instructions, worked out in several sessions between counsel over the last few days.

The jury then selected attorney Doug Roberts as its foreman, and told the court that it would take the three-day Presidents' Day weekend at home before returning Tuesday morning, February 18, to begin deliberations.

"We have a very intelligent jury and obviously a conscientious one," Breiner told the attorneys. "We'll see what happens."

It had to be an agonizing weekend for all: for Jim Mitchell, for his family, for his attorneys, for the prosecutor who wanted him imprisoned for life. And for the jurors too, who were not yet formally deliberating this case, but who could think of little else.

One juror's attention was diverted, though: Dorothy Diane Brabo's husband became ill with gall bladder trouble over the weekend and was hospitalized.

So Tuesday morning, Breiner was forced to excuse her and call yet another alternate onto the jury at the last possible moment. The two remaining alternates' names were placed into a hat and Pamela Covillo, Breiner's clerk, selected one: Patrick Ryan, the wry Australian who had been the last person picked to the panel. He was reached by telephone in San Francisco, but he was carless; a deputy was dispatched to get him, and it was almost noon by the time he got to the courthouse and deliberations started.

Because of the complexity of the instructions and the many options available to the jury, neither side expected the jury to come back quickly, but that didn't make the waiting any easier.

As the second day of deliberations began, Jim was surrounded by friends. Of course, Lisa was at his side, and so were the men of the O'Farrell's inner circle: Jeff Armstrong, Charlie Benton, Rocky Davidson, Johnny and Denny Morgan were all there, even though they had embarked on a marathon poker game the night before, determined to keep spirits up during the nail-biting time.

Posey waited quietly in his office, away from the press and the big defense contingent in the corridor outside the court.

Michael Kennedy sat in the hall and fiddled with a *New York Times* crossword, and when he could stand it no more, he threw it down on the bench and began pacing up and down the hall. He did not expect the jury to come back this day, or even the next, but he couldn't help being on edge. This was the brutal time, of worrying and second-guessing and hoping they'll come back soon and hoping they won't.

They did.

At 2:30 P.M., the jurors sent word that they had reached a verdict.

Judge Breiner was on his way to Los Angeles for a judicial conference, and so the clerks scrambled to find another judge to preside.

Jim walked into the courtroom with Lisa, then gave her a kiss and took his place at the table. It was entirely possible that they would not sleep together this night; Jim could be jailed immediately if he were found guilty.

Posey came in, a hint of a smile on his lips, sat down on the edge of his chair and shot a quick glance over at the other end of the table, where Michael and Eleanore and Nanci Clarence all huddled around Jim and offered him encouragement.

It was fifteen minutes before Michael B. Dufficy, who had just been named to the Superior Court a few days before, was able to get free and get down to Courtroom D.

As bad as waiting for a verdict was, this was worse. Knowing there was a verdict, but having to wait, was the epitome of suspense.

Eleanore turned from her seat behind her husband and, white-faced, scanned the courtroom for supportive faces. Jim, as he had done for the past five weeks, kept his eyes drilled straight ahead, betraying nervousness only by repeatedly removing his glasses and massaging the bridge of his nose.

Finally, Dufficy came, and asked the jury if it had indeed reached the verdict, and Roberts told him, yes, they had. He handed the verdict forms to Dufficy, who gave them to Pamela Covillo to read:

"In the *People of the State of California* v. *James Lloyd Mitchell,* Case Number SC12462A:

"Count One: We the jury in the above-entitled case find the defendant, James Lloyd Mitchell, not guilty of violating Section 187 of the Penal Code of the State of California, a felony, murder in the first degree;

". . . Not guilty of . . . murder in the second degree;"

Michael Kennedy put his arm around Jim Mitchell's shoulders, and John Posey's mouth set in a straight line. In the third row of seats, Lisa Adams began crying.

". . . We the jury in the above-entitled case find the defendant James

Lloyd Mitchell guilty of a lesser included offense, Section 192A of the Penal Code of the State of California, a felony, voluntary manslaughter."

The jury also convicted on the two lesser felonies, unlawfully discharging a firearm and brandishing a weapon at a police officer.

Now John Posey was on his feet, asking that Dufficy detain Jim Mitchell pending sentencing, and Dufficy quickly declined to do so, but set a hearing for the following morning at 9 A.M. before Breiner to consider the issue and set a sentencing date.

Kennedy put his arms around Jim in a bear hug, and he was joined by Eleanore and Nanci Clarence, the four of them hugging and grinning. Then Jim broke away and turned to Lisa, who was waiting at the rail, tears streaming down her face.

John Posey shouldered his way past and walked out of the courtroom. It took reporters, focused on the scene around Jim, a few moments to realize that he was about to get away before they scrambled after him.

"That's the way the system works," he told them. "I argued for what I believed the facts showed. I believe in our system of justice, and that's what the jury decided." He did point out that, "The defense went into this saying Jim Mitchell was not guilty and this was an accident."

But Michael Kennedy was ecstatic. "It's a great victory," he proclaimed happily. "The Mitchell family is very happy. We are not disturbed by the manslaughter conviction. If he is obliged to go to prison, he'll be fine," he said, but he added that the defense would undoubtedly appeal. He mentioned the video reenactment as a certain appellate issue, and said there would be others.

Jeff Armstrong, eyes red with tears, hugged Kennedy as he walked out. "Thank you, Michael," he choked.

Jim and Lisa, surrounded by a phalanx of friends, walked out of the courthouse arm in arm and got in the infamous Ford Explorer and sped away.

That night, in the office of the O'Farrell Theatre, Michael and Eleanore Kennedy and Nanci Clarence were toasted, highlights were replayed ("Don't glare at me, you little shit!") and somebody fired up a joint. Brave young women with satin skin wore lacy promises and smiled mysteriously, and Jim Mitchell drank champagne and played lowball with the boys.

It was Artie's kind of night.

J udge Breiner allowed Jim to stay free on bond pending sentencing, which he set for April 3.

The sentencing range was considerable. Breiner could conceivably give Jim Mitchell probation. He could also sentence him to three, six, or eleven years in prison, depending on mitigating and aggravating factors, plus four more years for the other two felonies and sentence "enhancements" from the use of firearms in the killing. What would it be? Probation, or fifteen years?

Nanci Clarence worked with Jim's probation officer as a report was prepared for the judge, and she and Tom Steel were also busy with the remaining civil suits pending against Jim, including those filed by Summit National Life Insurance, Julie Bajo, Karen Mitchell, and, perhaps most painfully for Jim and Georgia, Artie's three older children.

Meanwhile, the jurors began to decompress from the intensity of their experience. They all had agreed not to talk about the deliberations themselves, but some were willing to talk about the case in general terms.

Kentner Scott, pleasant, gray-haired Juror Number 1 with the astounding array of brightly colored sweaters, was the most vocal. And he was quite critical of John Posey.

"I started with an open mind about him, as I did about Jim Mitchell," Scott said. "He was aggressive, persistent, tireless, and had obviously done an immense amount of work preparing for this. The guy worked his tail off.

"But someplace along the way, I began to feel a mechanistic sense. He was like an automaton. And he was so aggressive I began to think of him as a little pit bull," Scott said.

Roboprosecutor.

Of the prosecution's expert case, he said, "It appeared to be solid, a house of bricks. But Tito Poza and Michael Kennedy made it look like a house of cards, and they just knocked it down."

He thought Julie Bajo was ludicrous, and fervently hoped that the manslaughter verdict would have a negative effect on her suit.

He said that he was convinced that "something just snapped" when Jim was outside the house, and added that he was very comfortable and pleased with the outcome.

He wouldn't say much about the deliberations themselves, other than to praise the foreman, attorney Dennis Roberts, and Father Nern, the Episcopal priest. "We were lucky to have two men so skilled and experienced in negotiation. They brought us back together when we were far apart."

Other jurors reported that a minority group on the panel, including Gil Brook and Betty Tutor, started deliberations favoring first-degree murder, with a larger group favoring involuntary manslaughter or acquittal. The voluntary manslaughter was a compromise position, but it was also a scenario in which they came to believe: Jim Mitchell killed his brother in the heat of passion.

Kentner Scott wrote Judge Breiner a letter thanking him for his patience and humor. The jurors were all extremely impressed with the cheerful, competent judge.

"He was so sharp, and had such a great sense of humor," Michael Williamsen said. "He was great."

(The jury's views of the judge were echoed by Kennedy, who called him "a joy," but Posey was far less complimentary. He felt that Breiner's rulings hamstrung him throughout, from pretrial through jury selection and on throughout trial.)

Williamsen said the jury was convinced the killing wasn't about money, despite the prosecution's efforts to build a money motive.

At the same time, most were not disposed to believe Jim Mitchell's claim of amnesia. In the end, it didn't enter into their deliberations.

Posey, exhausted but philosophical, kept telling the media "that's what this system is all about," but the disappointment in his tone was evident. He came down with a bad cold and sore throat right after the trial, and decided to take a few weeks of his accumulated leave.

The rest of the District Attorney's office was completely silent about the case. "It's just not mentioned. It's like it didn't happen," one attorney said.

Chuck Cacciatore certainly took no solace in the result, or in Posey's discomfiture. He knew the senior prosecutor was just doing his job. But he remained bitter about the way he was treated in the case—and he would always wonder if the outcome would have been different if he had been retained.

The defense wondered too. "Chuck Cacciatore would have been a lot tougher to handle," one member of the defense team said. "Like Kennedy, he's a pleasant, smooth, likable character, very good with juries. Posey was the perfect foil for Kennedy. Cacciatore would not have given him such a cheap target."

Other attorneys Monday morning quarterbacked it to death, of course. One frequently asked question: what if the prosecution had abandoned the first-degree murder approach and simply gone for second-degree? Some said that juries, when they can't find their way to first-degree murder, often slide right past second-degree to manslaughter. But try this, a couple of attorneys postulated: play on the natural sympathy for Jim by saying, "We agree, this isn't a first-degree murder, but look, how can you get by implied malice when he goes in the door firing like Rambo? It has to be second-degree murder . . ."

"That could have been very hard to deal with," one of the defense attorneys admitted.

John Posey doesn't see it that way. "I think it was a first-degree murder," he said stubbornly a couple of weeks after the trial. "I think Luke Haag's reconstruction was exactly what happened. He went in there to kill his brother."

Michael Kennedy was equally emphatic after the trial. "This case should never have been brought," he said. "It was so stupid of Posey. He's a pig-headed asshole, mean-spirited, overreaching. These domestic situations are almost invariably not first-degree murders. They are so steeped with emotion. They are situational.

"So was this case. I knew it, and the jury knew it."

Missy, Joanne, Kristal, and Bana all continue to mourn Artie Mitchell, deeply and grievously. All catch themselves speaking of him in the present tense. All know their lives will never be totally whole without him.

Missy will be busy with her family, with her life, and suddenly she will think of him and burst out crying. She knows her spiritual bond with Artie remains unbroken, and sometimes she feels his presence overwhelmingly.

Bana continues to fight the depression that has shadowed her for years, and as her poetry often reveals, Artie is at the center of her thoughts. She published a monograph entitled *Eight for Artie* soon after his death.

Kristal continues to dance, and to reminisce about the day the boss walked up, handed her a joint, and won her heart.

But Joanne is hanging on to his memory the most fiercely.

Her tiny San Francisco flat is a virtual monument to Artie Jay Mitchell. His underwear is in her top drawer, and a bottle of his favorite vodka, Absolut is in her freezer. His fuck-you grin beams out from every corner of the place, almost every square inch of wall space. Artie and Joanne in Mexico, Artie clowning, laughing, kissing her, kissing other women, nestling his bald head in some blonde's cleavage, performing oral sex upon the supine form of porn star Ginger Lynn on the set of *Grafenberg Spot,* romping with his kids, smoking a joint. Having a drink. Looking serious and slick in a suit and tie. Grinning that crinkled-up, little-boy grin. Artie Artie Artie Artie Artie Artie. *Artie.* The place vibrates with his presence.

Of course, he is not really there, is he? But Joanne is there, forty-three years old, her big brown eyes dulled with pain and bitterness. Alone. Sitting on her couch, where she had sat naked with him so many times, surrounded by the scraps of paper and silver emulsion that are all she has left of her man.

It is full on a year since Artie Mitchell died in the hallway of the Corte Madera house she found and rented for him a few years before, a house where, for a few golden months, she lived with him. One night, she screws up her courage and puts *Grafenberg Girls Go Fishing* in her VCR. It is emotional overload, to listen to it. She's very glad their lovemaking was preserved in that way, but it is high-tech torture, to be able to hear what she has lost forever.

Not surprisingly, Joanne Scott sees the case Posey's way. After all this time, she is the only one of all the people close to Art from the O'Farrell who remains vocally angry with Jim. Even Julie is quiet while her wrongful death suit is being negotiated.

In a letter published in the *Marin Independent Journal* after the verdict that was headlined "Mitchell Murder: Speaking Up for Art," Joanne wrote, "I've been overwhelmed by the massive publicity generated by the defense slanted toward excusing Jim Mitchell's actions and painting Artie in the worst possible light as a man who deserved to be shot.

"How can firing eight shots at an unarmed man, then fleeing the scene with a smoking rifle stuffed down a pantleg while Art's body lay in a pool of blood be thought of as a loving intervention for alcoholism?

". . . The Mitchell family rallied so strongly because they think the best thing for the family and the business financially is for Jim to remain out of jail and running the O'Farrell. Many acquaintances supported Jim because the Mitchell brothers contributed monetarily to many causes and political campaigns over the years. Jim is the survivor with the money. Art certainly can't help anybody financially now.

"Despite extensive testimony delivered to protect Jim, the Art Mitchell I knew was brilliant and loving. He possessed determination and strength enough to play a compelling role in legitimizing the sex industry in a country where the Puritan ethic has always been so predominant. Art's charisma contributed greatly to the success and the mystique of the O'Farrell Theatre.

"He was a loving, caring father to his six children, whom he most certainly would have wanted to watch grow to adulthood. I will always love and respect Art Mitchell, and it saddens me profoundly that he was killed in such a heartless way by a brother he trusted and loved."

Around 3 A.M. on February 27, 1992, the first anniversary of Artie Jay Mitchell's death, the cars began to show up in the O'Farrell Theatre parking lot.

One by one they came, Charlie Benton from Pleasant Hill and Jeff Armstrong from Walnut Creek and Jack Davis from Vallejo and Dan O'Neill from the old *War News* building in North Beach, where he was living as he worked on opening a club there. And Skip Dossett and Rocky and Johnny Morgan and James Lloyd Mitchell.

They climbed into a van, and headed across the Bay Bridge in the dark, and nobody said much.

A bottle of Rémy-Martin went from mouth to mouth as they rolled on east through the Delta. They passed Antioch, where the memories were still standing, 405 Grangnelli and Adelia Kimball Elementary and Hazel's Drive-In and Blu's Club and the building where the pool hall used to be, all behind them somewhere in the dark, quiet as the grave, and still nobody said much.

Then they stopped the van at the Cherokee Memorial Park in Lodi, and they all got out in the dark, and fumbled around with flashlights and tried to find the place where Artie was, and then they found it, and nobody said much.

The tears came, now, all of these men standing crying in the darkness, Jim Mitchell crying harder than anyone as he stared at his brother's grave. He cried out, "I'm sorry, Art, I really fucked up, I really fucked up bad."

Jeff Armstrong read some of Bana Witt's poetry, and Dan O'Neill took out a banjo and played an Irish love song, and nobody said much.

Then it was dawn, and they twisted up a big joint and smoked it, and cawed loudly, and cried, and drove into Lodi and had breakfast, and when a waitress told them they couldn't drink the Rémy in the restaurant, somebody snarled, "Lady, don't tell us what the fuck we can do in here," and she took another look at this odd group of red-eyed morose men, and served them their eggs and stayed out of their way until they left.

They went to a bar in Rio Vista and had a few more, and played some pool, just like the old days, almost.

Big Bob insisted that they go fishing. There was a spot right here in Rio Vista where he and Little Bob used to fish off the pier when they were kids, and so he went and bought tackle for everybody, and they all went fishing, just like the old days, almost, except Little Bob couldn't make it, and so they were just eight lonely desperate men fishing for everything they had lost, their youth and their fun and their happiness and their brother, off a pier in Rio Vista, California, in 1992.

Nobody caught anything. They drove back to the O'Farrell Theatre, and nobody said much.

EPILOGUE

In late March, the Marin County Probation Department asked for a psychiatric report on Jim Mitchell, which delayed sentencing until April 24.

As the sentencing approached, Breiner received an avalanche of letters supporting Jim and asking for leniency. He received more than 100 letters from an astounding variety of people. Jack Davis called in his political markers all over the area. Mayor Frank Jordan wrote on Jim Mitchell's behalf. So did San Francisco County Supervisor Terence Hallinan, Sheriff Michael Hennessey, and Jordan's new police chief, former sheriff Richard Hongisto. Letters came from everywhere, from Missy Manners, from Marilyn Chambers, from the teachers of Jim's children, from his uncle in Arkansas, and, of course, from his mother.

Jordan sounded the themes echoed by most of the letter writers. He told Breiner that a long prison term would serve "no useful rehabilitative purpose." He pointed out that Jim was now the primary source of financial support for ten children—his four and Artie's six. "I fear a lengthy incarceration would only further damage the lives of the children involved," Jordan wrote. "Jim will live for the rest of his life with the fact of his brother's death. I believe he deserves compassion." The mayor also cited Mitchell's support for charities, including the AIDS ward at San Francisco General Hospital.

Hennessey was less effusive, asking only that Breiner consider allowing Jim to remain free on bail pending appeal.

Nevertheless, for many it strained credulity that San Francisco's mayor and its two top law enforcement officers would go on record supporting Jim when the city had spent years and countless dollars fighting the theater. "It stinks," the *Examiner* said superciliously in an editorial.

But for insiders, it wasn't so surprising. The Mitchells had always been politically adroit in the extreme, and they had heavily supported Jordan in the mayor's race.

Breiner had more than the letters to consider. In her report, Probation Officer Rebecca Said quoted court-appointed psychologist Bruce Pither as saying that the circumstances of the shooting and the Mitchells' relationship were unique, and Jim did not pose a danger to others.

But Pither added that Jim exhibited "strong antisocial, paranoid, and narcissistic personality features," and was quoted in Said's report as saying that Jim is "rigid and inflexible with an ability to deal with stressful situations only where there is adequate structure."

Said's report also contained the tantalizing allegation that Jim Mitchell "flashed on the movie *Taxi Driver*" on the night of the killing, and thought he was Travis Bickle, the crazed protagonist who shot up a building on a misguided mission of mercy.

Said's report concluded by recommending a sentence of seven years and eight months.

Breiner certainly had no dearth of material to consider. And on the morning of April 24, he told Jim Mitchell and Michael Kennedy and John Posey and a courtroom jammed with Mitchell family and friends what he had decided.

"You became Travis Bickle and as a result Artie is dead. Despite his faults, Artie did not deserve to die and his children did not deserve to become orphans," Breiner told Jim Mitchell. "I know you feel remorse . . . but in a civilized community, such deeds cannot go without appropriate punishment."

Breiner said he couldn't remember ever receiving so many letters on behalf of a convicted criminal. "But I cannot make my decision in this case as if this were a popularity contest," Breiner said. "It is the judge, not the public, who has the responsibility to determine the sentence, and . . . the gravity of the crime itself—killing a human being—compels me to impose a prison sentence." He also said that Jim acted with "criminal sophistication."

That sentence was six years—three for voluntary manslaughter and another three for using a firearm in the killing. He also gave Jim sixteen months, to be served concurrently, for exhibiting a firearm to a police officer in a threatening manner. He issued a four-and-a-half-year sentence on the charge of discharging a firearm in a grossly negligent manner, but stayed it, which means that it will not have to be served if the other sentence is served.

But the biggest bit of news for Jim was that Breiner, against Posey's strong objection, agreed to continue bond for the duration of the appeal, meaning that Jim will not have to go to prison until appeals are exhausted. When Breiner announced the appeal bond, Jim allowed himself a little smile and hugged Nanci Clarence. A few moments later, he walked out of the courtroom with Lisa and Georgia Mae, a free man still.

A few minutes later, Kennedy told reporters that the case would be appealed on the basis of four claims of trial error:

- the animated video reenactment of the shooting should not have been shown to the jury;
- the 911 analysis by Hollien was not based on proven, accepted scientific methods;
- instructions to the jury were improper; and
- Rocky Davidson was improperly prevented from testifying.

"He came prepared to go to prison," Kennedy said of his client. "He has always been prepared for the worst and hoping for the best.

"He understands the sentence and he accepts it," he added. "But he also believes he will be vindicated on appeal."

At the time of sentencing, sources close to the case said, Mitchell's legal bills had reached $1.3 million. The appeal, likely to take at least a year or two, will no doubt push the tab much higher.

No one could say Jim didn't get his money's worth. Despite Breiner's stern words, the sentence means that even if the appeals fail, given good behavior and credit for the time he served before bail, Jim Mitchell will serve less than three years in prison. Had he been convicted of first-degree murder, he could have been in prison for the rest of his life.

But those who know Jim well say privately that however preferable freedom is to incarceration, no legal victory can ever truly set him free. For more than forty years, he took responsibility for his brother, and he is incapable of stopping now.

Jim Mitchell's jail is in his mind, and he will always be a prisoner there.

ACKNOWLEDGMENTS

With gratitude to:

—Georgia Mae Mitchell, for her faith, friendship and assistance.

—Missy Manners, for sharing both her pain and her memories so eloquently, and for her irrepressible spirit and humor that are so very evocative of Artie.

—Joanne Scott, for her patience, and kindness, and forthrightness; and Kristal Rose and Bana Witt, likewise. Never mind the bitterness: All four of your spoke to me with generosity and courage.

—Bill Boyer, who had the guts to talk to me.

—Martha Rauber, who was true to Artie and to this book.

—Ed Beitiks, who finishes first in my league every year, and hates this sort of thing; and David Dayton, who is owed a trip to Talladega or Winston-Salem, and just might get it.

—Burr and Jack and Ted and Richard and Frank and Danny and Charlie, for subsidizing my work.

—Cyra McFadden, who was an inspiration; she is one of the finest writers Montana ever produced, and that's saying something.

—Frank McCulloch, the best editor most of us will ever know.

—Jane Kay, for her kindness, and her insistence on fresh lime juice.

—Charlie Benton, for the lesson on how to play a pat jack.

—Jeff Armstrong, who helped me not at all.

—Hunter Thompson, for his friendship, and for pissing me off enough to get through this.

—Jim Silberman and Suzanne Gluck, for believing, and Dominick Anfuso, for making it work.

—Also, Chuck Rathbun, Geoff Precourt, Debra Weyermann, Lisa Palac, Richard Hertz, Jacqi, Kathy Miller, Alex Neill, Michael Dougan, Diane Curtis, Richard Barbieri, Howard Hanson, Donna Dressel, Patti Martini, Pam Day, Don Bennett, Mary and Gary Hammonds, Sono, Goat, George Cito, J.D. Sipes, Eric and Erica, Fanny, Vinnie, Kate and Cassie.

—And finally: Jerry Jeff Walker and Lyle Lovett, for those late nights when I don't find many answers but the music seems to help.

—And the 17-inch cutthroat trout who hangs out in the West Fork of the Bitterroot, on Alta Ranch, and there changed my life.

—dcm/6/3/92

INDEX

Adams, Lisa, 77, 122, 249, 271–72, 276–77, 334, 345, 407, 409–12, 415, 426, 427, 428, 429, 433, 448, 449, 450, 459
Adkins, Richard, 77–78
Alioto, Frank, 39
Alioto, Joseph, 39, 46
Anderson, Bruce, 395, 396
Anderson, Juliette, 121
Aquaviva, Fred, 25
Arjam, Farshid, 417–18
Armstrong, Jeff, 21, 22, 32, 58, 59, 60, 63, 64, 68, 86, 129, 253, 258, 264, 269, 291, 292, 293, 294, 310, 316, 334–35, 448, 450, 455
Armstrong, Neil, 36
Armstrong, Red, 58

Bajo, Julie, 158, 256, 257, 258, 259–61, 269, 270, 271, 272–74, 275, 277–80, 282–83, 288, 290, 294, 296, 299, 303, 306–9, 310, 314, 322, 337, 343, 346–47, 360, 364, 374–76, 377, 383, 392, 394, 399, 410, 413, 419, 422, 438, 442, 447, 451, 454, 440, 451
Baldassari, Frank, 282–83, 366
Banks, Annie Blanche "Tempest Storm," 101
Barrish, James, 316
Battaglia, Carolynne, 358, 359
Bell, Alexander Graham, 379
Benson, Jerome, 42–43, 44, 46, 49, 75, 76, 83
Benton, Alex, 198
Benton, Charlie, 68, 76, 177, 229, 253–54, 262, 263–64, 289, 291, 316, 333, 334, 415, 419–20, 448, 455
Berberian, Ed, 324
Bianchi, Albert, 341–42
Bird, Rose, 81
Blanchard, Ralph, 250, 251, 404
Blinder, Martin, 45, 314, 316, 356
Boren, Terry, 324
Boyden, Michael, 356
Boyer, Bill, 20, 22, 23, 32–33, 37, 47, 48, 50, 53–54, 55, 57, 58, 59, 63, 66, 67, 68, 70, 253, 302
Brabo, Dorothy Diane, 357, 359, 448
Bradford, Jennifer, 38
Bradford, William, 37
Brady, Phil, 304
Bragdon, Dona, 77, 78
Brautigan, Richard, 190
Breiner, Dorothy, 342
Breiner, Richard H., 341–43, 344, 347–48,

349–50, 353–54, 355, 356–57, 358, 360–61, 363, 365, 368–69, 378, 379, 381, 382–83, 384–86, 392–93, 396, 397, 401, 402, 403, 404–5, 409–10, 411, 412, 414, 415, 416, 418, 419–20, 423, 424, 432, 433, 435, 437, 438, 439, 440–41, 448, 449, 450–51, 452, 457, 458–59
Bright, Linda, 409–10
Brook, Gilbert, 357–58, 359, 451
Brosnahan, Jim, 327–28
Brown, Ira, 80
Brown, Jerry, 81, 341
Brown, Judith, 331, 342
Buckley, Jim, 60, 61, 62
Buckley, Stuart, 315, 322
Burroughs, William, 127
Bush, George, 392

Cacciatore, Chuck, 259, 296, 297, 305, 306–7, 309, 314, 321–24, 329, 331, 333, 338, 452
Caen, Herb, 191
Cameron, Ray, 355, 359
Card, Gordon, 293–94
Carpenter, David, 325–26
Ceccini, Richard, 25, 32, 63, 68
Chambers, Marilyn, 48–49, 50–51, 64, 85, 121, 193, 194, 205, 210, 302, 395, 457
Cheever, Susan, 395
Clancy, James, 84
Clarence, Nanci, 326–28, 329–30, 331, 333, 336–37, 345–46, 347, 348, 353, 354–55, 358, 361, 366, 371, 372, 376, 403, 407–408, 410, 417, 418, 422–24, 449, 450, 451, 459
Clark, John, 372
Cole, Gary, 206
Cooper, Sid, 371–72
Corazza, William, 309, 376, 380, 389
Covillo, Pamela, 448, 449
Cranston, Alan, 22
Creecy, Charles, 24
Crumb, Robert, 268
Curtis, Diane, 345, 381, 386

Dare, Barbara, 194
David, Peter, 359, 397
Davidson, Ben, 49, 51
Davidson, Bessie, 51
Davidson, Curtis "Rocky," 32, 51, 59, 68, 93, 129, 153, 173, 174, 178, 264, 276–77, 291, 303, 316, 334, 335–37, 396, 411, 414–16, 420, 425, 426–27, 428–29, 435–36, 455, 459, 415, 448

Davidson, Pete, 51
Davis, Angela, 46
Davis, Ed, 55–56
Davis, Jack, 233, 254, 262–63, 264, 412–13, 455, 457
Del Colletti, Billy, 20
DeLeon, Ray, 244–47, 259, 265, 273, 287–88, 294, 295–97, 298, 299, 330, 366–70, 372, 378, 440
Del Prete, Gino, 45
De Renzy, Alex, 38, 45
DeSalvo, Robert, 52, 60
Doda, Carol, 155
Dohrn, Bernardine, 40
Dossett, Donald "Skip," 91, 153, 241, 252, 253, 274, 275–77, 296, 373–74, 375, 408–09, 414, 447, 455
Dossett, Mary Joy, 274
Dougan, Michael, 370, 381
Douglas, Kirk, 350
Douglas, Michael, 350
Downing, Jenny, 9
Doyle, James, 328
Dufficy, Michael B., 449
Dzimian, Joan, 356

East Bay Ray, 152
Eichelbaum, Stanley, 58
Etheredge, Jeanette, 334
Evanoff, Mark Allen, 250, 251, 404

Feinstein, Dianne, 73–74, 76–77, 158
Felicity Split, 62
Fivis, Robert, 359
Florez, Elisa "Missy Manners," 145, 148–49, 158, 160, 162–70, 175–81, 183–89, 190, 191–92, 193, 194–95, 196–203, 204–207, 208, 209–16, 224, 225, 226, 227–28, 235, 239, 254, 291, 294–95, 299, 300–301, 302, 303, 304, 319, 321, 453, 457
Fluty, J. D., 20, 21, 22, 23, 24, 25, 58
Fontana, Jon, 32, 36–37, 48, 59, 68, 201–2, 204
Forbes, Hal, 305, 334, 371, 372
Freeman, Richard, 269, 290, 440
Freeman, Steven, 250, 251, 404
Freitas, Joe, 76
Fuller, Dana, 196, 316, 426
Furillo, Andy, 301

Garry, Charles, 328
Ghianina, 66–67
Gish, Jimmy, 68, 177
Goldstein, Al, 60, 61, 62, 79–80, 237, 238
Golson, G. Barry, 206
Gorra, Patricia, 359
Grangnelli, Frank, 17–18, 302
Graysmith, Robert, 325
Greaves, Debbie "Do," 91, 241, 373
Green, Aaron, 344
Green, Phil, 297, 369
Greth, Alan, 402

Haag, Lucien, 335, 354, 361, 363, 370, 375, 379, 384, 385, 387–95, 396, 397, 406, 420–22, 443, 445, 446, 447, 453
Haas, Kent, 279–82, 309, 365, 437, 440
Hallinan, Terence, 317, 457
Halvonik, Paul, 80
Hansan, Tilden, 403, 404
Harper, Dana, 77
Harrison, Nancy, 138–39, 271, 273, 303, 334, 410, 426, 440
Harrison, Ralph, 359
Hartley, Nina, 117–25, 194, 320
Hassall, Dave, 164, 165–66, 188
Hennessey, Michael, 457
Herman, Jerry, 321, 322, 324, 326, 333, 338
Hernandez, Rena, 77
Hill, Robert M., 53
Hinckle, Warren, 85, 214, 262, 264, 395–96
Hoffman, Clay, 296
Hoffman, Kathy, 259, 296, 322, 324, 371, 377, 441
Hollien, Harry, 334, 349, 350, 351–54, 361, 362, 364, 378, 379–81, 382–83, 384, 388, 391, 392, 394, 395, 396, 397, 398–99, 400, 406, 420, 422, 425, 443, 445, 447, 459
Hollien, Kevin, 380
Holmes, John, 64
Holmes, Ken, 377–78
Hongisto, Richard, 457
Howe, Charles, 39
Hunter, Heather, 243
Huntley, Ruth, 399

Jackson, George, 328
Jindrich, Ervin, 300, 309, 371, 388, 390
Johnson, Richard, 402
Jordan, Frank, 403, 412, 457–58

Keating, Charlie, 83–84, 424
Keen, Sam, 100
Keker, John, 346, 347
Kennedy, Eleanore, 329, 330, 356, 358, 449, 450
Kennedy, John F., 352
Kennedy, Robert F., 99, 352
Kessler, David, 439, 441
Keyes, Johnny, 50
Kinney, Nan, 136
Kirk, Paul, 420
Kopp, Quentin, 317

Lackey, Richard, 25
Lady T, 408–10
Lang, C. J., 66–67
Lawrence, Regina Kahn, 357
Leary, Timothy, 40, 150
Lee, Kristal Rose, 145, 146, 148–49, 158, 228–29, 231–35, 236, 37, 239–41, 243, 248, 254, 256–57, 295, 301, 302, 304, 335, 355, 453
Lesher, Dean, 32, 33, 54
Long, Huey, 388

Lords, Traci, 114
Lovelace, Linda, 197
Lucas, Malcom, 81
Lucchesi, Anthony Hill, 355, 357, 359

McDonald, George, 50
McDuffie, Michael, 309
McGrath, Robert, 115
McGuire, Robert, 84
McIlvenna, Ted, 45
McKnight, Sharon, 69, 91, 195, 197, 198, 199, 200, 203, 317, 319, 320
Maloney, Pete, 40–41, 44
Mapplethorpe, Robert, 45–46
Marlene, Lili, 122
Mason, Eric, 330, 371
Mattos, Jerry, 288, 296, 299, 309, 370, 371, 378, 390
Maurer, "Jockey," 60
Meese, Ed, 176, 192
Mercer, Otis, 27
Merrill, Jeffrey David, 331
Mezzavilla, Richard, 32, 46, 48, 57, 59, 68, 129, 310, 316, 334, 417
Mickle, James C., 314
Milk, Harvey, 45, 73
Milligan, Debbie, 271
Minetti, Diana, 131
Mitchell, Aaron James, 73, 86, 89, 90, 93, 218, 223, 235, 246, 260, 265, 268, 272, 294, 298, 313
Mitchell, Adrienne, 57
Mitchell, Austin, 235
Mitchell, Bill, 302
Mitchell, Caleb Robin, 89–90, 91, 179, 215, 218, 235, 249, 260, 265–66, 270, 272, 294, 295, 313
Mitchell, Charlie, 14, 15
Mitchell, Georgia Mae, 13, 15, 17, 18–19, 20, 21, 24, 26, 27, 33, 34, 38, 51, 52, 56, 65, 90, 171, 186, 260, 275, 288, 289–90, 291–92, 293, 294–95, 298, 299, 301, 302, 303, 305, 310, 311, 312, 313, 316, 320, 372, 404–05, 406–08, 440, 447, 451, 459
Mitchell, James Rafael "Rafe," 70, 218, 249
Mitchell, James Robert "J. R.," 13, 14, 15–16, 17, 18, 19–20, 21, 23, 24, 26, 27, 33–34, 41, 51, 52, 65, 72, 194, 405, 426
Mitchell, James Samuel, 14
Mitchell, Jasmine Monet, 87, 89, 90, 91–92, 179, 185, 186, 218, 235, 240, 260, 265, 294, 295, 298, 299, 304, 311, 313
Mitchell, Jennifer Skye, 70, 218
Mitchell, Justin Samuel, 70, 218, 302
Mitchell, Karen Kay Hassall, 70–71, 72, 86, 87, 88–89, 90, 91–94, 151, 157, 164, 170, 171, 172–75, 180, 181, 183, 184–85, 186–87, 188, 210, 213, 223, 226, 229, 233, 235, 242, 243–44, 245–46, 247, 253, 260, 265, 266–67, 272–73, 274, 279–80, 293–95, 296–97, 302, 304–5, 310, 311–314, 298–99, 356, 369, 406, 417, 444, 451

Mitchell, Karlan, 235
Mitchell, Liberty, 38, 45, 64, 65, 71, 73, 86, 88, 89–90, 91, 171, 181–82, 191, 218, 239, 249, 251, 265, 267–70, 295, 298, 299, 303–4, 310, 400–402
Mitchell, Lisa, 288, 289, 303, 316, 335
Mitchell, Mariah, 64, 71, 73, 86, 88, 90, 182, 218
Mitchell, Mary Jane Whitty, 69–70, 87, 88, 122, 196, 213, 216, 200, 302
Mitchell, Meredith Bradford, 37–38, 64–65, 71, 72, 73, 88, 89, 90, 92, 151, 171, 264–65, 266–67, 269, 288–89, 291–92, 302, 304, 305, 312, 401–402, 433
Mitchell, Meta Jane, 70, 218, 249
Mitchell, Minnie Lee Corbett, 14
Mitchell, Robert Lewis, 16–17, 289
Mitchell, Russ, 32, 59, 71, 198
Mitchell, Storm Sundown, 64, 71, 73, 86, 88, 89, 90, 182, 218, 249, 250, 251, 269, 295, 299, 303, 310, 424, 432, 433
Morgan, Bronwen, 101, 113–14, 115
Morgan, Denny, 291, 448
Morgan, Johnny, 291, 303, 396, 448, 455
Morrison, Jim, 319
Morton, Charles, 420–22
Moscone, George, 45, 73, 76
Musser, Sandra, 93, 170, 171, 172, 175

Nance, Andrew, 359
Natali, Les, 45
Neill, Alex, 345, 381
Nelder, Al, 40, 46
Nern, William Baker, 359, 397, 451
Newton, Huey, 40, 46, 197
Nolan, Angela, 114
Noltimier, Louis, 42

O'Connell, Carol, 175
Olick, David, 114–15
Olsen, Sharon, 364
O'Malley, William, 174–75
O'Neill, Dan, 196, 264, 289–90, 396, 425, 455
O'Neill, Maureen, 289–91

Page, Bonnie, 273, 279–80, 282, 287, 367
Page, Catherine, 21
Palac, Lisa, 50
Palladino, Jack, 411
Paraspolo, Tom, 279–80, 281–83, 288, 366, 437
Patrick, Dave, 162–63
Pawlcyn, Cindy, 176
Pérez, Tony, 237
Peters, William Wesley, 344
Pirazoli, Mike, 23
Pither, Bruce, 458
Portman, Barry, 327
Posey, John, 324–25, 330, 331, 333–34, 335–36, 337–38, 342, 345–46, 347, 348–350, 351, 352, 353, 354–55, 356, 357, 358, 359–61, 362, 363, 364, 365–66, 367,

Posey, John (*cont.*)
   368–69, 370, 372–74, 375–76, 377–79,
   380–81, 382–86, 371, 386–88, 389, 391–
   393, 395, 396, 397–98, 400, 401, 403,
   404–5, 406, 407, 411, 412, 413, 414, 415–
   416, 417, 418, 419–20, 422, 423, 424, 428,
   432–38, 439–41, 442–43, 444–45, 446,
   448, 449, 450, 451, 452, 453, 454, 458
Postel, Fred, 403
Poza, Fausto "Tito," 398–400, 447, 451
Pritchard; Ron, 23

Rajneesh, Bhagwan Shree, 103, 113, 114,
   115, 138
Rauber, Martha, 230–31, 240, 242, 244–45,
   246–47, 260–61, 271, 274–75, 294, 297,
   331, 367, 369, 440
Reems, Harry, 122
Reusswig, James, 27
Rhine, Joe, 39, 42, 43, 45, 46, 289
Ricardo, Rita, 155, 208, 302, 303
Richardson, Ruby, 68, 291, 297, 305, 310,
   311–12, 371, 372, 401–02, 417, 440
Richter, Ron, 288, 299, 370, 371, 390
Rio, Ellie, 224
Riordan, Dennis, 328, 329–31, 332–33,
   336–37, 338, 342, 343, 345–46, 349, 350,
   354, 378, 384, 387
Roberts, Dennis, 42, 43–44, 45, 78, 81–82,
   83, 84, 113, 174, 271, 289–91, 293, 314,
   315, 321, 322–24, 326, 329–30, 331, 333,
   335, 336, 337–38, 410, 411, 425, 426, 451
Roberts, Douglas, 359, 448, 449
Roberts, Sandy, 289
Rowe, Judy, 130, 131
Ryan, Patrick, 359, 448

Saia, Ben, 64
Said, Rebecca, 458
Salmon, Vincent, 396–98
Savitt, Beverly, 330–31, 337–38
Scaggs, Boz, 164
Schimmer, Claudia, 230
Scott, Joanne, 94, 130–31, 145, 146, 148–
   149, 153, 154–62, 167, 169–70, 187, 188–
   189, 190–91, 202, 203, 204, 207–8, 210,
   217–218, 223–24, 225–27, 229, 231, 232–
   233, 234, 237–38, 241–43, 248, 252, 254,
   256, 257, 258, 259, 270, 301, 302–3, 320,
   453
Scott, Kentner, 357, 359, 451, 452
Seger, Bob, 100
Seltzer, Gene, 187, 244
Sepulveda, Sandra, 267
Sharpe, Ivan, 66–67
Shaw, Frank, 80–81, 82, 83, 85, 130

Sheela, Ma Anand, 115
Sherman, Joseph Howard, 331
Sipes, J. D., 15–16
Skidmore, Sherryl, 441
Slater, Gail Palmer, 255
Smith, Arlo, 74, 76
Smith, Peter Allen, 314–15, 323, 324
Smith, Vernon P., 293
Smith, Warren, 358
Smith, William Kennedy, 346
Spain, Johnny, 328
Staller, Llona Cicciolina, 85
Stanich, Vince, 66, 68, 70, 80, 121, 132,
   133, 134, 135, 138, 163, 171, 190, 228,
   241, 243, 248
Steel, Tom, 81, 83, 84, 292, 315, 316, 322,
   326, 327, 328, 329–30, 410, 417–18, 426,
   427, 451
Stein, James, 359, 381
Strong, Jim, 266, 267
Sundahl, Debi, 135–36

Talbot, David, 206
Taylor, Lynn, 267
Thomas, Gary, 314, 315, 323
Thompkins, Sherri, 283, 287, 308–9, 334,
   364–65, 372, 375, 399
Thompson, Hunter S., 10, 85, 86, 127,
   189–90, 191, 253, 255–56, 374
Thompson, Phyllis, 356–57
Turer, L. Stephen, 414
Turner, Ron, 334
Tutor, Betty, 358, 359, 451

Vonnegut, Kurt, 381

Walter, Bernard, 74–76, 78–79, 80, 81, 82,
   83, 85, 115, 126, 136, 176
Wasserman, John, 42
Watkins, Mario, 299, 372, 377, 417, 440
Webb, Charles, 302, 303
Weiner, Sol, 40, 41, 44
Weldon, Mike, 303
White, Dan, 45
Williams, Cleveland, 393
Williamsen, Michael, 359, 434, 452
Willis, Danielle, 98, 127–28, 133, 247–48,
   259
Witt, Bana, 145, 146, 148–54, 190, 191–92,
   240, 244, 247–48, 252, 256, 258–59, 270–
   271, 301, 317–19, 453, 455
Wood, Jim, 77
Wright, Frank Lloyd, 343, 345

Zaffarano, Mickey, 60
Zane, Maitland, 36
Zenger, John Peter, 333